Blockchain and DLT

A comprehensive guide to getting started with Blockchain and Web3

Nakul Shah

www.bpbonline.com

FIRST EDITION 2024

REPRINT 2025

ISBN: 978-93-5551-928-3

LIMITS OF LIABILITY AND DISCLAIMER OF WARRANTY

Distributors:

BPB PUBLICATIONS
20, Ansari Road, Darya Ganj
New Delhi-110002
Ph: 23254990/23254991

DECCAN AGENCIES
4-3-329, Bank Street,
Hyderabad-500195
Ph: 24756967/24756400

MICRO MEDIA
Shop No. 5, Mahendra Chambers,
150 DN Rd. Next to Capital Cinema,
V.T. (C.S.T.) Station, MUMBAI-400 001
Ph: 22078296/22078297

To View Complete BPB Publications Catalogue Scan the QR Code:

Published by Manish Jain for BPB Publications, 20 Ansari Road, Darya Ganj, New Delhi-110002 and Printed by him at Manipal Technologies, Manipal

www.bpbonline.com

Dedicated to

*To my Mom (**Shalini Shah**),*

*Dad (**Satish Shah**)*

and

*Wife (**Mauli Shah**)*

About the Author

Nakul Shah, a seasoned professional with over nine years of experience in the software industry, currently serves as a subject matter expert in the emerging technology space. Holding a Master's degree in Financial Engineering from the University of Michigan, Nakul combines academic prowess with extensive practical knowledge.

Nakul's expertise lies in product development and technical content creation. A certificate in Blockchain and Crypto attests to his commitment to staying at the front of advancements in the field.

Nakul is an industry thought leader who authored the book Blockchain for Business with Hyperledger Fabric. He is proficient in explaining complex concepts and making them accessible to a broad audience. Nakul actively participates in affiliations and collaborations within the technology community, and conferences across the globe.

With a solid educational foundation, rich professional experience, and a commitment to ongoing learning, Nakul Shah continues to shape the landscape of blockchain technology, offering valuable insights and expertise to the global community.

About the Reviewer

Pradeep Selvaraj, a master in the domain of 3D web development, Metaverse innovation, AI Apps, Blockchain, and NFT development. He brings over 15 years of rich experience in the IT sector. He boasts an impressive array of certifications, including being a Google certified TensorFlow Developer, a certified blockchain developer from the Blockchain Council, and a Data Alchemist accredited by Covalent.

In addition to his reviewer role, he is the CEO and founder of Leogacy, a pioneer in AI SaaS, Metaverse, and 3D AR/VR initiatives. Under his visionary leadership, **Leogacy** has launched the NFT project '8lements'. His multifaceted expertise ensures a comprehensive and insightful review, enriching the reader's understanding of the dynamic world of blockchain and AI.

Our reviewer's expertise extends to offering nuanced, in-depth analyses of blockchain and AI, making his perspectives invaluable for both veterans and novices in these fields. He is at the forefront of pioneering work, currently dedicated to developing 3D Animated NFTs in the Metaverse named Diamond Floaters.

Acknowledgement

I extend my sincere appreciation to three key individuals who played crucial roles in the process of crafting this book—my parents and my wife.

To my parents, *Shalini Shah and Satish Shah,* your continuous support and confidence in me have been a driving force. Your belief in my pursuits has provided the confidence needed to navigate the complexities of this project and life. Your support is the foundation upon which my work stands, and for that I am sincerely grateful.

To my wife, *Mauli Shah,* your patience and consistent encouragement have been invaluable. Your belief in my abilities, and the time you dedicated to supporting my endeavors have contributed immensely to all my endeavors. Your support has provided stability throughout the challenges and triumphs of this process.

I express my deep gratitude to my family for their understanding and shared moments of joy. Your collective support has been an essential component in the development of this book.

To Mom, Dad, and *Mauli,* this book reflects on the impact of your support. I appreciate your crucial roles in this journey, and I thank you for being integral to the realization of this endeavor.

Preface

Blockchain is a transformative force, reshaping several industries and technologies and redefining data integrity. This book is designed to be your guide by providing a comprehensive explanation for engineering students and enthusiasts. It simplifies the complex concept of blockchain and **Distributed Ledger Technology (DLT)**.

In this book, you will learn about many topics, from the basics of blockchain and DLT to the real-world application of blockchain. You will also learn about Bitcoin, permissionless and permissioned blockchain, and will be provided with numerous practical examples to help you understand the concepts.

I hope you will find this book informative and helpful when unraveling the foundations of decentralized systems and exploring the limitless potential of blockchain.

Chapter 1: Cryptography and Distributed Systems – In this chapter, the focus is on the intersection of cryptography and distributed systems. The chapter begins by introducing the fundamental concepts of both cryptography and distributed systems, highlighting their importance in securing and managing data in a networked environment. It explores concepts like public-key cryptography, digital signatures, and secure multi-party computation are explored in the context of distributed systems. The chapter also explores the implementation of cryptographic primitives in blockchain technology and other distributed ledger systems. The importance of cryptographic algorithms in achieving consensus mechanisms, like proof-of-work or proof-of-stake, is also discussed.

Chapter 2: Introduction to Blockchain Technology – This chapter addresses the technical intricacies of blockchain technology and DLT. It also explores key theoretical aspects such as the CAP theorem, the Byzantine Generals Problem, and the nuances of consensus mechanisms, including types, cryptographic primitives, and data structures underpinning blockchain functionality.

Chapter 3: Bitcoin – This chapter discusses Bitcoin, covering its historical genesis, transaction dynamics, and foundational concepts. It also explores Bitcoin keys, addresses, and wallets, including elliptic curve cryptography, Base58 encoding, and BIP-38 encryption. In this chapter you will learn about transaction scripts, mining intricacies, and the structure of blocks, culminating in the pivotal genesis block. It will help you navigate the Bitcoin network, addressing core nodes, peer-to-peer architecture, and incentive-based engineering. The chapter concludes by exploring Bitcoin forensics, analyzing addresses and wallets precisely.

Chapter 4: Permissionless Blockchain: Ethereum – This chapter introduces Ethereum 1.0 and 2.0 and gives a detailed exploration of the Turing completeness inherent in the **Ethereum Virtual Machine (EVM)**, and a meticulous comparison with Bitcoin. The discourse extends to practical aspects such as Ether units, Ethereum wallets, and the utilization of Metamask. Transactional intricacies are examined, including structure, gas dynamics, and the conveyance of values to **Externally Owned Accounts (EOA)** and Contracts. The chapter culminates with a formal discussion on Smart Contracts and their deployment through Solidity.

Chapter 5: Permissioned Blockchain: Hyperledger Fabric – This chapter focuses on Hyperledger Fabric and encompasses an in-depth introduction to the framework, elucidating the tools and architecture integral to Hyperledger Fabric Blockchain. The chapter further delves into the intricate components of Hyperledger Fabric while addressing challenges related to interoperability and scalability within the blockchain landscape.

Chapter 6: Crypto Assets and Cryptocurrencies – This chapter dissects concepts like ERC20 and ERC721 Tokens, exploring the differences between ERC-721 and ERC-20 tokens, and talks about the significance of **Non-Fungible Tokens (NFT)**. This chapter serves as a guide to navigating complex digital assets and provides a great understanding of **Initial Coin Offerings (ICO)**, **Security Token Offerings (STO)**, and diverse cryptocurrencies.

Chapter 7: Blockchain Applications and Case Studies – This chapter introduces readers to the transformative impact of blockchain in IoT, AI, and cyber security. Explore how blockchain enhances security in the Internet of Things, ensures ethical AI applications, and fortifies cyber defenses. Real-world case studies exemplify the practical implications, making this chapter an essential guide to the evolving intersection of blockchain technology and these dynamic domains.

Code Bundle and Coloured Images

Please follow the link to download the
Code Bundle and the *Coloured Images* of the book:

https://rebrand.ly/er2r3cg

The code bundle for the book is also hosted on GitHub at
https://github.com/bpbpublications/Blockchain-and-DLT.
In case there's an update to the code, it will be updated on the existing GitHub repository.

We have code bundles from our rich catalogue of books and videos available at **https://github.com/bpbpublications**. Check them out!

Errata

We take immense pride in our work at BPB Publications and follow best practices to ensure the accuracy of our content to provide with an indulging reading experience to our subscribers. Our readers are our mirrors, and we use their inputs to reflect and improve upon human errors, if any, that may have occurred during the publishing processes involved. To let us maintain the quality and help us reach out to any readers who might be having difficulties due to any unforeseen errors, please write to us at :

errata@bpbonline.com

Your support, suggestions and feedbacks are highly appreciated by the BPB Publications' Family.

Piracy

If you come across any illegal copies of our works in any form on the internet, we would be grateful if you would provide us with the location address or website name. Please contact us at **business@bpbonline.com** with a link to the material.

If you are interested in becoming an author

If there is a topic that you have expertise in, and you are interested in either writing or contributing to a book, please visit **www.bpbonline.com**. We have worked with thousands of developers and tech professionals, just like you, to help them share their insights with the global tech community. You can make a general application, apply for a specific hot topic that we are recruiting an author for, or submit your own idea.

Reviews

Please leave a review. Once you have read and used this book, why not leave a review on the site that you purchased it from? Potential readers can then see and use your unbiased opinion to make purchase decisions. We at BPB can understand what you think about our products, and our authors can see your feedback on their book. Thank you!

For more information about BPB, please visit **www.bpbonline.com**.

Join our book's Discord space

Join the book's Discord Workspace for Latest updates, Offers, Tech happenings around the world, New Release and Sessions with the Authors:

https://discord.bpbonline.com

Table of Contents

Chapter 1
Cryptography and Distributed Systems

Introduction

Cryptography and distributed systems have emerged as the primary disciplines in the field of modern data security and efficient information exchange. Cryptography symbolizes the centuries-old quest for secure communication. Cryptography has transcended boundaries, from the cryptic hieroglyphs to the complex algorithms of the contemporary time. Meanwhile, the concept of distributed systems has germinated from the continuous evolution of computing and networked systems and aims to transform the way data is accessed, shared, and utilized across various platforms through collaborative data sharing, processing, and scalability.

This chapter will explore the intertwined disciplines of cryptography and distributed systems. Besides the histories and complexities of these groundbreaking technologies, we will learn about the nuances of encryption, digital signatures, key exchange, authentication mechanisms, and more.

Structure

This chapter contains the following topic:

- Routes of cryptography

- Emergence of distributed system
- Cryptography's basic concepts and terminologies
- Evolution of cryptography
- Encryption
- Principles of cryptography
- Encryption algorithms
- Working of Diffie-Hellman
- Cryptographic protocols
- Cryptographic key management
- Public key cryptography
- Hash functions
- Distributed file systems
- Distributed database
- Blockchain and cryptography
- Security protocols

Objectives

The chapter elucidates the interrelated relationship between cryptography and distributed systems and how their integration strengthens the security and integrity of decentralized networks. It aims to offer a comprehensive understanding of cryptography and distributed systems by shedding light on their evolution, fundamentals, features, and applications. The chapter will talk about encryption algorithms, encryption standards, cryptographic protocols, and more in detail. Through this, we will gain insights into their collaborative potential in addressing the technological challenges of contemporary times.

Routes of cryptography

Trails of cryptography trace way back in time, when simpler methods of encryptions were used, such as transposition ciphers, and polyalphabetic ciphers for high termed security contents. Encrypting things was fun during the childhood days for most of us, as we used to swap messages to our best buddies. Everyone might have used one or the other way to hide the message content from public like the use of invincible ink or wax. The necessity to hide messages has been present since we transitioned from living in caves to forming communities and embracing the concept of civilization. Once distinct groups or tribes emerged, the notion of competing against each other arose and was disseminated, accompanied by hierarchical aggression, covert communication, and manipulation of the masses. The most primitive forms of encryption were discovered in the birthplace of civilization, which is unsurprising, encompassing areas presently associated with Egypt, Greece, and Rome.

The earliest known form of cryptography dates back to ancient Egypt, where hieroglyphs were used to encrypt sensitive information. Throughout history, various forms of cryptography have been used, including substitution ciphers, transposition ciphers, and polyalphabetic ciphers.

The Caesar cipher, named after Julius Caesar (a Roman military general in 100BCE) who used it to encrypt his military messages, is one of the simplest and earliest known substitution ciphers. The Vigenère cipher and the Playfair cipher, developed in the 16th and 19th centuries respectively, are examples of polyalphabetic ciphers. These traditional methods of encryption can easily be broken by modern computers and are no longer considered secure for protecting sensitive information.

Monoalphabetic and polyalphabetic ciphers are two types of secret codes used in cryptography.

Monoalphabetic cipher

In a monoalphabetic cipher, each letter in a message is consistently replaced with a single, fixed letter. For instance, in a Caesar cipher, every *A* might always become a *G*, leading to a simple and predictable substitution. However, monoalphabetic ciphers are vulnerable to attacks like frequency analysis, where the frequency of letters in the encrypted message is analyzed to crack the code.

In this cipher, each letter in the plaintext is shifted by a fixed number of positions in the alphabet.

For instance, with a shift of 3, the following changes can be observed:

- **Original**: HELLO
- **Encrypted**: KHOOR

Here, each letter is replaced by the letter that is three positions ahead in the alphabet.

Polyalphabetic cipher

On the other hand, a polyalphabetic cipher adds complexity by using multiple substitutions for the same letter based on a secret key. The Vigenère cipher is a common example, where each letter in the key corresponds to a different shift in the alphabet. This dynamic substitution makes it more challenging for cryptanalysts to decipher the message, providing increased security compared to monoalphabetic ciphers. Poly means *many*, and in this case, it means many ways of encrypting each letter, adding an extra layer of protection to the coded message.

In this cipher, a keyword is used to determine different shift values for each letter in the plaintext.

For example:

- **Original**: HELLO
- **Key**: KEY
- **Encrypted**: RIJVS

Here, the first letter *H* is shifted by 10 positions (K in the alphabet), the second letter *E* by 4 positions (I in the alphabet), and so on.

The various roots of ancient cryptography are as follows:

Egyptians

The ancient Egyptians used a primitive form of steganography, which is the practice of hiding a message within another message or medium. They would carve hieroglyphs on the back of a stone slab, then cover the back with a layer of wax and write a harmless message on top of it, making it hard to detect that there was a hidden message. The method of steganography was also used by the Greeks and Romans, who would shave the head of a messenger and tattoo a message on his scalp, this reference is portrayed in a Hollywood movie, and then they used to wait for his hair to grow back before sending him on his way.

Greeks

The Greeks devised a slightly different and simpler method of encrypting messages by wounding a piece of tape around a stick. When the tape was unwound, the writing would appear gibberish. The intended recipient would then use a matching stick to decipher the message. On the other hand, romans used the Caesar Shift Cipher technique for encryption. It involved shifting letters by a fixed number, typically three, to create the coded message. To decode the message, the recipient would subsequently move the letters backwards by the identical magnitude. The Caesar Shift Cipher exemplifies a monoalphabetic cipher.

Emergence of distributed system

Likewise, the concept of distributed systems also has a long history. It dates back to the early days of computing when mainframe computers were connected through networks, where a universal flow of data always ends up with a certain particular node or few among the system. The initial development of distributed systems has been driven by the demand for expandability, dependability and availability. As the scope of internet broadened and more devices and resources were let out to explore the network, it was the best point to make entry for distributed systems, and to play a crucial role in contemporary computing infrastructure. In the early days of software architecture, monolithic systems were prevalent. These systems combined data access codes, business logic, and user-interface code, making it difficult to separate the layers, such as when the DBMS changes, or reuse components in other applications due to lack of modularity. The progression of distributed computing systems has been substantial since their origins. In the beginning, an individual computer could only execute one job at a time, and it was necessary to have multiple machines running concurrently to carry out multiple tasks.

However, this alone was inadequate to establish a fully distributed system, as it necessitated a method of intercommunication between different computers or software running on them. This resulted in the creation of message-based communication, where information is exchanged between computers using messages, as well as other techniques such as file and database sharing. The advent of multitasking operating systems and personal computers marked a new era in distributed systems. The emergence of operating systems such as Windows, Unix, and Linux enabled the execution of multiple tasks on a single machine. This, in turn, facilitated the construction and operation of entire distributed systems within one or a few interconnected computers via messaging. This development led to the emergence of the **service-oriented architecture** (**SOA**), wherein distributed systems were constructed by integrating a set of services running on one or multiple computers. The service interfaces were specified using WSDL (for SOAP) or WADL (for REST), and service consumers employed these interfaces for their client-side implementations. Please refer to the following *Figure 1.1*:

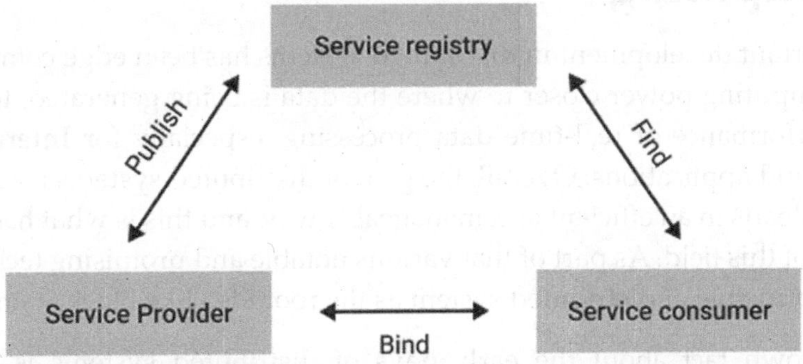

Figure 1.1: *Graphical representation of the SOA conceptual architecture.*

Note: There are two different kinds of application structure:

a. **A Monolithic application puts all of its functionality into a single process.**

b. **A microservices architecture puts each element of functionality into a separate service.**

- As the cost of computer power and storage went down, more and more companies started using distributed systems and IT systems that use **service-oriented architecture** (**SOA**). However, as the number of systems and services increased, it became hard to keep connecting them all together. To solve this problem, a new system called the service bus was created. This acts as a middleman, connecting all the different systems. This component is called the **enterprise service bus** (**ESB**) and it acts like a translator between different systems that communicate in different ways, like people speaking different languages. The main advantage of this model is that systems can communicate with each other without needing to worry about how the other systems communicate.
- After the introduction of tools like Docker and Kubernetes, which make it easy to move and manage multiple software applications, called containers, across multiple computer systems called hosts, the field of distributed systems has continued to focus on making this process even more convenient and efficient. This includes the use of cloud-native technology, which is specifically designed to work well in cloud computing environments and take advantage of the cloud's capabilities to handle large, complex workloads. Additionally, new technology like service meshes and serverless computing have been developed to improve networking and traffic management for these containerized applications and to deploy them only when they are needed. Edge computing is one of the most recent emerging advancements which involves distributed systems.

Edge computing

Another important development in distributed systems has been edge computing, which moves the computing power closer to where the data is being generated, to improve the speed and performance of real-time data processing, especially for **Internet of Things** (**IoT**) devices and applications. Overall, the goal of distributed systems is to handle large, complex workloads in an efficient and manageable way, and this is what has been driving the evolution of this field. As part of that various notable and promising techs present day uses the core principle of distributed system as the root idea like blockchain technology.

One lesser-known fact about the early days of distributed systems is that the very first distributed system was summoned in the early 1960s by a team of researchers at **Massachusetts Institute of Technology** (**MIT**) led by *Robert Taylor*. This system, the so-called **compatible time-sharing system** (CTSS), allowed multiple users to access a single mainframe computer concurrently through remote terminals. It was a remarkable breakthrough in computing at the time, as it allowed for more efficient use of expensive computer resources and laid the strong base columns for the development of todays distributed systems. Since then, the field has continued to evolve, driven by the need for increased scalability, reliability, and availability in computing systems. Blockchain technology is a digital ledger system that emerged in the late 2000s with the invention of bitcoin. It is based on the principles of distributed systems, which means that the data and computation are spread across multiple nodes in a network and there is no central point of control. Imagine a spreadsheet that is duplicated thousands of times across a network of computers. This is what a blockchain is, and it allows for a decentralized and transparent way of storing and sharing data.

Blockchains are built on top of distributed system technologies, such as peer-to-peer networks and consensus algorithms. A peer-to-peer network is a group of computers that share resources and information with each other without the need for a central authority. This is similar to a group of friends sharing music files with each other, where there is not one person in charge of the network. Consensus algorithms, on the other hand, are used to validate and process transactions on the network. These algorithms work to ensure that all nodes in the network have the same copy of the ledger and agree on the current state of the blockchain.

As blockchain technology has grown in popularity, its applications have expanded beyond just digital currencies. Many companies and organizations are now exploring the use of blockchain technology for various purposes such as supply chain management, digital identity, and more. For example, imagine a supply chain where every step of the process is recorded on a blockchain, this would provide transparency and traceability of the entire process, making it easy to identify any issues that may occur.

In conclusion, the history of distributed systems and blockchain technology have been closely intertwined, with blockchain technology building on the principles and technologies of distributed systems to create a decentralized, secure and transparent way of storing and sharing data. It is like building a new structure on the foundation of an old one, the new structure can have its own purpose and design but it relies on the foundation to stand.

The advancement of mechanical and electromechanical devices like The Enigma machine, the German cipher machine utilized during WWII in the early 1900s paved the way for the development of evolved and much more refined encryption tactics. With the arrival of computers and the internet, cryptography and distributed systems have gained significant importance in ensuring secure digital communication and information. They have a wide range of applications and are used to solve various problems that we face in today's world.

We might encounter more problems in the coming days, as we are still walking into much advanced era of modernization.

Cryptography's basic concepts and terminologies

Before deep diving into related concepts and further links of cryptography. Let us step out and familiarize ourselves with a few basic concepts and terminologies:

- **Encryption**: The process of converting plaintext into ciphertext, making it unreadable to unauthorized parties.
- **Decryption**: The act of deciphering the encoded message (ciphertext) back to its original form (plaintext) so that it can be read and understood by those who are authorized to do so.
- **Cipher**: The algorithm used for encryption and decryption.
- **Key**: A private value utilized in combination with an encryption algorithm to scramble and unscramble information.
- **Symmetric key**: A solitary private key utilized for both the procedures of encoding and decoding.
- **Asymmetric key**: A pair of keys, one for encryption and one for decryption, that are mathematically related but not identical.
- **Plaintext**: The original, unencrypted data.
- **Ciphertext**: The encrypted data.
- **Hash function**: A one-way function that takes an input (or message) and returns a fixed-size string of characters, which is typically a *digest* that is unique to the unique message.
- **Digital signature**: A digital code that is attached to an electronically transmitted document to verify its contents and the sender's identity.
- **Public key infrastructure (PKI)**: A collection of hardware, software, individuals, protocols, and protocols necessary for the establishment, administration, dissemination, utilization, storage, and revocation of digital certificates.
- **Certificate authority (CA)**: An organization that issues digital certificates and manages the PKI.
- **Non-repudiation**: The ability to prove that a specific individual was responsible for a particular action or message.
- **Authentication**: The process of verifying the identity of an individual or entity.

- **Key management**: The process of creating, distributing, storing, and protecting keys.

We will be looking at the above concepts in detail in the coming sections.

Know about cryptography

Cryptography is the practice of secure communication by converting plain text into an encoded message (ciphertext) and vice versa, using mathematical algorithms. As shown through *Figure 1.2*, cryptography is a combined version of two Greek words: **Kryptos** (Hidden) and **Graphia** (Writing):

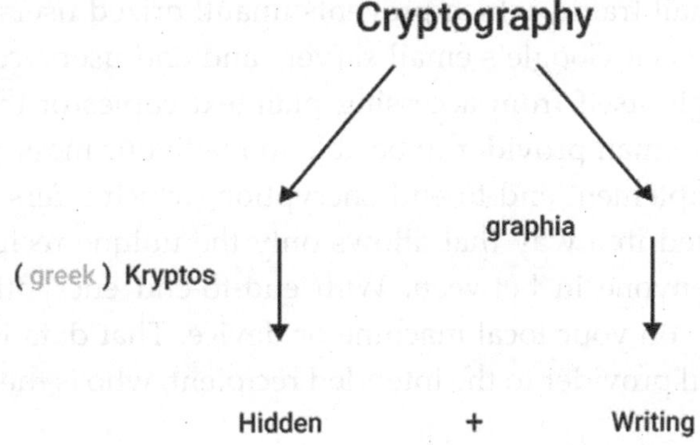

***Figure 1.2**: Cryptography has been derived from two Greek words*

Oxford dictionary quotes cryptography and cryptology as a secret manner of writing or solving ciphers. It is the science that embraces cryptography and cryptanalysis, but the term cryptology sometimes loosely designates the entire dual field of both rendering signals secure and extracting information from them.

Cryptography is the practice of secure communication by converting plain text into an encoded message (ciphertext) and vice versa, using mathematical algorithms. It is a fundamental element of computer security and is used in a wide range of applications, including online banking, e-commerce, and secure communications between governments and military organizations.

Cryptography encompasses more than just encryption, it also comprises other methods such as digital signature, which verifies the authenticity and ensures the integrity of a message, and secure key exchange, which enables two parties to establish a secure communication channel without the need of a pre-shared secret key. In decentralized systems, where there is no single central authority governing the flow of information, encryption becomes even more crucial as it enables honest users to securely exchange information and prevents malicious individuals from tampering with or deceiving the system.

Encryption: A way to secure system

Cryptography is often misunderstood as the seal of ultimate security. Cryptography may be a component of a secure system. Adding cryptography may not make a system secure, but it also does not weaken the same. How and at what layer your data is encrypted makes a huge difference. Just because a product or service uses encryption does not necessarily mean that everything that is stored on or sent over that platform is completely private. For example, Google now makes the HTTPS protocol, (HTTP over an encrypted connection) the default for all Gmail traffic, which prevents unauthorized users from reading emails while they travel between Google's email servers and end users' computers, but it does nothing to stop Google itself from accessing plaintext copies of those conversations. If you do not want your email provider to be able to read your messages, you have to take additional steps to implement end-to-end encryption, which refers to a system in which messages are encrypted in a way that allows only the unique recipient of a message to decrypt it, and not anyone in between. With end-to-end encryption, you encrypt the contents of a message on your local machine or device. That data is then transmitted as ciphertext by the email provider to the intended recipient, who is the only person who can decrypt and read it.

Here are a few lesser-known real-world applications of cryptography:

- **Secure voting systems**: Cryptography is used in securing electronic voting systems by protecting the privacy and integrity of the voting process. One key aspect of this is the use of **Voter-Verified Paper Audit Trails (VVPATs)**, which create a physical record of each vote cast. This allows for a tangible record to be used in case of any disputes or concerns about the integrity of the electronic vote. Additionally, digital signature algorithms are employed to confirm the authenticity of each vote and detect any signs of tampering. These measures work together to ensure that the voting process remains fair and transparent.
- **Secure email**: Cryptography is a powerful tool used to safeguard the confidentiality and integrity of email messages. Two widely used methods of email encryption are **Pretty Good Privacy (PGP)** and **Secure/Multipurpose Internet Mail Extensions (S/MIME)**. Both of these methods utilize public key cryptography, which allows for secure communication by providing a unique key for encrypting and decrypting messages. PGP and S/MIME are designed to protect the privacy of email messages by encrypting the contents of the message, so only the intended recipient can read it. Additionally, these methods provide a way to authenticate the sender of the message, which ensures that the message has not been tampered with and it is

coming from the intended source. These encryption methods are crucial for secure communication in various industries and organizations.

- **Secure audio and video conferencing**: Cryptography plays a vital role in ensuring the security of audio and video conferencing on platforms like **Zoom**. It allows for secure key exchange, digital signature verification, and encrypting audio and video streams.
- **Secure instant messaging**: Cryptography is utilized to protect instant messaging platforms, such as Signal and WhatsApp, through the use of end-to-end encryption.
- This ensures that messages are secured against interception or alteration while they are being transmitted.
- **Secure location-based services**: Cryptography performs an integral role in ensuring the security of location-based services, such as GPS navigation and location tracking. This is achieved through the implementation of various cryptographic techniques, including secure key exchange, digital signature verification, and encryption of location data. These techniques work together to protect the location information from being intercepted or tampered with by unauthorized parties, ensuring that the location-based services remain accurate and reliable.
- **Secure industrial control systems**: Cryptography plays a crucial role in safeguarding industrial control systems, which are widely used in various industrial settings such as power plants, oil refineries, and chemical facilities. These systems are responsible for controlling and monitoring various industrial processes, making them a prime target for cyber-attacks. The integrity and confidentiality of the control and monitoring data transmitted within these systems is vital to ensure the proper functioning and safety of the industrial facility. One example of a secure communication protocol that is commonly used in industrial control systems is the **International Society of Automation (ISA)** and **International Electrotechnical Commission (IEC)** 62443 standard. This standard provides a set of guidelines for the secure design, implementation, and maintenance of industrial control systems. It includes recommendations for secure communication protocols, such as the use of **virtual private networks (VPNs)** and **secure sockets layer (SSL)** certificates, as well as guidelines for digital signature verification and encryption of data.

Overall, the use of cryptography in industrial control systems is crucial in protecting the integrity and confidentiality of control and monitoring data transmitted within these systems, which can help to prevent unauthorized access, tampering and other malicious activities that could harm the industrial processes, and the safety of the employees, and the environment.

These are just a few examples of the real-world applications of cryptography. Cryptography plays a crucial role in securing various types of data and communication and it continues to evolve and be utilized in many different fields.

Industrial impact of cryptography

The advent of cryptography has rendered traditional methods of securing data and communications, such as the utilization of physical locks and keys, and simple substitution ciphers, obsolete. Cryptography offers a more sophisticated and robust method of protecting information by utilizing mathematical algorithms to encrypt and decrypt data. This makes it significantly more challenging for unauthorized individuals to gain access to or tamper with the information, akin to a safe that can only be unlocked with a complex combination rather than a simple key. Furthermore, cryptography enables secure key exchange, digital signature verification, and the ability to authenticate the identity of parties involved in a communication, which were not feasible with traditional methods, similar to a security guard that can only allow access to those with proper identification.

In industrial control systems, cryptography has supplanted the conventional approach of physical security, such as gates and security cameras, to safeguard the control and monitoring data transmitted within the system. The incorporation of secure communication protocols, digital signature verification, and encryption techniques, which are provided by cryptography, can ensure the integrity and confidentiality of the data. This can be likened to a fortress that has multiple layers of security, including a secure perimeter, guarded gates, and surveillance cameras, making it nearly impenetrable for unauthorized parties to access or tamper with the information. The secure communication protocols, digital signature verification and encryption techniques work together to secure the integrity and confidentiality of the data, protecting the industrial process and ensuring the safety of the employees and the environment.

Evolution of cryptography

Cryptography has been continuously evolving in response to technical advancements and security needs. Moreover, further advancements in technology and encryption methods continue to refine cryptography. Some of the key milestones in its evolution are as follows:

- The innovation of public-key cryptography in the 1970s brought forth the idea of utilizing a duo of keys, one for encoding and one for decoding, enabling secure correspondence without the prerequisite for pre-arranged secret key exchange.
- The extensive acceptance of the **Rivest–Shamir–Adleman** (**RSA**) algorithm, one of the initial viable public-key algorithms, during the 1980s, continues to persist in the contemporary times for safeguarding data transmission and authentication of digital signatures.

- The advent of **Elliptic-Curve Cryptography** (**ECC**) in the 1990s brought about a new cryptographic method that offers equivalent security to traditional algorithms but with reduced key sizes, rendering it more practical for use in devices with limited resources.
- The advancement of quantum computing, which has the potential to break many of the traditional encryption algorithms, prompted research and development into postquantum cryptography.
- The increasing use of cryptography in blockchain technology, which is the foundation of many decentralized digital currencies, such as Bitcoin and Ethereum.
- The utilization of cryptography in **Internet of Things** (**IoT**) devices has grown significantly in recent times, as these devices are frequently constrained by resources and require efficient and secure communication to safeguard sensitive data and personal information.
- The utilization of homomorphic encryption in cloud computing enables calculations to be performed on encrypted data, without the requirement for prior decryption, thus ensuring increased security and confidentiality for information retained in the cloud.

Public key cryptography

Public key cryptography involves a pair of keys, one public (known to everyone) and one private (known only to the owner). If Alice wants to send a secure message to Bob, she uses Bob's public key to encrypt it. Bob, with his private key, can decrypt and read the message.

Example: Think of it like sending a letter. Alice has a padlock (public key) that anyone can use to lock a box. Only Alice has the key (private key) to unlock the box and read the message inside.

RSA algorithm

Rivest-Shamir-Adleman (**RSA**) is a popular public key cryptosystem. Imagine Bob has two special numbers. He shares one of them (public key) with everyone. When Alice wants to send a secret message, she uses this number to lock it. Only Bob, with the other special number (private key), can unlock and read the message.

Some of its uses are:

- **Encryption**: Bob's public key is like a special lock, and Alice uses it to lock her message.

- **Decryption**: Bob's private key is like the unique key that opens the lock to read the message.

Elliptic curve cryptography

ECC is a powerful and innovative encryption method, revolutionizing the modern cryptographic techniques. It enhances security while requiring smaller key sizes compared to traditional cryptographic algorithms. Let us learn different aspects of ECC.

Key generation

Public Key (Q): Bob picks a curve and a point on it. He calls this point (G). His public key (Q) is a result of multiplying (G) by a secret number (d).

- Example: Q = d . G

Encryption: Generating a shared secret:

- When Alice wants to send Bob a secret message, she picks a random number (k).
- She computes a point (C) on the curve by multiplying (G) by (k).
- The x-coordinate of (C) is part of the encrypted message.
- The shared secret is derived by Bob multiplying (C) by his secret number (d).
- **Example: s = k . Q**

Decryption: Using the shared secret

- Bob, with his private key, multiplies (C) by (d) to get the same shared secret (s).
- Using a key derivation function, both Alice and Bob derive a symmetric key from (s).
- The symmetric key is used to decrypt the message.
- **Example: S = d . C**

Digital signatures

A digital signature is necessary to ensure message integrity and authenticity. It utilizes private keys to generate unique signatures, which provide a verifiable link between the signer and the message. Digital signatures are extensively used in cryptographic protocols.

Example:

- Bob uses his private key (d) to create a digital signature for a message.
- The signature involves multiplying a hash of the message by (d).
- This pair (H(m), s) serves as Bob's digital signature.

Example: s = d. H(m)

Strengths:

- ECC provides strong security with shorter keys.
- It is efficient, making it suitable for mobile devices and IoT.

Implementation note

ECC's security is based on the difficulty of a specific mathematical problem.

In essence, ECC uses curves and points on those curves to keep messages secure. The security comes from the complexity of certain mathematical operations, and ECC is chosen for its effectiveness and efficiency in securing communications.

These cryptographic methods help secure communication on the internet and ensure that only the intended recipient can access sensitive information.

The benefits of cryptography are as follows:

- Keeping information confidential through encryption
- Ensuring data integrity by detecting unauthorized changes
- Verifying the identities of those sending and receiving information
- Providing evidence of authenticity, making it impossible for the sender to deny sending a message

However, cryptography also has its drawbacks, such as:

- Being complex and difficult for non-experts to understand
- Incurring high costs for implementation and maintenance
- The challenge of properly managing and securing encryption keys
- Vulnerability to attacks from hackers or other malicious actors
- Limiting accessibility for those without the appropriate decryption key or knowledge.
- Adding computational overhead that can affect system performance

Encryption

Assume Alice and Bob possess a confidential key k. Alice intends to transfer a message m to Bob via a network, ensuring the confidentiality of m even in the presence of an eavesdropping adversary. Additionally, these same methods enable Alice to securely store a file on a disk, preventing anyone else with disk access from reading the file, while allowing Alice herself to access it later. Let us examine a fundamental technique to address this challenge.

Secure communication

Secure communication is the most critical element to ensure and preserve confidentiality and integrity. The intricate processes of encryption and decryption ensure that messages exchanged between parties stay immune to unauthorized accesses. Several elements play a crucial role in ensuring secure communication. They are as follows.

- **Encryption and decryption process:**

  Picture Alice wanting to securely send a message to Bob. They both share a secret key, let us call it k

  To maintain the message's confidentiality, Alice uses a special function E (encryption). She puts the key k and her message m into this function to produce a secret code c: $c=E(k,m)$ It is like locking the message.

  Bob, to read the message, uses another function D (decryption). He takes the key k and the secret code c to reverse the process and retrieve the original message: $m=D(k,c)$.

- **Shannon cipher functions:**

  In the world of cryptography, this system is known as a **Shannon cipher**. It consists of two functions: E for encryption and D for decryption.

  For instance, if k is the secret key, m is the message *Hello, World!* and c is the coded message, the process would be: Encryption: *E(k,"Hello, World!")*.

  Decryption: $m=D(k,c)$.

- **Key exchange:**

  Before Alice and Bob can use this cipher, they must agree on the same secret key k. They might do this through a secure channel or in person.

  Once they both have k, they can use it to lock and unlock messages securely.

- **Challenges with perfect security:**

  Achieving perfect security means having keys as long as the messages, which is impractical.

  In practice, a balance is sought. The key needs to be strong enough to keep messages secure but not excessively long.

- **Practical security example:**

  Imagine Alice wants to send the password *MySecurePassword* to Bob. She uses the key k and the encryption function E to create a secure code c.

Encryption: $c=E(k,\text{"MySecurePassword"})$

When Bob receives c, he uses the same key k and the decryption function D to retrieve the original password.

Decryption: $m=D(k,c)$.

In summary, Alice and Bob can communicate securely using a Shannon cipher. While achieving perfect security is challenging, they aim for strong, practical security by choosing suitable key lengths and encryption methods.

Principles of cryptography

Cryptography is the technique of securing information by converting it into a code that can only be read by those who are permitted to do so. The core ideas and rules of cryptography encompass:

- **Confidentiality**: Ensuring that confidential information is protected from those who are not authorized to access it.
- **Integrity**: The information is sensitive so its nature should not be tampered with or altered in any way.
- **Authentication**: Confirming the identity of the sender and receiver of the packet of information.
- **Non-repudiation**: Ensuring that the sender of the info cannot deny the origin of the content.
- **Key management**: Managing the generation, distribution, storage, and use of keys for encryption and decryption in a secure manner.
- **Algorithms**: Algorithms are math functions that help secure information by converting it into an unreadable form and making it readable again through decryption.
- **Public key cryptography**: Public key cryptography involves using a publicly accessible key to encrypt data and a privately held key to decrypt it. On the other hand, symmetric key cryptography employs a single secret key to encrypt and decrypt data.
- **Hash functions**: Mathematical functions that take an input (or *message*) and produce a fixed-length output, used to confirm the integrity of the original message

We will delve into these topics extensively as we progress forward. These notions and precepts are put into practice in diverse encryption techniques, including symmetric-key encryption, asymmetric-key encryption, and hash functions.

Encryption algorithms

Encryption algorithms are a fundamental aspect of cryptography, the practice of securing information through encoding it in such a way that it can only be accessed by authorized parties. These algorithms are mathematical functions that are used to encrypt and decrypt information. Like the unique identification methods, we have with our secure vaults. They play a crucial role in maintaining the confidentiality, integrity, and authenticity of the information being exchanged.

Two major types of encryptions are symmetric-key encryption and asymmetric-key encryption:

Symmetric-key encryption

Symmetric-key encryption, also known as secret-key encryption, utilizes a single shared key to both encrypt and decrypt data. This requires that the same key is exchanged between the sender and recipient of the information. Various examples of symmetric-key encryption algorithms include the following:

Data encryption standard

The **data encryption standard** (**DES**) is a symmetric-key encryption algorithm that was developed by IBM in the 1970s and was adopted as a standard by the US government in 1977. It uses a 56-bit key to encrypt and decrypt data. DES works by dividing the plaintext data into 64-bit blocks and then applying a series of mathematical operations, known as rounds, to each block. DES is a bit-oriented cipher. The key is used to control the operations performed in each round. DES was widely used for many years in various applications such as ATM transactions, e-commerce, and government communications. However, due to the advancement of computer power and the increasing need for stronger security, it was considered to be vulnerable to brute force attacks, where an attacker could use a computer program to try all possible keys until the correct one is found. In 2000, the US government announced that it was no longer considered secure for use in non-sensitive applications and the **Advanced Encryption Standard** (**AES**) was developed as a replacement. However, due to its widespread use, many legacy systems still use DES, and it is still used in some specific applications where its key size is considered sufficient. Overall, DES is considered to be a strong encryption algorithm for its time, but it is now considered to be too weak for most practical applications and should be replaced by more secure encryption algorithms such as AES.

Advanced encryption standard

The AES algorithm is widely employed today as it is considered one of the most secure symmetric-key encryption methods. AES is a specification for the encryption of electronic data established by the U.S **National Institute of Standards and Technology (NIST)** in 2001. AES is extensively utilized nowadays due to its superior security compared to DES and triple DES, even though it may be more challenging to implement. DES is a cipher that operates on bits, whereas AES is a cipher that operates on bytes. AES supports three different key lengths: 128, 192, or 256 bits. Our discussion will primarily focus on the 128-bit key length. Encryption involves 10 rounds of processing for 128-bit keys, 12 rounds for 192-bit keys, and 14 rounds for 256-bit keys. Apart from the last round in each case, all other rounds are identical. Each round of processing comprises a substitution step based on single bytes, a permutation step based on rows, a mixing step based on columns, and the addition of the round key. The order in which these four steps are executed differs for encryption and decryption.

That means it takes 128 bits as input and outputs 128 bits of encrypted cipher text as output. AES relies on substitution-permutation network principle which means it is performed using a series of linked operations which involves replacing and shuffling of the input data. AES was designed using the wide-trail strategy. As described in the publication security of a wide trail design by *Joan Daemen* and *Vincent Rijmen*, wide-trail design for a block cipher involves:

- A local nonlinear transformation (as *8 Computer and Network Security* by *Avi Kak* lecture 8 supplied by the substitution step in AES).
- A linear mixing transformation that provides high diffusion.

The phrase wide trail refers to the dispersal of the probabilities that one can associate with the bits at certain specific positions in a bit block as it propagates through the rounds.

Some points to remember in AES are as follows:

- AES is a block cipher.
- The key size can be 128/192/256 bits.
- Encrypts data in blocks of 128 bits each.
- AES is an example of key-alternating block ciphers.
- AES is a byte-oriented cipher.

One of the key disadvantages of symmetric-key encryption is that the key must be securely exchanged between the sender and receiver, before any communication can take place. This can be a significant challenge, especially in situations where the parties have not had the opportunity to share a key in advance.

Additionally, symmetric-key encryption may be vulnerable to brute force attacks, where an attacker uses a computer program to try all possible keys until the correct one is found. However, with the advancement of computer power and the increasing key size, this vulnerability has been mitigated.

In recent years, symmetric-key encryption is often used in combination with asymmetric-key encryption in order to securely exchange the symmetric key. This technique is known as **hybrid encryption** and is widely used in modern communication protocols such as **Transport Layer Security (TLS)** and **Secure Shell (SSH)**.

Overall, symmetric-key encryption is a robust encryption method that is widely used in various applications, it is considered to be fast, secure and efficient.

Originally, symmetric algorithms had a major flaw in that they only worked well if both parties already knew the shared secret. This made it hard to exchange a key securely without a third-party snooping in. Even if the key was obtained by a third party, they could easily break the encryption, making communication insecure.

However, the **Diffie-Hellman protocol** solved this issue by allowing strangers to exchange information over public channels to create a shared key. This shared key is difficult to crack, even if all the communications are monitored.

Working of Diffie-Hellman

Diffie-Hellman is a revolutionary cryptographic concept that enables secure key exchange over an untrusted network. Introduced by *Whitfield Diffie* and *Martin Hellman* in 1976, it forms the basis for secure communication by allowing two parties to independently generate a shared secret key without directly exchanging it. This key exchange method is crucial for establishing secure connections, underpinning protocols like HTTPS, SSH, and VPNs. The brilliance of Diffie-Hellman lies in its ability to facilitate secure communication in a world where transmitting secret keys openly would be highly vulnerable to interception The way this works is represented through *Figure 1.5*:

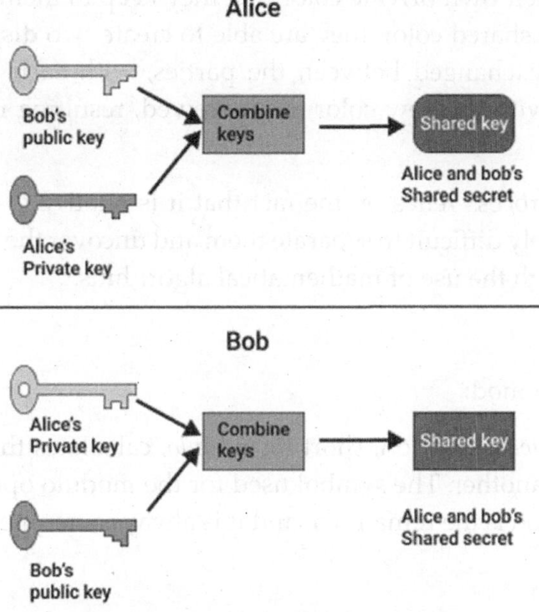

Figure 1.5: Working of Diffie-Hellman

We can get more clarity with the help of *Figure 1.6*. Here Alice and Bob have agreed upon a common starting point (which must be unique every time they communicate):

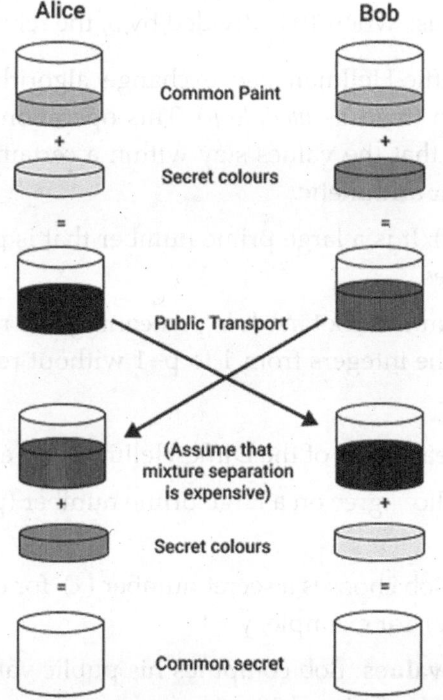

Figure 1.6: Color-based example of the Diffie-Hellman concept

Each party also has their own private color that they keep to themselves. By mixing their private color with the shared color, they are able to create two distinct new colors. These new colors are then exchanged between the parties, with each party then using their private color to mix with the new color they received, resulting in the same final secret color.

The security of this process relies on the fact that it is relatively simple to combine two colors, but it is extremely difficult to separate them and uncover the secret color. In practice, this is achieved through the use of mathematical algorithms.

For example:

First, we should know mod:

In mathematics, the *mod* operation, short for *modulo,* calculates the remainder when one integer is divided by another. The symbol used for the modulo operation is %. The result of the modulo operation is the remainder, and it is always a non-negative integer less than the divisor.

For example:

7mod 37mod3 is 1 because when 7 is divided by 3, the remainder is 1.

15mod 415mod4 is 3 because when 15 is divided by 4, the remainder is 3.

10mod 510mod5 is 0 because when 10 is divided by 5, the remainder is 0.

In the context of the Diffie-Hellman key exchange algorithm, the modulo operation is often denoted as modp (read as *modulo p*). This operation is applied to the result of exponentiation to ensure that the values stay within a certain range, typically from 0 to p–1 in the case of modular arithmetic.

- **Prime number (p)**: It is a large prime number that is publicly known and shared between the parties.
- **Base (g)**: It is a primitive root modulo p, meaning that raising g to different powers will generate all the integers from 1 to p–1 without repetition. The base g is also publicly known.

Now, Let us break down each step of the Diffie-Hellman key exchange process:

1. **Setup**: Bob and Alice agree on a large prime number (p) and a base (g). Let us say p = 29 and g = 5.
2. **Secret numbers**: Bob chooses a secret number (x), for example, x = 4. Alice selects a secret number (y), for example, y = 8.
3. **Calculate public values**: Bob computes his public value X using $X = g\text{^}x \bmod p$. Bob's calculation: $X = 5\text{^}4 \bmod 29 = 16$.

Alice computes her public value Y using $Y = g\^y \bmod p$. Alice's calculation: $Y = 5\^8 \bmod 29 = 24$.

4. **Exchange public values**: Bob sends his public value X to Alice. Alice sends her public value Y to Bob.
5. **Calculate shared secret**: Bob computes the shared secret K using $K = Y\^x \bmod p$. Bob's calculation: $K = 24\^4 \bmod 29 = 16$. Alice computes the shared secret K using $K = X\^y \bmod p$. Alice's calculation: $K = 16\^8 \bmod 29 = 16$.

   Result: Both Bob and Alice now have the same secret key (K = 16). This shared secret key (K) can be used for secure communication, and outsiders, even if they know X and Y, cannot easily deduce K.

Note: The brilliance lies in the fact that the shared secret (K) remains secure, even though the public values (X and Y) were openly exchanged. This ensures secure communication between Bob and Alice.

The security of this protocol relies on several key factors, as following:

- Generating prime numbers, even large ones like p, is relatively straightforward.
- Performing modular exponentiation, such as computing $X = g \wedge x \% p$, is also easily achievable.
- Extracting modular roots without knowing the prime factors is exceedingly difficult. It remains a challenging task to find K without possessing knowledge of x and y, even if one has access to the transmitted data, including p, g, X, and Y. This is based on the assumption of current computational power and mathematical understanding.

While it is relatively simple to perform the necessary mathematical operations to create the key, attempting to break the key through brute force is highly demanding and time consuming. Even if an attacker were to compromise the key, Diffie-Hellman ensures perfect forward secrecy. In summary, the process can be exemplified as follows:

- Alice and Bob independently select a secret key, and a function is applied to these keys to generate a public key. Only the resulting values, not the function itself, are shared. Even if a third party intercepts the communication, they will not possess all the necessary information to deduce the underlying function used. Subsequently, Alice and Bob each apply a new function using the received results, their own secret numbers, and the original prime value. This process leads them to a shared secret key that cannot be inferred by a third party. Alice and Bob can now communicate without concerns about potential eavesdropping.

- Alice and Bob privately select a confidential key, and a procedure is executed on these keys to generate a public key. The outcomes, rather than the procedure itself, are exchanged between them. Even if an eavesdropper is present, they will not possess all the relevant numbers, making it challenging to deduce the procedure used to derive the numbers.

- Subsequently, Alice and Bob individually employ a new procedure using the received outcomes, their own secret values, and the original prime number. Through this process, Alice and Bob arrive at a shared secret key that is indiscernible to third parties. As a result, Alice and Bob can freely communicate without concerns about the presence of eavesdroppers.

Limitations of Diffie-Hellman

The primary drawback of the basic form of Diffie-Hellman is its lack of authentication. When using Diffie-Hellman alone, there is a vulnerability to man-in-the-middle attacks. To mitigate this, it is recommended to combine Diffie-Hellman with a recognized authentication method, such as digital signatures, to verify the identities of users over a public communication medium.

Diffie-Hellman does not provide identity verification, meaning that anyone can claim to be a certain user without a built-in mechanism to verify their claims. Additionally, if the implementation is not carried out securely and with proper precautions, the algorithm can be susceptible to attacks with dedicated resources. For example, the strength of the implementation can be compromised if the random number generator lacks sufficient entropy to support the desired level of security. The degree of uncertainty injected into the generation of random numbers impacts the strength of the implementation.

Furthermore, in 2015, a vulnerability was demonstrated where the use of the same prime numbers for key exchanges by multiple servers weakened the overall security of Diffie-Hellman. Attackers could precompute attacks against those specific prime numbers, making it easier to compromise sessions of servers that used them. This issue arose because numerous servers were utilizing the same prime numbers. Precomputing such attacks still requires significant resources typically available to academic or nation-state actors, and it is unlikely to affect the majority of individuals.

Fortunately, for those concerned about nation-state attackers, there is an alternative method to achieve Diffie-Hellman key exchange using **Elliptic Curve Diffie-Hellman (ECDHE)**. ECDHE is beyond the scope of this book, but if you are interested in exploring the mathematical concepts behind this exchange, you can refer to the mentioned article. You can look ECDHE.

Application of symmetric encryption

Symmetric encryption is known for its speed and efficiency in handling large volumes of data. It safeguards sensitive information while ensuring swift data processing. Hence, it finds diverse applications across industries, with some of them are as follows:

- **Banking sector**: Symmetric encryption is often favored for its fast speed and efficient performance, making it a preferred choice for encrypting large quantities of data. Some banking services also rely on symmetric encryption for their security protocols.
- **Payment applications**: Applications used for financial transactions, such as card payments, require protection of sensitive information to avoid theft of personal identity and unauthorized charges without incurring high expenses. This approach minimizes the risks associated with handling payment transactions on a regular basis. Verification processes are in place to ensure the authenticity of the sender of a message.
- **Securing data at rest**: To secure data that is not actively being used, organizations can opt to encrypt confidential documents before archiving them or alternatively, encrypt the entire storage device.

Pros and limitations of symmetric encryption

Symmetric encryption has several notable advantages. However, this encryption method also faces significant limitations. Some limitations are as follows:

- Main advantage of symmetric cryptography is that it is much faster than asymmetric cryptography.
- Disadvantage that is spiking with this encryption is the key distribution problem and the key management problem for example when number of connected users increases, the number of keys is directly proportional the connected users number.
- To add more symmetric cryptography only ensures confidentiality of the transmitted or stored data. It cannot guaranty the integrity or authenticity.

Asymmetric-key encryption

Asymmetric-key encryption, also known as **public-key encryption**, utilizes a pair of keys: a public key and a private key. These keys are distinct and not identical. The public key is employed for encryption, while the private key is utilized for decryption. Therefore, the sender encrypts the information using the recipient's public key, and the recipient decrypts it using their private key. The public key is a key from the pair that can be shared with everyone, while the private key is the other key that is kept confidential. It is referred to as the private key. Any key can be used to encrypt a message, and the other key, which is not used for encryption, is employed for decryption. Examples of asymmetric-key encryption algorithms include RSA and **Elliptic Curve Cryptography** (**ECC**).

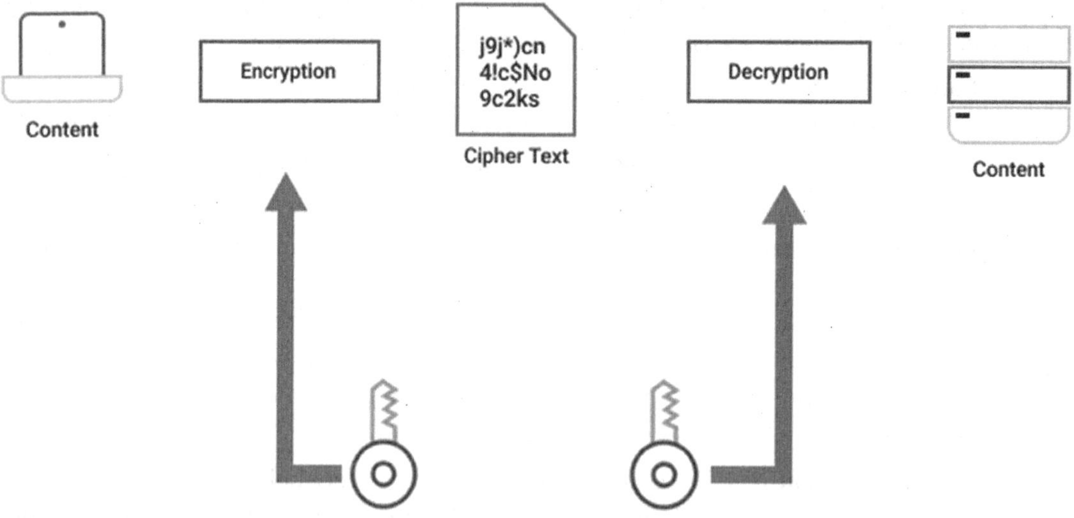

Figure 1.7: *In Asymmetric cryptography, public and private keys are not identical*

In asymmetric cryptography, the principles of authenticity and non-repudiation are upheld.

Encrypting a message with a private key establishes authenticity, providing proof of identity. Additionally, using a private key to encrypt a message ensures non-repudiation, as the sender cannot deny sending it. It is worth noting that either a public or private key can be used for encryption, and either a public or private key can also be used for decryption.

One of the key advantages of asymmetric-key encryption over symmetric-key encryption is that it allows for secure communication even if the parties involved have not previously shared a secret key. This is because the public key can be freely distributed, while the private key is kept secret. This is particularly useful in cases where the parties may not have had the opportunity to share a secret key in advance, such as in secure communication over the internet. Another important aspect of encryption algorithms is their ability to maintain the integrity of the information being exchanged. Hash functions are mathematical functions that take an input (or *message*) and return a fixed-size string of characters, known as a **hash**. These hashes.

The functionality of asymmetric encryption

Asymmetric encryption is a cornerstone in ensuring secure digital communication. This technique uses a pair of keys – private and public – to facilitate secure data exchange between entities, all while ensuring confidentiality and authenticity. Step-by-step illustration of the process is as follows:

- **Key generation**: The first step is to generate a pair of keys, a public key and a private key. These keys are mathematically related but not identical. The private key is kept secret and should not be shared with anyone, while the public key can be freely distributed.
- **Encryption**: When a message is to be sent, the sender will use the recipient's public key to encrypt the message. The encryption process uses a complex mathematical algorithm to scramble the message in such a way that it can only be read by someone who has the corresponding private key.
- **Transmission**: The encrypted message is then transmitted to the recipient over a secure communication channel, such as an encrypted email or a VPN connection.
- **Decryption**: Upon receipt of the message, the recipient utilizes their own private key to decrypt the message. The decryption process employs the same mathematical algorithm as was used for encryption, but in reverse order. This enables the recipient to read the initial message.
- **Digital signature**: The sender can also use their private key to create a digital signature of the message, which will be sent along with the encrypted message. The digital signature provides authenticity and non-repudiation, meaning that the recipient can confirm that the message was indeed sent by the sender and not tampered with.
- **Signature verification**: The recipient can use the sender's public key to verify the signature and confirm that the message was indeed sent by the sender and not tampered with.

In summary, Asymmetric encryption uses a pair of unique keys, one public and one private, to encrypt and decrypt messages. This ensures that only the intended recipient can read the message, and provides authenticity and non-repudiation by using digital signature. The private key is kept secret, while the public key can be freely distributed.

Refer to *Table 1.1* for the difference between symmetric and asymmetric encryption:

Symmetric	Asymmetric
Utilizes a single key for both encrypting and decrypting information.	Utilizes two keys, one for encryption and the other for decryption.
Encrypted data and keys are exchanged.	Only the encrypted data is exchanged, and the public key is available for anyone.
Quicker	Slow
Unmanageable if no of the participants become higher.	Operations can be streamlined with pairs of public and private keys.
Risk in exchanging the key in the network channel.	A private key is not exchanged.

***Table 1.1**: Difference between symmetric and asymmetric encryption*

Different types of asymmetric encryption algorithms

Following are the different types of asymmetric encryption algorithms:

- **Rivest-Shamir-Adleman (RSA)**: One of the most widely used asymmetric encryption algorithms, RSA is based on the mathematical properties of large prime numbers. It can be used for both encryption and digital signatures.
- **Elliptic Curve Cryptography (ECC)**: This algorithm is based on the mathematics of elliptic curves and is considered to be more efficient and secure than RSA for the same level of security.
- **Diffie-Hellman**: This algorithm is used for secure key exchange, and is often used in conjunction with other encryption algorithms such as AES.
- **Digital Signature Algorithm (DSA)**: This algorithm is based on the mathematical properties of large prime numbers and is used specifically for digital signatures.
- **ElGamal**: This algorithm is based on the discrete logarithm problem and is similar to the Diffie-Hellman algorithm in that it can be used for both encryption and digital signatures.
- **Quantum key distribution**: This is a new technology that uses the properties of quantum mechanics to secure the exchange of keys between two parties. It is considered to be highly secure and resistant to hacking, but is still in the early stages of development.

Each of these algorithms has its own set of advantages and disadvantages, and the choice of which one to use will depend on the specific requirements of the application.

Pros and cons of asymmetric encryption

Asymmetric encryption offers several advantages, but it has some limitations too. Here are the pros and cons of asymmetric encryption.

Pros

Pros of asymmetric encryption are as follows:

- **Enhanced security**: Asymmetric encryption uses two keys, a public key for encryption and a private key for decryption. The private key, being confidential, reduces the risk of unauthorized access. Even if the public key is intercepted, it cannot be used to decrypt the data without the corresponding private key.
- **Public key distribution**: Public keys can be freely distributed across networks, facilitating a straightforward key exchange. This simplicity is particularly advantageous in scenarios where secure communication needs to be established between parties that have not shared keys beforehand.
- **Digital signatures for trust**: The use of digital signatures in asymmetric encryption enhances accountability and trust in digital communication. Digital signatures verify the authenticity and integrity of a message or document, assuring the recipient that it comes from the claimed sender and has not been tampered with.
- **Versatility in use**: Asymmetric encryption supports various use cases, including data encryption, secure key exchange, digital signatures, and authentication in security protocols. Its versatility makes it suitable for a wide range of security applications.

Cons

Cons of asymmetric encryption are as follows:

- **Computational intensity**: Asymmetric encryption is computationally more intensive compared to symmetric encryption. The complex mathematical operations involved can impact the performance of systems, especially in resource-constrained environments.
- **Slower performance**: Due to the complexity of the algorithms used, the performance of asymmetric encryption is generally slower than that of symmetric encryption. This slowness may be a significant consideration in applications where real-time processing is crucial.
- **Private key management**: The storage and management of private keys can be strenuous. Losing a private key poses a significant risk, as it can lead to the

compromise of sensitive data. Proper key management practices are essential to mitigate this risk.

- **Inefficiency with large data sets**: Asymmetric encryption is considered less efficient when dealing with large data sets. The computational overhead becomes more pronounced, making symmetric encryption more suitable for scenarios involving extensive data encryption.

Practical limitations of asymmetric encryption are as follows:

- **Computational overhead**: Asymmetric encryption involves complex mathematical operations, leading to higher computational overhead compared to symmetric encryption. This can be a significant limitation in scenarios where computational resources are limited, such as IoT devices or systems with constrained processing power.
- **Slower performance in bulk operations**: The slower performance of asymmetric encryption becomes more pronounced when dealing with bulk data. Encrypting and decrypting large volumes of data using asymmetric algorithms may result in delays, impacting the responsiveness of applications.
- **Key length trade-offs**: To enhance security, longer key lengths are often recommended in asymmetric encryption. However, longer key lengths contribute to increased computational demands. Striking a balance between security and performance becomes a trade-off that organizations must carefully consider.
- **Key distribution challenges**: While the distribution of public keys is straightforward, ensuring the secure distribution of corresponding private keys is challenging. Any compromise or unauthorized access to private keys can lead to severe consequences, making robust key management crucial.
- **Limited efficiency in certain use cases**: Asymmetric encryption might not be the most efficient choice for certain use cases, such as encrypting large databases or streaming multimedia content. In these scenarios, symmetric encryption or hybrid approaches are often preferred for better performance.
- **Vulnerability to quantum computing**: The advent of quantum computing poses a potential threat to asymmetric encryption, especially those relying on mathematical problems like integer factorization or discrete logarithms. Quantum computers could potentially break widely used asymmetric algorithms, requiring the development of quantum-resistant cryptographic methods.
- **Resource-intensive key generation**: The generation of key pairs in asymmetric encryption is resource-intensive, especially for longer key lengths. This process can contribute to delays in setting up secure communication channels, impacting the user experience in applications that require rapid initiation of secure connections.

- **Need for ongoing management**: Asymmetric encryption systems require ongoing management of key pairs, including secure storage, periodic key rotation, and handling key compromises. This management overhead adds complexity and necessitates a robust security policy.

Understanding these practical limitations is crucial for organizations when deciding on the most suitable encryption approach based on their specific use cases, performance requirements, and the overall security landscape.

Cryptographic protocols

Cryptographic protocols, also known as **cryptographic mechanisms**, are sets of rules and procedures that are used to secure communication by providing confidentiality, integrity, authenticity, and non-repudiation. These protocols are designed to work in conjunction with cryptographic algorithms, such as those used for encryption, to provide a secure communication channel between two or more parties.

Some examples of cryptographic protocols are as follows:

- **SSL/TLS**: SSL and TLS, which stands for Secure Sockets Layer and Transport Layer Security respectively, are sets of rules and procedures that are utilized to ensure secure communication across the internet. These protocols ensure the confidentiality and reliability of data sent over a network, for example when accessing a website or conducting an e-commerce transaction.
- **Internet Protocol Security (IPSec)**: It is a set of protocols that are used to secure communication over an IP network. It is commonly used to secure communication between two private networks over the internet, such as when setting up a VPN.
- **Secure Shell (SSH)**: It is a cryptographic protocol that is used to secure remote login and other network services. It provides confidentiality and integrity for data transmitted over the network, and is commonly used for remote management of servers and other network devices.
- **Pretty Good Privacy (PGP)**: It is a protocol for encryption and digital signature which is commonly used for email and file encryption. It is a software package that uses a combination of symmetric-key and public-key cryptography.
- **Kerberos**: Kerberos is a network authentication protocol that is used to secure communication over a non-secure network. It provides authentication and confidentiality for network services and is commonly used in enterprise environments.
- **Open Authorization (OAuth)**: It is an open standard for access delegation, commonly used as a way for Internet users to grant websites or applications access to their information on other websites but without giving them the passwords.

Each of these protocols has its own set of advantages and disadvantages, and the choice of which one to use will depend on the specific requirements of the application.

Cryptographic key management

The management of cryptographic keys is the practice of handling the keys utilized for various purposes in a cryptographic network. Cryptographic keys function similar to physical keys that we use in our daily lives to unlock our belongings. A cryptographic key comprises a set of data used for securing or decrypting cryptographic features. The primary objective of cryptographic key management is to oversee the creation, distribution, preservation, application, replacement, and disposal of keys. This encompasses cryptographic protocol development, key servers, user protocols, authentication, authorization, encryption, and other pertinent protocols.

Just as physical keys come in various shapes and sizes and have distinct applications, cryptographic keys also vary in their form and function. These keys are classified into multiple categories based on their specific roles in cryptographic operations.

There are three main approaches to the management of cryptographic keys, which can be categorized as decentralized, distributed, and centralized. In the decentralized approach, end users bear sole responsibility for the management of their own keys, and the organization is not involved in the governance process of keys. On the other hand, the distributed approach involves each team or department within the organization implementing their own key management protocol based on their individual processes and policies. These teams may or may not collaborate or coordinate with each other in terms of key management.

In contrast, centralized key management entails a uniform policy that applies organization-wide and is followed by all teams and departments. Users across the organization adhere to the same key management protocol in this centralized approach.

Further cryptographic keys are classified into many varieties draw out from the basic ones on base of slight security mitigations added to make it crack proof.

Key management is very crucial to the security of cryptosystems. It is one of the most difficult processes of cryptography and involves wide range perspectives such as system policy, user training, institutional and departmental interactions.

Process of cryptographic key management

Cryptographic key management consist following stages:

- **Key exchange**: Cryptographic operations necessitate cryptographic keys. Public keys can be openly shared, while symmetric keys require a secure connection.

The conventional method involves transmitting keys through secure channels like diplomatic pouches and employing protocols such as Diffie-Hellman key exchange.

- **Key storage**: Key storage refers to the secure management of cryptographic keys, ensuring their proper allocation and protection. There are multiple approaches to securely store distributed keys. The application takes responsibility for handling the key and utilizes an access password to regulate its usage.
- **Key use**: As time period of keys in use increases, risk factors also pike. as the risk of a hacker is directly proportional to time duration of same key in use. That is why the keys should be frequently changed which limits chances of being compromised.

Public key cryptography

Public key cryptography employs two distinct keys for **encryption** and **decryption**; hence it is also referred to as asymmetric-key cryptography. Public key cryptography is derived from reversible mathematical function, making it fundamentally distinct from conventional symmetric key cryptography.

It is not that symmetric key cryptosystem is less effective than public key or the public key cryptosystem. The security of any cryptosystem relies solely on the key length and the computational effort needed to decrypt the encrypted cipher text.

Principles behind public key cryptography

In symmetric cryptography, ensuring confidentiality and authenticity are key concerns. In this type of cryptography, a shared secret key is used for both encrypting and decrypting the content. However, securely sharing this key between parties poses a risk. Additionally, symmetric key cryptography faces challenges when it comes to authentication. To address these issues and gain wider acceptance, digital signatures were introduced to provide assurance that a message has been sent by a specific individual. On the other hand, public key cryptography has successfully achieved both confidentiality and authenticity principles.

Let us analyze the process involved in public key cryptography.

Initially, to ensure data integrity and source authentication, the sender's private key is used to encrypt the content, thus acting as a digital signature. Additionally, this confirms that the encrypted content cannot be tampered without the sender's private key. Public key cryptography achieves authentication in terms of data integrity and source.

Afterward, the content that was encrypted with the sender's private key is encrypted again with the recipient's public key. The ultimate cipher text can only be decrypted using the recipient's private key, which is exclusive to them, ensuring confidentiality.

However, there is a drawback to this approach. Public key cryptography relies on mathematical functions, which make it more complex and computationally intensive. To achieve both confidentiality and authenticity, the public key algorithm must be applied four times.

Public key cryptography involves several steps to ensure secure communication between two parties:

- Firstly, each user must generate a pair of keys, one of which is for encrypting messages and the other for decrypting them.
- Secondly, each user must make one of their keys public while keeping the other private.

When a user wants to send a message to a specific recipient, they must encrypt the message using the recipient's public key and then transmit the encrypted message.

Upon receiving the message, the recipient can then decrypt it using their private key to read the original message. By following these steps, public key cryptography can provide secure communication while ensuring that only the intended recipient can read the message.

Public key cryptosystem applications

Public key cryptography is considered highly crucial in the fields of secure communication methods and identity verification mechanisms across digital platforms. It has various applications and some of the prominent ones among them are as follows:

- **Decryption/encryption**: If the objective of an application is to encode and decode the message, then the sender must encode the message using the intended recipient's public key, and the recipient can decode the message using their own private key.
- **Authentication**: It can certify that the message or user is legal or not. Authentication represent that users are who they request to be. Availability describe that resources are accessible by authorized parties such as denial of service attacks, which are the sensitive matter of national information, are attacks against availability.
- **Digital signature**: When the primary goal of an application is to confirm the authenticity of the sender, a digital signature can be used. This involves encrypting or signing the message using the private key of the sender. Since only the sender

has access to their private key, it assures all parties involved that the message is indeed sent by that particular individual.

- **Key generation**: Each user generates two keys including public key and private key. The private key maintain at user side and public key is freely accessible in the network.
- **Verification**: The signed signature is verified by the public key of concerned user.

RSA

RSA is named after its creators, Rivest, Shamir, and Adleman. It is an asymmetric cryptographic algorithm that facilitates the generation of public and private keys. RSA enables key exchange, where each party involved in a transaction is assigned their own set of public and private keys. Subsequently, a symmetric key is generated and securely communicated using the public/private key pairs. Asymmetric encryption, although typically slower than symmetric encryption and less scalable, is commonly employed for securely exchanging symmetric keys.

RSA using asymmetric cryptographic algorithm which works on a block cipher concept that converts plain text into ciphertext and vice versa at the receiver side. If the public key of User A is used for encryption, we have to use the private key of the same user for decryption.

To implement the RSA encryption algorithm, the following steps are taken:

1. First, two prime numbers *X* and *Y* are selected. These prime numbers must be large to ensure security.
2. The product of the two primes, denoted as $N = X*Y$, is calculated. This product forms the basis of the encryption algorithm.
3. Next, a public key *E* is chosen. It must not be a factor of $(X-1)$ and $(Y-1)$.
4. A private key *D* is selected such that the equation $(D * E) \bmod (X-1) * (Y-1) = 1$ holds true.
5. For encryption, the ciphertext *CT* is calculated as $CT = (plaintext)^E \bmod N$. The resulting *CT* is then sent to the receiver.
6. Finally, for decryption, the plaintext *PT* is calculated as $PT = (ciphertext)^D \bmod N$.

These steps form the basis of the RSA encryption algorithm, which is widely used in secure communication systems due to its effectiveness in ensuring confidentiality and authenticity.

Note: In the RSA algorithm, selecting and generating a public key and the private key is a critical task.

El Gamal cryptography algorithm

It is a public key cryptography algorithm. This cryptosystem is based on the difficulty of finding discrete logarithm in a cyclic group that is, even if we know *ga* and *gk*, it is extremely difficult to compute *gak*.

- Start by selecting two large prime numbers, *P* and *Q*, with *P* being the public key and *Q* being the private key.
- Choose the second encryption key as *E1*.
- Compute the third encryption key, *E2*, such that *E2 = E^Q mod P*, for *El* Gamal key encryption.
- Select a random number, *R*.
- Calculate the ciphertext as *CT = E1 ^R mod P*.
- Calculate the second ciphertext as *CT2 = (PT * E2^R) mod P*, for *El* Gamal key decryption. Finally, compute the plaintext as *PT = (CT2 * (CT^Q)^-1) mod P*.

Elliptic Curve Cryptography

Elliptic Curve Cryptography (**ECC**) is a contemporary family of public-key cryptographic systems, utilizing the algebraic structures of elliptic curves over finite fields and the **Elliptic Curve Discrete Logarithm Problem** (**ECDLP**) complexity. ECC provides all fundamental capabilities of asymmetric cryptosystems, including encryption, digital signatures, and key exchange. It is regarded as a natural successor to the RSA cryptosystem, thanks to its use of smaller keys and signatures that offer the same level of security as RSA but with faster key generation, key agreement, and signature processing speeds. Refer to *Figure 1.8* which deciphers how ECC functions.

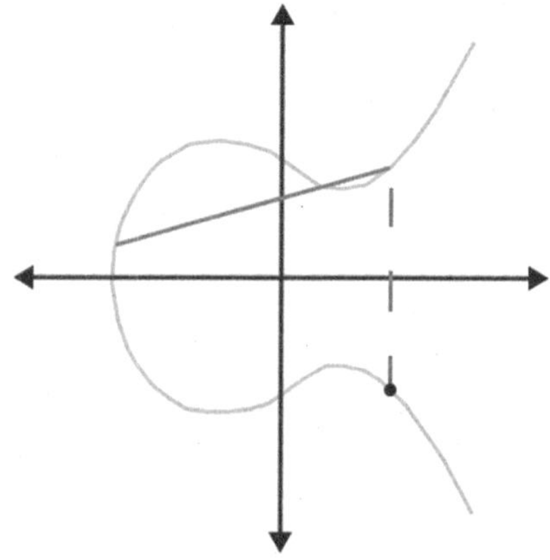

***Figure 1.8**: Operational mechanism of Elliptic Curve Cryptography*

Elliptic curves are utilized to create encryption schemes. They are defined over a special field and are discontinuous curves, meaning that they consist of a finite set of points. Elliptic curve cryptography forms the foundation of decentralized trust when transmitting and receiving transactions. In fact, it is employed to generate transaction signatures which, akin to physical signatures, can demonstrate a user's authority to participate in a transaction. In a decentralized system where there is no central authority to authenticate transactions, each transaction broadcasted to the network must possess a valid signature. These signatures must be capable of verifying that the transaction was initiated by a specific user. This is accomplished through asymmetric encryption where a user possesses one or multiple public/private key pairs. Signature schemes comprise a problem that can only be computed if the user has access to both the public and private key, but can be validated as a genuine signature by any other user with access to the public key.

One example of this is elliptic curve-based signature schemes, which enable a user to prove that they own the funds they are declaring in a transaction. This allows for the sending and receiving of transactions without the need for a central authority. Elliptic curves are chosen over other signature schemes such as RSA due to the smaller key sizes, which helps to reduce the amount of information held on the network.

Hash functions

A **hash function** is a mathematical algorithm that takes a variable number of characters, referred to as a message and converts it into a string with a fixed number of characters known as a hash value or hash. Hashing algorithms are one-way functions, meaning they are easy to perform in one direction but impossible to reverse. Hashing is valuable for ensuring the integrity of data and detecting any tampering, as even a slight change in the message will produce a completely different hash. Hash functions are fundamental tools in modern cryptography, used in information security to verify transactions, messages, and digital signatures. They have various applications in blockchain and distributed ledger technologies, including linking blocks and creating compressed data structures. *Figure 1.9* illustrates the sequential stages involved in the functioning of a hash.

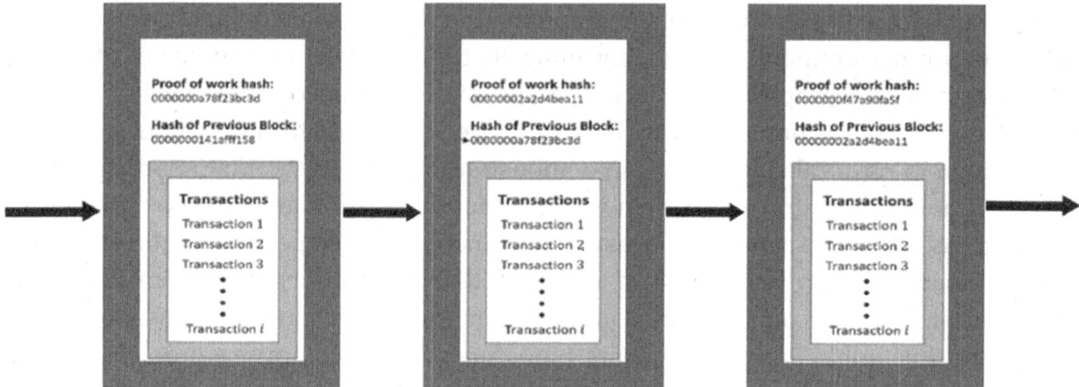

***Figure 1.9**: A visual representation of hash functions*

In a decentralized environment, where there is no central authority to control and verify the validity of transactions, the use of a hashing function ensures the integrity and traceability of each block in a blockchain. This creates an immutable record of events and allows for the tracking of assets from one block to the next.

Given the large amount of data transacted on distributed ledgers, it is necessary to use compressed data structures, such as Merkle trees, to store information within the block. This reduces the storage space required to run a node on the network.

Hashing functions are also used in the proof of work algorithm, which is the mechanism by which nodes on the network reach consensus on the state of transactions. A hashing function takes an input, or object, and generates a fixed-length output, known as a **digest**. Regardless of the size of the input, the output will always be the same size. Additionally, the same input will always produce the same digest when hashed using the same mechanism. Hashing functions are also collision-resistant, meaning that there is no discernible pattern between the digests of two different inputs.

The inner workings of hashing algorithms

A hash function usually works by initially dividing the input data into data blocks of a predetermined size and then utilizing an algorithm to calculate a hash value with a fixed length. The size of the data blocks might differ based on the particular algorithm employed, and padding may be applied if the blocks are too small. Irrespective of the algorithm, the resulting hash value is always of a fixed length, and the function is iteratively applied to each data block.

Encryption, on the other hand, involves the scrambling of data to create a coded message that can be unscrambled and decoded only by someone possessing a corresponding cipher. Unlike hashing, encryption is reversible and intended to be decrypted later by authorized parties. Hashing, by contrast, uses a formula that transforms data of any size into a fixed-length hash, making it computationally challenging to reverse. While encryption is primarily used to protect data in transit, hashing is employed to verify the authenticity of a file or data and to detect if it has been altered.

In essence, encryption is akin to placing data in a safe that opens only when the recipient knows the combination. Hashing, however, is more like a tamper-evident seal that provides assurance that the data has not been tampered with or altered.

Common cryptocurrency hash functions

The SHA-256 algorithm, which is employed by Bitcoin, is part of the **Secure Hash Algorithm (SHA)** family. Developed by the United States **National Security Agency (NSA)**, the SHA family encompasses various algorithms such as SHA-1, SHA-2 (which comprises of SHA-224, SHA-256, SHA-384, and SHA-512), and SHA-3 (with SHA3-224, SHA3-256, SHA3-384, and SHA3-512 being the members).

SHA-256 is a widely used and highly secure hashing algorithm. It is considered as one of the most robust and reliable encryption techniques among the SHA family.

Other common hashing algorithms include **Message Digest (MD)** algorithm, which includes MD2, MD4, MD5, and MD6. MD5 was previously a widely used algorithm, however, it has been deemed insecure due to hash collisions. Windows NT hash, also known as **Unicode hash** or **NTLM**, is another popular hash algorithm commonly used by windows systems. Other notable hashing algorithms include **RACE Integrity Primitives Evaluation Message Digest (RIPEMD)**, Whirlpool, and RSA.

Generally, the most commonly used hashing algorithms have a hash length that ranges between 160 to 512 bits. The SHA-256 algorithm is known for its high security and reliability, making it a popular choice among many cryptographic applications.

Digital signature

Digital signature is a mathematical process commonly employed to confirm the genuineness and completeness of a message, such as an email, credit card transaction, or digital document is known as a digital signature. These digital signatures produce a one-of-a-kind digital fingerprint that is specific to an individual or entity, which is used to identify users and safeguard information in digital messages or documents. In the context of emails, the email content itself is integrated into the digital signature. Digital signatures are significantly more secure than other types of electronic signatures and enhance transparency in online interactions, fostering trust among customers, business associates, and vendors.

Digital signatures work by proving that a digital message or document was not modified, intentionally or unintentionally, from the time it was signed. Digital signatures do this by generating a unique hash of the message or document and encrypting it using the sender's private key. The hash generated is unique to the message or document, and changing any part of it will completely change the hash.

Once completed, the message or digital document is digitally signed and sent to the recipient. The recipient then generates their own hash of the message or digital document and decrypts the sender's hash (included in the original message) using the sender's public key. The recipient compares the hash they generate against the sender's decrypted hash, if they match, the message or digital document has not been modified and the sender is authenticated.

Fundamentals of distributed systems

A distributed system is a collection of independent computers that work together to achieve a common goal. These systems can range from small networks of computers in a **local area network** (**LAN**) to large networks spanning the entire globe. The fundamental concept of a distributed system is that it allows multiple computers to work together as if they were a single computer.

One of the key components of a distributed system is the use of distributed algorithms. These algorithms are designed to coordinate the actions of multiple computers in a way that is both efficient and fault-tolerant. One example of a distributed algorithm is the distributed sorting algorithm. This algorithm allows multiple computers to sort a large dataset in parallel, and then combine the results in a way that ensures that the final result is sorted correctly. Another important concept in distributed systems is the use of consensus protocols. These protocols are used to ensure that all the computers in a distributed system agree on the state of the system. For example, a distributed database may use a consensus protocol to ensure that all the computers in the system agree on the contents of the database. One example of a consensus protocol is the Paxo's algorithm, which is used to ensure that all the computers in a distributed system agree on the order of a sequence of events.

Fault tolerance is another important aspect of distributed systems. This refers to the ability of a system to continue functioning correctly even when one or more of its components fail. Fault tolerance is achieved through the use of redundant components and mechanisms for detecting and recovering from failures. For example, a distributed storage system may use multiple copies of data to ensure that the data is still available even if one or more of the storage devices fail.

One example of a distributed system that many people are familiar with is the World Wide Web. The World Wide Web is a vast network of interconnected computers that are used to share information and resources. When you visit a website, your computer sends a request to a web server, which then sends back the requested information. This process is made possible by the use of distributed algorithms and protocols that ensure that the information is sent to the correct computer and that it is transmitted correctly.

Another example of a distributed system is the **distributed version control system (DVCS)**. This type of system is used to manage the source code of software projects. A DVCS allows multiple developers to work on the same codebase at the same time, and it ensures that their changes are merged correctly. Examples of popular DVCS include **Git** and **Mercurial**.

In conclusion, distributed systems are a powerful tool that allows multiple computers to work together to achieve a common goal. These systems use distributed algorithms and consensus protocols to ensure that the actions of the computers are coordinated, and they use fault tolerance to ensure that the system continues functioning correctly even when a component fails. Examples of distributed systems include the World Wide Web and distributed version control systems. With the growing popularity of technologies like cloud computing and the internet of things, distributed systems will become even more important in the future.

A quick glimpse of some terms from depth of DS are as follows:

- **Distributed algorithms**: A distributed algorithm is a type of algorithm utilized in a network of interconnected systems or nodes, where different processors work simultaneously on various parts of the algorithm. This allows for parallel processing and communication between the processors to ensure proper functioning of the software. The distinction between a regular algorithm and a distributed algorithm lies in the fact that the latter is designed to run on separate processors. Each processor executes a different portion of the overall algorithm concurrently and shares the results with each other. However, there are challenges associated with distributed algorithms. For instance, if a processor fails, it can disrupt the corresponding part of the algorithm. Additionally, communication issues between processors can hinder the progress of the distributed algorithm. Programmers often study distributed algorithms to address these challenges and ensure that the algorithm is successfully executed, even in the presence of technical errors.
- **Consensus protocols**: It is essentially the rules by which a network operates. The peers, or nodes, in the network are governed by a network's consensus protocol as it defines how decentralization is achieved within the network. A blockchain, or distributed ledger, is a network that is spread across many different computers.

These computers work together to make sure all the transactions on the network are correct and accurate. This is what makes blockchain special, as it does not rely on one central authority to control it.

Since anyone can add information to a blockchain, it is important to have rules in place that ensure everyone agrees on what information should be added and what should be ignored. These rules are called **consensus protocols**. They check transactions and help keep the network secure.

Normally, the consensus protocol is decided before the blockchain is first created. However, some networks like Ethereum can change their consensus protocol while they are still running. This means they can adapt and improve over time.

The consensus mechanism at the core of a blockchain network provides a specific approach to validate whether a transaction is valid or not. It offers a means of reviewing and confirming which data should be added to the blockchain's ledger. As blockchain networks typically lack a central authority determining correctness, nodes within the network must collectively agree on the network's state based on predefined rules or protocols.

In the case of Bitcoin, the consensus mechanism employed is proof-of-work, which involves the process of mining blocks to verify each transaction. Other types of consensus mechanisms include **proof-of-stake** (**PoS**) and **proof-of-authority** (**PoA**).

Understanding popular consensus mechanisms

The two most popular consensus protocols used today are called proof of work and proof of stake. Let us take a look at each one in more simple terms:

- **Proof of work** (**PoW**) is like a really hard math problem that needs to be solved. When someone solves the problem, they get a prize and a new block is added to the blockchain. This process is called *mining* and it happens over and over again. The problem with proof of work is that it uses a lot of energy and can hurt the environment. The first blockchain, Bitcoin, uses PoW To validate transactions to the Bitcoin blockchain *miners*, who are the nodes solve cryptographic, or mathematical problems, using their computers. Miners who solve a problem and validate and enable a block record are rewarded with bitcoin.
- **Proof of stake** (**PoS**) is a different kind of consensus protocol compared to PoW. Instead of using computational power to solve complex mathematical problems to add blocks to the blockchain, PoS selects validators randomly to add new blocks. The higher the amount of the network's own cryptocurrency that a validator has staked, the greater their chances of being chosen. PoS is considered

more environmentally friendly since it does not require as much energy as PoW. However, there are concerns that this could lead to centralization of power in the hands of a small group of validators. Ethereum is transitioning from PoW to PoS. In PoS, there are *forgers* instead of *miners*. These forgers stake a certain amount of cryptocurrency, which grants them a probability-based opportunity to become a block validator. The successful forger is then rewarded with the respective block transaction fees. By staking their own cryptocurrency on a block, forgers are disincentivized from attempting to deceive the network, as they would risk losing their stake if they are found to be incorrectly adding transactions to the network.

Major blockchains and their consensus are as follows:

- **Ethereum:**
    - o **Consensus mechanism**: Ethereum currently uses **proof of stake (PoS)** as its consensus mechanism and is transitioning to Ethereum 2.0, which fully adopts PoS for scalability and energy efficiency.
    - o **Advantages**: PoS reduces the environmental impact compared to **proof of work (PoW)** used in Ethereum's earlier versions. It also enhances scalability and reduces computational overhead.
    - o **Limitations**: Despite improvements, PoS may still face scalability challenges during high transaction volumes. Ethereum's transition to Ethereum 2.0 aims to address these limitations.
- **Polygon (formerly matic network):**
    - o **Consensus mechanism**: Polygon employs a customized PoS mechanism known as the **Matic PoS chain**. Validators are selected based on the number of tokens staked.
    - o **Advantages**: PoS enhances transaction throughput, reduces energy consumption, and provides faster confirmation times. Polygon's sidechain architecture further augments scalability.
    - o **Limitations**: While PoS is more energy-efficient, it may face challenges related to centralization if a significant portion of tokens is held by a few entities.
- **Solana:**
    - o **Consensus mechanism**: Solana utilizes a unique **proof of history (PoH)** combined with a PoS mechanism called **Tower Byzantine Fault Tolerance (BFT)**. PoH acts as a verifiable time source.
    - o **Advantages**: Solana achieves high throughput with low transaction costs, making it suitable for **decentralized applications (dApps)** and **decentralized finance (DeFi)**. The combination of PoH and PoS enhances security.

- o **Limitations**: The design complexity of Solana's consensus mechanism may pose challenges for some developers. Additionally, its reliance on PoH has led to debates on centralization concerns.

Other available consensus are as follows:

- **Delegated proof-of-stake** (**Proof-of-Stake**): This method operates similarly to PoS. However, instead of relying on probability, owners of cryptocurrency can use their stake to cast votes and select witnesses. These witnesses are responsible for securing and validating the blockchain, and they do not require their own cryptocurrency but depend on votes. This consensus protocol is more centralized compared to others. DPoS is utilized by **BitShares**, **Steem**, and **EOS**.
- **Proof-of-authority** (**PoA**): With PoA, block validators are predetermined, making it even more centralized. New blocks on the blockchain are created only when the validators are in the majority. The protocol resembles PoS. The validators are publicly known and accountable for determining their role and eligibility for PoS validation. PoA is employed by Elysian, a newer blockchain, as well as some Ethereum testnets or test blockchains.
- **Fault tolerance**: Fault tolerance is a property of the system that helps to continue its working when a fault occurs.

Nowadays, many computers work together on a shared task in a distributed manner. For example, imagine there are 10 different systems working together and if one system happens to have a problem, the other 9 systems will take over and continue the work without any interruptions to the user. This is similar to how big online stores operate, where even if one system malfunctions, the other systems will take control and customers can still purchase products without any issues. There are generally three types of issues that can arise in distributed systems: failures, errors, and faults. A fault refers to any problem that occurs within the system. When we investigate the system after a fault, we may find mistakes or errors in the code or the way it functions. A failure is when the system is unable to produce an outcome due to faults and errors. We need fault tolerance in distributed systems because of reliability, availability and security. Common example of fault tolerance applications are as follows:

- Air traffic control
- Banking services
- Patient monitoring system

Distributed file systems

A **distributed file system** (**DFS**) differs from conventional file systems such as NTFS and HFS by allowing direct access to the same file data from multiple sources. The data stored within a DFS can be located anywhere within the network, making it accessible to users who have the necessary permissions and access to the host. The primary objective of DFS is to facilitate resource and information sharing among users of geographically distributed systems through a shared **common file system (CFS)**. DFS is integrated into operating systems and operates as part of the overall system configuration, connecting workstations and mainframes within a LAN. The process of creating a namespace within DFS is transparent to clients. The services provided by DFS consist of two components.

- Local transparency
- Redundancy

Features of distributed file system

Some of the features of distributed file system are as follows:

- **Multi-protocol access**: Hosts can utilize standard NFS, SMB, or a POSIX client provided by the solution provider to access DFS data. Occasionally, NVMe-oF for files and (NVIDIA) GPU direct storage access can also be observed. This implies that the same file can be accessed using all the protocols supported by the DFS solution.
- **Data integrity**: Multiple users typically share a file system, and the file system must ensure the integrity of the data stored in transferred files. A concurrency control method is required to properly synchronize concurrent access requests from multiple users competing for access to the same file. A file system commonly offers atomic transactions as a high-level concurrency management system to maintain data integrity.
- **Transparent local access**: From the perspective of a host, the data is accessed as if it were local to the host accessing it.
- **Location independence**: Hosts may have no knowledge of the physical location of file data. The DFS manages data location, not the host accessing it.
- **Coherent access**: DFS file data is managed in such a way that it appears to the host(s) as if it all resides within a single file system, even though the data may be distributed across multiple storage devices/servers and locations.
- **Data-in-flight encryption**: Most DFS systems support encryption of data and metadata while it is being transmitted.
- **Local gateways and scale-out storage solution**: DFS systems may require server and storage resources at each location with access to file data. Local gateways often cache metadata and data referenced by hosts. These gateways can be scaled up or down as needed to meet performance requirements. In some cases where access and data reside together, gateways are not necessary.

Refer to *Figure 1.10* for an example of DFS:

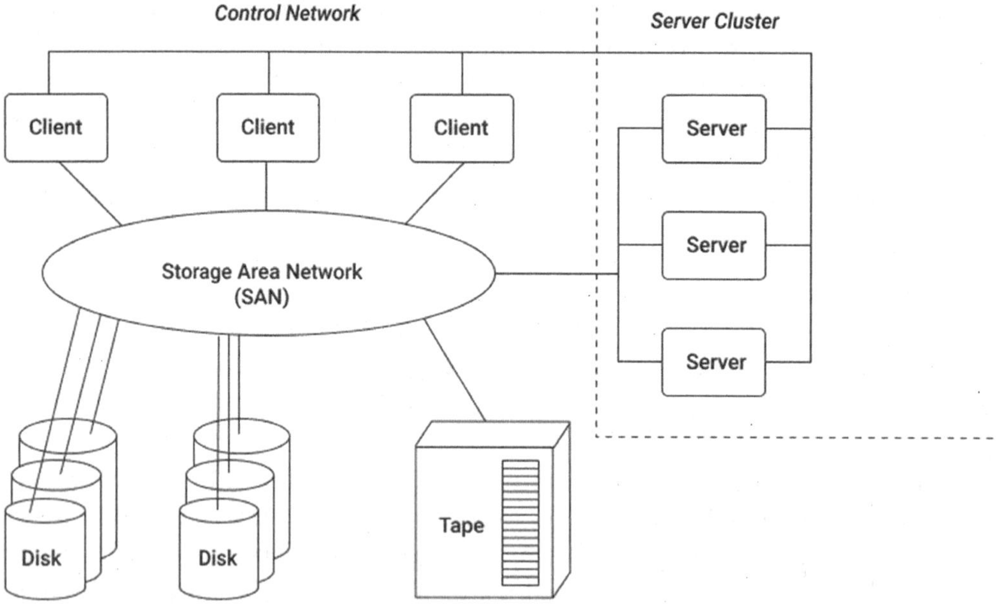

***Figure 1.10**: Graphical summary of the working of DFS*

Some pros and cons of DFS are as follows:

- **Storage management flexibility**: Storage management is very flexible and easy to modify it according to our need.
- **Availability**: High availability is also one of the best benefits of DFS. It keeps all the important data available all the time.
- **Security integration**: It is easy to implement security checks in DFS.
- **Load sharing**: Load sharing can be done with optimal results using the DFS.
- **Graphical way of administration**: Graphical view of administration window is available which reduces the cost by cutting down administration level.

Distributed database

Distributed databases are employed for horizontal scalability, and they are crafted to fulfil the workload demands without necessitating modifications in the database application or vertical scaling of a solitary machine. Distributed databases address diverse concerns such as accessibility, fault tolerance, throughput, response time, scalability, and numerous other challenges that can arise from employing a lone machine and a solitary database.

In a distributed system, multiple computers work independently on a common task. This can be seen in large e-commerce stores where multiple systems are used to handle the website's operations. If one system encounters a problem or failure, the other systems can take over and continue to operate without interruption. This type of system can also be seen in distributed databases, where multiple nodes work together to store and retrieve data. This approach allows for more efficient storage and retrieval, as well as increased availability and the ability to handle more requests. Additionally, distributed databases can scale horizontally by adding more nodes, providing more computing power, and eliminating the risk of a single point of failure.

There are mainly three types of problems (as discussed in previous section of fault tolerance) that can occur in distributed systems: failures, errors, and faults. A failure is when the system is unable to provide an outcome due to issues with the code or system. An error is a problem that is noticed when inspecting the system after a failure has occurred. A fault is a problem that occurs within the system. This approach helps to prevent single points of failure and increase overall system availability. A distributed database is spread across multiple physical locations, with processing tasks divided among processors on various database nodes. In a centralized **distributed database management system (DDBMS)**, the distributed data is managed as though it were stored in a single physical location. The DDBMS coordinates all data operations across databases and ensures that updates made in one database are automatically propagated to other sites.

Distributed databases are databases that are spread across multiple locations, nodes, or servers.

Different types of Distributed databases

There are various types of distributed databases, each designed to meet specific requirements. Here are some common types:

- Homogeneous distributed database:
  - **Definition**: All nodes have the same DBMS and data model.
  - **Advantages**: Uniformity simplifies management and maintenance.
  - **Example**: Oracle **Real Application Clusters (RAC)**.
- **Heterogeneous distributed database:**
  - **Definition**: Different nodes may run different DBMS or have different data models.
  - **Advantages**: Allows integration of diverse systems.
  - **Example**: Distributed databases connecting Oracle and Microsoft SQL server.
- **Replicated database:**
  - **Definition**: Complete copies of the database exist at multiple nodes.
  - **Advantages**: Increased availability and fault tolerance.

- **Example**: MySQL replication where changes made on one node are replicated to others.

- **Partitioned database:**
  - **Definition**: The database is divided into partitions, and each node contains a subset of the data.
  - **Advantages**: Enables scalability and parallel processing.
  - **Example**: Apache Cassandra, a NoSQL database that partitions data across nodes.
- **Client-server architecture:**
  - **Definition**: Nodes are divided into clients and servers, with clients requesting services from servers.
  - **Advantages**: Centralized management and efficient resource utilization.
  - **Example**: MongoDB, where clients interact with a cluster of server nodes.
- **Peer-to-peer architecture:**
  - **Definition**: All nodes have equal status and can act as clients or servers.
  - **Advantages**: Decentralized, fault-tolerant, and scalable.
  - **Example**: BitTorrent, a distributed file-sharing protocol.
- **Centralized database with distributed data:**
  - **Definition**: Database is centralized, but data is distributed across multiple locations.
  - **Advantages**: Combines centralization with data accessibility.
  - **Example**: Centralized cloud databases with distributed data centers.
- **Sharded database:**
  - **Definition**: Data is horizontally partitioned into shards, and each shard is stored on a different node.
  - **Advantages**: Enables horizontal scaling and improved performance.
  - **Example**: Google Cloud Spanner, which uses sharding for horizontal scalability.
- **Multi-version database:**
  - **Definition**: Maintains multiple versions of the database to support concurrent transactions.
  - **Advantages**: Allows for concurrent access without locking issues.
  - **Example**: Apache HBase, a distributed, scalable, and consistent NoSQL database.

Each type of distributed database has its own strengths and weaknesses, and the choice depends on factors like the specific use case, performance requirements, and the need for fault tolerance and scalability.

Table 1.2 shows a small comparison between homogeneous and heterogeneous databases:

Feature	Homogeneous Distributed Database	Heterogeneous Distributed Database
Definition	All nodes use the same DBMS and data model.	Different nodes may run different DBMS or have different data models.
Uniformity/ Diversity	Provides uniformity.	Allows for diversity.
Advantages	- Simplifies management and maintenance. Easier to implement.	- Enables integration of diverse technologies. Accommodates different application requirements.
Example	Oracle **Real Application Clusters (RAC)** where all nodes run Oracle DBMS.	Distributed databases connecting Oracle and Microsoft SQL Server.
Integration	May be easier to integrate due to consistent software and data structures.	Enables integration of diverse technologies, facilitating interoperability.
Complexity	Generally, it is less complex to implement and manage.	May be more complex due to diverse technologies and data models.
Flexibility	Less flexible when it comes to accommodating varied technologies.	More flexible, suitable for environments with diverse systems.
Use Cases	Well-suited for environments where uniformity is critical.	Useful in scenarios where different systems need to coexist, especially in large enterprises with diverse technologies.

***Table 1.1**: Comparison between homogeneous and heterogeneous databases*

Distributed database features

Some features of distributed database are as follows:

- **Distributed transaction management**: Ensures uniform distributed database by employing commit protocols, distributed concurrency control techniques, and distributed recovery methods in the event of multiple transactions and failures.
- **Location independence**: Data is stored at various locations and overseen by an autonomous DDBMS.

- **Network interconnection**: All databases within a collection are interconnected through a network and communicate with one another.
- **Transaction processing**: Transaction processing is a program including a collection of one or more database operations. Transaction processing is an atomic process that is either entirely executed or not at all.
- **Seamless integration**: Databases in a collection usually represent a single logical database, and they are interconnected.

Distributed database types

The two types of distributed databases are as follows:

- **Homogenous**: A homogenous distributed database is a network of identical databases that are located on multiple sites. These sites have the same operating system, **database management system (DDBMS)**, and data structure, which makes them easy to manage. This means that users can access data from each of the databases seamlessly without any difficulty.

  Simple example of homogeneous database is as follows:

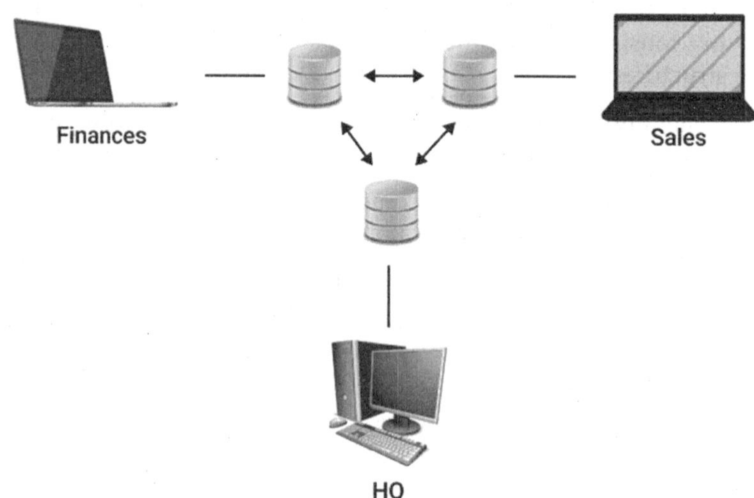

Figure 1.11: Diagram outlining DDBMS

- **Heterogenous**: A heterogeneous distributed database is a network of databases that have different schemas, operating systems, DDBMS, and data models. Because of these differences, a particular site may be completely unaware of other sites, causing limited cooperation in processing user requests. To overcome this limitation, translations are required to establish communication between different sites. This allows for data to be accessed and used by users from different locations or systems.

Example of heterogenous database is as follows:

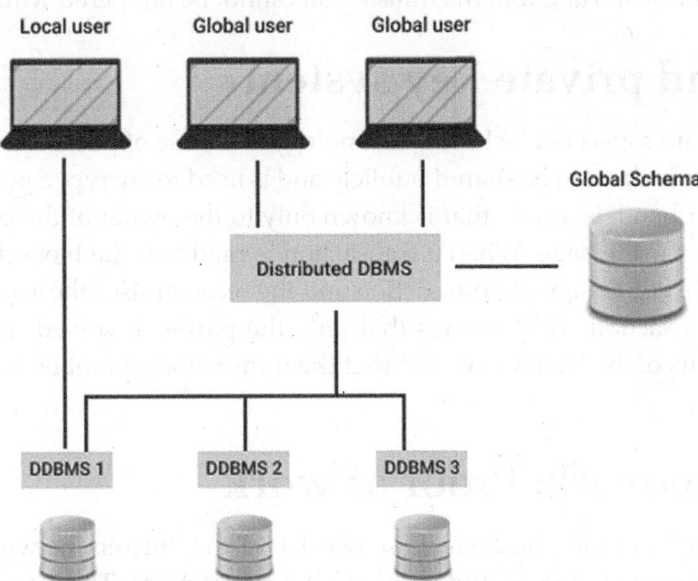

***Figure 1.12**: Chart showing the process of DDBMS functioning*

Blockchain and cryptography integration

Blockchain technology and cryptography are closely related and often used together to provide security for digital transactions. Blockchain is a digital ledger of transactions that is duplicated and distributed across the entire network of computer systems on the blockchain, making it extremely difficult for any one person or organization to tamper with the ledger. Cryptography, on the other hand, is the practice of securing communication by transforming plain text into a code that can only be deciphered by those who possess the key to the code. Together, blockchain and cryptography provide a secure, decentralized, and tamper-proof system for recording and verifying digital transactions.

One of the key features of blockchain technology is the concept of a decentralized ledger, which means that instead of having one central authority that maintains and verifies transactions, the ledger is distributed across a network of computers. Each computer in the network has a copy of the ledger, and transactions are recorded on all copies simultaneously. This makes it extremely difficult for any one person or organization to tamper with the ledger, as any changes would have to be made on every copy of the ledger simultaneously. In order to secure the transactions recorded on the ledger, cryptography is used. When a transaction is made, it is converted into a code using a cryptographic algorithm, such as SHA-256. This code is then added to the ledger as a new block. The code cannot be deciphered without the key to the algorithm, which is known only to the parties involved in the transaction. This ensures that only the parties involved in the transaction can see the details of the transaction and that the transaction cannot be tampered with by anyone else.

Public and private key system

Another important aspect of blockchain technology is the use of public and private keys. A public key is a code that can be shared publicly and is used to encrypt a message. A private key, on the other hand, is a code that is known only to the owner of the public key and is used to decrypt the message. When a transaction is made on the blockchain, the sender uses their private key to sign the transaction and the receiver uses the sender's public key to verify the transaction. This ensures that only the parties involved in the transaction can see the details of the transaction and that the transaction cannot be tampered with by anyone else.

Bitcoin network: Proof of work

One of the most popular blockchain networks is the Bitcoin network, which uses blockchain technology to record and verify digital transactions. The Bitcoin network uses a consensus algorithm called **proof of work** to validate transactions. In order to validate a transaction, a computer on the network must solve a complex mathematical problem. The first computer to solve the problem adds the block to the blockchain and receives a reward in the form of newly created bitcoins. This process is called **mining**, and it is the way new bitcoins are created.

Ethereum network: Proof of stake

Another popular blockchain network is the Ethereum network, which also uses blockchain technology to record and verify digital transactions. The Ethereum network uses a consensus algorithm called **proof of stake** to validate transactions. In this algorithm, instead of solving a complex mathematical problem, the network randomly selects a computer to validate a transaction based on the amount of ether, the cryptocurrency of the Ethereum network, that the computer holds.

In summary, blockchain technology and cryptography are closely related and often used together to provide a secure, decentralized, and tamper-proof system for recording and verifying digital transactions. The use of cryptographic algorithms and public and private key systems ensures that only the parties involved in a transaction can see the details of the transaction and that the transaction cannot be tampered with by anyone else. Popular blockchain networks such as the Bitcoin and Ethereum networks use different consensus algorithms to validate transactions and add new blocks to the blockchain.

Applications of blockchain technology

Blockchain technology has a wide range of applications beyond just cryptocurrency. Some of the most notable applications include:

- **Supply chain management**: Blockchain technology can be used to create an immutable record of transactions, making it possible to track products from the manufacturer to the end consumer. This can improve transparency and efficiency in supply chain management, making it easier to detect and prevent fraud.
- **Digital identity**: Blockchain technology can be used to create a secure and decentralized digital identity system. This can be used for voter registration, passport verification, and other forms of identity verification.
- **Smart contracts**: Blockchain technology can be used to create smart contracts, which are self-executing contracts with the terms of the agreement directly written into code. This can automate contract execution, reduce the need for intermediaries, and increase the efficiency of contract execution.
- **Decentralized applications (dApps)**: Blockchain technology can be used to create **decentralized applications (dApps)** that run on a blockchain network. These dApps can be used for a wide range of applications, including gaming, social media, and marketplaces.
- **Digital asset management**: Blockchain technology can be used to create a secure and transparent system for managing digital assets. This can include everything from digital art to real estate.
- **Internet of Things (IoT)**: Blockchain technology can be used to create a secure and decentralized network for the IoT. This can improve the security and efficiency of IoT networks and make it possible to create new types of IoT applications.
- **Banking and finance**: Blockchain technology can be used to create a secure and transparent system for financial transactions. This can include everything from payments and remittances to securities trading and fundraising.
- **Public administration**: Blockchain technology can be used to create a transparent and efficient system for public administration. This can include everything from land registry to public procurement.

Note: DLT and smart contracts are often mentioned together but they are distinct technologies. The emergence of DLT has provided a platform for hosting and executing smart contracts, bringing them into the mainstream. The derivatives industry is increasingly recognizing the potential of smart contracts and DLT to enhance operational efficiency and reduce expenses. These innovative technologies have the potential to revolutionize the execution and management of derivatives throughout their entire lifecycle, indicating that the derivatives market is on the verge of substantial modernization.

Smart contracts

A smart contract is a type of computer program that runs on a blockchain network. It is designed to automatically execute certain actions when certain conditions are met. Think of it like a digital version of a legal contract, where the terms and conditions are written in code and can be enforced automatically.

For example, imagine that you want to buy a house from someone. With a traditional legal contract, you would have to hire a lawyer, sign the contract, and then wait for the seller to transfer the ownership of the house to you. With a smart contract, all of this can be done automatically. Once the terms of the contract are met, such as you are paying the agreed upon price, the ownership of the house can be transferred automatically and recorded on the blockchain.

Smart contracts are useful for many different types of transactions, such as buying and selling goods and services, managing supply chains, and even voting in elections. Because they are stored on a blockchain, they are also secure and transparent, which can help to increase trust and reduce the need for intermediaries.

Different models of smart legal contracts

Outlined below are two contrasting models of intelligent legal agreements referred to as the external model and the internal model. It is presumed that the most probable implementations of smart contracts in the near future will pertain to operational clauses and Boolean logic, rather than non-operational clauses.

External

The external model for smart contracts involves using code to automatically perform certain actions in a legal contract. The code is separate from the contract and is only used to make sure the contract is carried out correctly. The legal contract still exists in its original form, written in natural language. If there is any difference between what the code does and what the contract says, the contract takes precedence. In this model, the code does not legally bind the parties and does not remove any ambiguity from the contract. The parties need to be sure that the code accurately reflects their obligations in the contract. This model is similar to the automation that is already used in some areas, such as daily collateral flows in certain margining arrangements. However, it could have a big impact if it becomes widely adopted.

In this model, it is the code that is *smart* and not the contract itself

Internal

In an internal model, a significant portion of the legal contract would likely remain unchanged. However, certain elements of the contract would be rewritten in a more formal representation of conditional logic, rather than its current natural human language form. This would allow a computer to automatically execute the conditional logic based on the formal representation. As a result, the contract would appear as a mixture of approaches. Some clauses would still be drafted in natural human language, while others would be represented in some form of code or other formal representation. Alternatively, the written contract could refer to a specific piece of code stored elsewhere, with the contract stipulating that the code is legally binding between the parties.

Distributed ledger technology

A distributed ledger is a type of technology that allows multiple parties to share and update a digital record in a secure and transparent way. It works by distributing copies of the same record across a network of computers, rather than having a single central authority controlling it.

An example of distributed ledger technology is blockchain, which is the technology that powers Bitcoin and other cryptocurrencies. In a blockchain, each block contains a record of multiple transactions, and each block is connected to the previous block. This creates a chain of blocks, or a blockchain. Each computer or node in the network keeps a copy of the entire blockchain, and when a new transaction is added, it is verified and recorded on all copies of the blockchain.

This makes it difficult for any one person or group to manipulate or corrupt the ledger, as any changes would have to be made on every copy of the blockchain. And since each participant has access to the same copy of the ledger, it is also transparent and easy to track the history of transactions.

Another example of distributed ledger technology is Hyperledger, which is a set of opensource tools and technologies that can be used to create and manage distributed ledgers. It is designed to be flexible and can be used to create private blockchains that are only accessible to certain participants, such as within a company or organization.

Impact of cryptography blockchain

Before delving into an explanation of blockchain cryptography, it is crucial to gain a detailed understanding of cryptography. In essence, cryptography refers to the concealment of secrets. Cryptography technologies are designed to ensure complete or pseudo-anonymity. It is the practice of securing information from unauthorized access or modification. The blockchain utilizes cryptography to ensure that network transactions remain secure, prevent double spending, and restrict access to sensitive information to only authorized individuals.

Through cryptography, information is encoded in a manner that only the intended recipients can decode it, protecting it from tampering or interception by unauthorized parties. Blockchain applications utilize the principle of tangible signatures by harnessing cryptographic techniques in conjunction with encryption keys. Cryptography methodologies employ sophisticated mathematical codes to securely store and transmit data values. Consequently, it guarantees that only the individuals for whom the transaction or data is intended can access, comprehend, and process the transaction or data, as well as verify the genuineness of participants and the transaction.

Understanding blockchain cryptography

Recollecting previous concepts like: key management, encryption, decryption, public key, and private key, let us analyze this pictorial representation in *Figure 1.13*. Here sender is trying to communicate with end receiver with help of secret keys that encrypts and decrypt the content to be communicated:

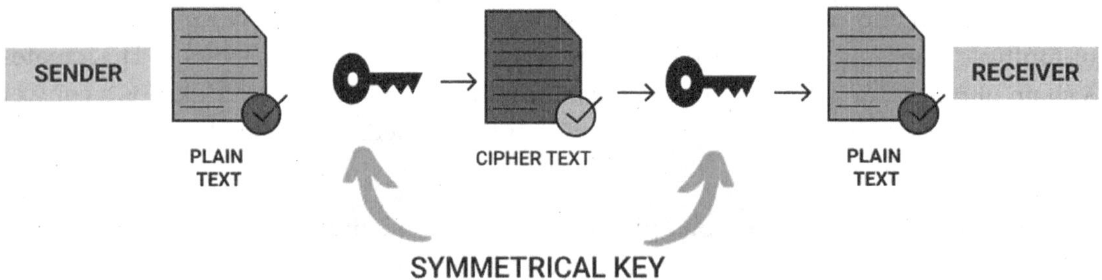

***Figure 1.13**: Visualization showcasing use of cryptography*

Blockchain cryptography is a complex topic, but it can be understood by looking at the basics of how it works. Imagine listening to a radio broadcast that is publicly available to everyone. But, now imagine a radio communication between two soldiers on a military mission, this type of communication is highly secure and encrypted, so that only the intended people can hear it. Blockchain cryptography works in the same way. It is a technique used to transmit secure messages between two or more people.

The sender uses a special key and algorithm to encrypt the message before sending it to the receiver. The receiver then uses a decryption process to read the original message. One of the most important aspects of cryptography is encryption keys. These keys make sure that only authorized people can read the message, data or transaction.

Many blockchain applications do not involve the use of secret, encrypted messages, especially in public blockchain. But new blockchain applications use different types of cryptography encryption to ensure the security and anonymity of transactions. Some of the tools used for this include hashing and digital signatures.

In summary, cryptography is the practice of creating protocols to prevent third parties from accessing and viewing data. It involves a combination of different fields such as physics, math, computer science, engineering, and others. The main focus of blockchain cryptography is on encryption, decryption, cipher, and keys. Digital signatures and hashing also play a significant role in blockchain cryptography.

Network security

Network security refers to the protection of information and data that is transmitted over a network, such as the internet or a private network. In a distributed system, where multiple devices or nodes are connected to the network and share information, network security becomes even more important to ensure the confidentiality, integrity, and availability of the data. Cryptography plays a key role as a component of network security in a distributed system. It uses mathematical algorithms and encryption keys to secure the communication between devices and protect against unauthorized access. For example, when a message is sent from one device to another, it is encrypted using a specific algorithm and a key known only to the sender and the intended recipient. This ensures that the message can only be read by the intended recipient, even if it is intercepted by an unauthorized party, as shown in *Figure 1.13*.

There are several types of cryptographic techniques that can be used for network security in distributed systems. These are as follows:

- **Digital signatures**: Digital signatures are used to verify the authenticity of the sender of a message. They are created by encrypting a message with the sender's private key and can be verified by decrypting it with the sender's public key.
- **Hashing**: Hashing is a one-way function that takes an input and produces a fixed length output. It is used to secure data integrity by allowing the recipient to verify that the data has not been tampered with during transmission.

- **Asymmetric-key cryptography**: This type of cryptography uses a pair of keys, one for encryption and one for decryption. It is considered more secure than symmetric-key cryptography, but is also more complex to implement.
- **Symmetric-key cryptography**: This type of cryptography uses the same key for both encryption and decryption. It is generally considered less secure than other types of cryptography, but is faster and easier to implement.

In addition to cryptography, other security measures can be used in distributed systems to protect against network attacks and unauthorized access. These can include firewalls, intrusion detection and prevention systems, and **virtual private networks** (**VPNs**).

Overall, network security in distributed systems is essential to ensure the confidentiality, integrity, and availability of data as it is transmitted over the network. Cryptography is a key component of network security, providing the necessary tools for encrypting and decrypting communications between devices. Along with other security measures, it helps to protect against unauthorized access, attacks and to ensure that data remains safe and secure.

Intrusion detection and prevention system

An **intrusion detection and prevention system** (**IDPS**) serves as a vigilant guardian for networks, actively scanning for potential threats, notifying administrators, and preventing possible attacks. Much like airport security checks, where passengers need tickets and pass security checks, an IDS monitors and alerts against malicious traffic or policy violations. It acts as a precursor to the **intrusion prevention system** (**IPS**), which not only monitors but also takes automated actions to thwart incidents.

IDS versus IPS: A security check analogy

In the analogy, an IDS is comparable to airport security monitoring and alerting against potential threats. On the other hand, an IPS, functioning like an advanced security check, goes beyond alerts. It takes automated actions to prevent potential incidents, ensuring a proactive approach to network security. This additional layer of protection, akin to stopping threats before they board the network *flight*, is crucial in safeguarding against data breaches and system failures.

Working mechanism of IDPS

An IDPS actively monitors network traffic, searching for patterns or anomalies that signal intrusion attempts. It can focus on known malicious activities or identify general suspicious patterns, such as an unusual surge in failed login attempts. When an intrusion is detected, the IDPS can take preventive measures, like blocking the suspicious IP address or shutting down a compromised service. This real-time identification and action help in preventing attacks and maintaining network security.

Significance in network security

For organizations relying on the security and integrity of their network, an IDPS is a critical security measure. By proactively identifying and blocking malicious activities, it minimizes the risk of data breaches and system failures. In the context of blockchain, where secure and tamper-resistant networks are paramount, integrating IDPS adds an extra layer of defense against potential threats.

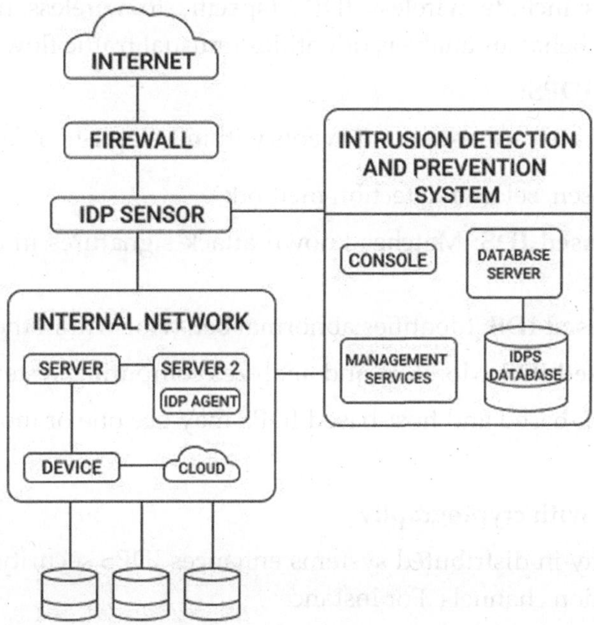

***Figure 1.14**: Illustration highlighting the IDPS working*

Basic functions of an IDPS are as follows:

- Guard technology infrastructure and sensitive data
- Review existing user and policies
- Gather network related
- Meet compliance regulations

Types of intrusion detection and prevention systems (IDPS)

When choosing an **intrusion detection and prevention system (IDPS)** for your organization, consider factors like network characteristics, objectives, and existing security policies. There are two main types of IDPS: network-based and host-based.

- **Network-Based IDPS:**
  - Monitors network segments, including wireless networks.
  - Analyzes network and application protocol activity for suspicious behavior.
  - Subtypes include wireless IDPS (specific to wireless network traffic) and network behavior analysis (identifies unusual traffic flows).
- **Host-Based IDPS:**
  - Monitors characteristics and events within a single host for suspicious activity.

Once the type is chosen, select a detection method:

- **Signature-based IDS**: Matches known attack signatures in a database to detect attacks.
- **Anomaly-based IDS**: Identifies abnormal behavior within the network.
- **Protocol-based IDS**: Monitors and analyzes computing system protocols.
- Both network-based and host-based IDPS may use one or more of these detection methods.

Enhancing security with cryptography

- Cryptography in distributed systems enhances IDPS security by ensuring secure communication channels. For instance:
  - **Encryption**: Protects data in transit, preventing interception and unauthorized access.
  - **Digital signatures**: Ensure message authenticity, preventing man-in-the-middle attacks.

In summary, IDPS is vital for securing distributed systems, monitoring malicious activity, and taking preventive measures. Cryptography strengthens security by safeguarding communication channels in the system.

Security protocols

Security protocols in distributed systems refer to a set of rules and procedures that are implemented to secure communication between different nodes or devices in a distributed network. These protocols are designed to ensure the confidentiality, integrity, and availability of data and resources in the network.

One widely used security protocol is **Secure Sockets Layer** (**SSL**) and its successor, **Transport Layer Security** (**TLS**). These protocols are used to establish a secure connection between a web server and a web client (such as a web browser) to protect the sensitive information being exchanged. SSL/TLS uses a combination of public key and symmetric key encryption to secure communication.

Another widely used security protocol is **Internet Protocol Security** (**IPsec**). IPsec is a set of protocols that provide security at the network layer of the OSI model. It is commonly used to secure communication between networks, such as between a company's internal network and a remote site. IPsec provides confidentiality, integrity, and authenticity of the data being transmitted by using a combination of encryption and authentication techniques.

Another security protocol is **Secure Shell** (**SSH**) which is used to securely access and manage remote systems. SSH uses a combination of public key and symmetric key encryption to secure communication and also provides secure file transfer capabilities. Security protocols such as SSL/TLS, IPsec, and SSH play an important role in ensuring secure communication in distributed systems by providing confidentiality, integrity, and authenticity of the data being transmitted. These protocols are widely used in various industries to protect sensitive information and ensure secure communication between systems.

Security standards

Security standards and protocols are essential for maintaining confidentiality, integrity, and availability in networked environments. They offer guidelines and specifications, forming a framework for secure design, implementation, and operation of distributed systems. These standards provide a common language and best practices to protect networks and data.

Some key security standards are as follows:

- **ISO/IEC 27001 and 27002:**
  - o Framework for **information security management system** (**ISMS**).
  - o Risk management approach to identify, assess, and mitigate information risks.
- **NIST SP 800-53:**
  - o Developed by the **National Institute of Standards and Technology** (**NIST**).
  - o Guidelines for security and privacy of federal information systems.
  - o Covers access control, incident response, and contingency planning.

- **Control Objectives for Information and Related Technologies (COBIT):**
  - o Developed by ISACA for IT governance and management.
  - o Focus on IT risk management, security, and compliance.
- **Payment Card Industry Data Security Standard (PCI DSS):**
  - o Developed by major credit card companies.
  - o Mandatory for organizations handling credit card information.
  - o Ensures protection against data breaches.

Security protocols in distributed systems are as follows:

- **Secure Sockets Layer/Transport Layer Security (SSL/TLS)**: Encrypts data for secure communication between web browsers and servers.
- **Internet Protocol Security (IPsec)**: Secures communication at the network layer through encryption and authentication.
- **Secure Shell (SSH)**: Provides a secure channel for remote system access, command execution, and file transfer.
- **Kerberos**: Network authentication protocol for secure user and device authentication.
- **Remote Authentication Dial-In User Service (RADIUS)**: Authenticates users and manages network access, commonly used in wireless networks and VPNs.
- **Terminal Access Controller Access Control System Plus (TACACS+)**: Authenticates users and manages network access, commonly used in Cisco networks.
- **Industry-specific security standards**: Developed by organizations like ISO and IEC to address specific security threats in different industries.

In summary, Security standards and protocols are crucial for ensuring the security and integrity of distributed systems. They provide a framework and technical means for secure design, implementation, and operation. Adhering to these standards and protocols is essential to protect networks and data against security breaches.

Limitations and challenges in implementing **intrusion detection and prevention systems (IDPS)**

- **False positives and negatives:**
  - o **Challenge**: IDPS may generate false positives, flagging normal activities as threats, or false negatives, missing actual attacks.
  - o **Limitation**: Balancing sensitivity to detect real threats without overwhelming administrators with false alarms is challenging.

- **Scalability Issues:**
  - o **Challenge**: Scaling IDPS for large networks with high traffic can be complex.
  - o **Limitation**: Handling increased data volume might impact system performance and response time.
- **Signature-based detection limitations:**
  - o **Challenge**: Relying solely on known attack signatures may miss novel or evolving threats.
  - o **Limitation**: IDPS effectiveness depends on regularly updated signature databases.
- **Anomaly-based detection challenges:**
  - o **Challenge**: Defining *normal* behavior is subjective and context-dependent.
  - o **Limitation**: Adapting to legitimate changes in network behavior while identifying malicious anomalies is complex.
- **Resource intensiveness:**
  - o **Challenge**: IDPS, especially when using deep packet inspection, can be resource-intensive.
  - o **Limitation**: High resource usage may impact network performance and increase hardware requirements.
- **Evolving threat landscape:**
  - o **Challenge**: Cyber threats continually evolve, making it challenging for static IDPS solutions.
  - o **Limitation**: Adapting to new and sophisticated attack techniques is an ongoing challenge.
- **Encrypted traffic handling:**
  - o **Challenge:** IDPS faces difficulties in inspecting encrypted traffic without compromising privacy.
  - o **Limitation:** Encrypted communications may hide malicious activities, limiting detection capabilities.
- **Lack of standardization:**
  - o **Challenge**: The absence of standardized formats for reporting and sharing threat intelligence.
  - o **Limitation**: Interoperability issues may hinder collaboration among different IDPS solutions.

- **High cost of implementation:**
  - o **Challenge**: Implementing and maintaining a robust IDPS can be costly.
  - o **Limitation**: Smaller organizations might face budget constraints, limiting access to advanced IDPS capabilities.
- **User awareness and training:**
  - o **Challenge**: Users need awareness and training to understand and respond to IDPS alerts.
  - o **Limitation**: Human error in responding to alerts can impact the effectiveness of IDPS.
- **Continuous monitoring:**
  - o **Challenge:** Achieving real-time monitoring for immediate threat response.
  - o **Limitation:** Delays in monitoring may allow attackers to exploit vulnerabilities before detection.
- **Privacy concerns:**
  - o **Challenge**: Balancing security needs with privacy regulations.
  - o **Limitation**: Overly intrusive monitoring may raise legal and ethical concerns.

In summary, effectively addressing these limitations and challenges requires a holistic approach, combining advanced technologies, regular updates, user education, and a continuous commitment to evolving security strategies.

Conclusion

The symbiotic relationship between cryptography and distributed systems have revolutionized the data exchange and digital communication in the modern technological landscapes. However, amidst their prowess, cryptography and distributed systems pose inherent challenges. As technological advancements continue to flourish, blockchain technology is headed towards a booming growth, which we will learn in the coming chapters.

In the next chapter, you will learn about the diverse architectures of centralized, decentralized, and distributed systems and types of blockchains. It will also explain the concepts related to blockchain ledgers, consensus mechanisms, and blockchain data structures. Furthermore, the chapter will explore the underlying protocols that facilitate the agreement and validation of transactions within the blockchain network. They will help you understand the nuances of blockchain technology.

Question and answers

1. **What role does cryptography play in blockchain technology?**

   Ans.: Cryptography is a critical element in the blockchain space. It secures data integrity, ensures transaction transparency, and enables user authentication. Cryptography provides cryptographic hashing for block validation and digital signatures for transaction verification.

2. **How do smart contracts work in blockchain technology?**

   Ans.: Smart contracts are self-executing contracts whose terms are written into code. They facilitate and verify the performance of an agreement when predefined conditions coded into the contract are met. It eliminates the need for intermediaries, ensuring transparency and security.

3. **What is a distributed file system?**

   Ans.: A distributed file system allows files to be stored on multiple servers or nodes across a network. It provides access to data files in a distributed manner. This way, it ensures improved scalability and increased reliability.

4. **What is the difference between symmetric and asymmetric encryption?**

   Ans.: Symmetric encryption deploys a single key for both encrypting and decrypting information. Contrary to this, a pair of keys is used in asymmetric encryption – a public key for encryption and a private key for decryption – which ensures confidentiality and authenticity.

5. **What to choose between symmetric and asymmetric encryption?**

   Ans.: The selection between symmetric and asymmetric encryption depends on the specific requirements and performance needs. Symmetric encryption offers faster processing but poses challenges in key management. Meanwhile, asymmetric encryption provides better security and functionalities. However, it faces challenges in handling large sets of data.

Multiple choice questions

1. **Which encryption method uses a single key for both encryption and decryption?**
   a. Symmetric encryption
   b. Asymmetric encryption
   c. Public-key encryption
   d. Private-key encryption

2. **What distinguishes asymmetric encryption from symmetric encryption?**
   a. Asymmetric encryption uses two different keys, while symmetric encryption uses a single key.
   b. Symmetric encryption is better than asymmetric encryption in handling large sets of data.
   c. Both are correct.
   d. Both are incorrect.
3. **What role does cryptography play in blockchain technology?**
   a. Verifying identities
   b. Ensuring confidentiality
   c. Securing data integrity
   d. All of the above.
4. **What cryptographic technique is used to verify the authenticity of a digital message?**
   a. Digital signature
   b. Public-key encryption
   c. Symmetric encryption
   d. Hashing
5. **What cryptographic method enables computations on encrypted data without decryption?**
   a. RSA encryption
   b. Digital signature
   c. Homomorphic encryption
   d. Elliptic-curve cryptography

Answers

1. a
2. c
3. d
4. a
5. c

Chapter 2
Introduction to Blockchain Technology

Introduction

The space of data exchange, transaction, and digital trust has been disrupted and revolutionized with the advent of blockchain technology. Since its documented inception in 2008, blockchain has become a hot topic in various sectors for its virtues like security, transparency and decentralization.

Blockchain is a distributed ledger. Simply put, it is a digital record that securely stores data across a network of computers. This makes it distinct from centralized systems, where information is stored in a single location controlled by a central authority. Blockchain functions on a decentralized network. This allows every participant to maintain a copy of the entire ledger. Eventually, it eliminates the need for intermediaries and fosters digital trust among users.

Although blockchain technology got its initial fame as the underlying infrastructure for Bitcoin, it is not limited to cryptocurrencies and has innumerable applications across industries, including healthcare, real estate, finance, supply chain management, and many more. This chapter aims to provide a comprehensive overview of blockchain technology and its transformative potential.

Structure

This chapter includes the following topics:

- Rise of blockchain technology
- Technical definition of a blockchain
- Different types of blockchain
- Distributed ledger technology vs. blockchain
- Byzantine generals problem
- Consensus mechanism
- Cryptographic primitives
- Data structure used in blockchain
- Block header hash and block

Objectives

Throughout this chapter, readers will get to explore the foundational concepts of blockchain technology. The chapter will elucidate blockchain's decentralized architecture, cryptographic principles, and the immutable nature of its distributed ledger system. Besides, it will examine the diverse applications of blockchain spanning a range of industries. The chapter will also conduct a comparative analysis between blockchain and centralized systems, and explain how the former fosters trust, transparency, and security. This will help readers envision the future trajectory of blockchain technology.

Rise of blockchain technology

New technologies that are emerging have the potential to revolutionize the way we live and work by altering our thoughts and processes. One of the significant transformative technologies of the 21st century is blockchain. Blockchain is a technology that is poised to usher in a new way of conducting business that will change everyday life for the better. Blockchains are virtual, and therefore, they have no physical form. *Figure 2.1* illustrates how they work:

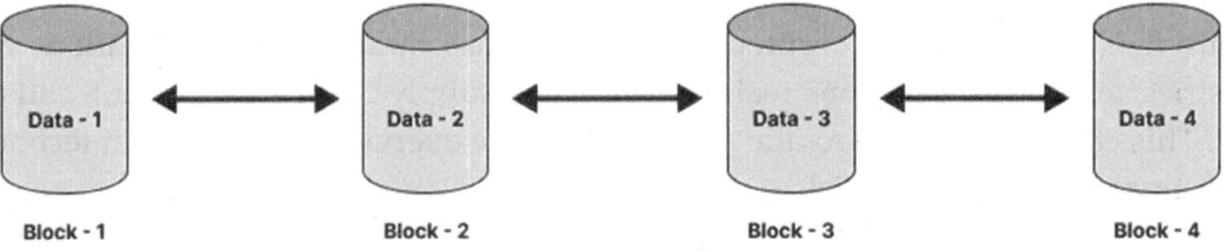

Figure 2.1: *Working of a blockchain network*

The graphic above shows a line of blocks, each containing data in the form of a distributed ledger. This is essentially a database that can be shared among multiple devices or institutions, and information can be shared instead of copied or transferred. The blocks that make up this ledger are arranged in chronological order.

Blockchain is a digital database that grows continuously and consists of a linked list of records. The database contains sensitive information, such as financial transactions, which are protected by cryptography and can be shared among a large, decentralized, and publicly accessible network. Each block in the chain includes a cryptographic hash of the previous block, a timestamp, and transaction data. This technology has emerged as a possible solution to the issue of declining trust in traditional institutions and online intermediaries, as it purportedly eliminates the need for trust between parties.

Defining blockchain

A blockchain is a decentralized, distributed ledger that records transactions on multiple computers in a way that cannot be altered retroactively. This allows for secure and transparent record-keeping, making it a popular technology for finance, supply chain management, and other industries.

In other words, a blockchain is a digital ledger that is used to keep track of transactions and information, much like a notebook in which you write down your daily expenses. This ledger is shared with many people, meaning that everyone can see and add to it, similar to a notebook that many friends can write in. When a transaction is made, it is recorded in the ledger and every participant in the blockchain has a copy of it. This makes it impossible for anyone to cheat or change past transactions, as once something is recorded in the ledger, it cannot be altered or erased.

Since many people have a copy of the ledger, there is no need for a central authority, such as a bank, to keep track of all the transactions. This makes the entire system more secure, transparent, and fair, as it operates like a group of friends who keep track of each other's expenses. A blockchain can be seen as a digital ledger that is used to keep track of transactions and information in a secure and transparent manner. The ledger is shared among a network of participants, much like a bulletin board where multiple individuals can post messages and keep track of each other's contributions.

Imagine that you and your friends have multiple copies of a bulletin board, and each time someone makes a contribution, the message is added to all the bulletin boards at the same time. This makes it nearly impossible for anyone to alter the information or cheat the system, as everyone has access to the same data and any changes would immediately become noticeable.

This concept is similar to how a blockchain operates. Transactions are recorded on numerous computers that are part of a decentralized network, with every participant having a copy of the ledger. This ensures the system is transparent, secure, and tamper-proof, as every individual in the network can see what is happening and any changes are immediately apparent. In this way, a blockchain operates as a decentralized network, where every participant has an equal say in how the system operates and no single person or entity can control it. This eliminates the need for intermediaries, and ensures that the transactions and information recorded on the blockchain are transparent and tamper-proof.

Problems with a centralized system

In the real world, most organizations fall somewhere in between a completely centralized and completely decentralized IT structure. To better understand the distinction between the two, a centralized network connects all users to a central server that houses all network data and user information. Conversely, a decentralized network is composed of multiple peer-to-peer user groups, each with its own server that stores data and information specific to that group. Originally, all communication networks were centralized until researcher *Paul Baran* introduced the concept of a decentralized network in 1964 to enhance telecommunications infrastructure. When an organization chooses centralization, it becomes the focal point of control and power, vested in the hands of only a select few. While centralization is touted as having many benefits, it also carries its own set of drawbacks, just like any other concept.

Some of the problems associated with a centralized system are as follows:

- **Higher security risk:** A single point of failure also increases the likelihood of disruption by a security breach or cybersecurity threat such as a DDOS attack, since there is only one target of the attack. Additionally, there are always inherent privacy risks with centralized systems since there is only one central repository for user data.
- If a core server becomes corrupted or goes offline, its data may be permanently lost.
- **Inefficient use of resources:** Centralized systems are often inefficient in terms of resource utilization, as resources are monopolized by the central authority, which may result in slower processing times and higher costs.
- **Limited scalability:** A centralized system can have difficulty scaling beyond a certain point since the only option is to add more storage, bandwidth, or processing power to the central server. When too many people try to use the network all at once and it gets too busy, it can slow down for people who are far away from the main computer. This happens because there is too much information trying to go through a small space, like cars on a congested road.

- **Limited accessibility:** Centralized systems can limit accessibility, as users are required to go through the central authority in order to use the system.
- **Opacity and lack of transparency:** Centralized systems are often opaque, meaning that the decisions and actions of the central authority are not always transparent or easily understood by the users, leading to potential privacy and security risks.

Centralized vs. decentralized vs. distributed architecture

The difference between centralized, decentralized, and distributed systems can be explained with the use of *Figure 2.2*:

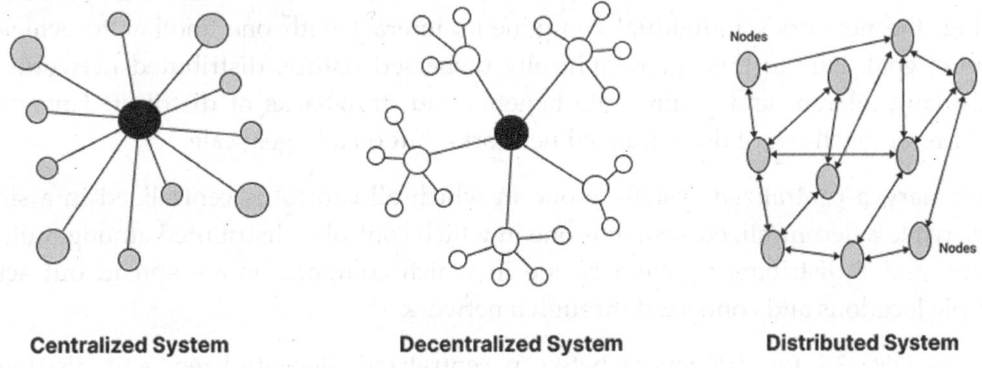

***Figure 2.2**: Difference between centralized, decentralized, and distributed systems*

Centralized architecture refers to a system in which all data and functions are controlled and managed by a single, central authority. In a centralized system, the central authority has complete control over the network and makes all decisions related to the functioning of the system. Centralized networks are currently the most widely used type of network on the web. These networks are dependent on a central network owner to connect all the other satellite users and devices, which means there is a single point of failure that can be deliberately exploited by malicious actors.

Decentralized architecture, on the other hand, refers to a system in which control is distributed among multiple entities, rather than being centralized in a single entity. Decentralized systems are stronger and less vulnerable to breakdowns because no one entity has complete control over the whole system. Thanks to recent advancements in technology, computers and other devices can work together to share processing power and create decentralized networks. It is important to note that decentralized networks are different from centralized networks because they do not rely on one central authority to manage everything. Instead, there are multiple servers that work together to manage the network.

Distributed architecture refers to a system in which components are spread out across multiple locations and connected through a network. In a distributed system, each component works together to achieve a common goal, and the system as a whole is more resilient and scalable than a centralized system. The term *distributed network* is used to refer to a network that is geographically dispersed and may follow a hierarchical node structure. However, in most cases, the term refers to a network where computational resources and node locations are evenly distributed. The decision-making process in a distributed network typically involves individual nodes voting for a new state, and the final behavior of the system changes in accordance with the aggregate results of the decisions each individual node votes on. The exact processes used for distributed decision-making depend on the network's consensus mechanism. In all forms of distributed decision-making, the network's individual components interact with one another to achieve a common goal. Due to their geographically dispersed nature, distributed networks are highly fault-tolerant and secure. The benefits and drawbacks of distributed networks closely resemble those of decentralized networks, but on a larger scale.

In summary, a centralized system is one in which all control is centralized in a single entity, while a decentralized system is one in which control is distributed among multiple entities, and a distributed system is one in which components are spread out across multiple locations and connected through a network.

Refer to *Table 2.1* for differences between centralized, decentralized, and distributed architecture:

Centralized	Decentralized	Distributed
All data and processing power is stored and managed by a single central authority.	The system is spread across multiple nodes, but there is still a central authority that manages and makes decisions for the system as a whole.	The system is spread across multiple nodes and there is no central authority controlling the system.
There is a single point of control, and communication is centralized through a central node.	Multiple nodes communicate with each other, but the central authority remains in control.	Each node communicates with other nodes and collaborates to make decisions for the system as a whole.
Centralized networks are typically the most costeffective options for small systems and require fewer resources to set up and maintain.	Decentralized networks improve user request speed by establishing local master nodes in high traffic areas, rather than routing to a central server.	Distributed networks offer robustness with node failure as computational workload is rebalanced among remaining nodes. They are more robust than other network architectures.

Centralized	Decentralized	Distributed
Easier to standardize interactions between the main server and client nodes. That can lead to a	Since decentralized networks do not have a single point of failure, they can continue to operate even	Distributed networks are more scalable than both centralized and decentralized networks.
more consistent and streamlined end user experience.	if a master node is compromised or shut down.	They generally exhibit lower latency as well due to the even distribution of network processing power and data.
Centralized networks have clear command chains, allowing for simple delegation and reducing cross-chatter between authorization levels. Adding or removing client nodes is also straightforward.	Decentralized networks speed up user requests by having local master nodes in high traffic areas, instead of routing to a central server over large distances.	In a distributed network, data is evenly shared and harder to modify, censor, or destroy, making the network more transparent. This is often further secured through cryptography.
Since centralized networks have a single point of failure, if the main server crashes, the entire network will likely shut down.	Decentralized networks offer an enhanced level of confidentiality to users, as the information stored on the network is spread across numerous points rather than going through a single entity. This means that there is no single point of vulnerability, reducing the risk of unauthorized access or data breaches.	Decentralized networks offer an enhanced level of confidentiality to users, as the information stored on the network is spread across numerous points rather than going through a single entity. This means that there is no single point of vulnerability, reducing the risk of unauthorized access or data breaches.
Centralized networks can be hard to **scale** past a certain point, since the only way to do so is to add more storage, bandwidth, or processing power to the central server.	In decentralized networks, master nodes act independently, leading to coordination issues for larger organizations trying to direct collective tasks.	Since it is difficult for any individual node to gain a global view of the entire network, it is therefore harder for individual nodes to make well-informed decisions based on the state of other nodes in the system.

***Table 2.1:** Difference between centralized, decentralized, and distributed architecture*

Blockchain: A comprehensive network architecture

When discussing the relative merits of different network architectures, it is important to keep in mind that no configuration is superior to any other across all environments. Blockchain technology offers a potential solution for various network needs by providing a secure, decentralized and transparent system for storing and transmitting data. In fact, blockchain is by far, one of the most disruptive and revolutionary technologies of our time. The decentralized nature of blockchain eliminates the need for a central authority and allows for secure, tamper-proof record-keeping and transfers. Additionally, blockchain's use of cryptographic algorithms makes it highly resistant to hacking and malicious activities. All these features make it a strong candidate for various network applications such as supply chain management, financial transactions, and digital identity management.

First and foremost, you must take into account that there is no central authority governing blockchain. This makes it a completely democratized system. Next, since the provided information is immutable, it can be easily shared and made open to the public allowing for unparalleled levels of transparency. These two pushing pods make blockchain the next big thing since the wide expansion of internet.

Table 2.2 shows real-world blockchain use cases through an issue and solution format:

Issue	Solution
Slow cross-border payments	Blockchain introduces a faster and more transparent payment gateway.
Accountability issues in traditional contracts	Smart contracts offer transparency and faster settlements
Costly supply chain management	Blockchain gets rid of fraud with real-time view and increases revenues
Slow government systems and public sectors	Provides faster, more secured, and cost effective governmental systems
Cybersecurity	Blockchain offers decentralized storage systems, Identity management, and traditional endpoint protection.

Table 2.2: *Real-world blockchain use cases through an issue and solution format*

Blockchain technology proposes itself as the ideal solution for various network needs by offering a secure, decentralized, and transparent way of storing and transmitting data. It eliminates the need for a central authority, providing a tamper-proof record-keeping system that is highly resistant to hacking and malicious activities. The cryptographic algorithms used in blockchain make it ideal for sensitive information such as financial transactions, supply chain management, and digital identity management. The consensus mechanism in the blockchain network ensures data cannot be altered or tampered with, providing increased efficiency and transparency. This makes it a valuable tool for various industries and an ideal solution for organizations looking to securely manage and transfer data.

One of the most important use cases of blockchain technology is in the financial sector. Blockchain allows for secure, tamper-proof financial transactions without the need for intermediaries such as banks. This not only increases the efficiency of financial transactions but also reduces the costs associated with intermediaries. For example, *Ripple* is a blockchain based real-time gross settlement system, currency exchange and remittance network that has been designed for fast and secure financial transactions.

In contrast to traditional financial systems, where transactions often involve multiple intermediaries and can take days to settle, blockchain streamlines the process by providing a decentralized and transparent ledger. In traditional systems, intermediaries play a crucial role in overseeing and validating transactions, which introduces delays and additional costs. Blockchain eliminates the need for these intermediaries, allowing for direct peer-to-peer transactions that are faster and more cost-effective.

Moreover, the traditional financial infrastructure may face challenges such as limited accessibility, especially for cross-border transactions, and susceptibility to fraud and errors. Blockchain addresses these issues by offering a decentralized and immutable ledger that enhances security, transparency, and accessibility. The cryptographic nature of blockchain ensures the integrity of transactions, reducing the risk of fraud.

Another important use case for blockchain is in supply chain management. Blockchain can be used to track the origin and movement of products from the point of production to the end consumer, providing greater transparency and accountability in the supply chain. For example, Walmart and IBM have developed a blockchain-based food traceability system to increase transparency and improve food safety.

Companies can leverage blockchain for supply chain management by creating a transparent and secure system to trace the journey of products. Each stage of the supply chain, from production to distribution and retail, is recorded on an immutable blockchain ledger. This decentralized and tamper-resistant database ensures that all participants in the supply chain have real-time access to accurate and unalterable information. By utilizing smart contracts, automated and self-executing agreements can be established, streamlining processes like payments and quality checks. This not only enhances transparency but also reduces the risk of errors and fraud. Blockchain's empower companies to build more efficient, accountable, and collaborative supply chains, fostering trust among stakeholders and improving overall supply chain management.

Blockchain is also being used in digital identity management. The decentralized nature of blockchain allows for secure and transparent management of digital identities, eliminating the need for a central authority. This has the potential to greatly improve the security of personal information and reduce identity theft. For example, Microsoft has developed a decentralized identity management system built on blockchain technology.

In addition to these use cases, blockchain is being explored in various other industries such as voting, real estate, and healthcare. The decentralized and cryptographic security of blockchain make it an ideal solution for organizations looking to securely manage and transfer data. Blockchain technology has proven to be a game-changer in the world of network architecture, offering an efficient, secure, and transparent solution for a variety of needs. Whether it is for financial transactions, supply chain management, or digital identity management, blockchain has the potential to revolutionize the way we store and transfer data. As the technology continues to evolve, we can expect to see even more innovative use cases and applications of blockchain in the future.

Let us look at how blockchain implementation can benefit organizations and enterprises with the help of some case studies:

- **Lower costs:** Keeping central databases, for example, in banks and in government institutions, and securing them from cybercrimes and other issues, can be expensive. The blockchain architecture can help reduce these costs.
    - A study by Santander InnoVentures estimates that blockchain technology could save banks up to $20 billion annually by 2022 in infrastructure costs.
    - The World Economic Forum suggests that blockchain implementation could generate over $1 trillion in new trade.
- **Tracking history:** The blockchain allows you to see the history of any transaction at any time, creating a permanent record.
    - In supply chain management, IBM's Food Trust network, built on blockchain, has demonstrated the ability to trace the origin of food products, reducing the time taken to trace the source of contaminated produce from weeks to seconds.
- **Increased security and accuracy:** Data entered into the blockchain is difficult to change and is validated by multiple independent networks, making it more secure and accurate.
    - The immutability of blockchain ledgers has been a key factor in preventing fraud. For example, Estonia's e-Government infrastructure, utilizing blockchain, has seen a reduction in identity theft cases.
- **Improved transparency:** With the blockchain, all participants have equal access to the data, making it a more transparent system.

- o The world bank has initiated projects leveraging blockchain to increase transparency and reduce corruption in financial transactions.

- **Fewer intermediaries:** The decentralized nature of the blockchain can reduce the need for intermediaries, making transactions faster and more efficient.
  - o Blockchain's decentralized nature eliminates the need for intermediaries in various industries. For instance, in real estate, startups like Propy aim to streamline property transactions by connecting buyers and sellers directly.
- **Enhanced privacy:** Users have control over their own data and can choose who to share it with, improving privacy and security.
  - o Self-sovereign identity solutions using blockchain, such as **uPort** and **Sovrin**, empower individuals to control their personal data, enhancing privacy.

Simplified architecture of blockchain

In a distributed blockchain network, each participant is responsible for maintaining, approving, and updating new entries. The system is not controlled by any single entity, but rather by all members of the network. This ensures that all records and procedures are valid and secure, allowing parties who may not trust each other to reach a common consensus.

Blockchain is a decentralized, distributed ledger that contains various types of transactions arranged in a peer-to-peer network. This network is made up of numerous computers, with each one playing a role in ensuring that data cannot be modified without the agreement of the entire network.

The structure of blockchain technology is represented by a series of blocks, each containing a set of transactions in a particular order. These blocks can be stored as a flat file or in the form of a simple database. Two essential data structures utilized in blockchain technology are pointers and linked lists. These structures help ensure the integrity and immutability of the data contained within the blockchain network. A brief explanation of pointers and linked lists are as follows:

- Pointers are variables that store information regarding the location of another variable. They serve to indicate the position of another variable.
- Linked lists, on the other hand, consist of a series of blocks in a specific order. Each block contains specific data and is linked to the next block through a pointer.

Refer to the following figure:

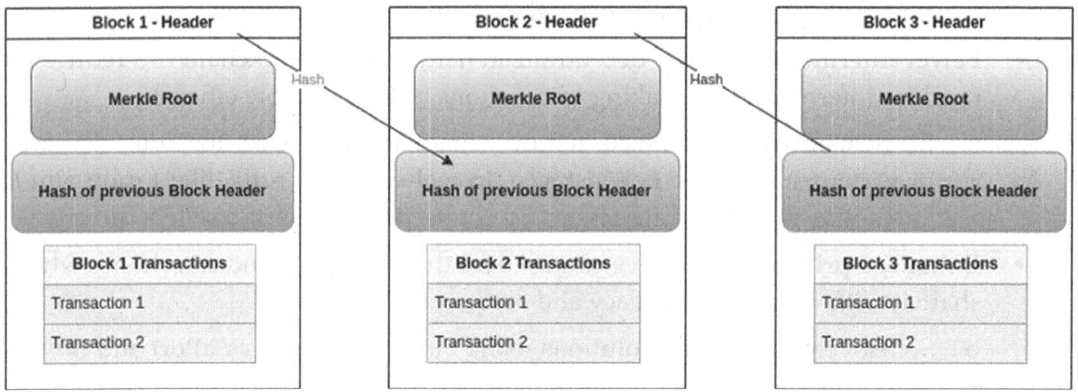

Figure 2.3: *Structure of blockchain architecture*

Figure 2.4 gives an accurate representation of blockchain for better understanding of concept:

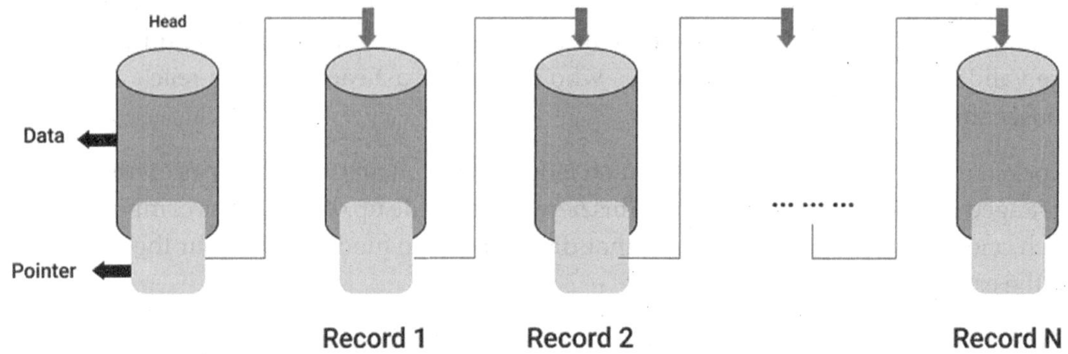

Figure 2.4: *Blockchain architecture*

Logically, the first block does not contain the pointer since this one is the first in a chain. At the same time, there is potentially going to be a final block within the blockchain database that has a pointer with no value.

Key characteristics of blockchain architecture

The blockchain architecture offers numerous benefits to businesses. Following are some of its key characteristics:

- **Cryptography:** Blockchain transactions are validated and trustworthy due to the complex computations and cryptographic proof among involved parties.
- **Immutability:** Any records made in a blockchain cannot be changed or deleted.

- **Provenance:** It refers to the fact that it is possible to track the origin of every transaction inside the blockchain ledger.
- **Decentralization:** Each member of the blockchain structure has access to the whole distributed database. As opposed to the central-based system, consensus algorithm allows for control of the network.
- **Anonymity:** Each blockchain network participant has a generated address, not user identity. This keeps users' anonymity, especially in a public blockchain structure.
- **Transparency:** The blockchain system cannot be corrupted. This is very unlikely to happen, as it requires huge computing power to overwrite the blockchain network completely.

This can suitably be explained through *Figure 2.5*:

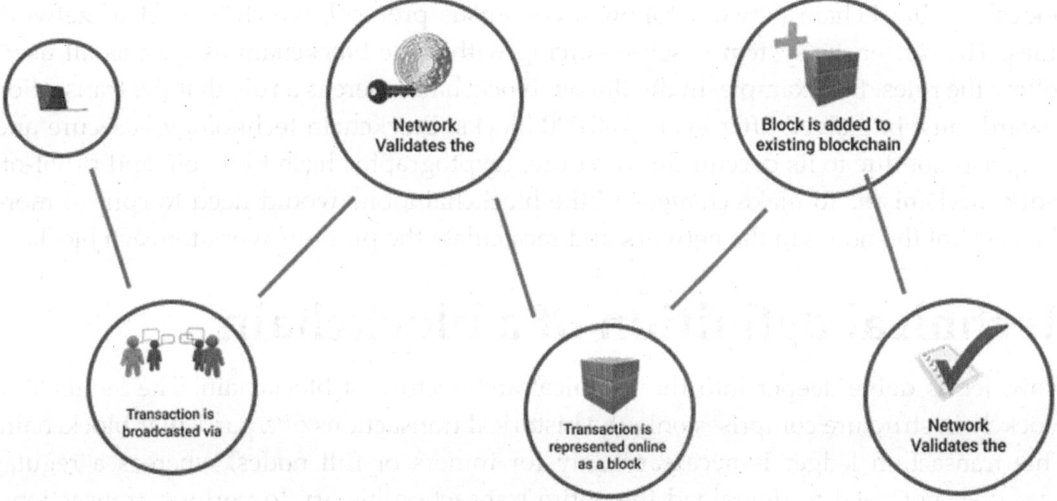

Figure 2.5: Blockchain functioning

Blockchain is a decentralized digital ledger that records transactions securely. The type of data stored in each block in a blockchain structure depends on the type of blockchain. For example, in the Bitcoin blockchain, the block contains information about the sender, receiver, and number of coins. One of the primary distinctions between a blockchain and a standard database is that the former enables encrypted information to be linked as blocks, rather than as raw data. Despite transactions being represented as cryptographic strings of data, the way in which these blocks are connected together provides significant value to the information.

Each block in a blockchain has a unique identifier, known as a **hash**. The hash is generated using a cryptographic algorithm and acts as a digital fingerprint for the block. Any changes to the block will result in a change in the hash, which helps detect tampering or corruption.

The blocks in a blockchain are linked together using the hash of the previous block, creating a chain of blocks. This is the main factor behind the security of blockchain architecture. The first block in the chain is called the **genesis block**, from which all other confirmed and validated blocks are derived. To prevent tampering or corrupt attempts, blockchain uses **proof-of-work**. This process slows down the creation of new blocks and requires powerful computer processors to make changes. Miners, special nodes in the network, perform this work and are rewarded with transaction fees.

When a new user joins the blockchain network, they receive a copy of the entire system. When a new block is created, it is sent to all nodes in the network, which then verify the block and add it to their local copy of the blockchain if the information is correct. The nodes in a blockchain network follow a consensus protocol, which is a set of network rules. The consensus system is self-enforcing within the blockchain as long as all users follow the rules. For example, in the Bitcoin blockchain, there is a rule that the transaction reward must be halved after every 200,000 blocks. Blockchain technology is secure and tamper-proof due to its decentralized nature, cryptographic hash function, and proof-of-work mechanism. To make changes to the blockchain, one would need to control more than 50% of the nodes in the network and recalculate the proof-of-work for each block.

Technical definition of a blockchain

Now, let us delve deeper into the technical architecture of blockchain. The ledger in a blockchain structure comprises only the historical transactions of a particular blockchain. This transaction ledger is necessary only for miners or full nodes, whereas a regular user does not need to download the entire transaction history to perform transactions. Instead, they can interact with client software that does not require complete copies of the blockchain.

A miner is a node that participates in the blockchain network and performs cryptographic hashing work to confirm transactions and add blocks to the blockchain. Miners add blocks in sequence, which make up the structure of the blockchain. The process of confirming transactions and adding blocks to the blockchain is referred to as mining.

The **Institute of Electrical and Electronics Engineers (IEEE)** defines blockchain as a **Distributed Ledger Technology (DLT)** that enables secure transactions and verifiable data sharing among multiple parties without the need for a central authority. According to the IEEE definition, blockchain is a decentralized technology that allows multiple parties to securely transact and share data in a transparent and verifiable manner. The ledger is maintained by multiple nodes in the network, rather than a central authority, making it resistant to tampering and corruption.

The definition of blockchain technology provided by the IEEE focuses on its key characteristics, such as decentralization, secure transactions, and verifiable data sharing. Despite its widespread use, there is still a great deal of confusion surrounding blockchain, as the technology is still in its early stages and can be implemented in various ways depending on the intended use case.

According to MIT Sloan Assistant Professor *Christian Catalini*, an expert in blockchain and cryptocurrency, blockchain technology allows a network of computers to regularly reach a consensus on the state of a distributed ledger. This ledger can contain various types of shared data, such as transaction records, attributes of transactions, credentials, or other pieces of information. The ledger is secured through a combination of cryptography and game theory, and does not rely on trusted nodes, as traditional networks do. This is what enables Bitcoin to transfer value globally without the need for intermediaries like banks. The usefulness of blockchain technology is heightened when it is combined with a crypto token and a distributed ledger.

Some key factors of blockchain architecture are as follows:

- **Decentralized structure:** The decentralized structure of a blockchain network is one of its defining features. It eliminates the need for a central authority and allows multiple nodes to participate in the network and validate transactions.
- **Blocks:** A block is a unit of data that contains a set of transactions, a timestamp, and a reference to the previous block, also known as a **hash**. This creates a chain of blocks, hence the name blockchain.
- **Nodes:** Nodes are the computers or devices that participate in the blockchain network. Each node stores a copy of the entire blockchain and helps to validate transactions and create new blocks.
- **Consensus mechanism:** In order to ensure the integrity of the data, the network uses a consensus mechanism. This allows the nodes to reach agreement on the validity of the transactions and helps prevent malicious actors from making unauthorized changes to the blockchain.
- **Public/private keys:** Public and private keys are used to create a digital signature for each transaction. The public key is used to encrypt the data, while the private key is used to decrypt it.
- **Hashes:** A hash is a fundamental element of the blockchain technology, serving as the backbone of its secure architecture. In the simplest terms, a hash is a unique representation of data, created through a cryptographic hash function. It acts

as a digital fingerprint for each block in the blockchain, providing a secure and unalterable way to identify and track the block.

- **Chain of blocks:** The hash of a block is linked to the hash of the previous block, creating a chain of blocks that forms the backbone of a blockchain's architecture.
- **Proof-of-work:** This is a mechanism that makes it difficult for anyone to change the information stored in a blockchain. It involves a process of computational work that must be performed in order to add a new block to the chain, making it time-consuming and resource-intensive.
- **Transactions grouped into blocks:** In a blockchain network, transactions are grouped into blocks. Each block contains a timestamp, a reference to the previous block (also known as a **hash**), and a set of transactions. This creates a chain of blocks, hence the name blockchain.
- **Verification by nodes:** The nodes in a blockchain network are responsible for verifying transactions and adding new blocks to the blockchain. For example, if a user wants to transfer funds to another user, the transaction needs to be verified by the nodes in the network before it is added to the blockchain.
- **Cryptography:** Cryptography is an important aspect of the blockchain architecture and is used to secure the data stored in the blockchain. For example, each block and transaction is encrypted, and a digital signature is used to verify its authenticity. Public and private keys are used to create a digital signature for each transaction, with the public key used to encrypt the data and the private key used to decrypt it.
- **Crypto tokens:** These are digital assets that can be traded on a blockchain and are often used to incentivize nodes to validate new blocks.
- **Smart contracts:** Another key aspect of the blockchain architecture is the use of smart contracts. A smart contract is a self-executing contract that automatically executes the terms of the agreement when certain conditions are met. This eliminates the need for intermediaries and helps to increase the efficiency and transparency of the blockchain network. For example, a smart contract can be used to automatically transfer funds from one user to another when a certain condition is met, such as the successful completion of a project.

Understanding blockchain ledgers

Original hard-copy ledgers were created to record all financial transactions, as well as to track asset acquisition and value. Ledgers are used as a double-entry system, with one column for debits and another for credits. There were three ledgers for assets, liabilities and equity, with equity calculated from assets minus liabilities. The accountant would create a balance sheet for each ledger and adjust the values based on market appreciation or depreciation. The balances were used to calculate overall equity. For example, if an individual bought a car in cash, it would be credited in the cash ledger and debited in the asset value column, keeping the overall equity the same. Today, the process has been digitalized, making it more efficient and less prone to errors. However, there is always a chance someone may forget to enter a piece of data.

An example of a distributed ledger that is commonly used is the torrent technology that allows users to download and seed data. In torrent technology, the user's data is distributed across multiple nodes, making it less vulnerable to file corruption, deletion, or malicious attacks. Any changes to the data would require the consensus of the majority of nodes in the network. It is important to note that not all distributed ledgers operate on a blockchain. While blockchain is one type of distributed ledger technology, there are also other forms of distributed ledgers that operate using different techniques and algorithms.

A blockchain is a type of distributed ledger that is open-source and operates through the cryptographic hashing of data. Each new piece of information is stored or encrypted within a block of the blockchain. The authentication and resolution of a consensus algorithm determines the cryptographic hashing of the data. Once authenticated, the data is encrypted, making the transaction transparent to all network nodes while limiting ownership to the holder of the private keys.

In layman's terms, a blockchain is created by a developer to be decentralized through the implementation of a distributed ledger framework. This framework ensures the secure transmission of data.

Additionally, the blockchain ledger is peer-to-peer, meaning transactions do not involve a third party. The decentralized nature of the ledger means the data is not stored in a single location. Instead, it is distributed across multiple nodes that store the blockchain ledger data and verify transactions each time a transaction is made.

Transactions in a ledger are recorded as a series of debits and credits, which are entries that either increase or decrease a specific account. In a double-entry bookkeeping system, the total of all debits must equal the total of all credits, as each financial transaction has two opposing effects.

For instance, let us consider a transaction where an individual named John Doe sells a car to Jane Smith for $10,000. The ledger entries for this transaction would be recorded as follows:

- Debit: John Doe's Asset Account (Car): $10,000
- Credit: John Doe's Cash Account: $10,000
- Debit: Jane Smith's Cash Account: $10,000
- Credit: Jane Smith's Asset Account (Car): $10,000

This example showcases how the transaction affects both parties involved. John Doe transfers ownership of the car to Jane Smith and receives cash in exchange, while Jane Smith gives up cash to acquire the car.

External applications can interact with blockchain ledgers in various ways, and each method provides different capabilities and benefits depending on the specific requirements of the application and use case.

One common method of interaction is through **application programming interfaces (APIs)**. An API is a set of protocols, routines, and tools for building software and applications that enable external applications to access data and interact with a blockchain ledger. They provide a standard way for different applications to communicate with each other and exchange data. For example, a cryptocurrency exchange can use an API to interact with a blockchain ledger and execute trades on behalf of users. The API acts as a bridge between the exchange and the ledger, enabling the exchange to access the ledger data, such as the current state of a user's balance, and execute transactions, such as buying or selling cryptocurrency.

Another way external applications can interact with blockchain ledgers is through smart contracts. Smart contracts are an innovative technology that has revolutionized the way external applications interact with blockchain ledgers. These contracts are self-executing, meaning that they automatically enforce the terms of an agreement between the parties involved. This eliminates the need for intermediaries, such as lawyers or banks, and greatly reduces the risk of fraud or miscommunication. The terms of the agreement are encoded as computer code and stored on the blockchain ledger, making them easily accessible and transparent to all parties.

One of the most significant benefits of smart contracts is their ability to automate complex processes, such as supply chain management. For example, consider a supply chain management application that is used to track goods from the manufacturer to the end consumer. Using a smart contract, the application can automate the process of updating the status of the goods and transferring ownership as they move through the supply chain. The smart contract is triggered by external transactions from the application, which provide information about the current state of the goods. Based on this information, the smart contract executes the necessary actions, such as updating the status of the goods and transferring ownership, without the need for human intervention.

The use of smart contracts in supply chain management provides several advantages over traditional methods. For instance, it provides a clear and transparent record of the current state of the goods and their ownership, which is accessible to all parties involved in the supply chain. This eliminates the need for manual record-keeping and reduces the risk of human error. Furthermore, smart contracts ensure that all parties involved in the supply chain have a clear and transparent record of the current state of the goods and their ownership. This increases trust and accountability between the parties, and reduces the risk of fraud or miscommunication. Smart contracts are a powerful tool for external applications to interact with blockchain ledgers. They provide a secure, transparent, and automated means of executing complex processes, such as supply chain management, without the need for intermediaries. As the use of blockchain technology continues to grow, we can expect to see more and more applications making use of smart contracts to provide innovative and efficient solutions to a wide range of industries.

Decentralized applications (dApps) are another way external applications can interact with blockchain ledgers. A decentralized application, commonly referred to as a dApp, is a software application that runs on a decentralized network. Unlike traditional applications that rely on a central server or authority, dApps are built on top of a blockchain ledger and can interact with the ledger to access data and execute transactions. dApps can be used to perform various tasks, such as financial transactions, digital identity verification, and asset management. For example, a decentralized voting application can interact with a blockchain ledger to securely and transparently count votes. The dApp sends transactions to the blockchain ledger to cast votes, and the ledger records and counts the votes. The transparency and immutability of the blockchain ledger ensure that the results of the voting process are tamper-proof and publicly available. One of the most well-known examples of a dApp is Bitcoin, a decentralized digital currency that enables peer-to-peer transactions without the need for intermediaries. Another example is Ethereum, a blockchain platform that enables developers to build decentralized applications and smart contracts. Another example of a dApp is Uniswap, a decentralized exchange that enables users to trade cryptocurrencies without the need for a central exchange.

Finally, wallets are another way external applications can interact with blockchain ledgers. Wallets are software programs that allow users to store, send, and receive cryptocurrencies. External applications can interact with blockchain ledgers through wallets by sending and receiving transactions on behalf of users. For example, a remittance application can use a wallet to send and receive payments on behalf of its users. The application sends transactions to the blockchain ledger through the wallet, which acts as a bridge between the application and the ledger. The wallet ensures that the transactions are executed securely and efficiently, and the ledger records the transactions and updates the state of the users' balances.

NFTs, unique digital assets representing ownership of specific items or content, are managed and stored in wallets. External applications, such as NFT marketplaces, leverage these wallets to enable users to store, buy, and sell NFTs seamlessly. When a user initiates a transaction on an NFT marketplace, the wallet acts as the intermediary between the application and the blockchain ledger.

For instance, consider an NFT art marketplace dApp. Users can connect their wallets to the dApp, which then interacts with the blockchain ledger to record ownership and transactions of NFT art pieces. The wallet ensures the secure execution of transactions, and the blockchain ledger maintains an immutable record of ownership and transaction history.

Blockchain events

A blockchain event refers to any action or occurrence that takes place within a blockchain network. These events can range from the creation of a new block to the execution of a smart contract. Blockchain events are a fundamental aspect of blockchain technology that enables the execution of transactions, updates to the ledger, and triggers specific actions within a blockchain network. They are triggered by specific conditions that occur within the network, such as the creation of a new block, the transfer of funds, or the execution of a smart contract. A blockchain event can be triggered in several ways, such as when a new transaction is added to the blockchain, when a smart contract is executed, or when a certain condition within the network is met. When an event is triggered, the information regarding that event is broadcasted to all nodes within the network, allowing them to update their copies of the blockchain ledger.

The creation of a new block is a significant blockchain event that occurs whenever a miner solves a complex mathematical puzzle and adds a block of transactions to the blockchain. This event is broadcasted to all nodes within the network, and upon validation, the block is added to each node's copy of the blockchain ledger. The creation of a new block confirms and records transactions, updating the state of the blockchain.

Smart contracts are self-executing contracts with the terms of the agreement between buyer and seller written in code. The execution of a smart contract is another example of a blockchain event. When specific conditions within the smart contract are met, the contract is automatically executed, triggering the blockchain event. For example, a smart contract can be designed to transfer funds from one account to another when a specific date is reached or to release funds from escrow when certain conditions are met.

In conclusion, blockchain events are actions or occurrences that take place within a blockchain network, and they can range from the creation of a new block to the execution of a smart contract. These events play a crucial role in the functioning and security of a blockchain network.

Features of blockchain

Blockchain technology is not just a backup network for cryptocurrencies, but it offers a lot more. Blockchain is a decentralized, distributed ledger technology that was originally created to support digital currencies such as Bitcoin. However, its features have made it a popular technology for a wide range of applications beyond just digital currencies.

Some of the key features of blockchain technology are:

Decentralization

The blockchain network is unique in that it is decentralized, which means that there is no governing authority or centralized control over the framework. Instead, a group of nodes maintains the network, making it decentralized. This decentralization is one of the core features of blockchain technology, as it allows for the distribution of data and control over the network among multiple participants, rather than relying on a single central authority.

This decentralized structure puts users in a more straightforward position, as they can access the system directly from the web and store their assets there without needing a governing authority. This feature is what sets blockchain apart from traditional centralized systems and has been one of the key factors in the rapid growth of blockchain technology. With blockchain, users can store a variety of assets, including cryptocurrencies, important documents, contracts, and other valuable digital assets, and they can have direct control over them using their private key. The decentralized nature of the system also makes it unique and appealing to a wide range of users, as it offers greater security against hackers and other malicious actors. Since there is no reliance on third-party companies, there is no added risk associated with using blockchain technology. Overall, the decentralized nature of blockchain is a significant advantage and offers greater control, security, and accessibility to users.

Immutable

Every year, a large amount of money gets stolen through regular channels. Businesses spend trillions of dollars to protect themselves from external hacks, but often these hacks come from internal sources who know about all the security measures. As a result, we end up paying the price for our trust. However, blockchain technology has many exciting features, and one of the best key features is its immutability. Immutability means that once data is stored on the network, it cannot be changed or deleted. This is because once a block is added to the blockchain, it becomes a permanent part of the ledger, and all transactions are verified by the network before being added to the blockchain. Every node on the system has a copy of the digital ledger, and to add a transaction, every node needs to check its validity. If the majority of nodes think it is valid, then it is added to the ledger. This promotes transparency and makes it virtually impossible for anyone to alter or corrupt the data.

With blockchain's corruption-proof nature, it is ideal for maintaining a secure, tamper-proof record of transactions. It is a technology that can change the game when it comes to creating a corruption-free environment. Therefore, businesses can benefit significantly from adopting blockchain technology to ensure that their data remains secure and untampered.

Efficient

Blockchain eliminates the need for intermediaries to manage transactions, reducing the time and costs associated with traditional financial transactions. This is particularly true for cross border transactions, where it can take several days for a transaction to be processed and for the funds to be transferred. With blockchain, transactions can be processed in a matter of minutes, making it a faster and more efficient technology for financial transactions.

Enhanced security

Blockchain technology provides a high level of security by using various methods, such as decentralization and cryptography. By eliminating the need for a central authority, blockchain ensures that no individual or entity can alter any characteristic of the network for their own benefit. Additionally, encryption is used to add another layer of protection to the system.

The use of cryptographic algorithms plays a crucial role in securing the network and protecting the data stored on it. This makes it extremely difficult for hackers to gain access to the information. Furthermore, the decentralized nature of the blockchain network makes it nearly impossible for any unauthorized user to modify the data.

Smart contracts and consensus algorithms automate the verification and execution of transactions, further reducing the risk of errors and fraud. Cryptography is a complex mathematical algorithm that acts as a firewall against attacks. Every piece of information on the blockchain is hashed cryptographically, which means that the true nature of the data is hidden from unauthorized users. The input data goes through a mathematical algorithm that produces a fixed-length value, adding another layer of protection to the information stored on the blockchain.

Each piece of data in a blockchain ledger is assigned a unique identifier, known as a **hash**. Each block in the ledger has its own unique hash and also contains the hash of the previous block. This means that if someone tries to alter the data, they would need to change the hash of every block in the chain, which is virtually impossible. In order to access the data, you need a private key, but for transactions, you only need a public key.

The cryptographic process of hashing in blockchain makes it highly secure and tamper-proof. Hashing creates a unique identification for each data, and any changes to the data will result in a completely different ID. This makes it impossible to reverse or alter the data. Each block in the blockchain has its own unique hash and contains the hash of the previous block, making it extremely difficult for anyone to tamper with the network. To do so, one would have to alter every data stored on every node in the network, which is next to impossible given the sheer number of nodes and the cost involved in accessing and hacking millions of computers. This feature of blockchain is one of its strengths and provides peace of mind to users by ensuring their digital assets are protected against hacking attempts.

Transparent

The transactions on the blockchain are transparent, meaning that they are publicly accessible and visible to everyone on the network. This makes it possible for users to see the history of a particular asset, such as a digital currency, or the status of a specific transaction. This feature is particularly useful for industries such as supply chain management, where it is important to track the origin and journey of a product.

The power of a tech which can be selectively transparent with authentic validation promises a whole new lot of use case for sure.

Some examples of industries that are using blockchain technology include finance, healthcare, real estate, and supply chain management. For instance, the finance industry is using blockchain to improve the speed and efficiency of financial transactions, while the healthcare industry is using it to securely store and manage medical records. The real estate industry is using blockchain to automate the process of tracking property ownership and transfer of ownership, while the supply chain management industry is using it to track the journey of a product from manufacturer to end consumer.

Different types of blockchain

It is undeniable that blockchain technology has undergone significant development in the last decade. At present, we are witnessing the existence of various blockchain types, each addressing specific challenges and fulfilling unique purposes. The primary function of blockchain technology is to provide a **DLT**, which eliminates the limitations of centralization. However, implementing DLT has brought about a new set of challenges that need to be resolved when deploying blockchain technology in diverse use cases.

Before we do an actual discussion of blockchain types, let us learn why we need them in the first place. The concept of DLT was introduced with the public blockchain type for cryptocurrency use. It solved the drawbacks of centralization but brought new problems, such as inefficiency. For instance, the consensus algorithm used, proof-of-work, required a lot of time and energy to solve mathematical equations, making it unsuitable for systems that need efficiency, such as banks with a high volume of transactions. The first generation of blockchain also faced issues such as scalability and lack of automation.

With its increasing popularity, various types of blockchain have been developed, each with unique features and purposes. The different types of blockchain can be broadly classified into three categories: public blockchains, private blockchains, and consortium blockchains.

Public blockchains

Public blockchains are open-source, decentralized networks where anyone can participate and contribute to the network. A public blockchain is the permission-less distributed ledger technology where anyone can join and do transactions. It is a non-restrictive version where each peer has a copy of the ledger. This also means that anyone can access the public blockchain if they have an internet connection. The most well-known example of a public blockchain is the Bitcoin blockchain, which was the first blockchain ever created. Public blockchains are secure and transparent, with every transaction being recorded on the blockchain ledger and verified by multiple nodes within the network. *Figure 2.6* is a visual representation of a public network:

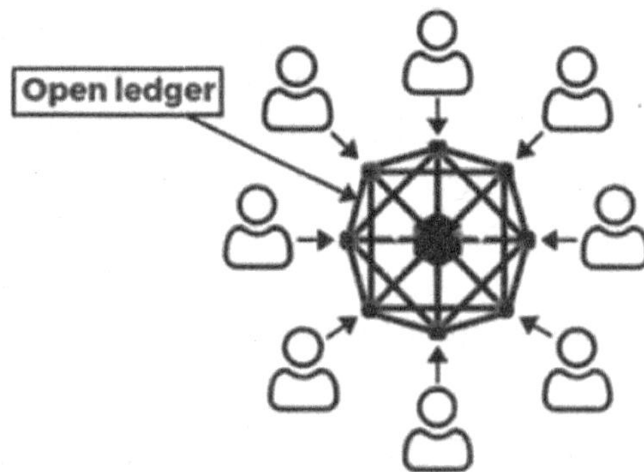

***Figure 2.6**: Public network*

The verification of the transactions is done through consensus methods such as **proof-of work (PoW)**, **proof-of-stake (PoS)**, and so on. The functioning of a public blockchain relies on participating nodes validating transactions. If there are not enough peers participating, the blockchain becomes non-functional. Different blockchain platforms use various types of blockchain as their foundation, each adding additional features to their platform.

Private blockchains

A private blockchain is one of the different types of blockchain technology, which is restricted to a specific group of participants and are typically used by organizations and institutions for internal purposes. It is also a permissioned blockchain that is under the control of an entity. Unlike public blockchains, private blockchains are not open-source, and only authorized participants have access to the network. By doing so, you can use the blockchain effectively and allow only selected participants to access the blockchain network. The organization can also set different parameters to the network, including accessibility, authorization, and the check list goes on. Transactions on private blockchains are usually faster and more secure, but they also lack the transparency and decentralization of public blockchains, that is, it takes less time for the network to reach consensus resulting in faster transactions. Private blockchains are more scalable in primitive comparison when considering major relying factors. A private network is portrayed through *Figure 2.7:*

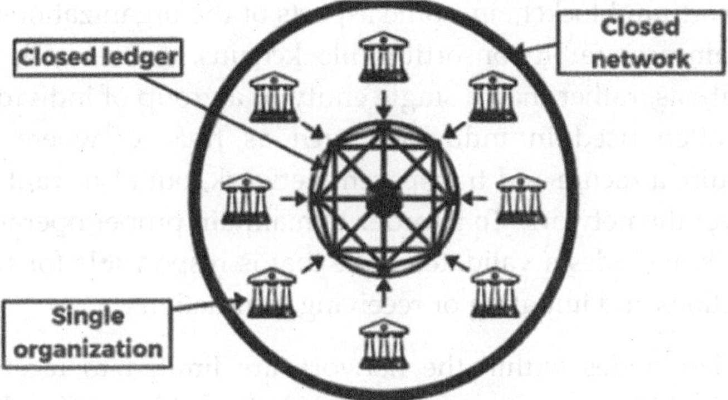

Figure 2.7: Private network

A permissioned blockchain does not have a decentralized theoretical nature. There are also various types of blockchain platforms that use private blockchain as the base of their platform. In many cases, a private blockchain is considered permissioned blockchain, but the concept of permissioned blockchain is much broader as it can include public blockchain as well. Lastly, as there are only a few nodes here, the security is not all that good. It is important to understand that it is possible to lose security if a certain number of nodes go rogue and compromise the consensus method utilized by the private network.

Consortium blockchains

Consortium blockchains are a hybrid of public and private blockchains, and they are designed to provide the benefits of both types of blockchains. It can be seen in *Figure 2.8*:

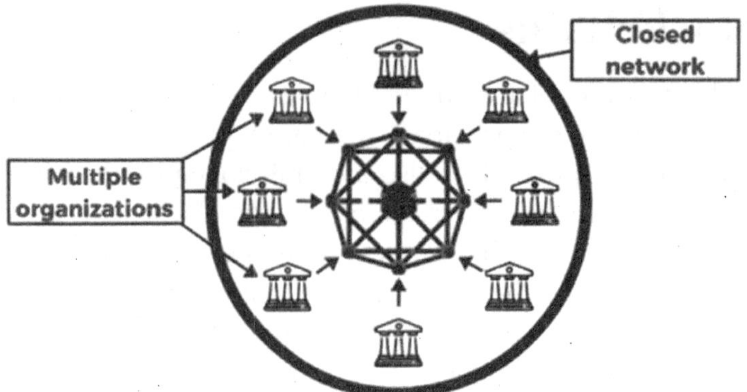

Figure 2.8: Consortium blockchain

A consortium blockchain, also known as **federated blockchains** is a creative approach to solving organizations' needs where there is a need for both public and private blockchain features. In a consortium blockchain, some aspects of the organizations are made public, while others remain private. In consortium blockchains, the network is controlled by a group of organizations, rather than a single entity or a group of individuals. Consortium blockchains are often used in industries such as finance, where the participating organizations require a secure and transparent network, but also want to maintain some level of control over the network. To in order to maintain proper operation, a consortium blockchain typically includes a validator node that is responsible for two key functions: validating transactions and initiating or receiving transactions.

Meanwhile, member nodes within the network are limited to receiving or initiating transactions only. In this way, a consortium blockchain is able to offer all of the benefits of a private blockchain, including transparency, privacy, and efficiency, without any single party having too much consolidated power or control over the network. By distributing power and responsibility across multiple entities, consortium blockchains are able to strike a balance between security, flexibility, and accessibility that is ideal for many different types of applications and use cases.

Even though it is secure, the whole network can be compromised due to the member's integrity. Needless to say, regulations and censorship can have a huge impact on network functionality. It is also less anonymous compared to other types of blockchain. A consortium blockchain can be used to share research data and results. Or may be of much use if a group of banks can work together and create a consortium. They can decide the nodes that will validate transactions.

Hybrid blockchain

Hybrid blockchain is the last type of blockchain that we are going to discuss here. More so, hybrid blockchain might sound like a consortium blockchain, but it is not. However, there can be some similarities between them. A hybrid blockchain is defined as a combination of a private and public blockchain. This type of blockchain allows organizations to leverage the benefits of both private and public blockchain, creating an ideal solution for their specific needs. A hybrid blockchain operates in a closed ecosystem, giving organizations the control and privacy, they need, while still allowing them to interact with a public network.

An example of a hybrid blockchain is **Dragonchain** and **XinFin**. These platforms offer a unique solution to organizations that want the best of both worlds. By combining the privacy and control of a private blockchain with the transparency and accessibility of a public blockchain, organizations can operate more efficiently and securely.

Some advantages of hybrid blockchain are as follows:

- **Works in a closed ecosystem**: The hybrid blockchain operates in a closed ecosystem, allowing organizations to work without having to make everything public. This provides organizations with more control and privacy over their data and operations.
- **Rules can be changed**: The rules of a hybrid blockchain can be changed according to the organization's needs, giving them more flexibility and control over their operations.
- **Immunity to 51% attacks**: Hybrid networks are immune to 51% attacks, making them more secure than public blockchain. This is because hybrid blockchain has a mix of private and public network participants who can validate transactions, making it more difficult for a single entity to control the network.
- **Privacy with public network connection**: A hybrid blockchain offers privacy while still connected to a public network. This means that organizations can still interact with the public network while maintaining control over their data and operations.
- **Good scalability**: Hybrid blockchain offers good scalability compared to the public network, making it ideal for organizations that deal with a large number of transactions.

Some disadvantages of hybrid blockchain are as follows:

- **Not completely transparent**: Although hybrid blockchain provides organizations with more control and privacy, it is not completely transparent. This is because only certain aspects of the operations are made public, while others are kept private.

- **Upgrading to hybrid blockchain can be a challenge**: Upgrading to a hybrid blockchain can be a challenge, as it requires organizations to change their existing infrastructure.
- **No incentive for participating**: There is no incentive for participating and contributing to the hybrid blockchain network, making it less attractive to potential participants.

Hybrid blockchain is a unique solution for organizations that want the best of both worlds. By combining the benefits of private and public blockchain, organizations can operate more efficiently and securely. The hybrid blockchain offers privacy, control, scalability, and immunity to 51% attacks, while still allowing organizations to interact with a public network. However, it is important to consider the disadvantages, such as lack of transparency and upgrading challenges, before deploying a hybrid blockchain solution.

Distributed ledger technology versus blockchain

DLT and blockchain are often used interchangeably, however, they are not exactly the same thing. Both DLT and blockchain are designed to solve the same problem of securely and efficiently sharing information and data between multiple parties. However, DLT is a broader term that includes other technologies, while blockchain is a specific type of DLT. Both technologies are related, but have some distinct differences that set them apart. Here is a comparison between DLT and blockchain:

DLT:

- DLT is a digital system that shares information and data across a network of nodes.
- It is a term that covers different types of technologies, including blockchain, that allow for secure and efficient sharing of data between multiple parties.
- DLT is often used for financial transactions and uses cryptography to keep the information on the ledger secure.

Blockchain:

- Blockchain is a type of DLT that creates an open and transparent ledger of transactions.
- It uses a series of blocks linked together with cryptography to form a growing list of records, called **blocks**.
- Each block has a unique hash, a timestamp, and information about transactions.

- This creates a secure and transparent ledger of transactions that is maintained by a network of nodes and is difficult to change.

DLT and blockchain are both digital systems used to maintain a secure and transparent ledger of information and data. However, they have some differences in terms of their network participants, transparency, security, and use cases. DLT can be used in both permissioned and permissionless networks, and it can maintain both private and public ledgers, while blockchain is primarily used in permissionless networks and is specifically designed for public ledgers. Both DLT and blockchain use cryptographic algorithms for security, but blockchain is considered more secure due to its use of blocks linked and secured by cryptography. DLT has a wide range of applications, including financial transactions, supply chain management, and voting systems, while Blockchain is primarily used in financial transactions and cryptocurrency applications.

CAP theorem

The CAP theorem is a concept that is often mentioned in relation to blockchain technology. CAP theorem implies to pointing out that the distributed system can deliver only two of three desired characteristics: consistency, availability, and partition tolerance. It is a principle that states that it is impossible for a distributed system to provide all three of the following guarantees: consistency, availability, and partition tolerance, at the same time. The C, A, and P in CAP are as follows:

- **Consistency**: Consistency means that all users see the same information at the same time, no matter which computer they use. For this to happen, when information is added to one computer, it must be sent to all the other computers in the system right away so that it can be saved.
- **Availability**: Availability means that when a user asks for information, they will get a response even if some computers are not working. All the computers in the system will give a response to any request made.
- **Partition tolerance**: A partition is when the connection between two computers breaks. Partition tolerance means that the system will still work even if there are problems with the connections between computers.

In a blockchain system, the CAP theorem is relevant because it can help us understand the trade-offs that must be made when designing a blockchain. For example, if we want to prioritize consistency, the blockchain may not be as available or able to handle network partitions as well. On the other hand, if we prioritize availability and partition tolerance, the blockchain may not be able to provide the same level of consistency.

In the context of blockchain, it is important to note that some blockchain systems prioritize consistency, while others prioritize availability and partition tolerance. For example, Bitcoin prioritizes partition tolerance and availability, while Ethereum prioritizes consistency. The CAP theorem is an important concept to understand when designing and building blockchain systems. By understanding the trade-offs between consistency, availability, and partition tolerance, we can make informed decisions about the design of our blockchain systems and the guarantees that they provide. Refer to the following figure:

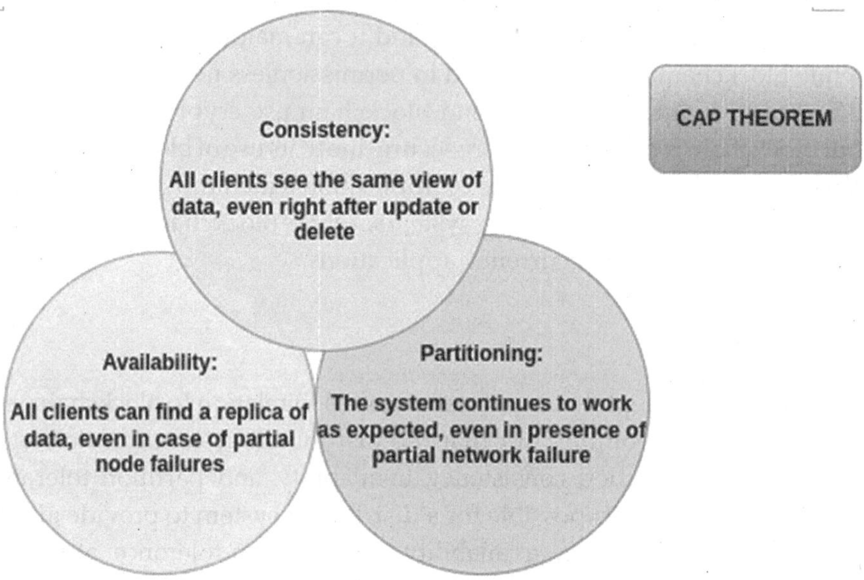

Figure 2.9: *CAP theorem*

In the context of blockchain, the Byzantine general problem becomes a crucial issue, as a decentralized system must ensure that all nodes agree on the state of the ledger, even in the presence of faulty nodes. This is where consensus mechanisms come in, as they provide a way for nodes to agree on the correct state of the system.

Byzantine generals problem

The consensus mechanism is a crucial component of any blockchain system. It ensures that trust, agreement, and security are maintained across a decentralized network of computers. The Byzantine generals problem, which involves the challenge of achieving consensus in a distributed system, is one of the key problems that consensus mechanisms aim to solve. There are multiple consensus mechanisms that exist, each with its own advantages and limitations. Some of the commonly used mechanisms include **proof of work (PoW)**, **proof of stake (PoS)**, **delegated proof of stake (DPoS)**, and **practical Byzantine fault tolerance (PBFT)**. The selection of a consensus mechanism is dependent on the specific requirements of the blockchain network and the trade-offs between factors such as security, scalability, and energy efficiency.

The Byzantine generals problem, named after the historical anecdote of the Byzantine army, is a problem in computer science related to the issue of reaching consensus in a decentralized system where some participants may be faulty or malicious. In such a system, it is challenging to ensure that all nodes reach the same agreement on a particular issue, such as the value of a transaction in a blockchain network, when some nodes may be sending false or conflicting information. Due to the communication channels not being secure, there runs a risk of a point of failure. This is known as a **Byzantine fault**, where components may fail and there is imperfect information on whether a component has failed.

When considering this matter within a contextual framework, society has traditionally turned to trusted third parties (or those deemed trustworthy) as the primary source of truth to address such issues. For instance, if an individual was to document that they had transferred you £100 and you were to record that you had only received £80, you both would rely on the bank as the trusted authority to establish a consensus.

A blockchain aims to solve this problem by creating a layer that can be trusted without needing to trust every individual. Miners and validators are the players of the game. The game they are playing is adding new entries to the ledger, and to do so, they need to follow the rules of the game. One widely used consensus mechanism that addresses the Byzantine generals problem is called **PoW**. In PoW, nodes in the network compete to solve a cryptographic puzzle, and the first node to solve it gets to add the next block to the chain. The other nodes then validate this block, and if they all agree on its validity, they add it to their copy of the ledger. This creates a decentralized and secure way of reaching consensus on the state of the system.

Another widely used consensus mechanism is called **PoS**. In PoS, nodes are chosen to validate transactions based on the amount of cryptocurrency they hold and are willing to stake as collateral. This creates an incentive for nodes to act honestly, as they stand to lose their staked funds if they act maliciously.

PBFT is a consensus mechanism that uses a consensus protocol to reach agreement on the next block to be added to the blockchain. In PBFT, nodes communicate with each other to reach agreement, and a node can only add a block to the blockchain if it has received enough votes from other nodes in the network.

In conclusion, the Byzantine generals problem is a challenge in decentralized systems, and consensus mechanisms are a way to solve this problem. There are several different consensus mechanisms, each with its own advantages and disadvantages, that have been developed to solve the Byzantine generals problem, including PoW, PoS, DPoS, and PBFT.

There are many other consensus mechanisms as well, each with its own strengths and weaknesses, and the choice of which one to use depends on the specific requirements of a given blockchain system. In general, the Byzantine generals problem and its consensus mechanisms are a critical part of ensuring the security and integrity of decentralized systems.

Consensus mechanism

Consensus for blockchain is a procedure in which the peers of a Blockchain network reach agreement about the present state of the data in the network. A consensus mechanism is a protocol or algorithm used in decentralized systems to reach agreement on a single version of data or state among all nodes in the network. In other words, it is a process by which all participants in a network come to a mutual agreement on a certain set of information.

Consensus mechanisms are critical to the functioning of decentralized systems, as they provide the necessary trust and security to enable participants to securely and confidentially transact with one another. Without consensus mechanisms, there would be no way for nodes in a network to agree on the current state of the network and to prevent conflicting transactions from being processed. Consensus mechanisms form the backbone of all cryptocurrency blockchains, and are what make them secure. There are many different types of consensus mechanisms, depending on the blockchain and its application. While they differ in their energy usage, security, and scalability, they all share one purpose- to ensure that records are true and honest.

Here is an overview of some of the best-known consensus mechanisms used by distributed systems to reach consensus:

- **PoW** is the first consensus mechanism and was used by cryptocurrencies such as **Bitcoin** and **Ethereum**. Miners compete to solve complex mathematical puzzles and the first to solve the puzzle is allowed to create a new block and validate transactions. The successful miner is also rewarded with cryptocurrency known as a block reward. PoW is regarded as a secure and reliable mechanism but requires large amounts of computational resources and energy, leading to high operating costs and environmental impact.
- **PoS** is a more environmentally-friendly alternative to PoW. In PoS, miners pledge a stake of cryptocurrency and are randomly selected to validate transactions. The more cryptocurrency a miner holds, the higher their chances of being selected. The system favors entities with a higher number of tokens leading to centralization concerns.
- **DPoS** is a variation of PoS where the network users vote to select witnesses to secure the network on their behalf. Only the top tier of witnesses with the most votes can validate blockchain transactions. The witnesses are incentivized to remain honest by being at risk of being replaced by those deemed more trustworthy.

- **Proof of activity (PoA)** is a hybrid of PoW and PoS, used by the **Decred** and **Espers** blockchain projects. The mining process starts like PoW, with miners competing to solve a mathematical problem, then switches to PoS where validators are selected to sign off on the block header. The block rewards are shared between the miner and validators. PoA has been criticized for its energy-intensive mining phase and its partiality towards validators holding a greater number of coins.
- **Proof of authority (PoA)** is a modified version of PoS where validators are selected based on their reputation. Validators must put their reputations on the line to validate blocks, rather than staking cryptocurrency. This mechanism requires very little computing power and is more resource-efficient, but has been criticized for its potential to centralize power in the hands of a few authoritative nodes.

Let us look at some real-world applications of consensus mechanisms:

- **Bitcoin - PoW:** Bitcoin, the pioneering cryptocurrency, employs the PoW consensus mechanism. Miners compete to solve complex mathematical problems, and the first one to solve it gets the right to add a new block to the blockchain. This resource intensive process ensures security but has led to concerns about energy consumption.
- **Ethereum - PoS:** Ethereum is transitioning from PoW to PoS, where validators are chosen to create new blocks based on the amount of cryptocurrency they hold and are willing to **stake** as collateral. This mechanism aims to be more energy-efficient than PoW.
- **Algorand - Pure proof of stake (PPoS):** Algorand utilizes a variation of PoS called **PPoS**, where a fixed number of randomly selected users are chosen as validators for each block. This enhances efficiency and scalability.
- **Tezos - Liquid proof of stake (LPoS):** Tezos employs LPoS, where token holders can delegate their coins to a validator of their choice, who then participates in block creation. This mechanism enhances decentralization and allows token holders to participate without the need for extensive technical knowledge.

By implementing consensus mechanisms like PoW, PoS, PPoS, or LPoS, blockchain networks ensure the trustworthiness and security of their transactions, enabling real-world applications ranging from peer-to-peer transactions to complex dApps in various industries.

PoS consensus mechanisms, designed for energy efficiency, encounter challenges linked to centralization and wealth concentration. PoS selects validators based on staked cryptocurrency, giving more influence on participants with larger stakes, fostering oligarchic control and reducing network diversity. The emphasis on financial stakes as a selection criterion creates barriers for smaller participants, diminishing decentralization.

Additionally, PoS faces challenges in resisting Sybil attacks and risks of contentious forks due to disagreements among major stakeholders. Addressing these issues is crucial to upholding decentralization, security, and inclusivity in evolving blockchain networks.

Cryptographic primitives

Cryptographic primitives are the basic building blocks that are used to construct cryptographic algorithms and protocols. Cryptographic primitives are fundamental building blocks of cryptographic protocols designed to create a highly secure network. In the context of blockchain, third parties or governments do not play a role in the process. Instead, transactions are conducted through a fully decentralized network, therefore, ensuring security is paramount in the blockchain ecosystem. The several types of cryptographic primitives are as follows:

- **One way hash functions:** These are mathematical tricks that take in a message and produce a fixed-sized string of numbers called the **hash** or **digest**. They help to make sure digital data is trustworthy and not changed. It is to be noted that a slight change in input can also change the hash function. This is known as the **avalanche effect**. A popular hash function is SHA-256.
- **Symmetric ciphers:** Assuming that a message has been encrypted using a key, the original message is transformed into a ciphertext that is readable but meaningless. The same key is used to decrypt the ciphertext back to its original form. A key is a variable that is used to encrypt or decrypt a message, essentially functioning as a means to lock or unlock data. Examples of key-based encryption algorithms include AES, DES, and Blowfish. While key-based encryption offers faster processing times compared to public-key cryptography, the sharing of keys can present a challenge. Examples are **Advanced Encryption Standard (AES)** and the **Data Encryption Standard (DES).**
- **Asymmetric ciphers:** These use two keys, one for hiding information (public key) and one for reading it (private key). Examples are RSA, DSA, and elliptic curve cryptography.
- **Block ciphers:** These scramble information in blocks of a set size, such as 64 or 128 bits. They are often used with hash functions to make sure long messages are kept safe.
- **Stream ciphers:** These scramble information bit by bit or byte by byte, making them good for keeping live information like audio or video secret.
- **Digital signatures:** These are a way to check if a digital message or information is really from the person who says it is. They use asymmetric ciphers to make a signature that can be checked using the sender's public key.

- **Message authentication codes:** These are similar to digital signatures but use symmetric ciphers to make a code that can be checked using the same secret key used to make it.

Developing new cryptographic primitives is a challenging task due to the complexity and potential for errors, requiring specialized expertise and thorough mathematical analysis. While traditionally seen as difficult, ongoing efforts aim to address emerging threats and vulnerabilities, illustrating the dynamic nature of cryptography. These cryptographic primitives serve as the foundation for building algorithms and protocols, ensuring various security services such as confidentiality, integrity, authenticity, and non-repudiation.

Data structure used in blockchain

Blockchain employs several key data structures that are crucial to its security and functionality. Primarily, a blockchain comprises two data structures – blocks and a linked list.

Relevance of block in blockchain

With the introduction of blocks in a blockchain, it becomes possible to store transactions in an organized and secure manner. In this section, we will delve deeper into the various aspects of blocks and understand their significance in the functioning of a blockchain. Block contains the information as a block header and transactions. Blocks are data structures whose purpose is to bundles sets of transactions and are replicated to all nodes in the network. A block in a blockchain acts as a container for transactions, grouping them together and verifying them before being added to the chain. The hash code generated for each block, using complex algorithms, ensures the permanent nature of the data stored in it, making it impossible to alter or delete.

Transparency is another crucial aspect of blocks in a blockchain. The data stored in a block is transparent and can be viewed by anyone on the network. This makes it possible for anyone to verify the authenticity of transactions in a block and ensures that the network operates with transparency. Security is further enhanced by the fact that blocks are verified by multiple computers on the network, making it difficult for anyone to manipulate or tamper with the data. The consensus mechanism used in a blockchain, such as PoW or PoS, helps to maintain the integrity of the data in a block and prevent malicious actors from interfering with the network. In addition to security and transparency, blocks in a blockchain also offer efficiency. Transactions can be processed and verified in real-time, reducing the time and cost associated with traditional methods of record keeping and transactions.

The different types of blocks are as follows:

- The majority of blocks serve to prolong the current primary blockchain, which also happens to be the longest chain within the network. These blocks are referred to as **main branch blocks**.
- In contrast, certain blocks may reference a parent block that does not belong to the longest blockchain. These blocks are known as **side branch blocks**.
- Additionally, there exist blocks that reference a parent block that is unknown to the node that is processing the block. These blocks are classified as **orphan blocks**.

The production of blocks within a blockchain is carried out by miners, who engage in a process called **mining** to create a valid block that will be approved by the wider network. Nodes play a crucial role in the blockchain by selecting pending transactions, verifying their cryptographic accuracy, and bundling them into blocks for storage within the chain. The block header serves as the metadata that enables the validation of the block's authenticity. The following *Figure 2.8* illustrates the details contained within a block's metadata:

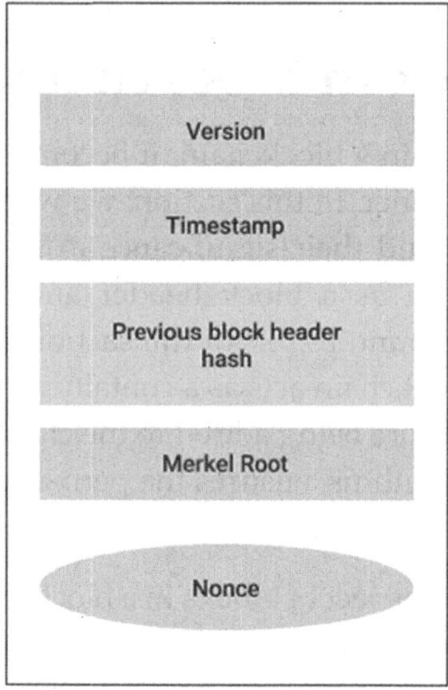

Figure 2.10: *Blocks in a blockchain*

A typical block hash looks like this:

08543b9176e4997111cffbd45b977826146678d0dd0e6fb13b0643fe57119468

Meta of the block may slightly change from different approach or type of blockchain.

A new block in a blockchain is created by connecting it to the previous block through a unique code called a **hash**. The new block includes the hash of the previous block, along with the new transaction and a random number called a **nonce**. All these elements are used to create the Merkle root, which is a hash that represents the block and all the transactions within it. This Merkle root helps link the blocks together, forming a chain. This process can be understood by *Figure 2.11*:

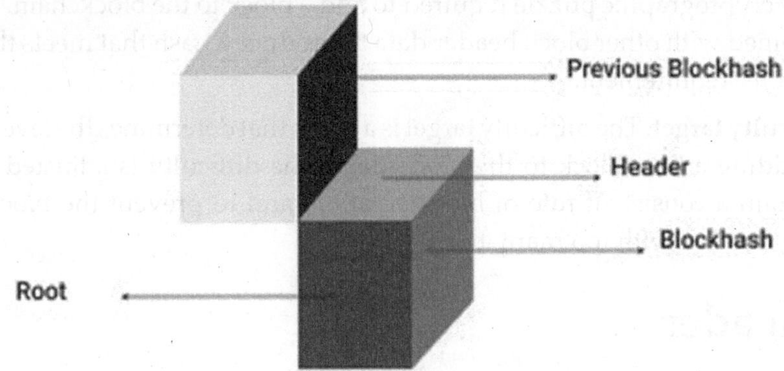

Figure 2.11: Blockchain process

Although there is some variation among different chains. This example shows a standard structure for a block.

A new block is added to the blockchain only after all the computers on the network have confirmed the transaction. This confirmation process is important because it makes the transaction permanent and unchangeable, which is a key feature of blockchain technology. The information in the block is compressed using a process called **hashing** to keep its size small. Each block contains all the confirmed transactions for that particular time period. As more blocks are added, they form a chain called a **blockchain**. This chain structure is what makes the blockchain secure.

Features of a block

Each block in the blockchain has a unique structure, which includes the following elements:

- **Header**: The header of a block contains metadata about the block, such as its unique identifier (the block hash), a timestamp, and the hash of the previous block in the chain. This links the current block to the previous one, forming a chain of blocks.
- **Transactions**: A block can contain multiple transactions, which represent transfers of digital assets from one user to another. The transactions in a block are processed and verified by the network participants (nodes) before being added to the block.
- **Merkle tree root**: To increase the efficiency of verifying the transactions within a block, a Merkle tree is used. A Merkle tree is a binary tree data structure that allows for efficient and secure verification of large amounts of data. The root of

the Merkle tree, which is a hash of all the transactions in the block, is stored in the block header.

- **Nonce**: A nonce is a random number that is used by the miners to find a solution to the cryptographic puzzle required to add a block to the blockchain. The nonce is combined with other block header data to produce a hash that meets the network's difficulty requirement.
- **Difficulty target**: The difficulty target is a value that determines the level of difficulty for adding a new block to the blockchain. The difficulty is adjusted regularly to maintain a consistent rate of block creation, and to prevent the blockchain from being flooded with too many blocks.

Block header

The block header stands as a vital element in a blockchain block, uniquely identifying it within the entire chain. It incorporates crucial information about the block's transactions and its own attributes. Through repetitive hashing, the header plays a key role in producing PoW, essential for securing mining rewards. This amalgamation of transaction details, nonce, data, and the Merkle root forms the foundation of each block in a blockchain, ensuring a distinct identification through individual block header hashes.

The block header contains three sets of block metadata. It is an 80-byte long string, and it is comprised of the 4-byte long Bitcoin version number, 32-byte previous block hash, 32-byte long Merkle root, 4-byte long timestamp of the block, 4-byte long difficulty target for the block, and the 4-byte long nonce used by miners.

The block header is then hashed, which means it is turned into a unique code. This is called the **block header hash** and is used to identify the block and its transactions. Since any change to the block header would result in a different block header hash, it makes it very hard to change the information in the block header.

Block header hash and block height

The blocks of a blockchain need an identification to refer them or distinguish them from other blocks. The two parameters used for this purpose are as follows:

- Block header hash is a unique identifier that is created by taking the hash of the block header in a blockchain. This value is obtained by cryptographic hashing of the header of the block. The hashing operation is performed twice. The block header contains important information about a block, such as the time it was added to the blockchain, the reference to the previous block in the blockchain, the root of a Merkle tree that summarizes the transactions in the block, a random number used to mine the block, and the difficulty target of the puzzle required to mine the block. The hash of the block header is created using a cryptographic function, which takes the block header as input and returns a fixed-length string of bytes. The block header hash ensures that the information in the block header cannot be easily altered, as any changes to the block header will result in a different block header hash. The hash of the block is not stored in the block's data whether the block is being transmitted to the other nodes or it is stored as part of the blockchain on some node.

- The second parameter used for identifying a block is its height. Block height, is the number that represents the position of a block in the blockchain. It starts from zero for the first block, also known as the **genesis block**, and increases by one for each subsequent block. The block height is used to maintain the chronological order of the blocks in the blockchain and to determine which block came first and which block came later.

Genesis block

The first block of a blockchain is known as the **genesis block**. This initial block holds significant importance, as it marks the beginning of the blockchain and serves as the foundation for all subsequent blocks. The genesis block of Bitcoin and other cryptocurrencies is the first-ever block that was mined on their respective networks. Each block within the blockchain stores information related to transactions on the network, and is identified by a unique header. However, the genesis block differs from all other blocks in that it does not have a preceding block. It typically includes specific data, such as a timestamp and message, which is used to initiate the blockchain.

The creation of the genesis block is a pivotal moment in the development of a blockchain, as it establishes the network's fundamental rules and characteristics. These rules, such as block size and mining rewards, are set in stone once the genesis block is created and cannot be altered. As the first block of the blockchain, the genesis block also plays a crucial role in shaping the story of the network's origins.

The decentralized nature of the Bitcoin network is one of its key features, meaning that there is no intermediary between users and the network. To ensure the validity of transactions on the network, complex mathematical problems are employed, which are solved by computers known as Bitcoin miners. Miners are unable to trade Bitcoins until they have completely solved the mathematical puzzle. Furthermore, all transactions on the Bitcoin network are permanently recorded, making it impossible to conceal any evidence of illicit activity.

One of the key features of the Bitcoin network is its decentralized nature, meaning there is no intermediary between the user and the network. The network uses complex mathematical problems to check and validate transactions, and these problems are solved by computers, or Bitcoin miners. Miners cannot trade Bitcoins until the mathematical puzzle is completely solved. Additionally, all transactions on the Bitcoin network are permanently recorded, making it impossible to hide any evidence of wrongdoing.

To help people understand the genesis block, a group of early Bitcoin enthusiasts formed the **Satoshi Nakamoto Institute (SNI)**. The institute provides information and insights about the history and vision of Bitcoin, as well as a collection of the forum posts written by *Satoshi Nakamoto*, the creator of Bitcoin, when he was working on the project.

Linking blocks in the blockchain

Linking blocks in a blockchain is an important process that keeps the blockchain secure and reliable. Each block in the blockchain contains information about transactions, and it is linked to the previous block by a reference called the **previous block hash**. The information stored in the blocks of a blockchain is permanent and can be checked. This information is divided into different blocks, and to make sure the blocks are in order, they are connected together in a chain. This reference is like a fingerprint and helps to keep the blocks in order.

To create the reference, the information in the block header is put through a cryptographic process. This process uses a mathematical algorithm to produce a unique identifier, which is the hash. If anything in the block header is changed, the hash will also change. This makes it easy for other computers in the network to see that the block has been altered. The chain is created using cryptography, with each block containing a special code, called a **hash**, that links it to the previous block. The hash also includes the time when the block was added to the blockchain. If any of the information in a block is changed, the hash of that block will be different and the chain will be broken.

Due to cryptography, once the information is written into the blockchain, it cannot be changed. Any node on the network can verify the entire blockchain by making sure the hash of each block matches the previous one.

The linking of blocks creates a chain of blocks that cannot be changed or deleted. This is because if a block is changed, the reference to the previous block will not match, which will alert other computers in the network. This creates a secure ledger of all the transactions in the blockchain, which is essential for the trust and security of the network.

Merkle tree

A Merkle tree, also called a **hash tree**, is a data structure in which every leaf node represents a cryptographic hash of a single data block, and every non-leaf node represents a cryptographic hash of its child nodes' hashes. This tree is commonly used to validate transactions in a blockchain network and is particularly efficient in doing so. The majority of Merkle trees have a binary structure, meaning that each node has only two child nodes, although some may have multiple child nodes. In computer science, Merkle trees are a widely used form of data structure that can efficiently summarize all the transactions in a block through a series of hash computations.

In a Merkle tree, transactions are organized into leaf nodes, and each leaf node contains the hash of a single transaction. The hashes of the leaf nodes are then paired and hashed again to create a set of intermediate nodes. This process is repeated until a single hash, known as the **Merkle root**, is generated.

A Merkle root is a simple mathematical method for confirming the facts on a Merkle tree. The Merkle root is included in the block header and acts as a summary of all the transactions in the block. When a new block is added to the blockchain, its Merkle root is included in the hash of the previous block, linking the two blocks together. They play a very crucial role in the computation required to keep cryptocurrencies like Bitcoin and ether running. *Figure 2.12* is a pictorial representation of a Merkle tree:

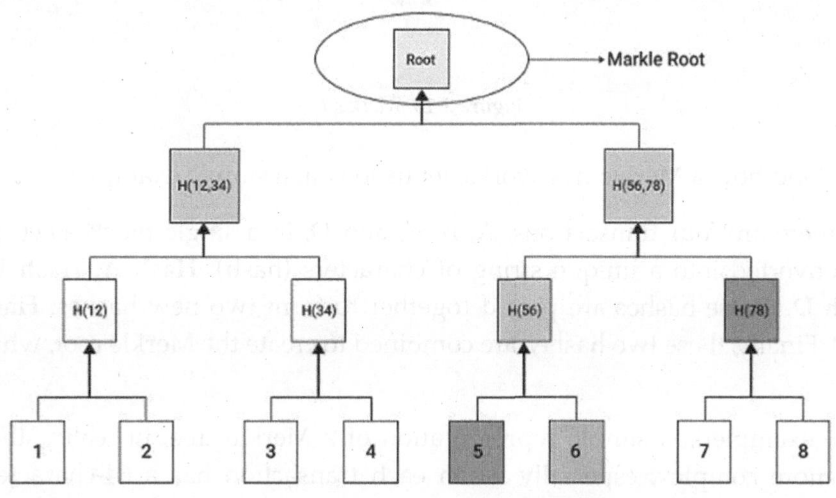

***Figure 2.12**: Merkle Tree*

One of the key advantages of using a Merkle tree is its efficiency. When a node wants to verify a transaction, it only needs to receive the portion of the tree that includes the relevant transaction, rather than the entire blockchain. This reduces the amount of data that needs to be transmitted and makes the verification process much faster. Another benefit of the Merkle tree is its ability to detect any tampering or modification of the transaction data. If a malicious actor tries to change a transaction, the hash of that transaction will be different from the original hash, which will break the cryptographic link between the leaf node and the rest of the tree. This makes it easy for other nodes in the network to detect the tampering and reject the altered transaction. A Merkle tree totals all transactions in a block and generates a digital fingerprint of the entire set of operations, allowing the user to verify whether it includes a transaction in the block. This process can be represented through *Figure 2.13:*

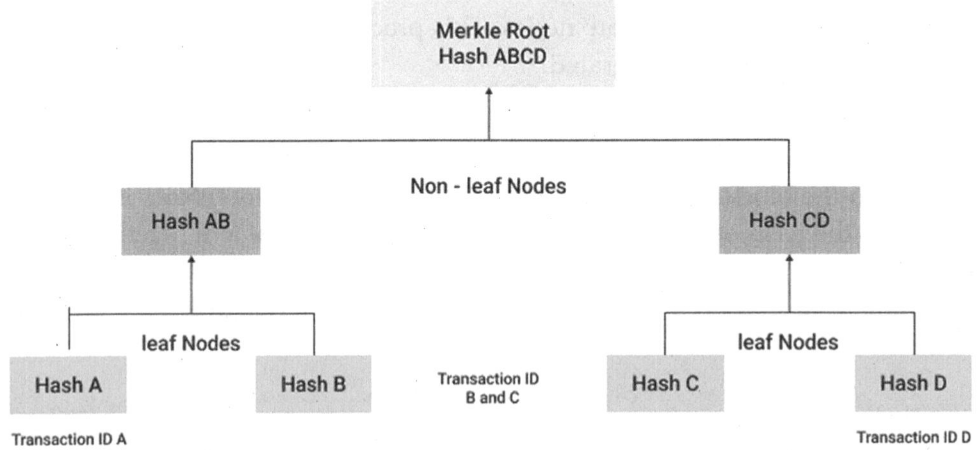

***Figure 2.13**: Merkle tree*

To understand how a Merkle tree works, let us look at a simple example:

Imagine there are four transactions, A, B, C, and D, in a single block. Each transaction is then converted into a unique string of characters (hash): **Hash A**, **Hash B**, **Hash C**, and **Hash D**. These hashes are paired together to form two new hashes: **Hash AB** and **Hash CD**. Finally, these two hashes are combined to create the Merkle root, which is **Hash ABCD**.

While the example is a simple representation of a Merkle tree, in reality, the structure is much more complex, especially when each transaction has a 64-character long ID. Nevertheless, this example provides a basic understanding of how the algorithm works and why it is so effective. a Merkle tree can be used to efficiently manage and verify the eligibility of participants for exclusive sales or events. Here is a step-by-step explanation:

- **Generating unique identifiers:**
  - o Each participant, or potential buyer, is assigned a unique identifier. This could be their Ethereum wallet address or any other unique identifier associated with their account.

- **Creating a whitelist:**
  - o The organizer of the NFT sale generates a whitelist containing the unique identifiers of participants eligible for the exclusive event. This whitelist is essentially a list of addresses allowed to participate.
- **Hashing participant identifiers:**
  - o The unique identifiers (addresses) of participants are hashed individually. This can be achieved using a hash function (for example, SHA-256), resulting in a hash for each identifier.
- **Building the Merkle tree:**
  - o The hashed identifiers are organized into a Merkle tree structure. The Merkle tree is constructed by pairing and hashing the individual hashes until a single root hash is obtained.
- **Publishing the Merkle root:**
  - o The organizer publishes the root hash of the Merkle tree. This hash serves as a concise and secure representation of the entire whitelist.
- **Participant verification:**
  - o Participants interested in the NFT sale can check their eligibility by hashing their identifier and comparing it to the published Merkle root. If the hash matches, the participant is on the whitelist.
- **Efficient verification process:**
  - o Verifying eligibility through the Merkle tree is computationally efficient. Participants do not need to reveal their identifier; they only need to present the hashed value. This ensures privacy while allowing efficient validation.
- **Event Access:**
  - o During the NFT sale or event, only participants with identifiers on the whitelist (matching the Merkle root) are granted access. This creates an exclusive environment for whitelisted participants.

By using a Merkle tree in this way, the NFT sale organizer can efficiently manage large whitelists and ensure that only eligible participants gain access to exclusive events. The process also maintains privacy for participants by not requiring the exposure of their actual identifiers during the verification process

Conclusion

Blockchain has emerged as a paradigm shift in the last decade. This decentralized system has revolutionized the essence of digital trust and collaboration. The journey of this chapter has unveiled the foundational concepts of blockchain, their types, and their applications. A strong understanding of technical concepts, like a Merkle tree, block header hash, block height, and more, will make it easy to decipher the ideas explored in the next chapter.

The next chapter will provide readers with a detailed knowledge of Bitcoin. It will explain Bitcoin's origins, evolution, and other fundamental concepts behind the King cryptocurrency. Readers will get to learn about Bitcoin concepts, like cryptographic keys, wallets, and addresses. Besides, advanced Bitcoin features like multi-signature addresses and **Base58** encoding are also covered in the next chapter.

Question and answers

1. **How does blockchain ensure security?**

   Ans.: Blockchain network ensures security through cryptographic techniques, including encryption and hashing. Under this, each block contains a cryptographic hash of the previous block. This creates an immutable chain.

2. **What are the different types of blockchains?**

   Ans.: Blockchains can primarily be categorized into three types – Public blockchains, which are open to anyone; Private blockchains, which offer restricted access; Consortium blockchains, which are semi-decentralized.

3. **What are the applications of blockchain?**

   Ans.: Blockchain technology has usability in various industries, including but not limited to finance and banking, healthcare, supply chain management, gaming, streaming, and more.

4. **What role does consensus play in a blockchain network?**

   Ans.: Consensus mechanisms are deployed to ensure agreement among parties on the validity of transactions. They play a vital role in decentralized decision-making and preventing fraudulent transactions.

5. **How does a blockchain network validate transactions?**

   Ans.: A blockchain network validates transactions through consensus mechanisms such as **PoW** and **PoS** or any other algorithms developed for that purpose. Miners or validators verify transactions before they are added to the blockchain.

Multiple choice question

1. **What is the fundamental concept of blockchain technology?**
    a. Centralized data storage
    b. Hierarchical database structure
    c. Peer-to-peer networking
    d. Decentralized ledger system

2. **Which data structure is crucial to blockchain formation?**
    a. Arrays
    b. Trees
    c. Linked lists
    d. Stacks

3. **Which blockchain type allows anyone to participate without permission?**
    a. Permissioned blockchain
    b. Public blockchain
    c. Private blockchain
    d. Consortium blockchain

4. **What role does a Merkle tree have in blockchain technology?**
    a. It encrypts data within blocks
    b. It validates the integrity of transactions
    c. It manages user permissions
    d. It ensures decentralized consensus

5. **What makes blockchain technology resistant to tampering?**
    a. User authentication
    b. Redundant data storage
    c. Encrypted transmission protocols
    d. Cryptographic hashing

Answers

1. d
2. d
3. b
4. b
5. d

Join our book's Discord space

Join the book's Discord Workspace for Latest updates, Offers, Tech happenings around the world, New Release and Sessions with the Authors:

https://discord.bpbonline.com

CHAPTER 3
Bitcoin

Introduction

In the past few decades, hardly a phenomenon has been able to capture as much attention as Bitcoin. It has evolved from a cryptographic experiment into a global digital currency. Moreover, it has disrupted the way we perceive and interact with money.

Bitcoin is a decentralized and transparent form of digital currency. It does not have any physical form, and its existence is in the digital world. Since Bitcoin is a decentralized currency, it is free from the control of any central authority. It is powered by blockchain technology and is based on the concepts of decentralization, cryptography, and immutable ledgers. Notably, Bitcoin aims to foster trust in financial transactions.

In this chapter, we will explore the multifaceted nature of Bitcoin, its origins, core principles, and technological intricacies. The chapter will shed light on how this digital currency has made its way to wider acceptance and integration into mainstream financial conversations.

Structure

This chapter contains the following topics:

- Bitcoin
- Consensus mechanism
- Encrypted private keys in blockchain
- Pay-to-script address
- Multi-sig addresses
- Vanity address
- Bitcoin wallet
- Transaction script
- Bitcoin mining
- Structure of a block
- Bitcoin relay network
- Blockchain fork
- Bitcoin testnet
- Basis of Bitcoin forensic

Objectives

The chapter aims to provide readers with a comprehensive understanding of Bitcoin. It will define and elucidate the fundamental principles that lie behind the meteoric rise of the King coin. It will also evaluate the broader implications of Bitcoin in the global financial sphere. The chapter will highlight emerging trends, innovative applications, and the disruptive potential of Bitcoin in shaping financial transactions in various industries. Thus, readers will get to learn the future prospects of Bitcoin and equip themselves with all the nitty-gritty of this digital currency.

Bitcoin

Bitcoin is a type of **digital currency** that can be used to buy and sell items online without the need for banks or financial institutions. Unlike traditional currencies, Bitcoin does not have a physical form and is solely existent in the digital realm. It can only be viewed on a computer screen or a smartphone. Bitcoin operates on a blockchain, a unique database that documents all Bitcoin transactions that have ever taken place. Whenever people conduct a purchase or sale using Bitcoin, the transaction is recorded on the blockchain. This ensures that no one can defraud the system or create counterfeit Bitcoins.

One can either purchase Bitcoins from an exchange or receive them as compensation for goods or services rendered. Once you acquire some Bitcoins, you can use them to purchase items online in the same manner as any other currency.

Bitcoin is a digital currency that was created in 2009 by an anonymous person or group under the name *Satoshi Nakamoto*. It operates on a decentralized network called the **blockchain**, which is a public ledger that records all transactions. In other words, Bitcoin is a digital currency that operates using blockchain technology, providing a secure and decentralized approach to buying and selling goods online.

With Bitcoin, people can send and receive digital currency without the need for a middleman like a bank. This is because Bitcoin is a decentralized payment system. The transactions on the Bitcoin network are verified by network participants and recorded on the blockchain. One of the unique things about Bitcoin is that there will only ever be 21 million Bitcoins in existence, making it a scarce commodity. Its value is determined by market demand and is highly volatile.

A practical use of Bitcoin is for international transactions. Someone in the United States can send money to someone in Japan using Bitcoin without needing a bank or currency exchange. The transaction is processed on the blockchain, and the recipient receives the equivalent value in Japanese yen. Bitcoin transactions are secure and decentralized, making them faster and less expensive than traditional international transfers.

Basics of Bitcoin

Bitcoin has several basic features that make it unique compared to traditional currencies, including:

- **Decentralization:** Bitcoin operates on a decentralized network, meaning that it is not controlled by a central authority like a bank or government. Instead, transactions are verified by network participants and recorded on the blockchain. This makes Bitcoin a trustless system. This means that users do not need to place their trust in a third party or intermediary for the validation and execution of their transactions. The decentralized nature of Bitcoin allows it to be used in places where traditional financial systems may not exist or may be unreliable. For example, people living in countries with unstable governments or weak financial systems may find Bitcoin to be a more stable and reliable way to store and transfer their wealth.
- **Limited supply:** Bitcoin has a limited supply of 21 million coins, which makes it a scarce commodity. This helps to prevent inflation and gives it value. It also means that Bitcoin is not subject to the same manipulations as traditional currencies, which can be subject to inflationary policies or fluctuations in supply.

- **Security:** Transactions on the Bitcoin network is secured using cryptography, which makes it difficult to hack or counterfeit. The network uses a public-private key system to ensure that only the owner of a particular Bitcoin address can access and spend their Bitcoins. This makes it a secure system for storing and transferring value.
- **Anonymity:** Bitcoin transactions are pseudonymous, meaning that they are not tied to the identity of the person making the transaction. However, the transactions are still recorded on the public blockchain, which makes it possible to trace the flow of funds. This can be beneficial in situations where transparency is needed, such as for auditing purposes or to track the flow of funds in a supply chain.
- **Transparency:** The blockchain is a public ledger that records every Bitcoin transaction. This makes the network transparent and helps to prevent fraud. Anyone can view the blockchain and verify the validity of a transaction, which helps to increase trust in the network.
- **Irreversibility:** Once a Bitcoin transaction has been confirmed on the blockchain, it cannot be reversed. This helps to prevent fraudulent transactions and chargebacks, which are common in traditional payment systems. However, it also means that users must take care to ensure that they are sending their Bitcoins to the correct address, as there is no way to reverse a transaction once it has been confirmed.

These features make Bitcoin an interesting and unique currency, with applications in many real-world scenarios. For example, Bitcoin can be used for international transactions, as it does not require a centralized intermediary such as a bank or currency exchange. It can also be used for micropayments, such as paying for online content or tipping creators on social media platforms. Additionally, Bitcoin can be used for fundraising, as it allows people to donate to causes and charities in a secure and transparent manner.

Bitcoin has various practical uses in the real world, such as:

- **International payments:** Bitcoin allows people to make cross-border payments directly to each other, without involving a middleman like a bank. This can be faster and less expensive than traditional payment methods, which can take a long time to process and may have high fees.
- **Investment:** Bitcoin has been used as an investment option, as its value has increased significantly over time. However, its value is highly volatile, which means that investing in it can be risky.
- **Remittances:** Bitcoin can be used to send money to friends and family members in other countries, especially in regions where traditional financial systems may be unreliable or unavailable.

- **E-commerce:** Some online merchants accept Bitcoin as a payment option, allowing customers to buy goods and services using their Bitcoins.

History of Bitcoin

Nakamoto's 2008 white paper revealed the blockchain system that would be the backbone of the cryptocurrency market. A blockchain is a digital ledger of transactions that is replicated and distributed across a network of computer systems to secure information. Although the maximum number of coins stipulated to be in existence is 21 million, experts believe that it will take until the year 2140 before the cap is reached.

After *Nakamoto* rolled out Bitcoin in 2009, he mined approximately 1.1 million Bitcoin and disappeared in 2010. He ceded control to *Gavin Andresen*, formerly known as **Gavin Bell**, who set out to decentralize the platform. This meant that there was no central authority, server, storage or administrator. All the parties were peer-to-peer and the blockchain was distributed to all. The network existed merely to legitimize and confirm the transactions. The price of Bitcoin dropped with the new uncertainty surrounding these actions.

Bitcoin has had a volatile history, with *Mark T. Williams*, a faculty member at Boston University's Questrom School of Business, once saying that Bitcoin has volatility seven times greater than gold, eight times greater than the S&P 500 and 18 times the U.S. dollar. Part of the extreme volatility in Bitcoin comes from the Gartner Hype Cycle, a life cycle common among new and innovative technologies. The five stages include: the innovation trigger, the peak of inflated expectations, the trough of disillusionment, the slope of enlightenment, and finally, the plateau of productivity. Many individuals created and then lost vast fortunes in Bitcoin, causing eight Nobel Prize winners in economic sciences to call Bitcoin a bubble, much like the often-cited Dutch tulip mania in the 1600s. However, bitcoin supporters point out that although Bitcoin has crashed five times, it has also returned to its previous price each time, while other bubbles have not recovered their value.

The strength of the economy is also a huge factor in Bitcoin pricing. In what has been designated as the 2022 **crypto winter**, sharp declines occurred in Bitcoin pricing as the Federal Reserve began aggressively increasing interest rates to stave off inflation. Investor appetite for risk all but disappeared, and liquidity became a major issue among the exchanges. Bitcoin's value decreased over 60% from a high of $68,990 in Nov 2021, and pessimism in the markets still persists.

Despite the controversy and volatility, more and more institutions, countries, and platforms are accepting the digital currency, and Bitcoin supporters hold hopes for it to become a global reserve currency. Bitcoin is legal in seven of the top 10 world economies by GDP, including the U.S. Nine countries have had an outright ban on Bitcoin, including

Egypt and Pakistan. Another 42 countries have implicitly banned Bitcoin, including Saudi Arabia and Taiwan.

Some countries have actively begun trading in Bitcoin, often due to global financial pressures. El Salvador adopted Bitcoin as its legal tender in 2021 to resolve deep economic woes. Unfortunately, the price of Bitcoin dropped precipitously since the country is still struggling to meet its debt obligations, and public adoption has been lackluster. Ukraine posted two crypto wallets at the beginning of the Russian invasion to raise funds, attracting more than $10.2 million within the first. Bitcoin has also attracted controversy due to its climate change implications. Mining Bitcoin requires significant electricity usage and is responsible for 0.10% of global greenhouse gas emissions. The University of Cambridge publishes the **Cambridge**

Bitcoin Electricity Consumption Index (CEBCI), which provides estimates on the greenhouse gas emissions related to Bitcoin, currently calculated at 48.35 million tonnes of carbon dioxide equivalent.

Bitcoin transaction

When you use Bitcoin to pay someone, it is important to understand how it works.

A Bitcoin transaction is like sending an email. The details of the transaction are signed digitally to make sure it is secure, and then sent to the entire network of Bitcoin users for verification. This information is public and can be found on a digital ledger called the **blockchain**. The blockchain is like a record of every Bitcoin transaction ever made, and it is constantly being updated by the Bitcoin network.

When you send Bitcoin to someone, it is important to know where the Bitcoin that you are sending came from. This is why the history of every Bitcoin transaction is recorded on the blockchain. There are no physical Bitcoins, and you do not have an account like you would with a bank. Instead, all transactions are recorded on the blockchain.

Let us say Mark wants to send 1 Bitcoin to Jessica. He uses his private key to sign a message that includes information about the Bitcoin he previously received, the amount he wants to send, and where it is going. This message is broadcast to the network, and everyone can see the details of the transaction. Refer to *Figure 3.1:*

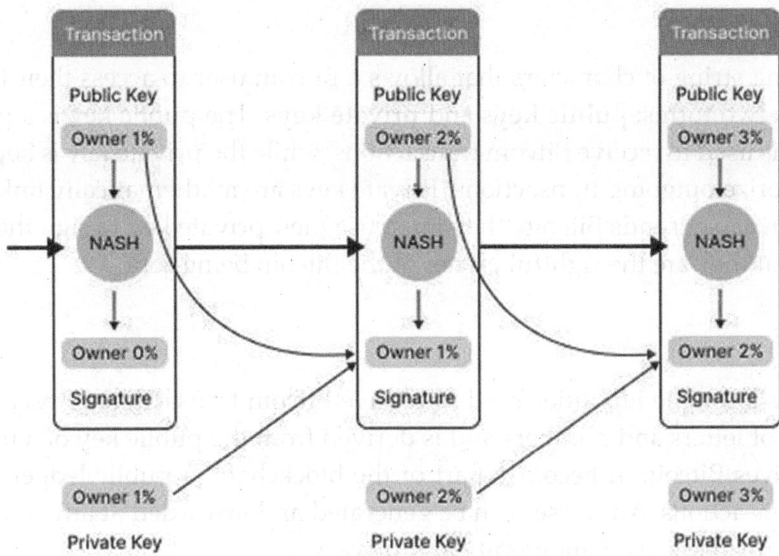

***Figure 3.1**: Bitcoin transaction process*

When *Mark* sends Bitcoin to *Jessica,* he might have received Bitcoin from multiple people in the past. To send 1 Bitcoin, he might need to use two different amounts that he previously received. The transaction will have two outputs: 1 Bitcoin to *Jessica's* address and 0.2 Bitcoin returned to *Mark* as change. This change is calculated by subtracting the amount *Mark* wants to send from the total he previously received.

While this might seem complicated, it is not necessary to understand all the details of Bitcoin transactions to use it. Your Bitcoin wallet takes care of the behind-the-scenes work so you can focus on sending and receiving Bitcoin easily.

Bitcoin transaction fees can vary a lot, from a few cents to $100. The fees depend on how many people want to use the Bitcoin network at the same time (supply and demand) and how big your transaction is. The bigger the transaction, the more inputs it has, and the higher the fee will be. Some wallets let you set the fee yourself so you can avoid paying too much. If you are not in a hurry, you can set a lower fee and wait for the network to be less busy. If you want your transaction to be processed quickly, you can pay a higher fee.

Bitcoin concepts

Bitcoin is a digital currency that operates on a decentralized platform. It was created to provide a peer-to-peer electronic cash system, allowing users to transfer funds without the need for intermediaries like banks or financial institutions. Bitcoin relies on a few key concepts to function effectively. In this section, we will discuss five of the most important concepts in Bitcoin: keys, addresses, wallets, Bitcoin transactions, and UTXOs.

Key

A key is a long string of characters that allows a Bitcoin user to access their funds. These keys come in two forms: **public keys** and **private keys**. The public key is a public-facing address that is used to receive Bitcoin transactions, while the private key is kept secret and used to authorize outgoing transactions. Private keys are mathematically linked to public keys, so when a user sends Bitcoin, they must use their private key to sign the transaction and prove that they are the rightful owner of the Bitcoin being sent.

Address

An address is a unique identifier used to receive Bitcoin transactions. Every address is a combination of letters and numbers and is derived from the public key of a user. Once an address receives Bitcoin, it becomes part of the blockchain, a public ledger that records all Bitcoin transactions. Addresses can be generated and discarded at any time, providing users with a greater level of anonymity and privacy.

Wallet

A wallet is a software application used to store Bitcoin. A wallet consists of two components: the public key and the private key. The public key is used to receive Bitcoin, while the private key is used to authorize outgoing transactions. Wallets can be stored on a computer, a mobile phone, or even a hardware device like a USB stick. They are usually protected by a password or PIN to prevent unauthorized access.

Bitcoin transaction

A Bitcoin transaction is a message that is digitally signed using cryptography and sent to the entire Bitcoin network for verification. Transactions contain information about the amount of Bitcoin being sent, the recipient's address, and the sender's address. Transactions are added to the blockchain once they are verified by a group of users known as **miners**. Miners use powerful computers to solve complex mathematical problems and validate transactions. Once a transaction is validated, it is added to the blockchain, and the transaction is complete.

Unspent transaction outputs

Unspent transaction outputs (UTXOs) are a critical concept in the Bitcoin ecosystem. When a user receives Bitcoin, it is stored as a UTXO. When that user sends Bitcoin, they must spend one or more UTXOs to complete the transaction. UTXOs are used to prevent double-spending, a situation where someone tries to spend the same Bitcoin twice. Once a UTXO is spent, it can never be used again.

In conclusion, Bitcoin relies on a few key concepts to function effectively. Keys, addresses, wallets, Bitcoin transactions, and UTXOs are all critical components of the Bitcoin ecosystem. Understanding these concepts is essential for anyone who wants to use Bitcoin, whether for investment or day-to-day transactions. While some of these concepts may seem complex, they are essential for maintaining the security and integrity of the Bitcoin network.

Validation of transaction

The validation of transactions is a crucial aspect of the Bitcoin network. It ensures the security and integrity of the system by preventing fraudulent transactions and double-spending. In this essay, we will explore the process of transaction validation in Bitcoin.

Bitcoin transactions are messages that are digitally signed using cryptography and sent to the entire Bitcoin network for verification. Transaction information is public and can be found on the digital ledger known as the blockchain. The history of each and every Bitcoin transaction leads back to the point where the Bitcoins were first produced or mined. The blockchain is a distributed ledger that is maintained by a network of nodes, each of which verifies the transactions. When a Bitcoin transaction is initiated, it is broadcast to the network and picked up by a node. This node then validates the transaction by checking that it is correctly formatted and signed, that the inputs are valid and that the sender has sufficient funds to complete the transaction. The node then relays the transaction to other nodes in the network.

Once the transaction is relayed to the network, it is included in a block. A block is a group of transactions that are bundled together and added to the blockchain. Each block contains a unique digital signature called a **hash** that identifies it and links it to the previous block in the chain.

To validate a block, nodes in the network must solve a complex mathematical puzzle. This process is known as **mining** and is performed by specialized computers called **miners**. The first miner to solve the puzzle and add the block to the blockchain is rewarded with newly minted Bitcoins and transaction fees.

Once a block has been added to the blockchain, the transactions it contains are considered validated and confirmed. It is practically impossible to alter the contents of a block without invalidating the entire chain, which would require a majority of the network's computing power. This makes the blockchain highly secure and resistant to tampering. In summary, the validation of transactions in Bitcoin involves a complex process that utilizes cryptography, distributed computing, and consensus mechanisms to ensure the security and integrity of the system. By preventing fraudulent transactions and double-spending, the validation process ensures that Bitcoin can function as a reliable and trusted digital currency.

To explain the validation of a Bitcoin transaction, let us use a hypothetical scenario involving two people, *Alice* and *Bob*. *Figure 3.2* is the visual representation of the process:

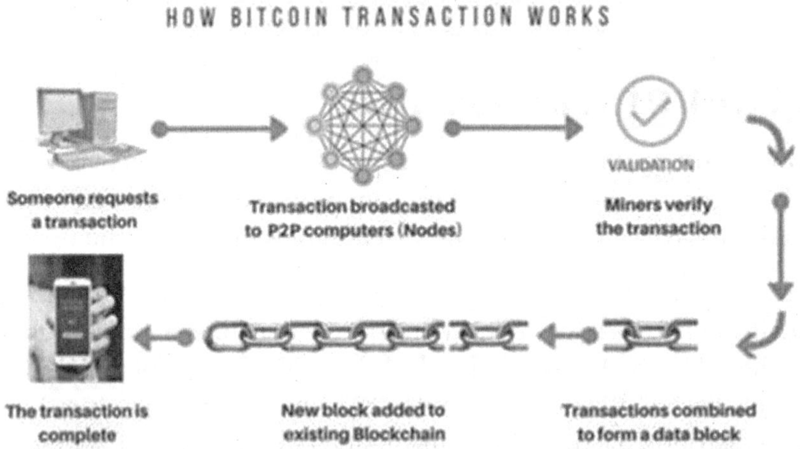

HOW BITCOIN TRANSACTION WORKS

VALIDATION

Someone requests a transaction

Transaction broadcasted to P2P computers (Nodes)

Miners verify the transaction

The transaction is complete

New block added to existing Blockchain

Transactions combined to form a data block

***Figure 3.2**: Bitcoin transaction*

Alice wants to send one Bitcoin to *Bob*, so she initiates a transaction. This transaction must be verified and validated by the network to ensure that *Alice* has the Bitcoin she wants to send and that she is not trying to double-spend it.

First, *Alice* creates a transaction with details including her private key, *Bob's* public key (known as a **Bitcoin address**), the amount of Bitcoin being sent, and a transaction fee. The transaction is then broadcasted to the Bitcoin network, where nodes validate it before adding it to the blockchain. Each node on the network checks the transaction's validity before adding it to a block. To do so, the node will confirm that *Alice* has the Bitcoin she is attempting to send by checking the blockchain's transaction history. This history includes all transactions that have ever taken place in the Bitcoin network, from the first ever transaction to the most recent.

Additionally, the node checks if the Bitcoin has already been spent in another transaction. If it has, then *Alice* cannot double-spend it, and the transaction is invalid.

Once the transaction is verified as valid, the node adds it to a new block, which is then added to the existing blockchain. At this point, the transaction is confirmed, and the Bitcoin is sent from *Alice's* address to *Bob's*.

This process is known as the **consensus mechanism**, which ensures that all transactions on the Bitcoin network are valid and that no one can manipulate the system.

Consensus mechanism

Consensus in the context of blockchain refers to the mechanism by which a distributed network of nodes agrees on the validity of transactions and the state of the blockchain. It ensures that all participants have a consistent view of the shared ledger. Achieving consensus is crucial in a decentralized environment where trust among participants is limited.

This is how consensus mechanism works:

- **Transaction propagation**:
  - o Users initiate transactions on the Bitcoin network by sending Bitcoins from one address to another.
  - o These transactions are broadcasted to all nodes on the network.
- **Transaction verification:**
  - o Nodes verify the validity of transactions by checking if the sender has sufficient funds and if the transaction follows the rules of the Bitcoin protocol.
- **MemPool:**
  - o Valid transactions are collected in a pool known as the **memory pool** (MemPool).
- **Mining begins:**
  - o Miners, specialized nodes in the network, compete to create a new block of transactions.
  - o They select transactions from the MemPool to include in the block.
- **Proof of work (PoW) puzzle**:
  - o Miners must find a specific value (nonce) that, when hashed with the block's data, produces a hash that meets certain criteria.
  - o These criteria involve the hash being lower than a specific target, which is adjusted regularly to maintain an average block time of 10 minutes.
- **Mining difficulty**:
  - o The difficulty of the PoW puzzle adjusts approximately every two weeks to ensure that, on average, a new block is mined every 10 minutes.
  - o This adjustment is based on the total computational power of the network. If miners collectively solve blocks too quickly, the difficulty increases; if too slowly, it decreases.

- **Finding the nonce**:
  - o Miners iterate through possible nonce values, repeatedly hashing the block's data until they find a hash that meets the criteria.
- **Block propagation:**
  - o Once a miner successfully solves the PoW puzzle, they broadcast the new block to the entire network.
- **Consensus confirmation**:
  - o Other nodes in the network verify the validity of the PoW by checking if the hash produced by the miner meets the required criteria.
  - o If valid, nodes accept the new block, and the transactions within it are considered confirmed.
- **Block reward**:
  - o The miner who successfully mined the block is rewarded with a fixed amount of newly created Bitcoins (the block reward) and transaction fees from the included transactions.
- **Continuation**:
  - o The process continues with the next block, creating a chain of blocks (blockchain) linked through PoW.
  - o This decentralized and competitive process ensures the security and immutability of the Bitcoin blockchain. Miners invest computational power and energy to compete for the opportunity to add a new block, making it economically and computationally infeasible to alter past transactions.

Bitcoin keys

Bitcoin, the world's first and most widely used cryptocurrency, has revolutionized the way people think about money and finance. Bitcoin operates on a decentralized network, which means that it does not rely on any central authority for its transactions. To ensure the security of the transactions, Bitcoin uses a system of public and private key cryptography. Bitcoin keys are a critical component of the Bitcoin network's security. Public key cryptography is used to receive funds, while private key cryptography is used to spend them. These two keys (or numbers) are related mathematically on the secp256k1 elliptic curve. The private key is a randomly generated number plotted on the curve, and the corresponding public key is a related point on that curve. An interesting fact is that the addresses are smaller, hashed versions of the public keys. Take a look at *Figure 3.3:*

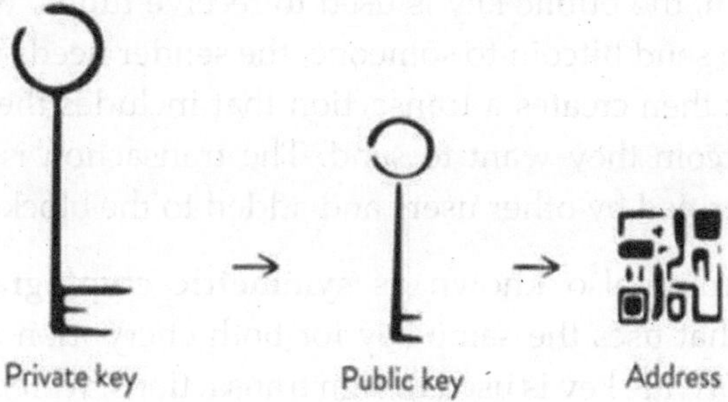

Figure 3.3: Bitcoin keys

The real point of this magical curve is that it creates **trap door functionality**, meaning that once we generate the first point on the curve, the private key, the corresponding second point, public key, is easily found but impossible to find in the opposite direction. If the user has the private key, then the user always has the public key, but if other users have the public key, it is mathematically impossible for them to do the reverse to find the private key.

Bitcoin users must keep their private keys secure to prevent unauthorized access to their funds. Let us dissect things on a much keener scale to understand both of them in detail.

You can think of public-key cryptography as a lock, but with two keys instead of one. *Figure 3.4* illustrates this process:

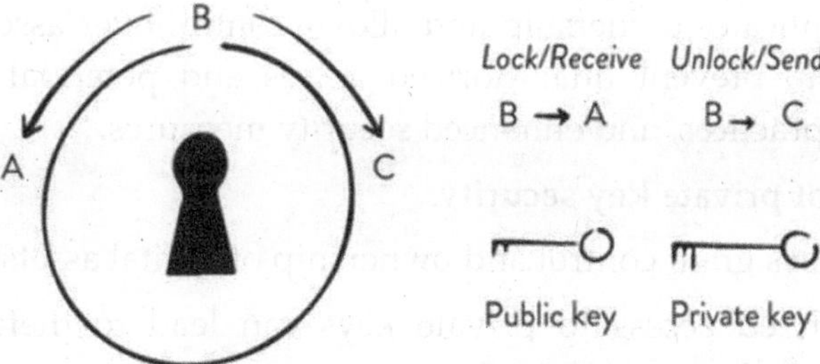

Figure 3.4: Public-key cryptography

In Bitcoin, a **public key** is an address that can be used to receive funds, and a private key is a code that is used to spend those funds. The public key is a long string of alphanumeric characters that is visible to anyone, while the private key is a secret code that only the owner of the Bitcoin wallet knows.

Public key cryptography, also known as **asymmetric cryptography**, is a method of encrypting messages that uses two different keys: a public key and a private key. The public key is used to encrypt messages, while the private key is used to decrypt them.

In the context of Bitcoin, the public key is used to receive funds, while the private key is used to spend them. To send Bitcoin to someone, the sender needs to know the recipient's public key. The sender then creates a transaction that includes the recipient's public key and the amount of Bitcoin they want to send. The transaction is then broadcast to the network, where it is verified by other users and added to the blockchain.

Private key cryptography, also known as **symmetric cryptography**, is a method of encrypting messages that uses the same key for both encryption and decryption. In the context of Bitcoin, the private key is used to sign transactions, which proves that the owner of the wallet is authorized to spend the funds. When a Bitcoin user creates a wallet, a pair of public and private keys is generated. The private key is stored securely on the user's device, while the public key is shared with other users to receive funds. The private key must be kept secret, as anyone who knows the private key can spend the funds in the associated wallet.

Bitcoin keys are essential to the security of the Bitcoin network. If a user's private key is compromised, their funds can be stolen by someone else. Therefore, it is crucial for Bitcoin users to keep their private keys secure and never share them with anyone else. There have been many instances in the past where users have lost their private keys, resulting in the loss of their Bitcoin funds.

Securing private keys in blockchain

The private key is a critical component in blockchain security, serving as the digital signature that authenticates ownership and allows control over assets. Securing private keys is paramount to prevent unauthorized access and potential loss. Here are key considerations, best practices, and enhanced security measures:

- **Importance of private key security**:
  - Private keys grant control and ownership of digital assets on the blockchain.
  - Unauthorized access to private keys can lead to theft, loss of funds, or compromised transactions.
  - Blockchain transactions are irreversible, emphasizing the need for heightened security.
- **Best practices for private key security**:
  - **Offline storage:** Keep private keys offline when not in use to mitigate exposure to online threats.
  - **Encryption:** Use strong encryption methods to safeguard private keys from unauthorized access.

- **Secure backups:** Create encrypted backups stored in multiple secure locations to prevent loss.
- **Avoid public networks:** Refrain from accessing private keys on public networks to minimize exposure to potential attacks.
- **Regular audits:** Periodically review and update security measures to adapt to evolving threats.

- **Security threats**:
  - **Phishing:** Malicious attempts to trick users into revealing private keys or sensitive information.
  - **Malware:** Viruses or malicious software designed to compromise security and gain unauthorized access.
  - **Brute force attacks:** Repeated attempts to guess the private key by systematically trying different combinations.
  - **Social engineering:** Manipulating individuals to divulge private key information through deceptive means.
- **Enhancing security with hardware wallets**:
  - **Isolation:** Hardware wallets keep private keys offline, isolated from internet connected devices, minimizing exposure to online threats.
  - **Secure elements:** Hardware wallets often include secure chips resistant to tampering, providing an additional layer of protection.
  - **Physical authentication:** Some hardware wallets require physical confirmation, adding an extra layer of security.
  - **Transaction verification:** Hardware wallets enable users to verify and approve transactions directly on the device.
- **Cold wallets for long-term storage**:
  - **Definition:** A cold wallet refers to keeping private keys completely offline, disconnected from the internet.
  - **Long-term storage:** Ideal for holding assets for an extended period, reducing the risk of online threats.
  - **Paper wallets:** A form of cold wallet, where private keys are printed or written on paper and stored securely.

The security of private keys is fundamental to safeguarding blockchain assets.

Elliptic curve cryptography

Elliptic curve cryptography is a key-based technique for encrypting data. ECC focuses on pairs of public and private keys for decryption and encryption of web traffic.

Here are the step-by-step details of how ECC works, along with a diagram to illustrate each step:

1. **Generate the curve**: The first step in ECC is to generate an elliptic curve. This curve is a two-dimensional plane that consists of points that satisfy a certain mathematical equation. The equation for the curve is $y^2 = x^3 + ax + b$, where a and b are constants that define the shape of the curve. An example of an elliptic curve is shown in the *Figure 3.5*:

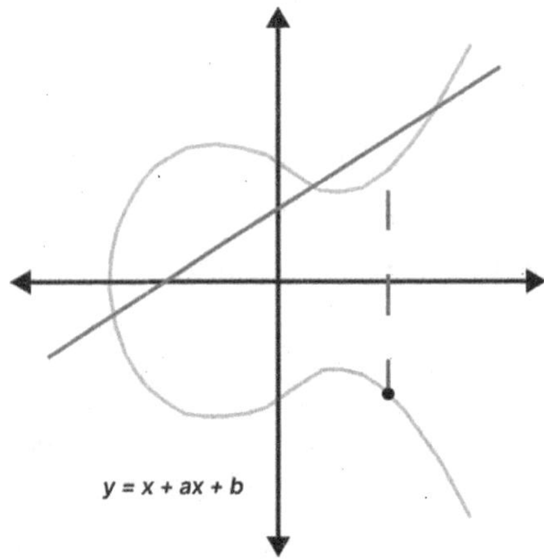

***Figure 3.5**: Elliptic curve cryptography*

2. **Choose a base point**: Next, a base point is chosen on the curve. This point is used as the starting point for all calculations involving the curve. The base point is chosen randomly, but it must have a specific set of properties that make it suitable for use in ECC. One property of the base point is that it must generate all other points on the curve when multiplied by a scalar.
3. **Generate the private key**: The private key is a randomly generated number that is kept secret by the owner. The private key is used to perform mathematical operations on the base point to generate a public key.
4. **Generate the public key**: To generate the public key, the private key is multiplied by the base point on the curve. The result of this multiplication is a new point on the curve that is the public key. The public key is then shared with anyone who needs to send a message to the owner of the private key.

5. **Encrypt the message**: To encrypt a message using ECC, the sender must first obtain the public key of the recipient. The sender then generates a random number called the **ephemeral key**, which is used to perform a calculation on the public key. The result of this calculation is a new point on the curve, which is the shared secret. The shared secret is then used to encrypt the message using a symmetric encryption algorithm.
6. **Decrypt the message**: To decrypt the message, the recipient uses their private key to perform the same calculation on the shared secret that was performed by the sender.

   This results in the original public key, which is used to decrypt the message.

Overall, elliptic curve cryptography provides a secure way to transmit messages over the internet. By using a mathematical function that is difficult to compute in one direction, but easy to compute in the opposite direction, ECC ensures that only the intended recipient can decrypt a message that has been encrypted using their public key.

ECC is a type of public key cryptography that uses elliptic curves to secure digital communications. It has become increasingly popular in recent years due to its security, efficiency, and scalability. The basic idea behind ECC is to use a mathematical function to generate a pair of keys, one public and one private. The public key can be freely shared, while the private key must be kept secret. Messages encrypted with the public key can only be decrypted with the corresponding private key, ensuring the confidentiality of the communication.

One of the key benefits of ECC is that it offers a higher level of security than other public key cryptography systems such as RSA. This is because ECC keys are typically shorter than RSA keys, while offering equivalent or better security. This makes ECC particularly well-suited for use in environments where resources are limited, such as mobile devices or embedded systems. To maintain high levels of performance and security, it is sensible to adopt ECC. ECC is increasingly being utilized by websites to enhance online security for customer data and mobile optimization. As more sites incorporate ECC for data protection, there is an increasing demand for simple guides on this type of cryptography. An elliptic curve used for ECC is a plane curve over a finite field consisting of points that satisfy the equation $y^2 = x^3 + ax + b$. In this example of elliptic curve cryptography, any point on the curve can be reflected over the x-axis without altering the curve. Also, a non-vertical line will intersect the curve in three or fewer places.

Public-key cryptography is a method that uses special math problems that are easy to solve in one direction but difficult to solve in the opposite direction. For example, RSA encryption works by multiplying prime numbers together to get a big number, which is easy to do. But it is difficult to figure out which prime numbers were used just from the big number.

However, to keep RSA secure, very long keys are needed. This makes the process slow and also means that key size matters a lot. ECC is a different method that has an advantage because it can achieve the same level of security as RSA, but with smaller keys. This is especially useful for mobile devices which have less power to do cryptography. ECC uses a different math problem that is easier to solve than RSA's math problem, so shorter keys can still provide strong security. In summary, ECC is a faster and more energy-efficient encryption method that can provide high security with smaller keys compared to RSA.

Even though ECC has some potential vulnerabilities that attackers can exploit to invalidate its security for private keys. Two common types of attacks are side-channel attacks and twist security attacks. Side-channel attacks include differential power attacks, fault analysis, simple power attacks, and simple timing attacks. These attacks typically result in information leaks, but simple countermeasures can be used to prevent them.

Twist-security attacks, such as invalid-curve attacks and small-subgroup attacks, can result in the victim's private key being exposed. However, these attacks can be mitigated with careful parameter validation and curve choices. Despite these vulnerabilities, the advantages of ECC for wireless security make it a more secure option overall. ECC is among the most commonly used implementation techniques for digital signatures in cryptocurrencies. Both Bitcoin and Ethereum apply the **Elliptic Curve Digital Signature Algorithm (ECDSA)** specifically in signing transactions. However, ECC is not used only in cryptocurrencies. It is a standard for encryption that will be used by most web applications going forward due to its shorter key length and efficiency.

Some applications of **elliptic curve cryptography (ECC)** are as follows:

- ECC is used in various security applications.
- The Diffie-Hellman protocol is one such application that enables secret key sharing between two parties, who agree on a curve, field size, and mathematical type.
- ECDSA is a popular digital signature algorithm used in cryptocurrencies like Bitcoin and Ethereum. It employs field inverse multiplication, arithmetic multiplication, inverse function, and modular operation to sign transactions.
- ECC is not just limited to cryptocurrencies but is also used in many online applications for single-way encryption of emails, data, and software due to its efficiency and smaller key size.
- ECC is also utilized in blockchain technology, such as Ethereum 2.0, which uses elliptic curve pairs with BLS signatures to verify specific Eth2 validator's verification of a particular transaction.

Bitcoin address

Bitcoin is a digital currency that enables secure and decentralized transactions without the involvement of a central authority like a bank. Instead, transactions are recorded on a public ledger called the blockchain, which is maintained by a network of nodes around the globe.

A Bitcoin address is a distinctive label that facilitates sending and receiving Bitcoin. It is a combination of alphanumeric characters, which generally starts with the number 1 or 3, that represents a particular destination on the Bitcoin network. Every Bitcoin address is associated with a private key that is used to prove ownership of the Bitcoin and sign transactions linked to the address.

Public key cryptography is used to create Bitcoin addresses. This type of encryption employs a pair of keys: a public key and a private key. The public key is used to create the Bitcoin address, whereas the private key is used to prove ownership of the Bitcoin and sign transactions. To create a Bitcoin address, a user first generates a public-private key pair using a Bitcoin wallet. Then, the public key is hashed using a cryptographic algorithm to produce the Bitcoin address. The outcome is a unique string of characters that denotes the user's location on the Bitcoin network.

When someone wants to send Bitcoin to a particular address, they transmit a transaction to the network containing the recipient's address and the amount of Bitcoin being sent. The transaction is verified by nodes on the network, and if it meets specific requirements, it is added to the blockchain.

To spend Bitcoin associated with a particular address, the owner of the address must sign a transaction using their private key. This action proves ownership of the Bitcoin and allows the transaction to be added to the blockchain. Once nodes on the network confirm the transaction, the Bitcoin is transferred to the recipient's address.

It is crucial to note that Bitcoin addresses can be used for numerous transactions, and the amount of Bitcoin associated with an address can be split into smaller amounts for transactions. This means that Bitcoin addresses can be reused, but it is generally recommended to use a new address for each transaction to improve privacy and security.

Bitcoin is new and exciting, but it is also relatively ambiguous, so it polarizes the general public. Its potential as a global currency exhilarates some people but terrifies others. Bitcoin addresses are 26-35 characters long, consist of alphabetic and numeric characters, and either begin with *1*, *3*, or *bc1*.

Currently, there are three Bitcoin address formats in use:

- P2PKH (address starts with the number 1)
- P2SH (address starts with the number 3)
- Bech32 (address starts with bc1)

To summarize, a Bitcoin address is a unique identifier used to send and receive Bitcoin on the decentralized Bitcoin network. It is generated using public-private key cryptography and is linked to a private key that is used to prove ownership of the Bitcoin and sign transactions associated with the address. Bitcoin addresses can be reused, but it is recommended to use a new address for each transaction to enhance privacy and security.

Base58

Base58 is a numerical system that is widely used in the field of cryptocurrencies and other digital applications. It is a variation of the Base64 system, which removes certain characters to reduce confusion and prevent errors when transmitting data.

Base58 is used to encode important data in the Bitcoin network, including Bitcoin addresses, public and private keys, and other data. The system includes the numbers 1 through 9 and the letters A through H, J through N, and P through Z. The letters I, O, and Q are not included in the Base58 system because they can be easily confused with the numbers 1 and 0.

Compared to traditional binary or hexadecimal encoding, Base58 offers a more compact representation of data. It is also more human-readable, as the characters used in Base58 are easy to distinguish and do not include confusing characters like the letters I and O. This makes it a preferred encoding system for transmitting data in a clear and efficient manner.

In addition to its compactness and readability, the Base58 system is often used with checksums to ensure data accuracy. A checksum is a mathematical function that generates a unique value based on the data being transmitted. This value is then included with the encoded data and can be used to verify that the data has not been corrupted or modified during transmission.

For example, let us say Alice wants to send a Bitcoin payment to Bob. Alice generates a Bitcoin address and encodes it using the Base58 system. She also includes a checksum with the encoded data to ensure its accuracy. Alice then sends the encoded data to Bob, who decodes it using the Base58 system and verifies the checksum. If the checksum matches, Bob knows that the data has not been corrupted or modified during transmission and can proceed with the transaction.

Overall, Base58 is a useful encoding system for transmitting data in a compact and human readable format, and is commonly used in the cryptocurrency industry for encoding Bitcoin addresses and other important data. It provides a level of data security and accuracy that is essential for secure and reliable transactions.

Refer to the following figure:

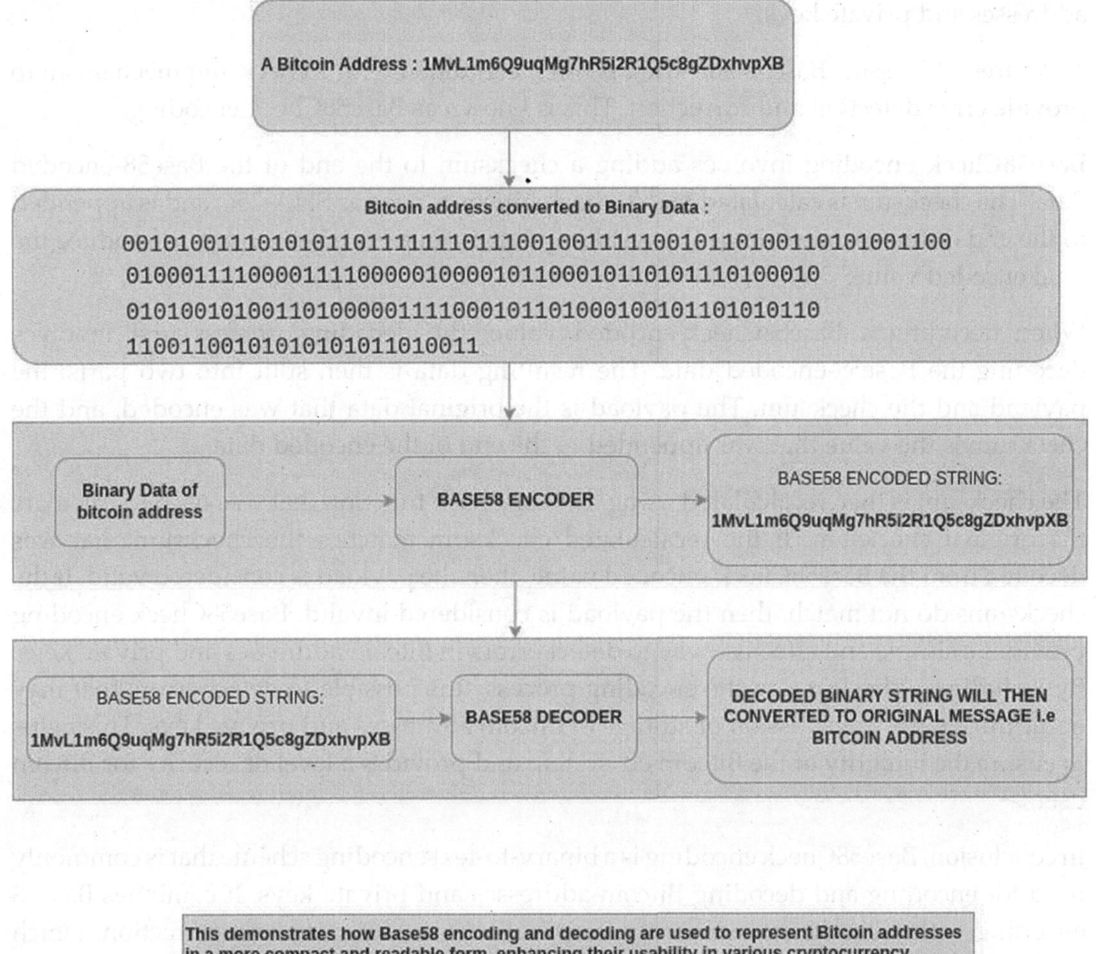

***Figure 3.6**: Base58 encoding and decoding*

Utility of Base58

Base58 is a **binary-to-text encoding scheme** that is commonly used for encoding and decoding Bitcoin addresses and private keys. The encoding scheme is a modification of the Base64 encoding scheme, which is used for encoding binary data in ASCII format. In Base58 encoding, the characters *0, O, I,* and *l* are removed to avoid confusion between them, and the + and / characters are also removed to avoid confusion with URL encoding.

Base58 encoding is commonly used in the Bitcoin ecosystem because it provides a compact and easy-to-read representation of Bitcoin addresses and private keys. However, the use of Base58 encoding alone does not provide any error detection or correction mechanism. This means that it is possible for errors to occur during the transmission or storage of Bitcoin addresses and private keys.

To address this issue, Base58 encoding is often combined with a checksum mechanism to provide error detection and correction. This is known as Base58Check encoding.

Base58Check encoding involves adding a checksum to the end of the Base58-encoded data. The checksum is calculated using a hash function, such as SHA-256, and is appended to the end of the encoded data. The resulting data is then Base58-encoded to produce the final encoded value.

When decoding a Base58Check-encoded value, the decoding process first involves decoding the Base58-encoded data. The resulting data is then split into two parts: the payload and the checksum. The payload is the original data that was encoded, and the checksum is the value that was appended to the end of the encoded data.

The checksum is then recalculated using the same hash function that was used to calculate the original checksum. If the recalculated checksum matches the checksum that was decoded from the Base58Check-encoded value, then the payload is considered valid. If the checksums do not match, then the payload is considered invalid. Base58Check encoding provides a simple and effective way to detect errors in Bitcoin addresses and private keys. By including a checksum in the encoding process, it is possible to detect errors that may occur during the transmission or storage of Bitcoin addresses and private keys. This helps to ensure the integrity of the Bitcoin ecosystem and provides a level of security for Bitcoin users.

In conclusion, Base58Check encoding is a binary-to-text encoding scheme that is commonly used for encoding and decoding Bitcoin addresses and private keys. It combines Base58 encoding with a checksum mechanism to provide error detection and correction, which helps to ensure the integrity of the Bitcoin ecosystem. Base58Check encoding is an important component of the Bitcoin infrastructure, and understanding how it works is essential for anyone who is involved in the Bitcoin ecosystem.

Encoding with Base58

The Base58 encoding process begins by taking the binary data that needs to be encoded and converting it into a Base58 string. The process involves the following steps:

1. Convert the binary data into a big-endian integer. This means that the most significant byte of the binary data is placed at the beginning of the integer.

2. Divide the integer by 58 (the base of the encoding scheme) and record the remainder.
3. Repeat step 2 with the quotient until the quotient is zero.
4. Convert each remainder into a Base58 character using a lookup table. The lookup table typically includes the characters *1* through *9*, *A* through *H*, *J* through *N*, *P* through *Z*, and *a* through *k*, *m* through *z*.
5. Concatenate the Base58 characters together to form the final encoded string.

Figure 3.7 illustrates the process:

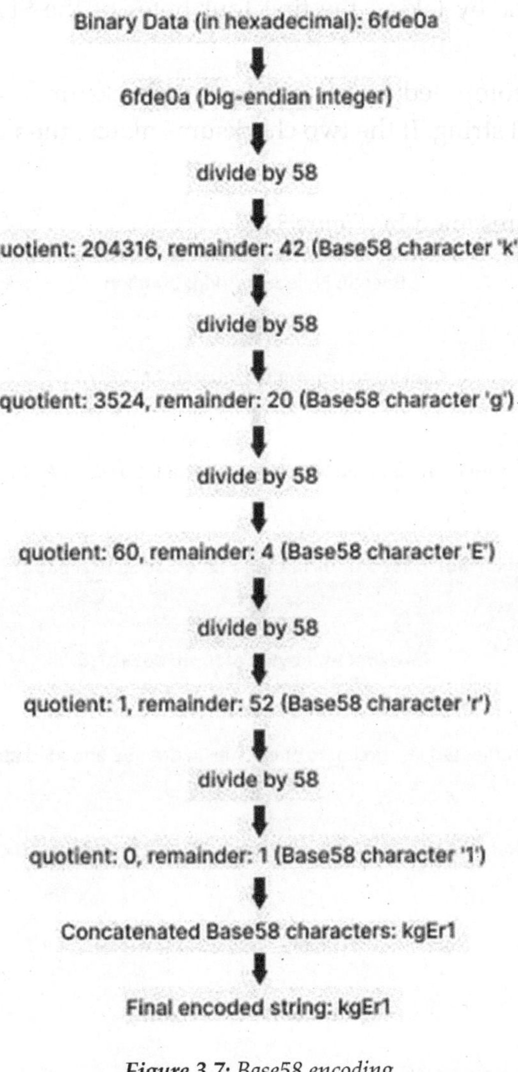

***Figure 3.7:** Base58 encoding*

Base58 decoding process

The Base58 decoding process involves the following steps:

1. Convert the Base58 encoded string into a big-endian integer. This involves decoding each Base58 character using a lookup table and multiplying it by the corresponding power of 58.
2. Convert the big-endian integer into a byte array by taking each 8-bit chunk of the integer and placing it in the byte array in big-endian order.
3. Verify the integrity of the data by computing the checksum of the byte array. This is typically done by taking the first four bytes of the SHA-256 hash of the byte array.
4. Compare the computed checksum to the checksum that was included in the Base58 encoded string. If the two checksums match, then the data is considered to be valid.

This process can be represented by *Figure 3.8*:

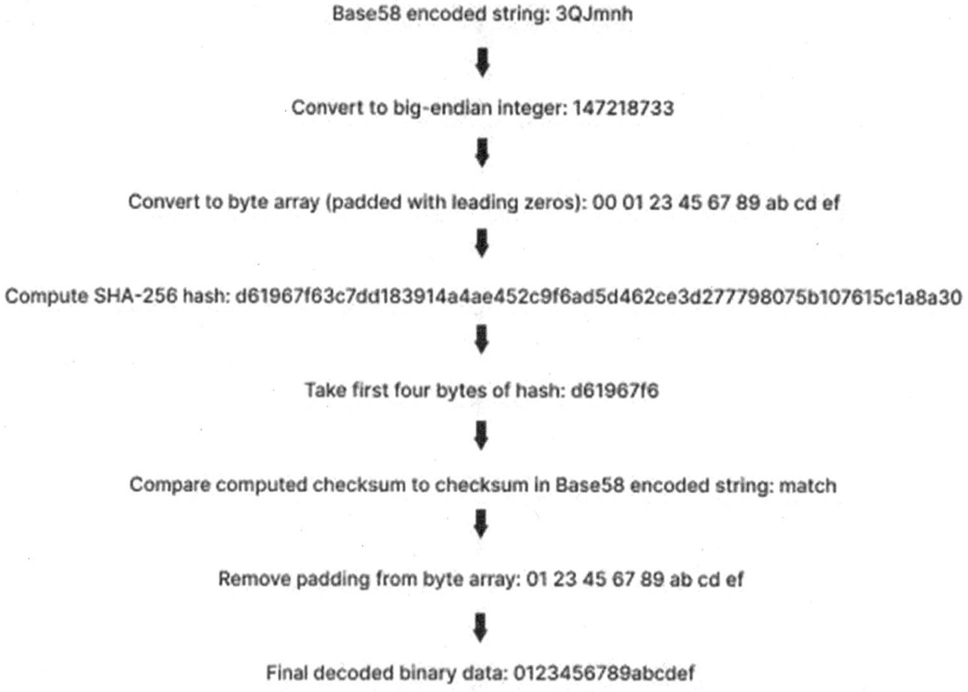

Base58 encoded string: 3QJmnh

⬇

Convert to big-endian integer: 147218733

⬇

Convert to byte array (padded with leading zeros): 00 01 23 45 67 89 ab cd ef

⬇

Compute SHA-256 hash: d61967f63c7dd183914a4ae452c9f6ad5d462ce3d277798075b107615c1a8a30

⬇

Take first four bytes of hash: d61967f6

⬇

Compare computed checksum to checksum in Base58 encoded string: match

⬇

Remove padding from byte array: 01 23 45 67 89 ab cd ef

⬇

Final decoded binary data: 0123456789abcdef

Figure 3.8: *Base58 decoding*

Encrypted private keys

The protection of private keys is critical in cryptocurrency transactions, and encrypted private keys, also known as **BIP-38,** offer a reliable method of ensuring this security. In this section, we will provide an in-depth analysis of encrypted private keys, highlighting their definition, functionality, and advantages and disadvantages.

As the cornerstone of cryptocurrency transactions, a private key serves as a secret code that grants access to digital assets. Private keys are used to sign transactions and verify ownership of funds, and hence their protection is crucial. One of the methods of securing private keys is encryption using a passphrase, and this is where BIP-38 comes in. BIP-38 is a standard for encrypting private keys used in cryptocurrencies, developed in 2013 by *Mike Caldwell.*

BIP-38 works by using a combination of **AES-256** encryption and ECDSA key pairs. AES-256 is a symmetric encryption algorithm that is widely used for securing data, while ECDSA is a digital signature algorithm that is used to verify the authenticity of transactions in Bitcoin. To encrypt a private key using BIP-38, a random passphrase is generated, and this passphrase is then used to encrypt the private key using AES-256 encryption. The encrypted private key is then encoded using Base58 encoding, resulting in a BIP-38 encrypted private key.

BIP-38 provides several advantages in securing private keys. One of the primary advantages is the additional layer of security it provides to private keys. Even if someone gains access to the encrypted private key, they cannot use it without the passphrase. Secondly, BIP-38 allows users to store their encrypted private keys offline, a process known as **cold storage**, which is considered one of the most secure ways to store digital assets.

However, BIP-38 also has some disadvantages. For instance, it can be cumbersome to use since users have to remember their passphrase and enter it every time they want to access their digital assets. In case the passphrase is forgotten or lost, the encrypted private key cannot be decrypted, and the digital assets will be lost permanently. Moreover, BIP-38 adds complexity to the process of managing digital assets, and users must take extra care to ensure that their passphrase is kept secure and not shared with anyone.

In conclusion, BIP-38 provides a reliable method of securing private keys used in cryptocurrency transactions. It employs AES-256 encryption and ECDSA key pairs to encrypt private keys, providing an additional layer of security to digital assets. While it has some drawbacks, its advantages make it a popular choice for users seeking to protect their private keys.

Pay-to-script address

In the world of cryptocurrencies, a **Pay-to-script-hash (P2SH)** address is a type of address used for transactions that involve complex scripts. P2SH is a mechanism that allows users to send Bitcoins to a script instead of a traditional Bitcoin address. Let us discuss the same in detail in the following paragraphs.

Bitcoin transactions are conducted using a public ledger known as the blockchain, where all transactions are recorded and publicly available for viewing. To conduct a transaction, a user needs to have a Bitcoin address, which is essentially a unique identifier for that user's wallet on the blockchain. There are several types of Bitcoin addresses, each with its own advantages and disadvantages.

One type of Bitcoin address is the P2SH address, which is a more complex form of address that allows users to send Bitcoins to a complex script that has been hashed. This type of address is useful in situations where a transaction requires multiple signatures, also known as **multi-sig transactions**, or when the transaction needs to fulfill specific conditions.

To understand how P2SH addresses work, we must first understand what scripts are. Scripts are small programs that are embedded in Bitcoin transactions and are used to determine the conditions under which Bitcoins can be spent. They allow for more complex transactions to be conducted on the blockchain. To create a P2SH address, the script is first hashed using the SHA-256 algorithm, resulting in a hash value. This hash value is then encoded using the Base58Check encoding method to create the P2SH address. The P2SH address is used to store the hash of the script, rather than the script itself, making it much shorter than the actual script. When someone wants to redeem Bitcoins from a P2SH address, they must provide the full script that was originally hashed and the corresponding signatures. The script is then evaluated, and if it meets the specified conditions, the Bitcoins are released.

The primary advantage of using P2SH addresses is that they allow for more complex transactions to be conducted on the blockchain. For example, a multi-sig transaction, where two or more signatures are required to spend the Bitcoins, can be conducted using a P2SH address. This adds an additional layer of security to the transaction, as all parties involved must agree before the transaction can be completed.

Another advantage of P2SH addresses is that they can help reduce transaction fees. This is because a P2SH transaction requires less space on the blockchain than a regular transaction. This means that miners can include more P2SH transactions in a single block, allowing them to earn more transaction fees while keeping the overall size of the blockchain smaller.

One analogy for P2SH addresses is that they are like a locked safe. The P2SH address is like the lock on the safe, and the script is like the combination needed to unlock the safe.

Only those with the correct combination can unlock the safe and access its contents, just like only those with the correct script can access the Bitcoins stored in a P2SH address. To create a P2SH address, a user can use a Bitcoin wallet that supports P2SH addresses, such as Electrum, Bitcoin Core, or Armory. The wallet will generate a P2SH address for the user, which can be used to receive Bitcoins from others. When the user wants to spend the Bitcoins, they must provide the full script and the required signatures to redeem the Bitcoins.

In the Bitcoin scripting system, scripts define the conditions that must be satisfied for spending bitcoins associated with a particular output. Bitcoin's scripting language is intentionally designed to be simple but flexible, allowing a variety of conditions to be specified. Here is an elaboration along with a real-world example.

Bitcoin script basics:

- **Script language:** Bitcoin uses a scripting language that is stack-based, allowing for the execution of simple programs. Scripts are part of transaction outputs and determine the conditions under which funds can be spent.
- **Unlocking script (ScriptSig):** When a user wants to spend Bitcoins, they must provide a script known as the **unlocking script** or **ScriptSig**. This script should satisfy the conditions set by the locking script.
- **Locking script (ScriptPubKey):** The conditions for spending Bitcoins are initially set by the **locking script** or **ScriptPubKey**, which is part of the output script. The spending transaction must satisfy the conditions specified in this script.

Conditions set by scripts:

- **Pay-to-public-key (P2PK):**
  - o **Locking script (ScriptPubKey)**: `<publicKey> OP_CHECKSIG`
  - o **Unlocking script (ScriptSig)**: `<signature>`
  - o **Condition**: The spending transaction must include a valid signature for the specified public key.
- Pay-to-Public-Key-Hash (P2PKH):
  - o Locking Script (ScriptPubKey): `<hash160(publicKey)> OP_EQUALVERIFY`
  - o `OP_CHECKSIG`
  - o Unlocking Script (ScriptSig): `<signature> <publicKey>`
  - o **Condition**: The provided public key must hash to the same value as the one specified in the locking script, and the signature must be valid.
- **Multi-signature (Multisig):**
  - o Locking Script (ScriptPubKey): `<m> <publicKey1> <publicKey2>`

- o **<publicKeyn> <n> OP_CHECKMULTISIG**
- o **Unlocking Script (ScriptSig): <signature1> <signature2> ... <signaturem>**
- o **Condition**: At least m out of n provided signatures must be valid for spending.

Real-world example of multi-sig wallet:

- **Use case:** Creating a wallet that requires signatures from multiple parties for any transaction.
- **Locking script (ScriptPubKey): <2> <pubKeyA> <pubKeyB> <pubKeyC> <3> OP_CHECKMULTISIG**
- **Unlocking script (ScriptSig): <sigA> <sigB>**

In this example, the funds in the wallet are locked with a 2-of-3 multisignature condition. To spend the bitcoins, at least two out of three private key holders (A, B, and C) must provide valid signatures.

Bitcoin's scripting system allows for various conditions and logic, enabling more complex spending conditions beyond simple transfers. This flexibility is crucial for implementing advanced features such as smart contracts and complex multi-signature wallets.

Multi-sig addresses

Multi-sig addresses are a unique type of Bitcoin address that requires multiple private keys to access the funds. Multi-sig addresses are an important tool for increasing the security of Bitcoin transactions, as they provide an additional layer of protection against unauthorized access and theft.

In this section, we will explore multi-signature addresses in detail, including how they work, the benefits they offer, and some examples of their use in practice.

Working of multi-sign addresses

At its core, a multi-signature address is simply a Bitcoin address that is associated with multiple public keys. In order to access the funds stored in the address, multiple private keys must be provided. The number of keys required to unlock the address can vary depending on the specific implementation, but typically ranges from two to four.

The process of creating a multi-signature address is relatively straightforward. To begin, the users involved in the transaction must agree on the number of keys required to unlock the address, as well as the specific public keys that will be associated with the address. Once this is done, the users can use a special software tool to generate a new multi-signature address that incorporates the specified public keys.

When a user wants to send Bitcoin to a multi-signature address, they must provide the required number of private keys to unlock the address. For example, if a multi-sig address requires three private keys to access the funds, all three keys must be provided in order to complete the transaction. This process ensures that multiple parties must agree to a transaction before it can be executed, which greatly reduces the risk of unauthorized access or theft.

Creating a multi-sig address involves a series of steps, and the process of signing and verifying transactions with multiple keys. They are as follows:

- **Choose signers and set parameters:**
    - o Decide how many signers (m) are needed out of a total possible (n) for a transaction.
    - o Obtain public keys from each signer involved in the multi-signature setup.
- **Create the locking script (ScriptPubKey):**
    - o Construct a locking script that includes the number of required signatures (m), public keys, and the total number of keys (n).
    - o The locking script typically looks like `<m> <publicKey1> <publicKey2> ... <publicKeyn> <n> OP_CHECKMULTISIG.`
- **Generate the multi-signature address:**
    - o Hash the locking script to create a unique address.
- **Signing and verifying transactions:**
    - o Construct the Spending Transaction:
        - ▪ When spending from a multi-signature address, create a transaction as usual but include the specific conditions in the unlocking script.
- **Create the unlocking script (ScriptSig):**
    - o For each signer, generate a unique signature.
    - o The unlocking script typically looks like `<signature1> <signature2> ... <signaturem>.`
- **Combine signatures and execute the transaction:**
    - o Combine the required number of signatures (m) from the signers.
    - o Execute the transaction with the combined signatures.
- **Verify the transaction:**
    - o The network verifies the transaction against the locking script.
    - o If the combined signatures meet the specified conditions (m out of n), the transaction is valid.

This process ensures that a transaction is only executed if the predetermined number of authorized signers provide their signatures. It enhances security by requiring consensus among multiple parties to spend funds.

Benefits of multi-signature addresses

The use of multi-signature addresses offers several important benefits to the users. Perhaps the most obvious benefit is that they provide an additional layer of security for Bitcoin transactions. By requiring multiple private keys to access the funds stored in an address, multi-sig addresses make it much more difficult for an attacker to steal Bitcoin through hacking or other means.

Another key benefit of multi-signature addresses is that they provide a mechanism for implementing complex transaction workflows. For example, a multi-sig address could be used to require approval from multiple parties before a large Bitcoin transaction can be executed. This feature is particularly useful for businesses and other organizations that need to manage large Bitcoin holdings in a secure and responsible way.

Multi-signature addresses also offer increased flexibility and control over Bitcoin transactions. By allowing multiple parties to participate in the transaction, users can ensure that all parties involved have a say in how the transaction is executed. This can help to reduce disputes and misunderstandings and ensure that all parties are satisfied with the outcome.

Examples of multi-signature address use

There are many different scenarios in which multi-signature addresses can be used to improve the security and efficiency of Bitcoin transactions. Here are a few examples:

Cold storage

One common use case for multi-signature addresses is to provide a secure storage solution for large Bitcoin holdings. By creating a multi-sig address that requires multiple private keys to access, users can ensure that their Bitcoin holdings are protected from theft or other forms of unauthorized access.

For example, a company might create a multi-sig address that requires three private keys to access. The first key might be held by the company CEO, the second key by the company CFO, and the third key by a trusted third-party escrow service. By requiring all three keys to access the funds, the company can ensure that no single person can gain access to the funds without the approval of multiple parties.

Escrow services

Multi-signature addresses can also be used to facilitate secure transactions between two parties. For example, an escrow service might create a multi-sig address that requires the buyer.

Vanity address

A vanity address is a customized Bitcoin address that is created with a specific word, phrase or pattern that the user chooses. The word **vanity** refers to the fact that the address is created for aesthetics or branding purposes rather than security purposes. The creation of a vanity address involves a process of trial and error until the desired pattern is found. In this section, we will discuss in detail what a vanity address is, how it is created, and its special traits. A vanity address is a Bitcoin address that is customized to include a specific word or pattern chosen by the user. For example, a user may want to create an address that starts with their name, their company name or their favorite word. The process of creating a vanity address involves generating a large number of public and private key pairs until one is found that meets the desired criteria.

Vanity addresses are not inherently more secure than regular Bitcoin addresses. However, they do provide a way for users to create unique, memorable addresses that can be used for branding purposes. For example, a business might create a vanity address that includes their company name or slogan, which can help to establish their brand and make their address more recognizable.

The creation of a vanity address involves the generation of multiple public and private key pairs. The first few characters of the public keys are then scrutinized to see if they match a specific pattern chosen by the user. If a public key matches the criteria, the corresponding private key is used to generate the Bitcoin address. If it does not meet the desired pattern, the process is repeated with a new key pair. The complexity of the pattern affects the time it takes to create a vanity address. A simple pattern such as the word Bitcoin may take only a few minutes to generate, while a more intricate pattern like a company slogan may take several hours or days.

Vanity addresses have unique traits that set them apart from regular Bitcoin addresses. They are personalized to meet specific criteria chosen by the user, making them more memorable and recognizable. They can be used for branding purposes, allowing businesses to create addresses that include their company name or slogan, thus, establishing their brand and making their address more recognizable. Creating a vanity address requires a significant amount of trial and error. The process can be time-consuming and may necessitate a considerable amount of computational power, depending on the complexity of the desired pattern. However, vanity addresses do not provide additional security over regular Bitcoin addresses.

For instance, let us say Alice wants to create a vanity address that starts with the word *crypto*. Alice first generates a large number of public and private key pairs. She then checks the first few characters of each public key to see if it matches the desired pattern. After several hours of generating key pairs and checking for the desired pattern, Alice eventually discovers a public key that starts with the word *crypto*. She employs the corresponding private key to generate the Bitcoin address that she can use for transactions.

Generating vanity addresses involves a process of trial and error, where a user attempts to find a specific pattern or characters in a cryptocurrency address. This process is computationally intensive because it requires generating numerous cryptographic key pairs and hashing them until a match is found. The more complex or longer the desired pattern, the more computational power and time are needed.

The potential security risks in generating vanity addresses include:

- **Resource intensity:** Vanity address generation can be resource-intensive, requiring significant computational power. This might lead to high electricity costs or prolonged processing times.
- **Key security:** The security of a vanity address depends on the strength of the cryptographic key pair. If the key generation process is not secure, there is a risk of weak keys that could be vulnerable to attacks.
- **Privacy concerns:** Vanity addresses are customized, making them potentially traceable to the user generating them. If privacy is a concern, users should be cautious about associating specific patterns with their identities.
- **Software risks:** Using unreliable or malicious software for vanity address generation poses security risks. Users should rely on reputable tools and follow best practices to mitigate these risks.

Bitcoin wallet

Bitcoin is a decentralized digital currency that operates on a peer-to-peer network. To use Bitcoin, users must have a Bitcoin wallet, which is a software program that stores the private keys necessary to access and manage their Bitcoin funds. There are several types of Bitcoin wallets, each with its own unique features and characteristics. Desktop wallets, mobile wallets, web wallets, and hardware wallets are the most common types of Bitcoin wallets.

Desktop wallets are software programs that can be downloaded and installed on a desktop computer. They are generally more secure than web wallets, as they are not vulnerable to hacking attacks. Electrum, Exodus, and Bitcoin Core are popular desktop wallets. Mobile wallets are designed for use on smartphones and tablets. They offer convenience and portability and can be used to make payments in physical stores by scanning a QR code.

Mycelium, Bread wallet, and Co-pay are popular mobile wallets.

Web wallets are online services that allow users to store their Bitcoin funds in the cloud. They are generally less secure than desktop or mobile wallets, as they are vulnerable to hacking attacks. **Coinbase**, **Blockchain.info**, and **BitGo** are popular web wallets. Hardware wallets are physical devices that are designed to store the private keys necessary to access and manage Bitcoin funds. They are considered the most secure type of Bitcoin wallet, as they are not vulnerable to hacking attacks. Trezor, Ledger Nano S, and KeepKey are popular hardware wallets.

Bitcoin wallets offer several features that are designed to enhance security, privacy, and usability. Private keys are used to sign transactions and prove ownership of Bitcoin funds. Address management is important for maintaining privacy and security, as it allows users to use a different address for each transaction. Please refer to the following figure:

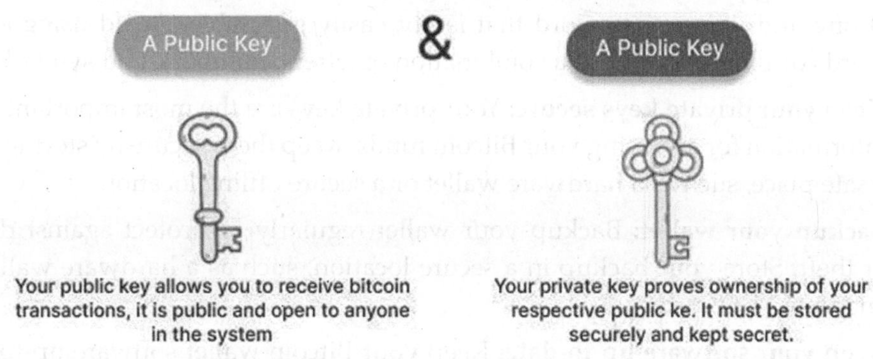

Figure 3.9: Bitcoin wallet

Private keys are 256 digits long, making them impractical for storing, transacting and securing your money. This is why they are protected in a Bitcoin wallet that will automatically activate them for transacting, in pair with a public key. When you create your Bitcoin wallet, a seed or recovery phrase is automatically generated to retrieve your funds in case you lose access to your private key. A seed, mnemonic or recovery phrase is a succession of 12 or 24 words that will be used to generate any Bitcoin key you need to send and receive Bitcoin.

There exist different types of Bitcoin wallets, depending on the situation and need. One should be very careful while deciding the right one for the use, in particular custodial wallets that third party controls. It is highly recommended that you follow the guidance below to avoid costly mistakes and risk losing funds:

- Do not use a paper wallet unless you are an advanced user and recognize the risks involved.
- Large amounts of Bitcoin should preferably be stored in multi-sig wallets.
- Remember to set up recovery instructions for your heirs or respective nominees.
- Do not use a wallet that does not give you the recovery data.

Transaction history is kept to record all transactions, including the amount sent and received, the date and time of the transaction, and the transaction fee. Encryption is used to protect the private keys and transaction data from unauthorized access. Using Bitcoin wallets requires a certain level of knowledge and understanding of how they work. Following are some of the best practices for using Bitcoin wallets:

- **Use a hardware wallet:** Hardware wallets are considered the most secure type of Bitcoin wallet. If you are serious about Bitcoin security, consider investing in a hardware wallet.
- **Use strong passwords:** When creating a password for your Bitcoin wallet, use a strong and unique password that is not easily guessable. Avoid using common words or phrases, and use a combination of letters, numbers, and symbols.
- **Keep your private keys secure:** Your private keys are the most important piece of information for accessing your Bitcoin funds. Keep them secure by storing them in a safe place, such as a hardware wallet or a secure offline location.
- **Backup your wallet:** Backup your wallet regularly to protect against data loss or theft. Store your backup in a secure location, such as a hardware wallet or an encrypted USB drive.
- **Keep your software up-to-date:** Keep your Bitcoin wallet software up-to-date to ensure that you have the latest security patches and bug fixes. This will help to prevent hacking attacks and keep your Bitcoin funds secure.

Bitcoin HD wallet

Bitcoin **Hierarchical Deterministic (HD)** wallet is the type of wallet that use a single seed to generate an unlimited number of private keys. This is accomplished through the use of advanced cryptographic algorithms that generate a unique private key for each transaction. The key advantage of an HD wallet is that it eliminates the need for multiple backups and reduces the risk of losing Bitcoins due to a hardware failure or theft.

The most common technology used in Bitcoin HD wallets is **Bitcoin Improvement Proposal 32 (BIP32)**, which provides a set of guidelines for creating hierarchical deterministic wallets. BIP32 specifies the use of a master key, which is a 256-bit random number used to generate all subsequent private keys. It also defines a set of rules for generating private keys from the master key, including the use of **HMAC-SHA512**, a hash-based message authentication code that ensures the integrity of the keys.

Another technology used in Bitcoin HD wallets is BIP39, which provides a set of guidelines for creating mnemonic phrases that can be used to generate the master key. The mnemonic phrase is a sequence of words that are randomly generated and can be easily remembered. This makes it easy for users to back up their wallets by writing down the mnemonic phrase and storing it in a safe place.

Refer to the following table:

Wallet Type	Description	Security	Usability	Anonymity
Hardware Wallet	Physical device for storing private keys offline.	High	Moderate	High
Software Wallet (Desktop)	Software installed on a desktop or laptop computer.	Depends on computer security.	Easy	Moderate
Software Wallet (Mobile)	Wallet apps on mobile devices.	Depends on device security.	Easy and portable	Moderate
Web Wallet	Wallets accessed through a web browser.	Depends on platform security.	Convenient but less secure	Low to moderate
Paper Wallet	Private and public keys printed or written on paper.	High if generated securely and kept physically secure.	Low (requires manual entry for transactions)	High
Brain Wallet	Keys generated based on a passphrase memorized by the user.	High (depends on passphrase strength)	High	Low
Multi-Signature Wallet	Requires multiple private keys to authorize a transaction.	High (depends on the number and security of keys)	Moderate to High	Depends on setup

Wallet Type	Description	Security	Usability	Anonymity
Deterministic Wallet	Uses a seed to generate a sequence of key pairs.	High (if seed is kept secure)	Moderate	Moderate

Table 3.1: *Different types of wallets*

Creating an HD wallet from the seed

To create an HD wallet from the seed, the user needs to follow a set of steps that include generating the **master key**, generating the **mnemonic phrase**, and deriving the **private and public keys**. The first step is to generate the master key, which is a 256-bit random number that is used to generate all subsequent private keys. This can be done using a software tool that implements the BIP32 standard.

The second step is to generate the mnemonic phrase, which is a sequence of words that are randomly generated and can be easily remembered. This can also be done using a software tool that implements the BIP39 standard. The user should write down the mnemonic phrase and store it in a safe place, as it can be used to recover the master key and all subsequent private keys.

The final step is to derive the private and public keys from the master key. This can be done using a software tool that implements the BIP32 standard. The user can then use the private key to sign transactions and the public key to receive Bitcoins.

Derive private child key

To generate a private key in Bitcoin wallets, a seed is required to be generated first. This seed is a randomly generated 256-bit number which serves as the basis for generating a master private key. The master private key is then used to generate a series of child private keys, which are used to sign transactions.

The process of generating a private key in Bitcoin wallets involves the following steps:

1. **Generating a seed:** A secure random number generator is used to create a 256-bit random number seed. The seed is essential to generate the master private key. It is important to ensure that the random number generator used is secure to eliminate predictability and maintain the security of the private keys derived from it.
2. **Generating a master private key:** To generate a master private key, the seed is used as input into a key derivation function. This function generates a sequence of pseudorandom numbers based on the seed. The first pseudo-random number is selected as the master private key. In Bitcoin, the key derivation function

employed to generate the master private key is called **BIP32**, which is a standard for hierarchical deterministic wallets.

3. **Generating child private keys:** The third step involves generating a series of child private keys from the master private key. HD key derivation is used to achieve this. HD key derivation allows a large number of private keys to be generated from a single master private key.

In Bitcoin, a series of child private keys is generated through HD key derivation. Each child private key is generated by combining the master private key with a unique index number. This results in a unique private key for each index number, which can be used to sign transactions for that specific index.

In summary, to derive a private key in Bitcoin wallets, a secure random number generator is used to generate a 256-bit seed. The seed is used as input into a key derivation function to generate a master private key, which is then used to generate a series of child private keys through hierarchical deterministic key derivation.

Derive public child key

In order to derive a public key in Bitcoin wallets, we need to start with the private key. The private key is a 256-bit number that is generated using advanced cryptographic algorithms. The public key is derived from the private key using ECC.

ECC is a mathematical algorithm that is used to create and verify digital signatures. It is based on the properties of elliptic curves, which are smooth, continuous curves that can be used to generate points on a two-dimensional plane. The curve is defined by a set of mathematical parameters, including a prime number, a base point, and a coefficient.

To derive a public key from a private key in Bitcoin wallets, we need to follow the given steps:

1. **Generate a nonce:** A nonce is a random number that is used to generate a unique point on the elliptic curve. In Bitcoin, the nonce is generated using a deterministic algorithm, which means that the same nonce will be generated for the same private key every time.

2. **Generate a point on the elliptic curve:** To generate a point on the elliptic curve, we use the private key and the nonce as inputs to the elliptic curve equation. The equation is defined as:

$$y\^2 = x\^3 + ax + b$$

where a and b are the parameters of the curve. We plug in the values for a and b, as well as the x-coordinate of the nonce and the private key, and solve for y. The resulting point is a point on the elliptic curve.

3. **Convert the X-coordinate to a public key:** To convert the x-coordinate of the point on the elliptic curve to a public key, we perform a series of mathematical operations. First, we append a prefix to the x-coordinate to indicate whether the y-coordinate is even or odd. Then we hash the result using the SHA-256 algorithm. Finally, we apply the RIPEMD-160 algorithm to the hash to generate the public key.

Transaction script

A transaction script is a set of instructions or rules that determine the conditions under which a transaction can be executed on a blockchain network. The script defines the requirements for the sender and the recipient, as well as the conditions under which the transaction can be executed. These scripts are written in a programming language specific to the blockchain network and are executed by the nodes on the network.

In Bitcoin, the transaction script is written in a scripting language called **script**. Script is a simple stack-based language that allows for complex conditions to be defined for a transaction to be executed. Script is used to define the conditions under which the output of a transaction can be spent. The output of a transaction is locked using a script, which contains instructions that must be met to unlock the output and spend the funds.

The script is attached to the output of the transaction, and it is evaluated by the nodes on the network when a new transaction is submitted to the network. The nodes check whether the script conditions have been met before validating and adding the transaction to the blockchain.

The script language is a limited programming language with a set of predefined operations that can be performed on data. It is designed to be simple to reduce the risk of bugs and to maintain the security of the blockchain network. Some of the operations available in the script language include:

- **Arithmetic operations**: These are basic mathematical operations such as addition, subtraction, multiplication, and division.
- **Comparison operations**: These are operations used to compare data values such as equal, greater than, less than, and not equal.
- **Logical operations**: These are operations used to perform logical operations such as and, or, and not.
- **Conditional operations**: These are operations used to define conditions for executing a particular script.

The transaction script is responsible for validating a transaction, and it is used to ensure that only authorized parties can spend the funds. The script can specify various conditions, including the public keys of the sender and recipient, the amount of the transaction, and the time of execution. These conditions must be met for the transaction to be executed successfully.

In Bitcoin, the transaction script is used to implement a variety of features such as multisignature transactions, time-locked transactions, and multi-party transactions. Multisignature transactions require more than one signature to spend the funds, while time-locked transactions require a specific period to pass before the transaction can be executed. The transaction script can also be used to implement smart contracts, which are self-executing contracts that automate the negotiation and execution of a contract agreement. Smart contracts use the transaction script to define the conditions under which the contract is executed.

One of the limitations of the transaction script is that it is limited to a set of predefined operations. This means that it cannot perform complex operations, such as accessing data from external sources or interacting with external systems. However, this limitation is intentional, as it helps to maintain the security and stability of the blockchain network.

The stack-based architecture in Bitcoin's scripting language plays a fundamental role in how transactions are executed on the blockchain. Here is a more detailed exploration of the stack-based nature.

Stack-based architecture:

- **Data storage:**
  - o Bitcoin's script operates on a data structure known as a stack. The stack is a **last-in, first-out (LIFO)** data structure where data elements are added or removed only from the top.
- **Script execution:**
  - o During the execution of a script, data elements are pushed onto the stack, and operations are performed using the top elements of the stack.
  - o Instructions in the script manipulate the stack by pushing or popping data elements, creating a dynamic and evolving structure.
- **Operations:**
  - o Script operations include arithmetic, comparison, logical, and conditional operations, each interacting with the stack.
  - o For example, the addition operation (**ADD**) would take the top two elements from the stack, add them, and push the result back onto the stack.
- **Simplicity and security:**
  - o The stack-based approach simplifies the scripting language, making it less prone to errors and vulnerabilities.

 - o The limited set of operations ensures that scripts are concise, reducing the potential for complex bugs that might compromise security.

A comparison with traditional languages are as follows:

- **No registers or memory:**
  - o Unlike traditional programming languages that use registers or memory for data storage and operations, Bitcoin's script relies solely on the stack.
  - o This minimalist approach aligns with Bitcoin's goal of simplicity and security.
- **Script evaluation:**
  - o Script evaluation involves sequentially processing instructions, pushing or popping data onto or from the stack based on the operation being executed.
  - o Traditional languages, by contrast, may use a combination of registers, memory, and a call stack for execution.
- **Security emphasis:**
  - o The stack-based architecture enhances security by minimizing the complexity of the scripting language.
  - o Security vulnerabilities related to memory access or unintended side effects are reduced, contributing to the robustness of Bitcoin's scripting system.
- **Transaction verification:**
  - o During the verification of transactions, nodes evaluate scripts by executing operations on the stack.
  - o The stack-based model ensures that only valid transactions, meeting the specified conditions, proceed to be added to the blockchain.

Understanding the stack-based architecture is crucial for developers, as it defines how scripts are processed and transactions are verified on the Bitcoin network. The simplicity of the stack-based approach aligns with Bitcoin's core principles, emphasizing security and reliability in the execution of smart contracts and transaction scripts.

Script address

The scripting language used in Bitcoin is called **script**, and it is a simple stack-based language that is used to define the conditions under which a transaction can be spent. The script language is designed to be flexible and powerful, and it can be used to create a wide range of transaction types, including multi-signature transactions, time-locked transactions, and more. Script addresses are created by combining a public key hash and a script. The public key hash is a unique identifier that is derived from a public key, and it is used to identify the recipient of a transaction. The script, on the other hand, is a set of conditions that must be met in order to spend the Bitcoins sent to the address. Script addresses can be created for a variety of different purposes, such as for multi-signature transactions, time-locked transactions, and more.

One of the most common types of script addresses is the **Pay-to-Public-Key-Hash (P2PKH)** address. This type of address is used to send Bitcoins to a recipient who has a public key that is associated with a particular hash. When someone sends Bitcoins to a P2PKH address, they are essentially locking the Bitcoins in a script that requires the recipient to provide a signature that matches their public key in order to spend them. This ensures that only the intended recipient can spend the Bitcoins, making it a secure way to send and receive Bitcoins.

Another type of script address is the **Pay-to-Script-Hash (P2SH) address.** P2SH addresses are used to send Bitcoins to a script rather than a public key hash. The script in this case is typically a multi-signature script that requires multiple signatures in order to spend the Bitcoins. P2SH addresses are commonly used for things like escrow services, where multiple parties must agree to release funds. This type of script address adds an extra layer of security and trust to the transaction.

Script addresses can also be used for more complex transaction types, such as time-locked transactions. In a time-locked transaction, the Bitcoins are locked in a script that requires a certain amount of time to pass before they can be spent. This type of transaction can be used for things like insurance policies or other contracts that require a certain amount of time to pass before funds can be released. Time-locked transactions can also be used for things like crowdfunding, where the funds are released only when a certain goal is met.

One of the key advantages of script addresses is their flexibility. They can be used to create a wide range of transaction types, which makes them a powerful tool for developers and users alike. However, they also come with some potential drawbacks. Since they are more complex than traditional addresses, they can be more difficult to use for beginners. Additionally, they can also be more expensive to use, as they require more space on the blockchain to store.

In conclusion, script addresses are an important part of the Bitcoin ecosystem. They allow users to perform a wide range of transaction types, and they provide a flexible and powerful tool for developers. While they may be more complex and expensive to use than traditional addresses, their benefits make them a valuable addition to the Bitcoin network. As Bitcoin continues to evolve and gain mainstream adoption, script addresses will play an increasingly important role in the future of digital finance.

Bitcoin mining

Bitcoin mining is a crucial component of the Bitcoin ecosystem, and it is the process through which new Bitcoins are created and transactions are confirmed on the blockchain. Mining is a competitive process that involves solving complex mathematical problems, and it is a key part of the Bitcoin network's security and stability. In this section, we will delve into the history of Bitcoin mining, how it works, the difficulties and troubles behind it, and how the mining difficulty is calculated.

Bitcoin mining is the critical process that involves adding new transactions to the blockchain, which serves as a public ledger of all Bitcoin transactions. The miners are the ones responsible for verifying and validating transactions and adding them to the blockchain. As compensation for their work, miners receive newly generated Bitcoins. The mining process involves solving complex mathematical problems, and the first miner to solve the problem receives Bitcoins as a reward.

The importance of mining cannot be overstated, as it is a crucial component that provides security and stability to the Bitcoin network. Mining ensures that transactions are confirmed and that new Bitcoins are created at a predictable rate, which helps to maintain the integrity of the network. Without mining, the Bitcoin network would be unable to function correctly, and transactions would not be processed and verified.

In recent years, Bitcoin mining has gained significant attention due to the increasing demand for the cryptocurrency. The popularity of Bitcoin has made mining more competitive and challenging. It requires advanced equipment and substantial computing power, which can be expensive and time-consuming to acquire. Despite these challenges, mining remains an essential and profitable activity for those willing to invest in the resources required.

Bitcoin mining has its roots in the early days of the cryptocurrency, and it has evolved significantly since its inception. In the early years, anyone with a computer and internet connection could mine Bitcoins. However, as the network grew more significant and more miners joined, the process became more challenging and required specialized hardware.

Mining difficulty is continually changing as the network's hash rate fluctuates. The hash rate is a measure of the computing power required to solve the mathematical problems necessary for mining. When the hash rate increases, mining difficulty also increases, making it more challenging to mine Bitcoins. Similarly, when the hash rate decreases, mining difficulty decreases, making mining easier.

The mining difficulty is calculated using a formula that takes into account the current hash rate and the amount of time it takes to solve a block. The Bitcoin network is designed to maintain a constant rate of block production, with a new block created roughly every ten minutes. To achieve this, the difficulty of mining adjusts automatically every 2016 blocks, which is approximately every two weeks.

Despite the benefits of mining, there are also some difficulties and troubles associated with the process. The high energy consumption required for mining has been a significant concern, with some estimates suggesting that Bitcoin mining consumes more electricity than some small countries. The environmental impact of mining has also been a point of criticism, with concerns raised about the carbon footprint of the mining process.

History of Bitcoin mining

Bitcoin mining was first introduced in 2009, when the Bitcoin network was created. At the time, mining was a relatively simple process that could be done using a personal computer or laptop. However, as the Bitcoin network grew and more people started mining, the difficulty of mining increased significantly.

In the early days of Bitcoin mining, miners could earn up to 50 Bitcoins per block. However, as the number of Bitcoins in circulation increased, the reward for mining a block decreased.

Today, miners are rewarded with 6.25 Bitcoins for each block they mine.

As the Bitcoin network has grown, so too has the complexity of mining. Today, mining requires specialized hardware and software, and it is a highly competitive process that is dominated by large mining operations located in areas with cheap electricity.

Working of bitcoin mining

Bitcoin mining is a complex process that involves solving complex mathematical problems. These problems are designed to be difficult to solve, and they require a significant amount of computational power to solve. Miners use specialized hardware called **application-specific integrated circuits (ASICs)** to solve these problems.

The first step in the mining process is to gather transactions into a block. Once a block of transactions has been assembled, miners compete to solve a mathematical problem. The problem is designed to be difficult to solve, and it requires miners to make many guesses before they find the correct answer.

When a miner solves the problem, they broadcast their solution to the network, and other miners check to make sure that the solution is correct. Once the solution has been verified, the miner who solved the problem is rewarded with Bitcoins.

The difficulties and troubles behind Bitcoin mining are as follows:

- Bitcoin mining is a complex and competitive process that comes with a number of difficulties and troubles. One of the biggest challenges facing miners is the cost of electricity. Mining requires a significant amount of energy, and the cost of electricity can eat into miners' profits.

- Another challenge facing miners is the complexity of the mining process. As the Bitcoin network has grown, the difficulty of mining has increased significantly, and it is now almost impossible for individual miners to compete with large mining operations.
- In addition to these challenges, Bitcoin mining also comes with environmental concerns. Mining requires a significant amount of energy, and this energy is often generated by burning fossil fuels. As a result, mining is often associated with high carbon emissions.

Environmental impact and energy consumption in Bitcoin mining:

- **Energy consumption**:
  - o Bitcoin mining involves solving complex mathematical puzzles to validate transactions and add new blocks to the blockchain.
  - o The **PoW** consensus mechanism, used by Bitcoin, requires miners to compete by solving these puzzles, which demands significant computational power.
  - o The energy consumption of Bitcoin mining is substantial, with estimates varying. It is often compared to the energy consumption of entire countries.
- **Carbon footprint**:
  - o The environmental impact of Bitcoin mining is largely attributed to the carbon footprint associated with electricity generation.
  - o Mining operations often rely on fossil fuels, contributing to greenhouse gas emissions.
- **Global comparisons**:
  - o Bitcoin's annual energy consumption has been likened to that of some small countries, raising concerns about its environmental sustainability.
- **Renewable energy integration**:
  - o Some mining operations aim to mitigate environmental impact by using renewable energy sources, such as solar or hydroelectric power. **China's Ban on Bitcoin Mining.**
- **Government crackdown**:
  - o China was a dominant player in the global Bitcoin mining industry, hosting a significant percentage of mining operations.
  - o In 2021, the Chinese government imposed a ban on cryptocurrency mining, citing environmental concerns and financial risks.

- **Mining exodus**:
    - o The ban led to a mass exodus of mining operations from China, impacting the global distribution of mining activities.
- **Increased electricity charges**:
    - o Some Chinese regions increased electricity charges for cryptocurrency mining, further discouraging these activities.
    - o The move aimed to address the strain on local power grids and reduce the environmental impact associated with mining.
- **Shift in global mining landscape**:
    - o The ban prompted miners to relocate to other countries with more favorable regulatory environments and access to cleaner energy sources.
    - o This shift contributed to a redistribution of the global Bitcoin mining landscape.

Impact on Bitcoin's environmental perception:

- **Debate on sustainability:** China's actions fueled the ongoing debate about the environmental sustainability of Bitcoin and its PoW consensus mechanism.
- **Calls for alternatives:** The environmental concerns have intensified calls for alternative consensus mechanisms, such as **proof-of-stake** (**PoS**), which is considered more energy efficient.
- **Industry innovation:** The challenges posed by the environmental impact have spurred innovations within the cryptocurrency industry to explore and implement greener technologies and consensus mechanisms.

Evolution of Bitcoin mining hardware:

- **CPU mining era;**
    - o In the early days of Bitcoin (around 2009), mining could be done using **Central Processing Units** (**CPUs**) commonly found in personal computers.
    - o CPUs were quickly outpaced by the increasing complexity of mining algorithms, making them inefficient and slow.
- **GPU mining era**:
    - o Miners transitioned to **graphics processing units** (**GPUs**) as they offered parallel processing capabilities, significantly boosting mining speed.
    - o GPU mining became the norm due to its improved efficiency over CPUs.
- **FPGA mining (Field-Programmable Gate Arrays)**:
    - o Miners then experimented with FPGAs, which allowed for more flexibility in programming and optimizing mining algorithms.

- FPGAs were more energy-efficient compared to GPUs but still faced competition from emerging technologies.

- **Application-Specific Integrated Circuits (ASIC) mining**:
  - The introduction of ASICs marked a significant shift in the mining landscape.
  - ASICs are custom-designed chips specifically tailored for Bitcoin mining.
  - ASICs surpassed the efficiency of previous hardware, offering unprecedented hashing power and energy efficiency.
  - This advancement made other mining hardware obsolete, concentrating mining power in the hands of those with access to ASICs.
- **ASIC dominance**:
  - Currently, ASICs dominate the Bitcoin mining industry. They are purpose built for hashing the SHA-256 algorithm used in Bitcoin mining.
  - ASICs are highly efficient in terms of both processing speed and energy consumption, but their centralized production and usage have raised concerns about the decentralization of mining power.
- **Hardware development timeline**:
  - **CPU era (2009-2010):** Bitcoin mining commenced with CPUs, providing the foundation for the network.
  - **GPU era (2010-2013):** Miners adopted GPUs, offering improved mining capabilities.
  - **FPGA era (2011-2013):** FPGAs provided a middle ground between GPUs and ASICs, with enhanced efficiency.
  - **ASIC era (2013-present):** ASICs revolutionized Bitcoin mining, dominating the landscape with unprecedented speed and efficiency.
- **Mining duration and halving events**:
  - Bitcoin undergoes a halving event approximately every four years, reducing the reward miners receive for successfully mining a block.
  - The reward started at 50 BTC per block and has halved several times, reaching 6.25 BTC per block as of the latest halving in 2020.
  - Mining duration is influenced by factors such as the mining hardware's efficiency, electricity costs, and the overall network hash rate.
- **Market dynamics**:
  - The Bitcoin mining hardware market is dynamic, with continuous innovation and improvements in efficiency.

- o Market trends are influenced by technological advancements, regulatory developments, and the overall health of the cryptocurrency ecosystem. In conclusion, the evolution of Bitcoin mining hardware reflects the industry's constant pursuit of efficiency and speed. From the early days of CPU mining to the current dominance of ASICs, the landscape has seen significant shifts. Ongoing innovations aim to address concerns related to centralization and energy consumption in the quest for a more sustainable and decentralized mining ecosystem.

Structure of a block

In the cryptocurrency world, blocks play a key role in the functioning of the blockchain network. A block is a collection of transactions that are bundled together and added to the blockchain. The basic structure of a block can be understood through *Figure 3.10:*

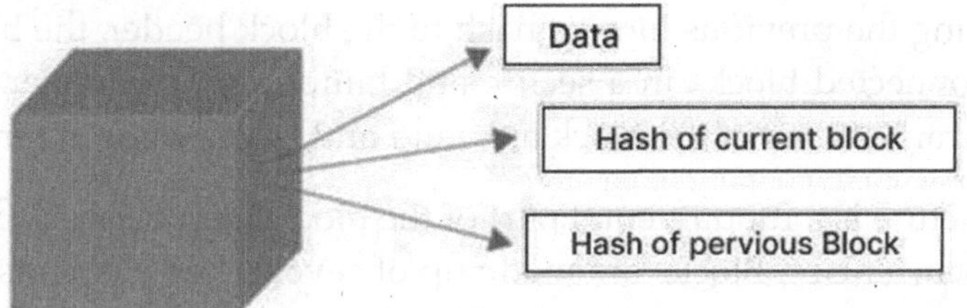

***Figure 3.10:** Basic structure of block*

A few takeaways regarding a block are as follows:

- A block refers to a large volume of trade that occurs at once.
- Exchanges typically define a block as more than 10,000 shares of stock or a trade that has a notional value in excess of $200,000.
- Block trades are sometimes done outside of the open markets to lessen the impact on the security's price.
- In order not to influence market prices, large block orders may be broken up into smaller orders and executed through different brokers to mask the true size.

The blocks have a specific structure that is important in maintaining the security and integrity of the network. The structure of a block can be broken down into several key elements. The first component is the block header, which contains information about the block, for example, B. Version number, previous block hash, timestamp and difficulty target. A block header is an 80-byte section that is always contained in a block.

Another element is the transaction counter, which determines the number of transactions in the block. This is followed by a list of the transactions themselves, which may vary in size and complexity depending on the blockchain network.

Another important element of the block is the Merkle tree, a mathematical structure used to verify the integrity of the transactions in the block. The Merkle tree is built by taking all transactions in a block and encrypting them individually. These hashes are then matched and shuffled again, repeating the process until only one hash remains. This final hash is known as the **Merkle root**, which is included in the block header.

The block structure also includes a nonce, which is a random number added to the block header to give the block hash a specific purpose. This goal is determined by the difficulty level of the network, which is regularly adjusted to ensure blocks are added to the blockchain at a constant rate.

All of these components are combined into a complete block, which is then added to the blockchain. Blocks are added to the blockchain in a process called mining, which involves solving complex mathematical problems to create new blocks.

The block structure is important for maintaining the security and integrity of the blockchain network. By adding the previous block's hash to the block header, the blockchain creates a chain of interconnected blocks in a secure and tamper-proof manner. The Merkle tree ensures that the transactions in the block are valid and have not been tampered with.

So, the block structure is a fundamental part of the blockchain network, including Bitcoin and other cryptocurrencies. Blocks are made up of several key elements, including block header, transaction counter, transaction list, Merkle tree, and nonce. By understanding the structure of the block, we can better assess the security and integrity of the entire blockchain network.

Block header

A block header is a crucial component that serves as the first line of defense against fraudulent or invalid transactions. The header of an Ethereum block contains different fields of metadata which are as follows:

- **Hash of the previous block:** Every block header gives information about the previous or parent block. This field contains the hash value of the previous block and this reference connects all the blocks. The size of this field is 32 bytes.
- **Version:** This field stores the version number to show software upgrades. The size of the version field is 4 bytes.
- **Difficulty:** The mining difficulty at the time of the block creation is stored in this field.

The concept of mining would be explained in the upcoming articles. Its size is 4 bytes.

- **Timestamp:** This field contains the time at which the block was created. The size of this field is 4 bytes.

- **Nonce:** A nonce is a value used during the mining of the block. This field's size is also 4 bytes.
- **Merkle tree root:** A Merkle tree is a structure obtained from hashing the transactional data of a block. The root of this tree is stored in the block header under this field. 32 bytes is the size of the Merkle tree root field.

Figure 3.11 visually represents the block header:

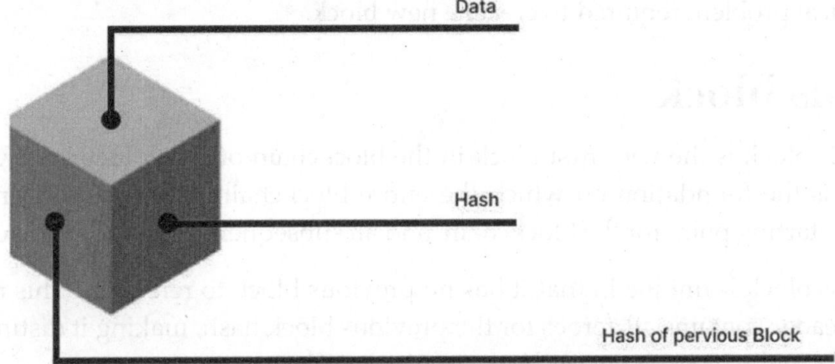

***Figure 3.11:** Block header*

The block header is a crucial component of the blockchain. It serves to identify and verify the contents of a particular block, and contains a range of information, including its size, version, timestamp, and other key details. The block header is simply **a piece of metadata** that is attached to a block of transactions, and includes various fields, each serving a specific purpose. These fields include the block version number, the previous block hash, the Merkle root hash, the timestamp, the target, and the nonce.

The block version number is used to identify the format of the block. As the Bitcoin protocol has evolved over time, new versions of the block format have been introduced, each including new fields and features to improve the security and reliability of the blockchain. The previous block hash serves as a unique identifier for the block that came before it. This hash is generated by taking the SHA-256 hash of the previous block's header, and it is used to link each block in the blockchain to the one that came before it.

The Merkle root hash is used to verify the contents of the block. It is generated by hashing together all of the transactions included in the block, using a special algorithm called a **Merkle tree**. The Merkle root hash provides a way to quickly and efficiently verify that all of the transactions in the block are valid and have not been tampered with.

The timestamp field is used to record the time at which the block was created. This timestamp is important for a range of reasons, including helping to prevent double-spending attacks and providing a way to track the evolution of the blockchain over time.

The target field is used to adjust the difficulty of mining new blocks on the Bitcoin network. This field is updated every 2016 blocks, or approximately every two weeks, and it is used to maintain a consistent rate of block creation.

Finally, the nonce field is used by miners to try and solve the mathematical puzzle required to create a new block. This field is essentially a random number that miners can change in order to try and find a hash that meets the target difficulty level. By changing the nonce repeatedly, miners are able to effectively brute-force their way through the complex mathematical problem required to create a new block.

Genesis block

The genesis block is the very first block in the blockchain of a cryptocurrency, including Bitcoin. It is the foundation on which the entire blockchain is built. The Genesis block serves as a starting point for the blockchain, and all subsequent blocks are built on top of it.

The genesis block is unique in that it has no previous block to reference. This means that its block header contains all zeroes for the previous block hash, making it distinct from all other blocks in the blockchain, as shown in *Figure 3.12:*

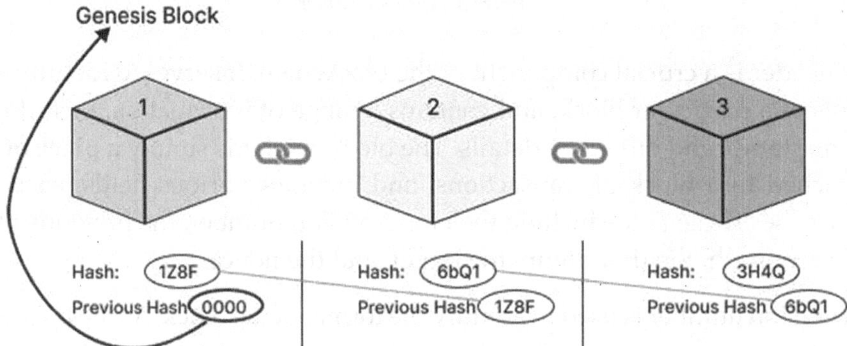

Figure 3.12: *Genesis block*

The creation of the genesis block was a significant milestone in the history of cryptocurrencies. It represented the birth of a new type of decentralized, peer-to-peer currency that operates independently of any central authority. The genesis block contains the first-ever transaction on the Bitcoin network, which was a reward of 50 Bitcoins that was given to the creator of the block, known as *Satoshi Nakamoto.*

The structure of the genesis block is similar to that of all other blocks in the blockchain. It contains a block header, which includes a version number, a timestamp, a reference to the previous block hash, which is all zeroes in the case of the genesis block, a Merkle root hash, and a nonce.

The Merkle root hash is a cryptographic hash of all the transactions in the block. This hash is used to ensure that the transactions in the block are valid and have not been tampered with. The nonce is a 32-bit value that is used in the mining process to find a valid hash for the block header.

Refer to *Figure 3.13* for the structure of the genesis block:

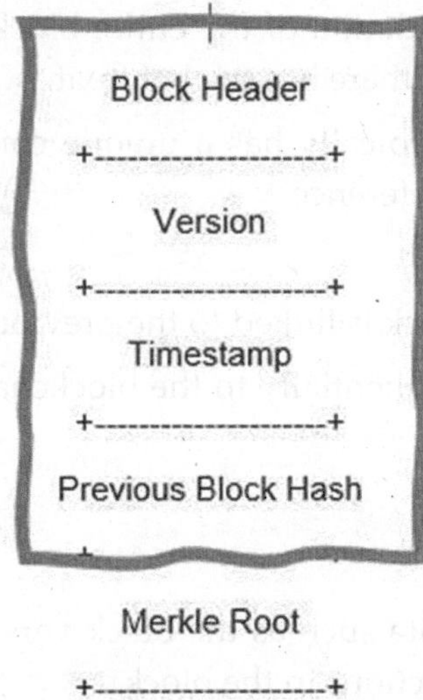

Figure 3.13: *Structure of the genesis block*

The creation of the genesis block was a key milestone in the development of cryptocurrencies, as it represented the birth of a new type of decentralized, peer-to-peer currency. The genesis block served as the starting point for the Bitcoin blockchain, and all subsequent blocks are built on top of it. Its structure is similar to that of all other blocks in the blockchain, containing a block header with various pieces of information, including a Merkle root hash and a nonce.

Linking of blocks

Linking of blocks refers to the process of connecting individual blocks of data within a blockchain network. Each block in a blockchain contains a set of transactions or data that are recorded in a secure and tamper-evident manner. These blocks are then linked together in a specific order, creating a chain of blocks or a blockchain. The linking of blocks in a blockchain is achieved through the use of cryptographic hashes. Each block in a blockchain network contains a unique hash value that is generated using a cryptographic algorithm. This hash value is based on the contents of the block and is unique to that block. The hash value is also used to link the current block to the previous block in the chain.

Bitcoin core node and API are fundamental aspects of the Bitcoin network that are crucial for users to understand.

Here is how a simple flow of the chronology of block order works:

- **Genesis block:**
  - The first block in the blockchain is called the genesis block.
  - It serves as the foundation of the entire blockchain and does not reference a previous block since there is none before it.
  - The genesis block typically has a unique coinbase transaction, containing a special message or reference.
- **Subsequent blocks:**
  - Each subsequent block is linked to the previous one, forming a chain.
  - Blocks are added sequentially to the blockchain through a process known as **mining.**
- **Block structure**:
  - **Block header**:
    - Includes metadata such as the block version, timestamp, and the Merkle root of all transactions in the block.
    - Contains a reference to the previous block's hash, creating a link between blocks.
    - The block header is hashed using the SHA-256 algorithm.
  - **Transactions**:
    - A block contains a list of transactions, including coinbase transactions that reward miners and regular transactions transferring value.
  - **Merkle tree:**
    - The Merkle tree structure is used to efficiently summarize and verify the transactions in a block.
    - Leaves of the tree represent individual transactions, and each non-leaf node is a hash of its children.
- **Mining process**:
  - Miners compete to solve a cryptographic puzzle by finding a specific nonce value that, when combined with the block header, produces a hash below a certain target.
  - The first miner to solve the puzzle broadcasts the solution to the network, and other nodes verify the validity of the solution.

- **Block validation**:
  - o Nodes on the network validate the block's transactions, ensuring they adhere to consensus rules.
  - o The block header's hash must be below the target to meet the PoW requirement.
- **Propagation**:
  - o Once a block is mined and validated, it is broadcasted to all nodes in the network.
  - o Nodes update their local copy of the blockchain, appending the new block.
- **Consensus mechanism**:
  - o The consensus mechanism ensures that all nodes in the network agree on the validity and order of blocks.
  - o In Bitcoin, the PoW mechanism secures the network and determines the miner who gets to add the next block.
- **Continuous cycle**:
  - o The process repeats for each subsequent block, with miners competing to find the next valid block and append it to the existing blockchain.
- **Blockchain growth**:
  - o As more blocks are added, the blockchain grows linearly, creating an immutable and sequential ledger of transactions.
- **Halving events**:
  - o Periodic halving events reduce the reward miners receive for successfully mining a block.
  - o These events occur approximately every four years, influencing the economic incentives and supply dynamics of the network.

Understanding the chronology of block order provides insights into the secure and decentralized nature of blockchain systems, emphasizing the role of mining, consensus mechanisms, and the continuous growth of the blockchain ledger.

Type of full nodes

There are two types of full nodes in the Bitcoin network: **pruned nodes** and **non-pruned nodes**. Pruned nodes only store a portion of the blockchain data, which reduces storage requirements but limits their ability to validate transactions independently and the non-pruned nodes store the entire blockchain, allowing them to validate transactions and blocks independently.

Bitcoin core application programming interface

Bitcoin core **application programming interface (API)** is a set of software interfaces that allows developers to interact with the Bitcoin network. This API provides access to various functionalities of the Bitcoin core software, including transaction creation, validation, and broadcasting. The API can be used to develop applications that interface with the Bitcoin network, such as wallets, exchanges, and other blockchain-related services.

Some of the key features of the Bitcoin core API include:

- **JSON-RPC interface:** The API uses a **Remote Procedure Call (RPC)** interface that allows remote access to the Bitcoin Core software. This interface uses the JSON format to communicate data between the Bitcoin Core node and other applications.
- **Security:** The Bitcoin Core API is designed with security in mind. It provides robust authentication mechanisms and encryption to ensure that the interactions between applications and the Bitcoin network are secure.
- **Customization**: The API allows developers to customize their interactions with the Bitcoin network. For example, developers can customize transaction fees, set up custom block filters, and customize network parameters.

Understanding Bitcoin core node and API is essential for anyone who wants to use, develop or interact with the Bitcoin network. Different types of full nodes provide different levels of validation and storage requirements. The Bitcoin core API is a powerful tool that provides developers with access to the Bitcoin network, and it has features like a JSON-RPC interface, robust security, and customization options.

Peer-to-peer network

Peer-to-peer (P2P) network architecture is a fundamental component of the Bitcoin and blockchain technology. A P2P network is a distributed network that allows nodes or peers to communicate directly with each other without the need for a centralized server. This can be represented through *Figure 3.14:*

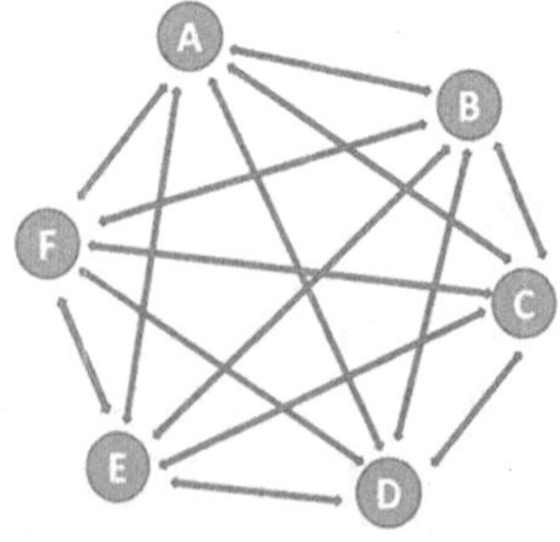

Figure 3.14: *Peer to peer network*

In a P2P network, every node acts as both a client and a server, which means that all nodes are equal and can initiate and respond to requests. *Figure 3.15* explains the working of nodes:

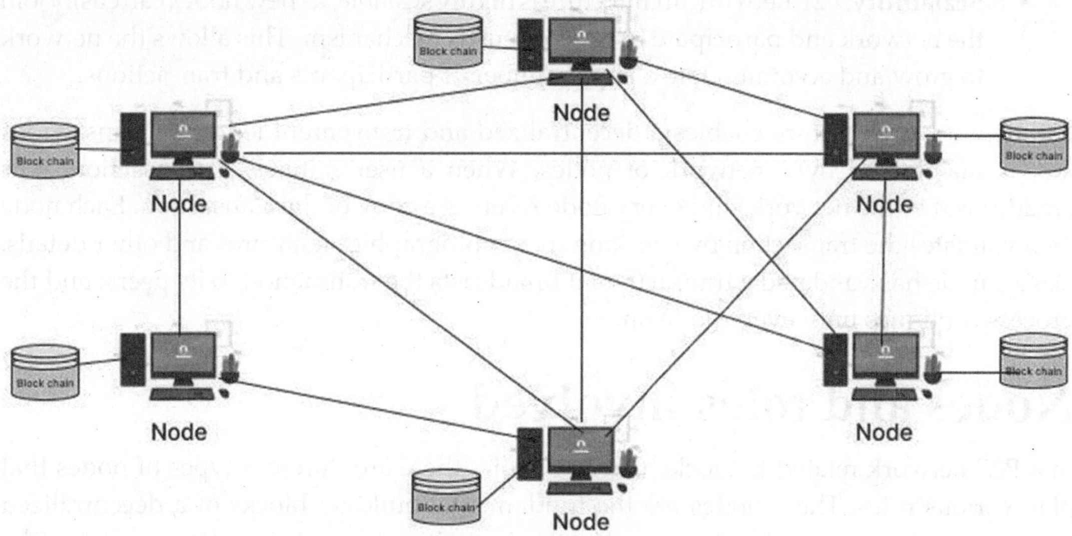

Figure 3.15: Functioning of nodes

The Bitcoin network is a decentralized P2P network that enables users to send and receive transactions without the need for a trusted intermediary or central authority.

In a P2P network, each node can act as both a client and a server, meaning it can initiate or respond to communication requests. This creates a network of nodes that can share resources and information with each other, without relying on a central server.

The following are some key characteristics of P2P network architecture in blockchain and Bitcoin:

- **Decentralization:** P2P network architecture is completely decentralized, meaning there is no single point of control or authority. Every node on the network is equal and has the same authority.
- **Consensus mechanism:** To ensure that transactions are verified and recorded in a secure and transparent manner, P2P network architecture uses a consensus mechanism. In Bitcoin, the consensus mechanism is PoW, which requires nodes to compete to solve complex mathematical problems to validate transactions.
- **Resilience:** P2P networks are resilient to attacks or failures as there is no central point of control or failure. This means that the network can continue to function even if some nodes go offline or become compromised.

- **Privacy and security:** P2P network architecture can provide high levels of privacy and security by encrypting communications between nodes and using public-key cryptography to ensure that transactions are secure.
- **Scalability:** P2P network architecture is highly scalable, as new nodes can easily join the network and participate in the consensus mechanism. This allows the network to grow and accommodate a large number of participants and transactions.

P2P network architecture enables a decentralized and transparent ledger of transactions that is maintained by a network of nodes. When a user initiates a transaction, it is broadcasted to the network, and every node receives a copy of the transaction. Each node then validates the transaction by checking the cryptographic signatures and other details. Once a node has validated a transaction, it broadcasts the transaction to its peers, and the process continues until every node on.

Nodes and roles involved

In a P2P network related to blockchain or Bitcoin, there are different types of nodes that play various roles. These nodes are the fundamental building blocks of a decentralized network and work together to maintain the integrity and security of the system. The various types of nodes are:

- **Full nodes:** Full nodes are the backbone of the blockchain network, responsible for verifying transactions and ensuring that the blockchain is kept up-to-date. These nodes keep a complete copy of the entire blockchain ledger, which allows them to validate transactions and blocks independently.
- **Mining nodes:** Mining nodes are a type of full node that participates in the process of adding new transactions to the blockchain. These nodes use powerful computing resources to compete with other miners to solve complex mathematical puzzles and add new blocks to the blockchain.
- **Light nodes:** Light nodes are a simplified version of full nodes, which only store a small subset of the blockchain's data. These nodes rely on full nodes to validate transactions and blocks, making them less resource-intensive but also less secure.
- **Super nodes:** Super nodes are a type of node that helps to facilitate communication between different nodes in the network. These nodes act as hubs that relay information between other nodes, improving the overall efficiency and speed of the network.

In addition to these node types, there are also various roles that nodes can play in a P2P network related to blockchain or Bitcoin, including:

- **Seed nodes:** Seed nodes are a type of super node that serves as an initial point of contact for new nodes joining the network. These nodes maintain a list of other nodes in the network and help new nodes establish connections with existing nodes.

- **Master nodes:** Master nodes are a type of full node that performs additional functions beyond basic transaction verification. These nodes help to secure the network by providing additional layers of security and privacy and are often used in specialized blockchain applications such as **decentralized finance (DeFi).**
- **Wallet nodes:** Wallet nodes are a type of light node that store private keys and allows users to send and receive cryptocurrency transactions. These nodes communicate with full nodes to validate transactions and update the user's account balance.

Overall, the different types of nodes and roles involved in a P2P network related to blockchain or Bitcoin work together to create a decentralized system that is secure, transparent, and efficient.

In a **peer-to-peer (P2P)** blockchain network, various types of nodes play distinct roles in maintaining network integrity and security. Full nodes serve as the backbone, independently validating transactions and ensuring the consistency of the entire blockchain. Mining nodes engage in competitive mining to add new blocks, contributing to the network's security through PoW consensus. Light nodes, a simplified version of full nodes, rely on their more resource-intensive counterparts for transaction validation. Super nodes act as efficient communication hubs, relaying information between nodes to enhance overall network speed. Seed nodes facilitate network growth, serving as initial contact points for new nodes. Master nodes, a type of full node, provide additional security and privacy layers, often employed in specialized blockchain applications like **DeFi**. Wallet nodes store private keys, allowing users to send and receive cryptocurrency, while communicating with full nodes for transaction validation. This intricate network of nodes collaboratively ensures decentralization, efficiency, and user accessibility in the blockchain ecosystem.

Let us look at the following table:

Feature	Full nodes	Mining nodes
Primary function	Validate and store a complete copy of the blockchain, ensuring its integrity.	Validate transactions and actively participate in the mining process to create new blocks.
Block creation	Do not engage in the block creation process.	Actively participate in mining to solve cryptographic puzzles, creating new blocks.
Consensus mechanism	Contribute to consensus by validating and relaying transactions	Contribute to consensus by solving PoW puzzles, adding new blocks to the blockchain.

Feature	Full nodes	Mining nodes
Reward system	Typically, full nodes do not receive direct rewards for their activities.	Rewarded with cryptocurrency (block rewards and transaction fees) for successfully mining new blocks.
Resource intensity	Less resource-intensive compared to mining nodes.	More resource-intensive due to the computational effort required for mining activities.
Blockchain storage	Store and maintain the entire blockchain ledger.	Store a copy of the blockchain but with a focus on recent transactions rather than the entire history.
Participation in mining	Do not actively participate in the mining process.	Actively engage in solving PoW puzzles to validate and add new blocks to the blockchain
Role in network security	Contribute to the overall security by validating and relaying transactions.	Contribute to security through the mining process and maintaining the integrity of the blockchain.

Table 3.2: *Difference between full nodes and mining nodes*

Incentive based engineering

Incentive-based engineering is an approach that aims to design and implement systems in a way that aligns the interests of its participants towards a common goal. In the context of blockchain and Bitcoin, this approach is used to incentivize network participants to behave honestly and contribute to the network's security and functionality. In a peer-to-peer network, nodes are incentivized to participate in the network and contribute their resources to maintain the network's integrity. In the case of Bitcoin, nodes that participate in the network and perform the computational work required to validate transactions and create new blocks are rewarded with newly minted Bitcoins and transaction fees.

The incentive-based approach is crucial to the security and sustainability of the Bitcoin network. Without adequate incentives, nodes may be less motivated to contribute their resources to the network, leading to a reduction in the overall security and functionality of the network.

Additionally, the incentive-based approach also helps prevent malicious behavior such as double-spending and 51% attacks. In a 51% attack, a malicious actor gains control of a majority of the network's computational power and can manipulate the network's transactions. However, such an attack is expensive and requires a significant amount of computational power, making it economically unfeasible for most participants. In total, this approach helps ensure the network's security and sustainability by aligning the interests of its participants towards a common goal.

Extended bitcoin network

The extended Bitcoin network refers to the ecosystem of various services, tools, and technologies built around the core Bitcoin network. These include wallets, exchanges, mining pools, and other third-party applications that use the Bitcoin network as their underlying infrastructure. The extended Bitcoin network comprises multiple layers, each with its unique set of actors and services. These layers can be visualized as a stack, with the Bitcoin protocol at the bottom, followed by the network layer, the transport layer, and the application layer at the top.

At the bottom of the stack is the Bitcoin protocol, which defines the rules and procedures for how transactions are processed, validated, and recorded on the blockchain. The Bitcoin protocol is maintained by the core developers of the Bitcoin network and is constantly evolving to improve the network's security, scalability, and functionality.

Above the protocol layer is the network layer, which consists of the nodes that form the Bitcoin network. Nodes are the computers that run the Bitcoin software and communicate with each other to validate transactions and propagate blocks. The network layer also includes mining pools, which are groups of miners that work together to mine blocks and earn rewards. The transport layer sits on top of the network layer and is responsible for transmitting data between nodes. This layer includes the Internet, as well as other communication protocols such as TCP/IP and UDP.

Finally, at the top of the stack is the application layer, which includes the various services and applications that use the Bitcoin network. These include Bitcoin wallets, which allow users to store and manage their Bitcoin holdings, as well as exchanges, which enable users to buy and sell Bitcoin with fiat currencies or other cryptocurrencies.

Other applications and services that use the Bitcoin network include payment processors, merchant services, and blockchain explorers, which provide information about the status of transactions and the state of the blockchain. The extended Bitcoin network is decentralized, meaning that no single entity controls it. Instead, it is made up of a diverse set of actors and organizations that contribute to its growth and development. This decentralization is one of the key features of the Bitcoin network, as it makes it more resilient to attacks and provides greater security for users.

Bitcoin relay network

The Bitcoin relay network is a network of computers that are specifically designed to facilitate the transfer of data between different nodes in the Bitcoin network. It is a peer-to-peer network that helps to reduce the amount of time and resources required to transfer data between nodes, improving the overall efficiency of the Bitcoin network.

Following are some important points to know about the Bitcoin relay network:

- **Purpose:** The primary purpose of the Bitcoin relay network is to improve the speed and efficiency of transaction propagation within the Bitcoin network. By using specialized nodes and protocols, the relay network can quickly and securely relay transactions and blocks between different nodes in the network.
- **Node types:** There are two types of nodes that participate in the Bitcoin relay network: regular nodes and relay nodes. Regular nodes are simply nodes that participate in the standard Bitcoin network, while relay nodes are specialized nodes that are designed to participate in the relay network specifically.
- **Protocol:** The Bitcoin relay network uses a specialized protocol known as the **FIBRE protocol**. This protocol is designed to facilitate high-speed data transfer between different nodes in the network, and it is optimized for low latency and high throughput.
- **Benefits:** One of the main benefits of the Bitcoin relay network is that it can help to reduce the amount of time required for transactions to be confirmed. By improving the speed and efficiency of transaction propagation, the relay network can help to reduce the risk of double-spending and other types of fraud within the Bitcoin network.
- **Security:** The Bitcoin relay network is designed to be secure and resistant to attacks. It uses a variety of security measures to protect against malicious nodes and other types of attacks, including encryption, authentication, and reputation systems.

Overall, the Bitcoin relay network plays an important role in the functioning of the Bitcoin network. By improving the speed and efficiency of transaction propagation, it helps to ensure that the Bitcoin network remains secure and reliable.

Network discovery

Network discovery is the process of discovering and connecting to peers in a peer-to-peer network, such as the Bitcoin network. In the context of Bitcoin, network discovery is an essential part of the protocol as it allows nodes to find and connect to each other, enabling the network to function as a decentralized system. The network discovery process in

Bitcoin is initiated when a node joins the network. The node sends out a message to a set of pre-defined seed nodes that it knows about, requesting a list of other nodes that are currently active on the network. The seed nodes respond with a list of IP addresses of other nodes that they know about, allowing the new node to start connecting to them.

Once a node has connected to a few other nodes on the network, it can start to exchange information with them, such as transactions and blocks. The node can also ask the other nodes for more information about the network, such as the current difficulty level and the latest block height.

One of the challenges of network discovery in Bitcoin is that it needs to be resistant to attacks and malicious behavior. For example, an attacker could attempt to flood the network with fake IP addresses or nodes, which would disrupt the network and prevent nodes from discovering each other. To address this, Bitcoin uses a variety of techniques to ensure that the network discovery process is reliable and secure.

One such technique is the use of DNS seeds, which are DNS servers that are run by trusted parties and contain lists of IP addresses of active nodes on the network. Nodes can query the DNS seeds to get a list of initial nodes to connect to, which helps to bootstrap the network discovery process.

Another technique used in Bitcoin to ensure reliable network discovery, is the use of peer banning. Nodes can ban other nodes that are behaving maliciously or attempting to disrupt the network, preventing them from connecting to the node in the future.

Full node

A full node is a computer program that validates transactions and blocks and maintains a copy of the entire blockchain network. Full nodes play a critical role in the decentralized architecture of the Bitcoin network by enforcing the consensus rules and relaying transactions and blocks to other nodes in the network. To become a full node, a user must download and run the Bitcoin core software, which is the reference implementation of the Bitcoin protocol. Once a user has downloaded and installed the software, the full node will download and verify the entire blockchain, which is a record of all Bitcoin transactions that have ever occurred.

By running a full node, users can independently verify the validity of their own transactions and the transactions of others on the network. This means that they do not need to trust any third-party service providers or intermediaries, which is one of the core principles of the Bitcoin network. Full nodes also serve as a backbone for the Bitcoin network by relaying transactions and blocks to other nodes in the network. By doing so, they help to ensure that all nodes in the network have access to the latest transactions and blocks, which helps to prevent double-spending and other types of fraud.

Additionally, full nodes can participate in the process of mining new blocks, which involves solving complex mathematical problems to validate transactions and add them to the blockchain. However, mining requires specialized hardware and significant computing power, so it is not feasible for most individual users. Full nodes are a critical component of the decentralized architecture of the Bitcoin network. By running a full node, users can independently verify the validity of transactions and blocks, relay transactions and blocks to other nodes in the network and participate in the process of mining new blocks.

Exchange network

An **exchange inventory** specifically refers to the list of transactions and blocks that a node has received from other nodes and is willing to share with them in return. When a node receives a request for a specific item, it can respond with the appropriate data from its exchange inventory.

The exchange inventory plays an important role in maintaining the integrity and efficiency of the Bitcoin network. By sharing information about transactions and blocks with each other, nodes can verify the validity of the data and ensure that all nodes have a consistent view of the blockchain. This helps to prevent double-spending and other malicious activity. Furthermore, by maintaining an up-to-date exchange inventory, nodes can reduce the amount of unnecessary data transfer on the network. If a node knows that another node already has a certain transaction or block, it does not need to request that data again, which can save time and bandwidth.

Overall, the exchange inventory is a key component of the Bitcoin peer-to-peer network, allowing nodes to efficiently share information and maintain the security and consistency of the blockchain.

In a peer-to-peer network like Bitcoin, the exchange inventory plays a crucial role in enhancing network efficiency and maintaining the integrity of the blockchain. When a node maintains an exchange inventory, it essentially keeps a record of the transactions and blocks it has received from other nodes and is willing to share with them in return. The following points should be considered for efficiency enhancement:

- **Preventing redundant data transfer:** The exchange inventory helps reduce unnecessary data transfer on the network. If node A knows that node B already possesses a specific transaction or block, node A does not need to request that data again. This optimization saves both time and bandwidth by preventing redundant transmission of information.
- **Consistent blockchain view:** By sharing information about transactions and blocks, nodes collectively work towards maintaining a consistent view of the

blockchain. This ensures that all nodes are operating with the same dataset, preventing discrepancies and inconsistencies in the blockchain's history.

Nodes communication

Nodes maintain a shared understanding of each other's inventories through a process often associated with the gossip protocol. The gossip protocol is a communication mechanism where nodes propagate information across the network. Let us look at how it works:

- **Node requests:** When a node, let us say Node A, needs information about a specific block or transaction, it sends a request to its connected peers, including Node B.
- **Response from node B:** Node B responds with the requested data if it has it in its inventory. This response includes the relevant block or transaction details.
- **Inventory announcements:** Additionally, nodes periodically announce their current inventories to their peers. This announcement includes a list of blocks and transactions they possess.
- **Peer-to-peer communication:** Nodes communicate with each other, sharing their inventories and responding to requests. This creates a dynamic and updated network where nodes can learn about each other's inventories over time.

By leveraging the gossip protocol, nodes continuously update their knowledge of the network's state, making informed decisions about data exchange and reducing redundancy.

Simplified payment verification

Simplified payment verification (SPV) is a type of lightweight node in the Bitcoin network. Unlike a full node that stores a complete copy of the blockchain, an SPV node only stores a subset of the blockchain necessary to verify transactions relevant to the node's own wallet.

An SPV node does not need to download the entire blockchain to function, which makes it more efficient and less resource-intensive than a full node. Instead, it relies on block headers and a Merkle tree to validate transactions. The Merkle tree provides a cryptographic proof that a specific transaction is included in a specific block in the blockchain.

Salient features of an SPV node are:

- **Lightweight:** SPV nodes are lightweight nodes, as they only store a subset of the blockchain.
- **Fast sync:** SPV nodes synchronize with the network quickly, as they only download block headers instead of the entire blockchain.
- **Reduced storage requirement:** SPV nodes require significantly less storage space than full nodes.

- **Limited trust model:** SPV nodes trust full nodes to provide accurate information about the blockchain, as they do not store the entire blockchain themselves.
- **Improved privacy:** Since SPV nodes do not store the entire blockchain, they do not have access to all the transaction data, which can improve privacy.
    - o **Mobile compatibility:** SPV nodes are often used in mobile wallets, as they do not require as much storage or processing power as full nodes.

SPV nodes and privacy

SPV nodes are lightweight nodes in the Bitcoin network that do not store the entire blockchain. Instead, they only download and store the block headers, which contain a summary of transactions in each block. SPV nodes use this information to verify the authenticity of transactions without downloading the entire blockchain.

In terms of privacy, SPV nodes provide a level of anonymity because they do not reveal the user's transaction history. However, since they do not download the entire blockchain, they rely on other nodes to provide transaction information. This means that the user's privacy is only as strong as the privacy of the nodes they connect to.

One potential privacy concern with SPV nodes is that they rely on a technique called **bloom filters** to request transaction information from full nodes. Bloom filters are probabilistic data structures that allow SPV nodes to request a subset of transactions from full nodes without revealing which specific transactions they are interested in. However, they are not perfect and there is a risk that a determined attacker could use them to de-anonymize SPV users.

Another potential privacy concern is that SPV nodes can be targeted by **Sybil attacks**, where an attacker creates many fake nodes to manipulate the information provided to the SPV node. This could potentially be used to link a user's transactions together and compromise their anonymity.

Transaction pool

A transaction pool, also known as a **mempool**, is a list of unconfirmed transactions that have been broadcasted to the Bitcoin network but have not yet been added to a block by a miner.

Think of the transaction pool as a waiting room for transactions. When you send Bitcoin to someone, your transaction is first broadcasted to the network and added to the mempool. Miners then select transactions from the pool and add them to the next block they mine. However, not all transactions can fit into a single block, so transactions with higher transaction fees tend to get prioritized by miners. To further explain this with an analogy, imagine a busy restaurant with a queue of customers waiting to be seated. Customers arrive and join the queue, and when a table becomes available, the next customer in the queue is seated. However, if the restaurant is too busy and there are not enough tables available, some customers may have to wait longer than others. In the same way, transactions are added to the mempool and wait to be included in the next block. Transactions with higher transaction fees are prioritized, like customers who have made a reservation and are seated first.

The transaction pool is important because it allows nodes to validate transactions and ensure they comply with the network's rules before they are included in a block. It also helps to prevent double-spending by ensuring that a Bitcoin cannot be spent twice. Additionally, transactions can be removed from the pool after a certain period of time if they are not added to a block, which helps to prevent spam attacks on the network.

Blockchain fork

A blockchain fork is a split that occurs when the blockchain network is divided into two separate chains due to conflicting versions of the software. This results in two independent blockchain networks with different transaction histories.

This can happen when some nodes on the network have different versions of the blockchain software and are unable to agree on which transactions are valid. For example, let us say that there are two miners on the blockchain network, Miner A and Miner B. They both work on adding new blocks to the blockchain, but they have different versions of the software. Miner A adds a new block to the blockchain, but Miner B rejects it because it does not meet the requirements of their version of the software. This causes a split in the blockchain network, with some nodes following Miner A's version of the blockchain and others following Miner B's version.

This split results in two separate chains with different transaction histories. Each chain is now its own separate blockchain network, and they will continue to operate independently of each other. This is known as a **fork** in the blockchain.

There are two types of blockchain forks: **soft forks** and **hard forks**. Soft forks are changes to the blockchain that are backward-compatible, meaning that nodes that have not updated to the new software can still participate in the network. Hard forks, on the other hand, are changes to the blockchain that are not backward-compatible, meaning that nodes that have not updated to the new software will not be able to participate in the network.

Bitcoin testnet

Bitcoin testnet is a network that runs in parallel with the main Bitcoin network and is specifically designed for testing and experimentation purposes. It is essentially a copy of the main network with a few key differences that make it distinct.

One of the main differences is that testnet Bitcoins have no value and can be obtained for free from various sources, including **testnet faucets**. This means that developers and users can experiment with Bitcoin transactions without having to use real Bitcoins, which could be risky and expensive. Another important difference is that testnet blocks are not added to the main Bitcoin blockchain. This means that any transactions or blocks created on testnet do not affect the actual Bitcoin network and cannot be used to spend or receive real Bitcoins.

Testnet also has a different network identifier and a separate set of DNS seeds, which means that it operates as a completely separate network from the main Bitcoin network. This ensures that any testing or experimentation done on testnet does not interfere with the main network.

For example, let us say a developer wants to test a new Bitcoin application or feature. They can use testnet to run simulations and experiments without risking any real Bitcoins. They can create transactions, mine blocks, and test the application's functionality in a safe and controlled environment. Once the testing is complete and the application is ready to be deployed, the developer can switch to the main network and use real Bitcoins.

Basics of Bitcoin forensic

Bitcoin forensic analysis is a process of examining transactions on the Bitcoin network to identify patterns or evidence of illicit activities such as money laundering or fraud. One aspect of this analysis involves the examination of Bitcoin addresses and wallets.

A Bitcoin address is a unique identifier that represents the location of Bitcoin on the blockchain. It consists of a string of alphanumeric characters and can be used to receive and send Bitcoin. A Bitcoin wallet, on the other hand, is a software program that stores private keys which are necessary for accessing Bitcoin stored in a particular address.

One way to analyze a Bitcoin address is by examining its transaction history. By looking at the inputs and outputs of the address, it is possible to determine the flow of Bitcoin in and out of the address. This information can be used to identify patterns or anomalies that could be indicative of illicit activity.

For example, if an address has received large amounts of Bitcoin from multiple sources and then suddenly sends out all of its Bitcoin to a single address, this could be a sign of money laundering. Similarly, if an address is receiving Bitcoin from known fraudulent sources, this could be evidence of involvement in fraudulent activities.

Another aspect of Bitcoin forensic analysis involves examining Bitcoin wallets. This can be done by analyzing the metadata associated with a particular wallet, such as the creation date, the number of transactions associated with the wallet, and the types of transactions. This information can be used to identify the owner of the wallet and potentially link it to other addresses or transactions.

For example, if a particular wallet is associated with multiple addresses that have been involved in illicit activities, it is possible that the owner of the wallet is also involved in these activities.

Clustering of address

Clustering is a technique used in Bitcoin and blockchain forensics to identify and group together addresses that are controlled by the same entity. This technique involves analyzing transactions on the blockchain to determine the flow of funds between different addresses.

When a Bitcoin transaction is made, it typically involves multiple inputs and outputs. The inputs are the addresses from which the funds are being spent, and the outputs are the addresses to which the funds are being sent. By analyzing the inputs and outputs of transactions, it is possible to identify patterns of behavior that can help to identify which addresses are controlled by the same entity.

For example, if a transaction involves multiple inputs that are all controlled by the same address, it is likely that the owner of that address is consolidating their funds. On the other hand, if a transaction involves multiple outputs that are all controlled by the same address, it is likely that the owner of that address is sending funds to different destinations.

Once clusters of addresses have been identified, it is possible to perform further analysis to try to identify the real-world identity of the owner of those addresses. This may involve looking for clues such as the IP addresses associated with transactions or analyzing the timing and frequency of transactions.

However, it is important to note that clustering alone does not necessarily mean that the addresses are all controlled by the same person or entity. There may be cases where multiple people or entities use the same address for different purposes, or where an address is controlled by multiple parties.

While clustering addresses in Bitcoin and blockchain forensics can provide valuable insights into the flow of funds and potential connections between addresses, it has certain disadvantages and limitations:

- **Privacy concerns:** Clustering poses a significant privacy risk as it can potentially reveal the financial activities and connections of users. Individuals may prefer to keep their financial transactions private, and clustering undermines this privacy.
- **False positives:** The technique of clustering may lead to false positives, where addresses are grouped together incorrectly. This can happen when multiple users or entities use the same address for legitimate and unrelated transactions, creating misleading connections.
- **Shared wallets and services:** Clustering might incorrectly associate addresses used by shared wallets, exchanges, or other services. Many users interact with cryptocurrencies through third-party services, and addresses belonging to these services can be erroneously linked.
- **CoinJoins and mixing services:** Privacy-enhancing techniques, such as CoinJoins and mixing services, deliberately aim to obfuscate the connection between input and output addresses. Clustering may struggle to accurately identify addresses involved in such privacy-focused transactions.

Conclusion

The chapter tries to explore and highlight the profound impact of Bitcoin on the financial landscape and technological innovation. In recent years, Bitcoin has transcended conventional financial spheres. Moreover, despite facing challenges like scalability issues, security concerns, and regulatory uncertainties, Bitcoin has continued shaping the future of finance, digital currencies, and decentralization. In the next chapter, you will learn about Ethereum, a permissionless blockchain.

The chapter will explore the significance of Ethereum in the blockchain world. Topics like EVM, gas, Ethereum Wallet, and more are covered in the upcoming chapter.

Questions and answers

1. **What is Bitcoin, and how does it differ from traditional currencies?**

   Ans.: Bitcoin is a decentralized digital currency based on blockchain technology. It operates on a peer-to-peer network without the need for intermediaries like banks and other financial institutions. Bitcoin exists purely in a digital form and is free from any central authority or government.

2. **Who created Bitcoin and why?**

   Ans.: Bitcoin was created by an individual or group with the pseudonym of *Satoshi Nakamoto* in 2009. The real identity of *Satoshi Nakamoto* is still a mystery. It is aimed at providing an alternative to traditional banking systems.

3. **What is the process of creating new Bitcoins?**

   Ans.: New Bitcoins are created as rewards for miners who add computing power to validate and verify transactions on the network. Bitcoin mining means solving complex mathematical problems using specialized hardware and adding new transactions to the blockchain.

4. **What is the Bitcoin relay network?**

   Ans.: The Bitcoin relay network is an additional layer in the Bitcoin ecosystem. It facilitates the rapid propagation of transactions and blocks across nodes. It is a network of specialized nodes that are strategically positioned to relay transaction data more efficiently than the standard peer-to-peer network.

5. **What is the importance of Bitcoin forensic analysis?**

   Ans.: Bitcoin forensic analysis consists of several investigative techniques to interpret transactional data on the network. It assists cybersecurity firms and law enforcement agencies in tracking illicit activities, such as fraud and money laundering.

Multiple choice questions

1. **What is the maximum supply cap of Bitcoins that can ever exist?**
   a. 10 million
   b. 21 million
   c. 50 million
   d. Unlimited

2. **What process adds new transactions to the blockchain by solving complex mathematical puzzles?**
   a. Hashing
   b. Staking
   c. Mining
   d. Minting

3. **Which type of node stores the entire Bitcoin blockchain and independently validates transactions?**
   a. Mining node
   b. Light node
   c. SPV node
   d. Full node

4. **What is the primary difference between the Bitcoin mainnet and the testnet?**
   a. The testnet uses a different blockchain protocol than the mainnet.
   b. Testnet Bitcoins have no value and can be obtained freely, while mainnet Bitcoins have monetary value.
   c. Testnet transactions cannot be validated by miners, unlike the mainnet.
   d. The testnet operates at a faster transaction speed compared to the mainnet.
5. **Which term describes a blockchain fork causing an incompatibility between older and newer versions of the software?**
   a. Hard fork
   b. Soft fork
   c. Merge fork
   d. Temporary fork

Answers

1. b
2. c
3. d
4. b
5. a

Join our book's Discord space

Join the book's Discord Workspace for Latest updates, Offers, Tech happenings around the world, New Release and Sessions with the Authors:

https://discord.bpbonline.com

Chapter 4
Permissionless Blockchain: Ethereum

Introduction

In the blockchain world, Ethereum has emerged as a pioneering development that has redefined the sphere of decentralized technologies. It has shot to fame and recognition due to its groundbreaking usability. Ethereum has expanded the capabilities of blockchain technology beyond only financial transactions. It has been the primary force behind the rollout of revolutionary developments like smart contracts and decentralized applications.

This chapter will delve deeper into the concepts and workings of Ethereum. From the **Ethereum virtual machine** (**EVM**) to the ever-evolving upgrades like **Ethereum 2.0**. The chapter will also cover all the aspects related to this disruptive technology. It aims to provide a comprehensive understanding of Ethereum's architecture and its impact on the blockchain world and the future of decentralized applications.

Structure

This chapter includes the following topics:

- Introducing to Ethereum
- Understanding Ethereum 1.0 and 2.0
- Beacon Chain

- The shard Chains
- Ethereum virtual machine
- Smart contracts and gas
- Comparing Bitcoin and Ethereum
- Types of accounts in Ethereum
- Contract transactions on Ethereum
- Smart contracts and Solidity
- Basics of Solidity
- Introduction to MetaMask
- Truffle
- Remix and test networks

Objectives

The objective of this chapter is to provide a comprehensive understanding of the Ethereum Blockchain. It will provide a detailed explanation of Ethereum's core technology and its upgrades, usability, and future prospects. Elucidating these topics, the chapter will establish the significance of Ethereum in the blockchain space. By the end of the chapter, readers will have a sound understanding of Ethereum and its potential to disrupt various sectors through decentralized applications.

Introducing Ethereum

In the vast landscape of digital currencies, there exists a remarkable innovation known as **Ethereum**. As a decentralized, open-source blockchain platform, Ethereum has revolutionized the way we envision transactions, contracts, and applications in the digital age. This section aims to provide a comprehensive understanding of Ethereum, exploring its fundamental concepts, real-world applications, development ecosystem, challenges, and future directions.

At its core, Ethereum is a decentralized, open-source blockchain platform that facilitates peer-to-peer transactions and enables the creation of smart contracts and **decentralized applications (dApps)**. Unlike traditional centralized systems, Ethereum empowers individuals by eliminating intermediaries, such as banks or governments, fostering a transparent and inclusive ecosystem. Ethereum's foundation lies in blockchain technology, a decentralized ledger where transactions are recorded and secured across multiple nodes. This technology ensures transparency, immutability, and security, as each transaction is verified by the network consensus. By removing the need for trust in a central authority,

Ethereum enables secure and tamper-proof digital transactions.

Some major characteristics of Ethereum are as follows:

- **Immutability**: Ethereum's immutability ensures data permanence on the blockchain.
- **Transparency**: Ethereum's transparency allows open scrutiny of all transactions.
- **Security**: Ethereum's security relies on cryptographic techniques and decentralized consensus.
- **Decentralization**: Ethereum's decentralization removes single points of control.
- **Programmability**: Ethereum's programmability allows self-executing smart contracts.
- **Censorship resistance**: Ethereum's censorship resistance prevents external control over transactions.
- **Tokenization**: Ethereum's tokenization creates digital tokens representing various real world and digital assets.

Turing completeness

Ethereum brings Turing completeness to the blockchains which made it unique to Bitcoin. Turing completeness is a concept derived from the work of *Alan Turing*, a renowned British mathematician and computer scientist. In simple terms, a system or language is considered Turing complete if it can simulate a universal Turing machine. A universal Turing machine is a theoretical model of a computing machine that can simulate the behavior of any other Turing machine. It can perform any computation that can be described algorithmically.

The EVM, as the runtime environment for executing smart contracts on the Ethereum blockchain, achieves Turing completeness. This means that any computation that can be expressed algorithmically can be executed within the EVM. Smart contracts written in Ethereum's programming language, Solidity, can contain loops, conditionals, and other constructs that enable complex computations and decision-making processes. The EVM's Turing completeness empowers developers to create sophisticated and versatile applications on the Ethereum blockchain.

Let us now understand a few closely related topics:

- **EVM**: To execute smart contracts, Ethereum utilizes the EVM. Acting as a runtime environment, the EVM ensures compatibility and consistency across different nodes on the Ethereum network. It executes the code of smart contracts and manages the state of the Ethereum blockchain, guaranteeing reliable and uniform results across the network.

- **Ether (ETH) and gas**: ETH serves as the native cryptocurrency of the Ethereum network. It powers transactions, executes smart contracts, and incentivizes participants. Additionally, the concept of gas comes into play, where users pay a fee in Ether to perform operations on the Ethereum network. This fee ensures the proper allocation of network resources and prevents misuse.

Use cases and real-world applications

Some use cases and real-world applications of Ethereum are as follows:

- **Decentralized finance (DeFi)**: Enabling financial services like lending, borrowing, and trading without intermediaries.
- **dApps**: Powering applications across sectors such as supply chain, gaming, identity verification, and asset tokenization.
- **Smart contracts**: Facilitating automated agreements, reducing the need for intermediaries in various transactions.
- **Tokenization of Assets**: Representing real-world assets digitally, improving liquidity and accessibility.
- **Supply chain management**: Enhancing transparency and traceability in supply chains through decentralized ledgers.
- **Gaming and virtual assets**: Enabling ownership and trade of in-game assets securely.
- **Identity Verification**: Providing secure and decentralized methods for identity verification.
- **Content monetization**: Allowing creators to monetize content directly without intermediaries.
- **Immutable record keeping**: Ensuring data on the blockchain remains tamper-resistant and secure.
- **Decentralized autonomous organizations (DAOs)**: Creating and managing organizations without a central authority and so on.

Understanding Ethereum 1.0 and 2.0

In the fascinating world of blockchain technology, Ethereum has emerged as a groundbreaking platform with the potential to revolutionize various industries. Ethereum 1.0, also known as the Eth1.0 or the Ethereum Mainnet, has already made significant strides in enabling dApps and smart contracts. However, as the ecosystem evolved and encountered challenges, the need for Ethereum 2.0, or Eth2, became apparent.

Ethereum 1.0: Creating decentralized ecosystems

Ethereum 1.0, the initial version of the Ethereum network, introduced a paradigm shift by enabling the development and execution of smart contracts. Smart contracts are self-executing agreements written in code, which automatically execute when predefined conditions are met. Think of them as digital agreements that automatically trigger and execute actions when predefined conditions are met. Let us consider a scenario where you wish to sell your car to a friend. Instead of navigating a protracted process involving lawyers and paperwork, you can create a smart contract on Ethereum. This contract would encapsulate the transaction details, such as the car's price and the sale date. Once the specified conditions are fulfilled, the smart contract autonomously executes, transferring car ownership to your friend. It is akin to having a virtual intermediary that ensures adherence to the agreed-upon terms.

This capability opened up a world of possibilities, allowing developers to build decentralized applications and tokenized ecosystems on top of the Ethereum blockchain. One of the most prominent use cases of Ethereum 1.0 is **DeFi**. DeFi applications leverage smart contracts to create financial instruments such as lending and borrowing platforms, decentralized exchanges, and yield farming protocols. These applications provide users with access to financial services without relying on traditional intermediaries like banks. Smart contracts on Ethereum 1.0 have been instrumental in various real-world use cases. For instance, consider a crowdfunding scenario where an entrepreneur seeks financial support for a new project. With Ethereum 1.0, the entrepreneur can create a smart contract that specifies the funding goal, rules for participation, and the release of funds once the goal is met. Participants can contribute **Ether (ETH)** to the smart contract, and if the funding goal is reached within the specified timeframe, the funds are automatically released to the entrepreneur. This eliminates the need for intermediaries, such as banks or crowdfunding platforms, streamlining the process and ensuring transparency.

Besides, Ethereum offers a diverse range of real-world applications that have the potential to revolutionize various industries.

A noteworthy example is the utility of NFT's are unique digital assets that represent ownership of items such as art, music, or even virtual real estate. Let us imagine you are an artist who has crafted a stunning digital artwork. Instead of relying on traditional galleries or agents to sell your work, you can create an NFT on Ethereum. This NFT serves as a digital certificate of ownership, validating the uniqueness and authenticity of your artwork. Collectors can bid on your NFT, and when it is sold, the transaction is immutably recorded on the Ethereum blockchain, guaranteeing the provenance and value of your creation.

Beyond the realms of finance and art, Ethereum possesses the capacity to transform numerous other industries. It can be employed for supply chain management, guaranteeing transparency and authenticity in the movement of goods. Voting systems can be fortified with Ethereum, ensuring heightened security and invulnerability to manipulation. Additionally, Ethereum facilitates the development of decentralized applications, commonly known as dApps, that operate on its blockchain. These dApps can encompass an array of activities, ranging from games and social networks to prediction markets and decentralized storage solutions.

However, Ethereum 1.0 faced challenges in terms of scalability and efficiency. As the popularity of Ethereum grew, so did the demand for transactions and computational resources. The limited scalability of Ethereum 1.0 became evident during periods of high network congestion, resulting in increased transaction fees and slower confirmation times. To address these issues, the Ethereum community embarked on the journey towards Ethereum 2.0.

Ethereum 2.0: Bringing scalability and efficiency

Ethereum 2.0, also referred to as Serenity, represents a major upgrade by aiming to address the scalability challenges of Ethereum 1.0. At its core, Ethereum 2.0 seeks to transition from a **proof-of-work (PoW)** consensus mechanism to a more efficient **proof-of-stake (PoS)** consensus mechanism. This shift in consensus mechanism is expected to significantly enhance the scalability, security, and energy efficiency of the Ethereum network.

Note: PoW is a consensus mechanism used in blockchain networks to validate and secure transactions. It is the underlying algorithm that enables participants in a network to agree on the state of the blockchain without relying on a central authority. miners compete to solve complex mathematical puzzles or algorithms in order to add new blocks to the blockchain. The puzzles are designed to be computationally intensive and require a significant amount of computational power. Miners employ powerful hardware devices, such as specialized mining rigs or GPUs, to perform these computations.

The key innovation Ethereum 2.0 proposed in the roadmap is the concept of shard chains. Sharding involves dividing the Ethereum network into multiple smaller chains, known as **shards**, each capable of processing transactions and executing smart contracts. This allows for parallel processing and increases the overall throughput of the network. Shard chains work in harmony with the Beacon Chain, which serves as the coordination mechanism for the shards, facilitating communication and maintaining the overall consensus of the Ethereum 2.0 network.

At the heart of Ethereum 2.0 lies the Beacon Chain, the coordination mechanism for the entire network. The Beacon Chain serves as a validator registry and a consensus mechanism for Ethereum 2.0. Ethereum 2.0 introduces a **PoS** consensus mechanism through the Beacon Chain. In a PoS system, validators are chosen to create new blocks and validate transactions based on the number of tokens they hold and are willing to stake as collateral. This introduces economic security into the network, as validators have a financial incentive to act honestly. If a validator behaves maliciously or fails to perform its duties, it risks losing a portion of its staked tokens. This transition to PoS provides multiple advantages, including increased energy efficiency and reduced centralization risks.

Beacon Chain

The Beacon Chain is a crucial component of Ethereum 2.0, the major upgrade to the Ethereum blockchain. It served as the backbone of Ethereum's transition from a **PoW** to a **PoS** consensus mechanism. The Beacon Chain introduces PoS by allowing participants, known as **validators**, to propose and attest to new blocks without the need for traditional mining.

Some key features of the Beacon Chain are as follows:

- **PoS consensus**: Validators are chosen to propose and attest to new blocks based on the amount of cryptocurrency they *stake* as collateral.
- **Validator committees**: Validators are grouped into committees that take turns proposing and attesting to blocks, enhancing security and efficiency.
- **Validator rewards and penalties**: Validators are incentivized with rewards for good behavior and face penalties for malicious actions, ensuring the security of the network.
- **Centralized control avoidance**: The Beacon Chain helps avoid centralization concerns associated with PoW mining pools.

While the Beacon Chain is a significant step toward Ethereum 2.0, it is important to note that the full implementation of shard chains, which further enhances scalability, will be completed in the road map.

The shard chains: Scaling Ethereum

One of the most significant innovations in Ethereum 2.0 will be the introduction of shard chains. Shard chains enable Ethereum to achieve scalability by dividing the network into smaller chains or shards. Each shard operates as an independent blockchain, capable of processing its transactions and executing smart contracts. This parallel processing allows for increased network capacity and improved transaction throughput. In Ethereum 2.0, the network will be divided into multiple shard chains, each capable of processing its own set of transactions and smart contracts. These shard chains operate in parallel, allowing for greater throughput and reducing congestion. Each shard chain is responsible for a subset of the network's total transactions, enabling Ethereum 2.0 to scale to accommodate a vast number of users and applications.

Ethereum virtual machine

The EVM is a key component of the Ethereum blockchain platform. It is a runtime environment (which executes code) that executes smart contracts, which are self-executing agreements written in programming languages like solidity and vyper. The EVM ensures that these smart contracts are executed consistently across all nodes in the Ethereum network.

EVM has the capability to execute any computable function, making it a powerful and flexible platform for developing decentralized applications. This means that developers can write smart contracts with complex logic and perform a wide range of computations within the Ethereum ecosystem.

To better understand this concept, let us consider an example. Imagine you want to create a decentralized voting system on the Ethereum platform. With the EVM, you can write a smart contract that can handle all the necessary computations and logic for the voting process. The smart contract can manage voter registration, vote casting, and result tabulation, all in a decentralized and transparent manner. The EVM ensures that the smart contract's code is executed correctly and consistently across the Ethereum network.

It also allows for the development of DeFi applications on Ethereum. DeFi applications enable various financial activities such as lending, borrowing, and trading without relying on traditional intermediaries like banks. The EVM's capability to execute complex computations enables the creation of sophisticated DeFi protocols and smart contracts that can automate and manage these financial activities. Furthermore, EVM connects the Ethereum platform to the real world by allowing developers to interact with external data sources called **Oracles**.

For instance, you can create a smart contract that fetches real-time price data from an external source and uses it to execute certain actions or trigger specific conditions within the contract. This integration with real-world data enhances the functionality and utility of Ethereum based applications.

Role of EVM

The EVM plays a crucial role as a runtime environment for executing smart contracts on the Ethereum blockchain. In simple terms, you can think of the EVM as a virtual computer that runs the code of smart contracts. When a smart contract is created and deployed on the Ethereum network, it is written in a high-level programming language, such as solidity. However, the EVM does not directly understand these high-level languages. so, the smart contract code is compiled into bytecode, which is a low-level, machine-readable format.

The EVM is responsible for interpreting and executing this bytecode. It reads and processes each instruction step by step, like how a traditional computer executes machine code. The EVM's execution is deterministic, meaning that given the same inputs, it will produce the same outputs every time.

The EVM provides a sandboxed environment for executing smart contracts. This means that the execution of a smart contract is isolated from the rest of the Ethereum network and other smart contracts. The EVM also manages the storage and memory required by smart contracts during their execution. Each smart contract has its own storage space, where it can store and retrieve data. This storage is persistent and remains on the blockchain even after the contract execution is complete. The EVM also provides temporary memory for storing intermediate results during contract execution.

One crucial aspect of executing smart contracts on the EVM is the concept of gas. Gas is a measure of computational effort required to execute operations on the EVM. Each operation in the bytecode has a predefined gas cost associated with it. Gas acts as a unit of payment for executing smart contracts, and users need to provide sufficient gas to cover the computational cost of their contract execution.

Gas serves two important purposes. Firstly, it prevents malicious or poorly written smart contracts from consuming excessive resources and causing network congestion. Secondly, it incentivizes efficient coding and allows users to prioritize their transactions by adjusting the gas price they are willing to pay. If a smart contract execution runs out of gas, it will be reverted, and any changes made during the execution will be discarded. This ensures that the Ethereum network remains stable and prevents infinite loops or resource exhaustion. The following *Figure 4.1* shows the flowchart of the process:

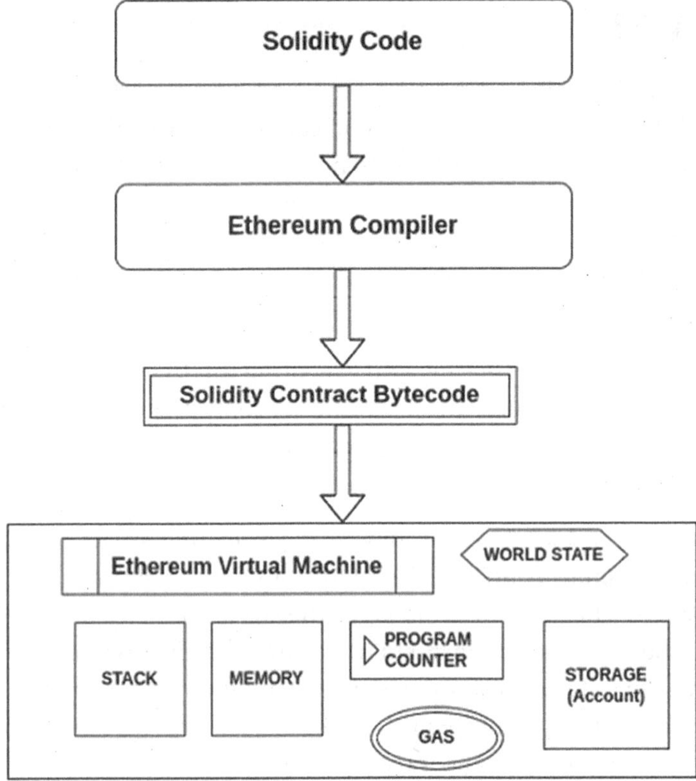

***Figure 4.1**: Visual representation using flowchart*

Stack based architecture of EVM

The EVM functions by interpreting and executing bytecode instructions. When a smart contract is deployed on the Ethereum network, its high-level code is converted into bytecode, a low-level format that the EVM can understand. Subsequently, the EVM processes each bytecode instruction to carry out the corresponding operation. A key aspect of the EVM's architecture is its stack-based approach. In simpler terms, the EVM utilizes a stack to store and manipulate data during the execution of smart contracts. Imagine a stack of books, where you can add or remove books from the top. The EVM stack follows a **Last-In, First-Out** (**LIFO**) pattern, meaning that the most recently added item is the first one to be removed.

To comprehend the workings of the EVM's stack-based architecture, let us consider an example.

Suppose we have the instructions called **Op-codes**: `PUSH1 10, PUSH1 5, ADD`.

The **PUSH1** instruction adds or pushes a value to the stack, while the **ADD** instruction retrieves the top two values from the stack, adds them together and stores the result back on the stack.

Executing these instructions, the EVM would proceed as follows:

- **PUSH1 10**: Adds the value 10 to the stack. Stack: [10]
- **PUSH1 5**: Adds the value 5 to the stack. Stack: [10, 5]
- **ADD**: Retrieves the top two values (10 and 5) from the stack, adds them, and stores the result (15) back on the stack. Stack: [15]

This stack-based approach allows the EVM to efficiently manipulate data and perform computations within smart contracts.

Another critical aspect of the EVM is memory management. When executing smart contracts, the EVM offers temporary memory space to store intermediate results during computation. It is important to note that this memory is separate from the persistent storage of smart contract data on the Ethereum blockchain. The EVM's memory is organized as a linear array of bytes and can be expanded dynamically as required during contract execution.

The EVM's instruction set consists of a collection of opcodes, which are specific codes representing different operations. Each opcode corresponds to a particular task or computation that the EVM can perform. For instance, the **ADD** opcode adds two values, the **MSTORE** opcode stores a value in memory, and the **JUMP** opcode alters the program counter to a different location within the bytecode.

The EVM's instruction set is designed to be Turing complete, meaning it can perform any computation expressible through algorithms. This Turing completeness empowers smart contract developers to create complex and sophisticated applications on the Ethereum blockchain. It is worth noting that the EVM's instruction set is deterministic, ensuring that executing the same bytecode instructions under identical conditions will always produce the same results. This determinism guarantees consistency and predictability in the execution of smart contracts across all nodes on the Ethereum network.

Smart contracts and gas

Let us consider a Simple Solidity contract, as shown in the following code:

```
constructor() {

    // Set the initial counter value to zero

    counter = 0;
```

```
    }

    // Function to increment the counter value by one

    function incrementCounter() public {

        counter++;

    }

    // Function to retrieve the current counter value

    function getCounter() public view returns (uint256) {

        return counter;

    }

}
```

Explanation:

- **contract MathContract**: This line declares a new smart contract named `MathContract`.
- **uint256 public result;**: This declares a state variable result of type `uint256` (unsigned integer of 256 bits). The `public` keyword automatically generates a getter function, allowing external parties to read the value.
- **function addNumbers(uint256 _a, uint256 _b)**: This function takes two parameters `_a` and `_b`, both of type `uint256`. It adds these two numbers and stores the result in the `result` state variable.
- **function getResult() public view returns (uint256)**: This function has the view modifier, indicating that it does not modify the contract's state. It returns the stored `result` when called.

In summary, this contract allows you to add two numbers by calling the `addNumbers` function and retrieve the result using the `getResult` function. The `result` variable holds the last calculated sum.

If this contract is executed, logic will be permanently stored in blockchain. This applies same to not only storing and adding numbers but storing land details to digital education certificates immutably.

Gas: Efficient execution on the EVM

Gas is a fundamental concept in the Ethereum network, representing the computational effort required to execute operations on the EVM. In simple terms, gas measures the amount of work a specific operation or computation consumes. Each operation in a smart contract, such as calculations, storage modifications, or interactions with other contracts, requires a certain amount of gas to be executed.

Gas fees refer to the transaction fees users need to pay to execute immutable contracts on the EVM. Gas fees serve multiple purposes, including incentivizing miners to include transactions in blocks and ensuring that the network remains secure and efficient. Users must pay gas fees to execute functions and transactions on the Ethereum network. The fees are determined by the complexity and computational requirements of the executed operations.

Gas optimization is crucial when writing smart contracts to ensure efficiency and cost effectiveness. By optimizing gas usage, developers can reduce the computational resources required and, consequently, lower the associated gas fees. There are various techniques and best practices for gas optimization, including minimizing unnecessary computations, reducing storage usage, and avoiding expensive operations. Careful consideration of gas optimization can lead to significant cost savings and enhance the overall performance of smart contracts.

Comparing Bitcoin and Ethereum

Bitcoin and Ethereum are two prominent cryptocurrencies that have made significant impacts on the world of blockchain technology and digital finance. While both are decentralized digital currencies, they differ in their underlying purposes, functionality, and implications. Understanding the differences between Bitcoin and Ethereum is crucial for investors, enthusiasts, and those interested in the potential of blockchain technology. In this comparison, we will delve into various aspects of these cryptocurrencies to uncover their distinctions and real-world implications. By exploring these sub-topics, we will gain a comprehensive understanding of the similarities, differences, and real-world implications of Bitcoin and Ethereum. So, let us dive into the world of cryptocurrencies and unravel the unique characteristics that define these two remarkable digital assets.

Purpose and functionality

Purpose and functionality of Bitcoin and Ethereum are as follows:

Bitcoin:

- Created as a digital currency to facilitate peer-to-peer transactions.
- Focuses on secure, decentralized monetary transfers.
- Primarily serves as a store of value and a medium of exchange.

- Example: Bitcoin allows users to send and receive bitcoin directly without the need for intermediaries, enabling cross-border transactions with lower fees compared to traditional banking systems.

Ethereum:

- Designed as a decentralized platform for executing smart contracts and building dApps.
- Provides a Turing-complete programming language for creating complex applications.
- Enables the creation of custom tokens and crowdfunding through **initial coin offerings (ICOs)**.

Example: Ethereum powers a wide range of dApps, such as DeFi protocols, **non-fungible token** (**NFT**) marketplaces, and decentralized exchanges, offering users financial services, digital art ownership, and secure token trading.

Blockchain architecture

Blockchain architecture of Bitcoin and Ethereum are as follows:

Bitcoin:

- Utilizes a simpler blockchain architecture focused on transaction processing.
- Transaction validation is done through the **PoW** consensus mechanism.
- Block time is approximately 10 minutes.

Example: Bitcoin's blockchain acts as a public ledger, recording every transaction to ensure transparency and immutability, serving as an alternative to traditional banking systems.

Ethereum:

- Features a more advanced blockchain architecture accommodating smart contracts.
- Implements the **EVM** for executing decentralized applications.
- Moving towards **PoS** consensus mechanism to improve scalability and energy efficiency.

Example: Ethereum's blockchain enables the creation and execution of self-executing smart contracts, allowing developers to build innovative applications with various real-world use cases, such as DeFi, supply chain management, and decentralized identity solutions.

Tokenomics

Tokenomics and monetary policy of Bitcoin and Ethereum is as follows:

Bitcoin:

- Limited supply capped at 21 million coins.
- Deflationary monetary policy as the number of coins decreases over time.
- Halving events every four years reduce block rewards to miners.

Example: Bitcoin's scarcity and predictable issuance have contributed to its status as a digital store of value, with some investors considering it a potential hedge against inflation and a digital equivalent to gold.

Ethereum:

- Currently utilizes a monetary policy similar to traditional fiat currencies.
- Plans to transition to Ethereum 2.0 with a new economic model and fee burning mechanism.
- Uses **ETH** as a utility token for paying transaction fees and accessing network resources.

Example: Ethereum's economic model ensures the network's sustainability and incentivizes miners and validators to secure the network while also providing developers access to computational resources for executing smart contracts.

Developer community and ecosystem

Developer community and ecosystem of Bitcoin and Ethereum are as follows:

Bitcoin:

- Known for its robust and passionate community of developers and enthusiasts.
- Primarily focuses on maintaining Bitcoin's core protocol and enhancing its security and scalability.

Example: Developers contribute to the Bitcoin ecosystem through the creation of wallets, exchanges, and other infrastructure supporting the use and adoption of Bitcoin as a digital currency.

Ethereum:

- Boasts a vibrant ecosystem with a large and diverse community of developers.
- Actively fosters the creation of decentralized applications and innovative solutions.

Example: Ethereum's ecosystem includes popular projects like **MetaMask**, **Uniswap**, and Compound, which provide users with access to dApps, decentralized exchanges, and lending platforms, offering new financial opportunities and user experiences.

Types of accounts in Ethereum

The following *Table 4.1* shows a comparison between Ethereum accounts and traditional banking:

Aspect	Ethereum accounts	Traditional banking
Control and ownership	Decentralized, user controlled with private keys	Centralized, bank-managed accounts with customer access
Transactions and settlement	Peer-to-peer, decentralized consensus mechanisms	Centralized, mediated by banks, longer settlement times
Access and availability	24/7 availability, unrestricted access	Business hours, limited access on weekends and holidays
Privacy and anonymity	Pseudonymous transactions, some privacy	KYC regulations, transactions linked to real identities
Fees and costs	Variable transaction fees, user-selectable	Various fees (transaction, maintenance, currency conversion)
International transactions	Borderless transactions, potentially faster	Involves multiple intermediary banks, higher fees, longer times
Risk and security	User-managed private keys, smart contract vulnerabilities	Bank-provided security, regulatory protection, fraud prevention

***Table 4.1**: Comparison between Ethereum accounts and traditional banking*

In the Ethereum blockchain, two primary types of accounts exist: **externally owned accounts (EOAs)** and contract accounts. These accounts play distinct roles in the Ethereum ecosystem, reflecting the dual nature of Ethereum as both a cryptocurrency and a decentralized computing platform. Let us discuss these accounts in detail:

- **Externally owned accounts (EOAs)**: EOAs are the most straightforward and common type of Ethereum account. These accounts are controlled by private keys held by individuals or entities. An EOA has an Ethereum address associated with it, derived from the account's public key. EOAs are used to manage and control Ether, the native cryptocurrency of Ethereum. Individuals use EOAs to hold and transfer Ether, sign transactions, and participate in various activities on the Ethereum network. Transactions initiated by EOAs involve simple value transfers or interactions with smart contracts. Importantly, EOAs are not associated with any executable code; their primary function is to facilitate the transfer and management of Ether.

- **Contract accounts:** In contrast, contract accounts are linked to the deployment and execution of smart contracts on the Ethereum blockchain. A smart contract is self-executing code that resides at a specific Ethereum address, essentially transforming it into a contract account. These accounts contain both the contract's bytecode and its state. When a smart contract is deployed, a unique Ethereum address is assigned to it, and this address becomes the identifier for the associated contract account. Contract accounts hold Ether and interact with other smart contracts or EOAs through the execution of transactions. Unlike EOAs, contract accounts are associated with executable code, allowing them to perform complex operations and autonomously execute predefined functions based on the conditions specified in the smart contract's code.

The following table shows the differences between EOA and contracts:

Feature	EOA	Contract account
Control	Controlled by a private key owned by an individual	Controlled by the logic encoded in the associated smart contract
Primary purpose	Facilitates the transfer and management of Ether	Executes programmable logic through deployed smart contracts
Address type	Derived from the account holder's public key	Assigned to a deployed smart contract, becoming its unique identifier
Transaction role	Initiates value transfers and interactions with smart contracts	Executes code in smart contracts, typically in response to transactions
Executable code	Does not contain executable code	Contains bytecode and state associated with the deployed smart contract
User control	User controls the account through a private key	Code execution is automated, with conditions defined in the smart contract
Interactions	Involved in sending/receiving Ether and interacting with other accounts	Engages in complex operations as per the programmed logic in smart contracts
Common use cases	Holds Ether, participates in token transfers, general transactions	Powers dApps, DeFi protocols, and customized functionalities

***Table 4.2:** Differences between EOA and contracts*

In summary, EOAs and contract accounts cater to different roles within Ethereum – one focusing on cryptocurrency management and user interactions, and the other enabling programmable and decentralized functionalities through the execution of smart contracts.

To initiate a transaction, you need to provide specific instructions or data to the smart contract. This data is sent as part of a transaction, which consists of several components:

- **Sender**: The sender is the external owned account initiating the transaction. It is the account that holds the Ether or tokens being used to interact with the smart contract.
- **Receiver**: The receiver is the address of the smart contract to which the transaction is directed. It identifies the specific smart contract that will process the transaction.
- **Value**: The value represents the amount of Ether being sent in the transaction. It can be a numeric value representing Ether or the value of another token associated with the smart contract.
- **Gas**: Gas is a measure of computational effort required to execute the transaction on the Ethereum network. It acts as a fee that you pay to the network to have your transaction processed.

Let us consider an example to illustrate how these components come together in a contract transaction. Imagine you want to purchase a digital collectible, such as a unique piece of artwork, from an online marketplace running on Ethereum. The marketplace would have a smart contract that handles the buying and selling of these collectibles.

To initiate the purchase, you would use your Ethereum wallet to send a transaction to the smart contract's address. In this transaction, you would specify the value of Ether you are willing to pay for the collectible, along with any additional data required by the smart contract. You would also include the necessary gas to cover the computational effort required to process the transaction.

Once the transaction is sent, it is added to a pool of pending transactions awaiting verification by Ethereum miners. Miners are responsible for validating transactions and adding them to the blockchain, ensuring the integrity and security of the network. They prioritize transactions based on the amount of gas provided, as higher gas transactions are processed faster.

Once your transaction is verified and included in a block, the smart contract will execute the necessary code to complete the purchase. The ownership of the digital collectible would be transferred to your Ethereum address, and the corresponding amount of Ether would be transferred to the seller's address.

The Ethereum wallet serves as a digital tool for managing your Ethereum assets, including Ether and tokens. It provides access to your external owned account, which acts as your unique identifier on the Ethereum network. Through the Ethereum wallet, you can initiate contract transactions by sending specific data to smart contracts. These transactions consist of components such as the sender, receiver, value, and gas. By understanding the structure of these transactions, you can participate in various Ethereum-based applications, including decentralized marketplaces, financial services, and more.

We will delve into the details of Ethereum wallets, including their definition, features, pros and cons, and essential points to keep in mind. Whether you are new to Ethereum or looking to deepen your understanding, this section will provide you with valuable insights.

An Ethereum wallet is a software application that allows users to securely store, send, and receive ETH, the native cryptocurrency of the Ethereum network. It also enables users to manage other Ethereum-based tokens, such as ERC-20 tokens, which are widely used in dApps built on the Ethereum platform. In essence, an Ethereum wallet serves as a digital vault for your Ether and tokens, providing you with control over your assets and facilitating transactions on the Ethereum network.

Features of Ethereum wallets are as follows:

- **Secure storage**: Ethereum wallets employ robust cryptographic mechanisms to ensure the security of your private keys, which are used to access and manage your funds. They provide a secure storage environment, protecting your assets from unauthorized access or potential hacking attempts.
- **Transaction management**: Ethereum wallets enable you to send and receive Ether and tokens, allowing you to interact with smart contracts, participate in token sales (ICO/IEO), and conduct peer-to-peer transactions. They provide an intuitive user interface to manage and track your transactions.
- **Token management**: Ethereum wallets typically support a wide range of ERC-20 tokens, making it convenient for users to store and manage various tokens within a single wallet. This feature is essential for participating in token sales, decentralized exchanges, and other Ethereum-based applications.
- **Address book**: Ethereum wallets often include an address book feature, allowing you to save and label frequently used addresses. This makes it easier to send transactions to known recipients without having to manually enter their address every time.
- **Integration with dApps**: Many Ethereum wallets offer seamless integration with dApps. This enables you to interact with a wide range of decentralized services, such as DeFi platforms, digital collectibles, and decentralized exchanges, directly from your wallet.

Some of the pros of Ethereum wallets are as follows:

- **Ownership and control**: With an Ethereum wallet, you have full ownership and control over your funds. Unlike traditional banking systems, where financial institutions act as custodians of your assets, Ethereum wallets empower individuals to be their own bank, managing their assets independently.
- **Accessibility**: Ethereum wallets provide users with easy access to their funds from anywhere in the world, as long as they have an internet connection. This accessibility allows for quick and convenient transactions, regardless of geographic location or traditional banking hours.
- **Diverse applications**: Ethereum wallets open up a world of possibilities, as they provide access to a wide range of dApps and decentralized services. From lending platforms and decentralized exchanges to gaming and digital collectibles, Ethereum wallets enable users to explore and participate in various innovative applications.

Some of the cons of Ethereum wallets are as follows:

- **Security risks**: While Ethereum wallets offer robust security measures, the responsibility of safeguarding your private keys falls on the user. If private keys are lost or compromised, there is a risk of losing access to your funds. It is crucial to follow best practices for security, such as using strong passwords and enabling **two-factor authentication (2FA)**.
- **Learning curve**: Ethereum wallets may have a learning curve, especially for individuals new to cryptocurrencies and blockchain technology. Understanding concepts such as private keys, gas fees, and transaction confirmations may require some initial research and learning.
- **Potential scams**: The decentralized nature of Ethereum also attracts scammers and fraudulent activities. Users must exercise caution and be vigilant to avoid phishing attempts

Although Ethereum wallet faces some challenges, it is still one of the most popular services in the blockchain world. Nonetheless, here are some of the things to keep in mind:

- **Wallet backup**: It is essential to create secure backups of your wallet's private keys or seed phrases. This ensures that you can recover your wallet and funds in case of accidental loss or device failure. Store backups in offline and secure locations.
- **Verify authenticity**: When choosing an Ethereum wallet, ensure that you download it from official sources or reputable app stores. Beware of phishing websites or fraudulent applications that may attempt to steal your private keys.

- **Stay updated**: Keep your wallet software and any associated plugins or extensions up to date. Developers regularly release updates that address security vulnerabilities and improve performance.
- **Research wallet options**: There are various Ethereum wallet options available, including desktop, mobile, hardware, and web wallets. Research and compare different wallets based on factors such as security features, user interface, community reputation, and compatibility with your device.
- **Gas fees**: Ethereum transactions require gas fees to incentivize miners and secure the network. Gas fees can vary depending on network congestion and the complexity of the transaction. It is important to consider gas fees when sending transactions to ensure you include an appropriate fee and avoid delays.
- **Test small transactions**: When using a new Ethereum wallet or interacting with unfamiliar dApps, it is advisable to start with small transactions to ensure everything works as expected before committing larger amounts.

EOAs function as the gateway for individuals and entities to interact with the Ethereum network. Each EOA is associated with a unique Ethereum address, which acts as the identifier for that account. The private key corresponding to this address is required to access and manage the funds associated with the account.

When it comes to transactions, EOAs can initiate two types: value transfers and contract interactions. Value transfers involve sending ETH, the native cryptocurrency of the Ethereum network, from one EOA to another. Contract interactions, on the other hand, involve invoking functions within smart contracts, which are self-executing agreements with predefined rules encoded on the Ethereum blockchain.

EOAs initiate transactions by signing them with their private keys, ensuring that only the account owner can authorize and execute these actions. Once a transaction is signed, it is broadcasted to the Ethereum network, where it is validated and included in a block by miners. The significance of externally owned accounts in Ethereum:

- **Ownership and control**: EOAs provide individuals and entities with complete ownership and control over their funds and transactions. Unlike traditional financial systems where intermediaries have significant control, EOAs empower users to manage their assets directly without relying on third parties.
- **Decentralization**: EOAs contribute to the decentralized nature of the Ethereum network. By allowing individuals to participate directly in transactions and interactions, Ethereum reduces the need for intermediaries, fostering a more inclusive and transparent financial ecosystem.
- **Accessibility**: Ethereum's EOAs offer global accessibility, allowing users from anywhere in the world to create an account and participate in the network. This

accessibility is not limited by geographical boundaries or traditional banking hours, providing users with greater flexibility and financial inclusivity.

- **Interoperability**: EOAs can interact with various dApps and smart contracts deployed on the Ethereum network. This interoperability enables users to access a wide range of services, such as DeFi platforms, digital collectibles, and decentralized exchanges, all from their EOA.

Some of the things to keep in mind are as follows:

- **Private key security**: As the private key is the key to accessing and controlling an EOA, it is of outmost importance to keep it secure. Users must take necessary precautions to protect their private keys from theft, loss, or unauthorized access. It is recommended to use hardware wallets or secure password management solutions to safeguard private keys.
- **Transaction confirmation**: Once a transaction is initiated, it needs to be confirmed by miners on the Ethereum network. This confirmation ensures that the transaction is added to the blockchain and considered final. It is important to be patient and allow sufficient time for transaction confirmations, especially during periods of high network congestion.
- **Gas fees**: Ethereum transactions require gas fees to be paid by the sender. Gas fees compensate the miners for their computational efforts in processing and validating transactions. Users should consider gas fees when initiating transactions to ensure sufficient fees are provided for timely processing.
- **Network upgrades**: Ethereum is a rapidly evolving platform, and network upgrades, such as the transition to Ethereum 2.0, may introduce changes to the EOA functionality and network dynamics. Staying informed about network upgrades and their implications is crucial for EOA users.

Real-world examples

Let us consider a real-world example to better understand the concept of EOAs in action. Suppose you want to participate in an **initial coin offering (ICO)** for a promising blockchain project. To do so, you would need to create an EOA, generate a unique Ethereum address, and send Ether from your EOA to the ICO's designated address. By utilizing your EOA, you have full control over your funds and can directly participate in the ICO without relying on intermediaries.

Contract transactions on Ethereum

Contract transactions are considered the cornerstone of Ethereum's functionality. Understanding of contract transactions unveils the backbone of the execution of programmable agreements.

Before delving into contract transactions, let us briefly review the basics of Ethereum transactions. A transaction in Ethereum represents a transfer of value or an interaction with a smart contract. It consists of several essential components, including:

- **Sender**: The Ethereum address of the account initiating the transaction.
- **Recipient**: The destination addresses where the transaction is directed.
- **Value**: The amount of ETH being transferred in the transaction.
- **Nonce**: A unique identifier for each transaction, preventing replay attacks.
- **Gas price**: The fee paid per unit of gas to incentivize miners.
- **Gas limit**: The maximum amount of gas that the transaction can consume.

In a contract transaction, the To field specifies the address of the smart contract to which the transaction is directed. This address is unique to each smart contract and serves as the identifier for the contract on the Ethereum network. Some other concepts related to contract transactions are:

- **To address**: In a contract transaction, the to field specifies the address of the smart contract to which the transaction is directed. This address is unique to each smart contract and serves as the identifier for the contract on the Ethereum network.
- **Data**: The data field in a contract transaction contains the encoded instructions for the smart contract to execute. It includes the function to be called and any input parameters required by that function. The data field is essential as it tells the smart contract what action to perform upon receiving the transaction.
- **Gas**: Gas plays a crucial role in executing contract transactions. It represents the computational effort required to perform the desired operations within the smart contract. The sender of the transaction must provide enough gas to cover the execution cost, determined by the complexity of the contract's logic and the operations it performs.
- **Gas price**: Similar to regular transactions, contract transactions require a gas price, which is the amount of Ether the sender is willing to pay for each unit of gas. Miners prioritize transactions with higher gas prices, as they provide a greater incentive for them to include the transaction in a block.
- **Gas limit**: The gas limit determines the maximum amount of gas that the transaction can consume. It serves as a safety mechanism to prevent infinite loops or excessive

resource consumption. If the execution of a contract transaction exceeds the gas limit, the transaction is reverted, and any changes made by the contract during execution are rolled back.

Understanding the structure of contract transactions is crucial for several reasons. Some of them are:

- **Smart contract interactions**: Contract transactions enable users to interact with dApps and execute specific functions within smart contracts. These interactions facilitate various use cases, including DeFi, NFTs, gaming, and more.
- **Atomicity and consistency**: Contract transactions adhere to the principles of atomicity and consistency, ensuring that operations within a transaction either fully succeed or fail. If a contract transaction involves multiple function calls, the entire transaction will be reverted if any of the calls encounter an error or exception, ensuring data integrity and reliability.
- **Contract upgrades and interoperability**: The structure of contract transactions allows for seamless contract upgrades and interoperability. By deploying new versions of a smart contract, users can interact with updated functionalities while maintaining compatibility with existing applications that reference the old contract's address.

Structure of transaction

Transactions form the backbone of the Ethereum blockchain, facilitating the transfer of value and execution of smart contracts. Understanding the structure of transactions is essential for navigating the Ethereum ecosystem effectively. Transactions in Ethereum follow a specific structure that consists of various components. Let us examine each element in detail:

- **Sender**: The sender, also known as the **From address**, represents the Ethereum account initiating the transaction. It is a unique identifier associated with an individual or an organization on the Ethereum network.
- **Recipient**: The recipient, also known as the **To address**, specifies the destination of the transaction. It can be the address of another Ethereum account or a smart contract deployed on the blockchain.
- **Value**: The value field represents the amount of ETH being transferred in the transaction. It denotes the financial aspect of the transaction, allowing users to send and receive digital currency.
- **Nonce**: The nonce is a unique identifier attached to each transaction. It prevents replay attacks by ensuring that each transaction is executed only once. The nonce

value increments with each subsequent transaction sent from the same sender's address.

- **Gas price**: Gas price refers to the amount of Ether paid per unit of gas, representing the fee the sender is willing to pay to execute the transaction. Higher gas prices incentivize miners to prioritize the transaction during block creation.
- **Gas limit**: The gas limit specifies the maximum amount of gas the transaction can consume. It acts as a safety mechanism, preventing infinite loops and resource exhaustion within smart contracts.
- **Data**: The data field contains additional information or instructions accompanying the transaction. In regular transactions, this field is typically empty. However, in the case of contract transactions, it contains encoded instructions for the smart contract to execute.

Transaction flow

It refers to the sequence of events that take place when a transaction occurs on the Ethereum blockchain. To better understand the transactional flow in Ethereum, let us explore the sequential steps involved:

- **Transaction creation**: The transaction creation process begins when a user initiates a transaction from their Ethereum wallet. They provide the recipient address, value, gas price, gas limit, and any additional data required.
- **Transaction signing**: Once the transaction is created, it is digitally signed using the sender's private key. This ensures the authenticity and integrity of the transaction.
- **Transaction broadcast**: The signed transaction is then broadcasted to the Ethereum network. It propagates through nodes, reaching miners who validate and include it in a block.
- **Transaction confirmation**: Miners compete to include the transaction in the blockchain by solving complex mathematical puzzles. Once a miner successfully mines a new block, the transaction becomes confirmed and permanently recorded in the Ethereum blockchain.

Transaction nonce

A transaction nonce is a sequential number assigned to each transaction initiated from a specific Ethereum account or address. It acts as a safeguard against replay attacks and ensures that each transaction is executed only once. The transaction nonce plays a crucial role in protecting users from replay attacks. By requiring a unique nonce for each transaction, the Ethereum network ensures that even if an attacker intercepts a transaction, they cannot replay it to execute unwanted actions on behalf of the user. The transaction nonce serves multiple purposes in the Ethereum network. They are as follows:

- **Preventing replay attacks**: By requiring a unique nonce for each transaction, Ethereum ensures that transactions cannot be duplicated or replayed, protecting users from potential malicious activities.
- **Maintaining transaction order**: The nonce ensures that transactions from the same account are executed in a specific order, preserving the integrity of the transaction history and preventing inconsistencies.

Nonce generation and sequential ordering

Nonce generation and sequential ordering are crucial components of the Ethereum's transaction processing mechanism. They contribute to the security, integrity, and validity of transactions. A brief explanation of nonce generation and sequential ordering are as follows:

- **Nonce generation**: When a user initiates a transaction from their Ethereum account, the nonce value is generated by counting the number of transactions previously sent from that account. It starts with zero for the first transaction and increments by one for each subsequent transaction.
- **Sequential ordering**: The nonce enforces a strict sequential order for transactions from the same account. Miners validate transactions based on their nonce value and ensure they are included in the blockchain in the correct order of nonce sequence. This prevents transactions from being skipped or executed out of order.

Note: A few other concepts that you must be aware of are:

- **Nonce Incrementation: It is important to increment the nonce value correctly for each subsequent transaction to ensure its acceptance by the network. Failure to do so may result in rejected transactions or incorrect ordering.**
- **Nonce Reset: In some cases, such as when recovering a compromised account or using multiple devices, the nonce count may be disrupted. It is crucial to restore the correct nonce value to resume transactional activities from the account accurately.**
- **Nonce Synchronization: When interacting with external services or applications, ensure that the nonce value remains synchronized across different platforms to avoid nonce-related errors and transaction failures.**

In conclusion, the transaction nonce in Ethereum acts as a fundamental security measure, ensuring the integrity, order, and uniqueness of transactions. By assigning a sequential identifier to each transaction, Ethereum prevents replay attacks and maintains the correct sequence of transactions from an account. Understanding the concept of transaction nonces is essential for secure and reliable interactions within the Ethereum ecosystem, allowing users to confidently participate in DeFi, smart contracts, and various blockchain-based applications.

Definition and importance of transaction gas

In the Ethereum blockchain, gas is a unit of measurement that quantifies the computational resources consumed by each transaction. As explained earlier, gas is the transaction fees a user needs to pay while executing contracts on the Ethereum blockchain. Here, we will delve into the concept of transaction gas, exploring its significance, calculation, and practical examples to enhance your understanding of this crucial aspect of the Ethereum network. It serves multiple purposes, including:

- **Resource allocation**: Gas ensures a fair distribution of network resources. By attaching a gas limit to each transaction, Ethereum prevents infinite loops, malicious activities, and denial-of-service attacks. It establishes a balance between computational complexity and network efficiency.
- **Fee calculation**: Gas is used to calculate transaction fees, denominated in ETH. Each operation in a transaction, such as arithmetic calculations, storage operations, or smart contract interactions, consumes a specific amount of gas. The total gas consumed determines the fee paid to miners for including the transaction in a block.

Gas price and gas limit

In Ethereum, gas price and gas limit are essential concepts tied to transaction processing within the network. Gas price represents the amount of cryptocurrency (usually measured in Gwei) users are willing to pay for each unit of gas in a transaction. It acts as an incentive for miners to include a transaction in a block. Transactions with higher gas prices are prioritized because miners are more likely to include them to earn higher fees.

Impact on transaction confirmation

Higher gas prices generally result in faster confirmation times, as miners are more motivated to include transactions with lucrative fees. Conversely, lower gas prices may cause delays in transaction confirmation.

Gas Limit refers to the maximum amount of gas units a user is willing to spend on a transaction. It serves as a safeguard against infinite loops or computational heavy operations, preventing malicious or unintentional resource exhaustion. If the gas limit is set too low, a transaction may run out of gas before completion. Miners stop processing a transaction when it reaches its gas limit, and unspent gas is refunded. However, if the gas limit is too high, users may end up paying more fees than necessary.

Gas fee calculation

The total fee (transaction cost) is calculated by multiplying the gas price and gas used (gas limit). Users need to find a balance between setting a competitive gas price for faster confirmation and setting a sufficient gas limit for the intended operation.

In summary, gas price determines the transaction's priority, and gas limit prevents excessive resource consumption. Finding the right balance ensures efficient transaction processing on the Ethereum network.

Factors affecting transaction gas calculation

Gas fees are determined by the computational resources that are required for executing smart contracts or processing transactions. Gas consumption in a transaction depends on various factors. A sound understanding of these factors will help users make informed decisions when initiating transactions on the Ethereum network. Some factors affecting transaction gas calculation are as follows:

- **Operation complexity**: Each operation in a transaction has an associated gas cost. Complex operations, such as executing loops or accessing large data structures, consume more gas than simpler operations. For example, a simple arithmetic calculation may consume less gas compared to a transaction that updates multiple storage variables in a smart contract.
- **Execution path**: The execution path followed within a smart contract affects gas consumption. Different inputs or conditions may result in divergent execution paths, leading to varying gas costs.
- **External calls**: Interacting with other smart contracts or external services incurs additional gas costs. These costs include the gas consumed by the called **contract** and any associated data storage or computation.

Gas limit and out-of-gas errors

Every transaction specifies a gas limit, which defines the maximum amount of gas that can be consumed. If a transaction exceeds its gas limit before completion, it is considered out-of-gas and is reverted, resulting in a failed transaction. It is crucial to set an appropriate gas limit to ensure successful execution.

Practical examples of gas usage

To illustrate the concept of transaction gas, consider the following examples:

- **Sending ether**: A simple transaction involving sending Ether from one account to another consumes a small amount of gas. The gas cost primarily covers the validation and storage of the transaction on the blockchain.
- **Executing a smart contract function**: Interacting with a smart contract function involves more complex operations, such as reading or updating data on the blockchain. Each operation consumes gas, and the total gas cost depends on the complexity of the function and the amount of data involved.
- **Token transfers**: Transferring tokens on the Ethereum blockchain, typically using the ERC-20 standard, involves invoking smart contract functions. These transfers consume gas for both the token transfer itself and the execution of any associated logic in the smart contract.

Gas optimization

Gas optimization is a crucial consideration when developing smart contracts on Ethereum. It plays a pivotal role in conducting transactions and interacting with smart contracts on the Ethereum network. Gas optimization aims to minimize gas consumption and maximize efficiency to reduce transaction costs. Here are a few tips for efficient gas usage:

- **Minimize unnecessary operations**: Avoid unnecessary computations, redundant storage operations, and excessive looping to reduce gas consumption.
- **Gas-efficient code patterns**: Follow gas-efficient coding patterns recommended by the Ethereum community, such as using modifiers, avoiding unnecessary state changes, and minimizing storage writes.
- **Gas estimation**: Use gas estimation tools provided by Ethereum development frameworks to estimate the gas required for a transaction before submitting it. This helps set an appropriate gas limit and avoid out-of-gas errors.

Transaction recipient

The transaction recipient is identified by its unique Ethereum address, also known as the **To address**. This address is a string of alphanumeric characters, typically represented as a hexadecimal value. It serves as a virtual identifier for the recipient, ensuring accurate and secure delivery of the transaction.

The transaction recipient can be a person, a business, or even an automated program. When a transaction is sent to a person's Ethereum address, it is akin to sending funds to their digital wallet. The recipient can then access and manage the received value through their Ethereum wallet. In the case of a smart contract, the transaction recipient refers to the contract's address. Smart contracts are self-executing agreements with the terms of the agreement directly written into code. When a transaction is sent to a smart contract's address, the contract's code is executed, and predefined actions or computations are performed. These actions can range from distributing tokens to executing complex business logic.

Let us consider an example to illustrate the concept of transaction recipient. Suppose Alice wants to purchase tokens in a new dApp through an ICO. She initiates a transaction from her Ethereum wallet, specifying the ICO contract's address as the transaction recipient. In this scenario, the ICO contract acts as the recipient, receiving Alice's transaction and executing the logic to allocate the purchased tokens to her Ethereum account.

Furthermore, the transaction recipient can be a multisig wallet address. Multisig wallets are designed to require multiple signatures or approvals from different parties to authorize a transaction. This adds an extra layer of security and control, making it suitable for businesses, joint accounts, or governance mechanisms within decentralized organizations.

Transaction values and data

In the Ethereum blockchain, transactions are at the core of value transfer and smart contract execution. To delve deeper into the workings of Ethereum, it is crucial to grasp the concepts of transaction values and data. In this section, we will explore these elements in detail, uncovering their significance and real-world applications within the Ethereum ecosystem.

Transaction values

Transaction values in Ethereum refer to the transfer of digital assets, primarily ETH, between participants. Following are the key aspects of transaction values:

- **Ether as a medium of exchange**: Ether serves as the native cryptocurrency of the Ethereum blockchain, enabling participants to exchange value. It acts as a unit of account, store of value, and medium of exchange within the Ethereum network.
- **Value transfer**: Transactions allow individuals to send and receive Ether, enabling peer-to-peer transfers of digital currency. This is particularly useful for various financial activities, such as making payments, remittances, or settling debts.
- **Token transfers**: In addition to Ether, Ethereum supports the creation and transfer of tokens. Tokens represent fungible or non-fungible assets, such as utility tokens, security tokens, or digital collectibles. Transactions facilitate the movement of these tokens between addresses on the Ethereum network.

Real-world example: During **initial coin offerings (ICOs)** or token sale events, transactions play a pivotal role in distributing newly created tokens to investors. Participants send Ether to a designated address in exchange for the newly minted tokens, representing their investment in a particular project.

Transaction data

Transaction data carries additional information or instructions accompanying a transaction. While regular transactions may have empty data fields, smart contract transactions utilize this feature extensively. The significance of transaction data is as follows:

- **Execution of smart contracts**: Smart contracts are self-executing agreements written in programming languages like Solidity. Transactions include data that triggers specific functions within smart contracts, allowing for the execution of complex logic and automation. This functionality enables a wide range of dApps and DeFi protocols.
- **Function invocation**: Transaction data specifies the function to be invoked within a smart contract, along with any required parameters. This allows users to interact with dApps, initiate token transfers, or access specific features within a decentralized ecosystem.

Real-world example: In a **Decentralized Exchange (DEX)**, transaction data is used to execute trades between different tokens. Users provide data specifying the desired trade parameters, such as the token pair, amount, and price. This information guides the smart contract to execute the trade on behalf of the user. Transaction data can also include supplementary information, such as a reference ID, memo, or message, for tracking or communication purposes. This feature enhances the versatility and practicality of Ethereum transactions.

- **Security and privacy considerations**: While Ethereum transactions are transparent and recorded on the blockchain, certain aspects related to transaction values and data require attention.
- **Confidentiality**: While Ethereum transactions do not inherently offer confidentiality, users can utilize techniques such as encryption or privacy-focused solutions to protect sensitive data within transactions.
- **Gas fees**: Every transaction on Ethereum incurs a cost known as **gas fees**. These fees are paid in Ether and compensate miners for processing and including transactions in blocks. Users must consider gas fees when sending transactions, as they can vary based on network congestion and transaction complexity.

Transaction values to EOA and contracts in Ethereum

Transactions in Ethereum involve the transfer of value between different entities, including EOA and smart contracts. Understanding how transactions interact with EOAs and contracts is vital for navigating the Ethereum ecosystem. In this section, we will explore the concept of transaction values, their significance, and their relationship to EOAs and contracts.

The **transaction value** in Ethereum refers to the amount of cryptocurrency (Ether) or other digital assets being transferred from one account to another. It represents the financial aspect of the transaction and plays a crucial role in various scenarios within the Ethereum network.

EOAs are accounts owned and controlled by individuals or organizations on the Ethereum blockchain. These accounts are associated with a unique Ethereum address, represented by a combination of letters and numbers. EOAs interact with the Ethereum network by initiating transactions, executing smart contracts, and storing Ether and other digital assets.

Transaction value to EOAs

When a transaction occurs between two EOAs, the transaction value represents the amount of Ether being sent from the sender's account to the recipient's account. This can be seen as a simple peer-to-peer transfer of value, similar to sending money from one bank account to another.

For instance, suppose Alice wants to send 2 Ether to Bob. Alice initiates a transaction from her EOA, specifying Bob's EOA address as the recipient and setting the transaction value to 2 Ether. Upon confirming and mining the transaction, the 2 Ether is transferred from Alice's account to Bob's account on the Ethereum blockchain.

Example: Suppose there is a decentralized voting application deployed as a smart contract on the Ethereum blockchain. To cast a vote, a user sends a transaction to the voting contract, specifying their chosen candidate and setting the transaction value to 0 Ether. In this case, the transaction value does not represent a financial transfer but rather acts as a parameter to record the user's vote within the smart contract's logic.

Importance and real-world examples are as follow:

- **Efficient financial transactions**: Transaction values enable smooth and secure transfers of Ether and other digital assets between EOAs, facilitating peer-to-peer transactions and financial interactions.

- **Interaction with decentralized applications**: Transaction values are used to trigger specific actions and provide inputs to smart contracts, allowing users to interact with decentralized applications and leverage their functionalities.

Real-world use case: In DeFi applications, transaction values are critical for interacting with protocols such as lending, borrowing, and decentralized exchanges. For example, a user may provide liquidity to a liquidity pool by sending a transaction with a specific value of Ether and receiving corresponding tokens in return.

Smart contracts and Solidity

Smart contracts are at the core of the Ethereum blockchain, revolutionizing the way agreements are made and executed in a trust less and decentralized manner. In this module, we will delve into the concept of smart contracts and explore Solidity, the primary programming language used for developing smart contracts on the Ethereum platform. By understanding the principles, features, and real-world applications of smart contracts and Solidity, readers will gain the knowledge necessary to harness the full potential of dApps on the Ethereum blockchain. Smart contracts are self-executing agreements written in code, with the terms of the agreement directly embedded into the contract itself. They automatically enforce the rules and conditions defined within, removing the need for intermediaries and enabling trustless interactions between parties. Smart contracts are immutable, transparent, and operate based on predefined conditions.

Some benefits and advantages are as follows:

- **Transparency and trust**: Smart contracts eliminate the need for intermediaries, fostering transparency and trust between parties. All actions and outcomes are recorded on the blockchain, ensuring an immutable and auditable record of transactions.
- **Efficiency and automation**: By automating contract execution, smart contracts streamline processes, reduce costs, and eliminate manual errors. They enable self-executing transactions based on predefined conditions, allowing for automatic payments, escrow services, and complex logic.
- **Decentralization and security**: Smart contracts operate on a decentralized blockchain network, ensuring that no single entity has control over the contract. This eliminates the risk of censorship, manipulation, or single points of failure, enhancing security and resilience.

Solidity: The language of smart contracts

Solidity is a high-level programming language specifically designed for writing smart contracts on the Ethereum platform. It is statically typed, supports inheritance and complex data structures, and facilitates the creation of reusable and modular contracts.

Some key features of Solidity are as follows:

- **Contract-oriented**: Solidity is a contract-oriented language, focusing on defining the behavior and data structures of smart contracts. It allows the creation of contract templates that can be deployed multiple times with different parameters.
- **Turing complete**: Solidity is Turing complete, meaning it can perform any computation that can be expressed algorithmically. This flexibility enables the creation of complex and sophisticated decentralized applications.
- **Security and error prevention**: Solidity includes built-in mechanisms to prevent common vulnerabilities, such as integer overflow and reentrancy attacks. It also encourages developers to follow best practices, including code reviews and extensive testing.

Solidity development tools

Developers can utilize a range of tools to write, test, and deploy Solidity smart contracts. These include development environments like **Remix** and **Truffle**, testing frameworks like Truffle and **Mocha**, and deployment tools like the **Ethereum Development Toolkit**, **Hardhat** and **Ganache**. Smart contracts and Solidity have revolutionized various industries, enabling innovative decentralized applications.

Best practices and considerations

Developers should adhere to best practices when writing Solidity smart contracts to ensure security, efficiency, and compatibility. Some considerations include:

- **Code auditing**: Perform comprehensive audits of smart contract code to identify vulnerabilities and ensure compliance with industry standards.
- **Gas optimization**: Optimize smart contract code to reduce gas costs, as excessive gas consumption can lead to higher transaction fees and slower execution.
- **Upgradability and maintenance**: Plan for upgradability and maintenance of smart contracts by implementing upgradeable contract patterns and modular design.

Development environment and client

In order to effectively develop and deploy smart contracts on the Ethereum blockchain, it is crucial to understand the development environment and client tools available. This section will explore the development environment and client software that enable developers to write, test, and interact with smart contracts using Solidity, the primary programming language for Ethereum. By gaining a comprehensive understanding of these components, developers can efficiently create and deploy secure and functional smart contracts.

Development environment

The development environment refers to the set of tools and software used to write, compile, test, and deploy smart contracts. It provides developers with the necessary resources to build and interact with the Ethereum blockchain. Following are the key components of the development environment:

- **Integrated development environment** (**IDE**): An IDE is a software application that provides a comprehensive environment for writing, testing, and debugging code. Ethereum developers commonly use IDEs specifically tailored for smart contract development. Examples include Remix, Truffle, and visual studio code with appropriate extensions. These IDEs offer features like syntax highlighting, code completion, debugging, and deployment capabilities, facilitating efficient development and debugging processes.
- **Solidity compiler**: Solidity is the primary programming language used for writing smart contracts on the Ethereum blockchain. A Solidity compiler translates the human readable Solidity code into bytecode that can be executed on the EVM. The Solidity compiler ensures the correctness and compatibility of the code, generating the necessary bytecode for deployment.
- **Testing frameworks**: To ensure the functionality and reliability of smart contracts, developers use testing frameworks to write and execute test cases. Frameworks like Truffle and **OpenZeppelin** provide powerful testing tools and utilities, enabling developers to simulate various scenarios and validate the behavior of their smart contracts. Testing frameworks help catch bugs, prevent vulnerabilities, and enhance the overall quality of smart contracts.

Client software

Client software refers to the software that interacts with the Ethereum blockchain. It allows developers to deploy smart contracts, interact with existing contracts, and perform various operations on the blockchain. Following are the two main types of client software used in Ethereum:

- **Ethereum node clients**: Ethereum nodes are computer programs that maintain a copy of the entire blockchain and participate in the consensus mechanism. Ethereum node clients, such as **Geth** and **Parity**, enable developers to connect to the Ethereum network, synchronize with the blockchain, and interact with smart contracts. These clients provide APIs and **command-line interfaces (CLIs)** for sending transactions, querying data, and managing accounts.
- **Web3 libraries**: Web3 libraries, such as Web3.js and ethers.js, provide a convenient interface for developers to interact with the Ethereum blockchain from web applications. These libraries abstract the complexities of interacting with the blockchain, offering functions and methods for contract deployment, function invocation, and transaction handling. Web3 libraries simplify the process of integrating Ethereum functionality into web-based applications.

Basics of Solidity

Solidity is a powerful programming language specifically designed for writing smart contracts on the Ethereum blockchain. In this section, we will delve into the basics of Solidity, exploring its features, syntax, and functionality. By the end of this section, you will have a solid understanding of Solidity and be ready to start developing your own smart contracts on Ethereum. Solidity serves as the primary programming language for developing smart contracts on Ethereum. It is a statically-typed, high-level language with similarities to JavaScript and C++. Solidity empowers developers to write code that governs the behavior of smart contracts, defining their rules, conditions, and interactions with other contracts and users. Solidity's robustness and versatility make it a popular choice among Ethereum developers worldwide.

Solidity syntax and some of its features are as follows:

- **Contract structure**: In Solidity, a contract is the fundamental building block of a smart contract. It encapsulates the code, data, and functions required to define the behavior of a contract. Contracts are declared using the **contract** keyword, followed by the contract name and a set of curly braces.
- **Data types**: Solidity supports various data types, including integers, Booleans, strings, arrays, and structs. These data types enable developers to store and manipulate different kinds of information within a smart contract.
- **Functions and modifiers**: Functions in Solidity define the behavior and actions that can be performed by a smart contract. They can have input parameters and return values. Additionally, modifiers allow developers to impose conditions or restrictions on functions, enhancing the security and efficiency of the contract.

- **Events**: Events are an essential feature of Solidity that allow contracts to communicate with external applications. They are used to notify interested parties about specific occurrences within the contract. Events serve as a log of important contract events and provide transparency and traceability.
- **Control structures**: Solidity supports control structures such as **`if-else`** statements, loops, and switch cases, enabling developers to implement conditional and iterative logic within their smart contracts.
- **Inheritance and libraries**: Solidity provides support for inheritance, allowing developers to create hierarchical relationships between contracts. Inheritance enables code reusability and simplifies contract development. Additionally, Solidity allows the creation of libraries, which are reusable code components that can be imported into multiple contracts.

Solidity development process

To develop smart contracts in Solidity, developers follow a structured process:

- **Writing the contract**: Developers write the smart contract code using the Solidity syntax, defining the contract's structure, functions, data types, and events.
- **Compiling the contract**: The Solidity code is then compiled into bytecode, a low-level representation of the contract that can be executed on the EVM.
- **Deploying the contract**: The compiled bytecode is deployed onto the Ethereum blockchain, creating an instance of the smart contract. Deploying the contract requires interacting with the Ethereum network and paying gas fees to miners for processing the transaction.
- **Interacting with the contract**: Once deployed, the smart contract can be interacted with using external applications, wallets, or other contracts. Users can call functions, retrieve data, and trigger events based on the contract's functionalities.

Pros and cons of Solidity

Here are some pros and cons of Solidity.

Pros:

- Solidity is designed specifically for Ethereum smart contract development, ensuring compatibility and seamless integration with the Ethereum ecosystem.
- It provides a wide range of features and functionality, empowering developers to build complex and innovative decentralized applications.
- Solidity's popularity and active community support make it easier to find resources, documentation, and community-driven libraries.

- Ethereum's widespread adoption and active developer community offer ample opportunities for developers proficient in Solidity.

Cons:

- Solidity's learning curve can be steep for developers new to blockchain and smart contract development.
- Writing secure Solidity code requires careful attention to best practices and security considerations.
- The immutability of smart contracts on the blockchain can make updates and bug fixes challenging once a contract is deployed.
- Solidity's dynamic nature can sometimes lead to unexpected behaviors, requiring thorough testing and auditing of smart contracts.

Life cycle of a smart contract

The life cycle of a smart contract encompasses various stages. Each stage plays a pivotal role in the integrity and longevity of the contracts. By properly understanding it, developers can create robust and secure contracts. This encourages users to interact confidently with contracts and stakeholders to maintain and manage contracts effectively. The life cycle of a smart contract is as follows:

1. **Creation stage**: The creation stage marks the birth of a smart contract. Following are the key steps involved:
    a. **Design and development**: The process begins with defining the purpose, functionality, and requirements of the smart contract. Solidity, a high-level programming language, is commonly used for writing smart contracts on the Ethereum platform. Developers use Solidity's syntax and features to code the contract's logic and behavior.
    b. **Compilation**: Once the smart contract is written in Solidity, it needs to be compiled into bytecode, a low-level language that the EVM can understand. The compiler translates the Solidity code into bytecode, which can be deployed on the Ethereum blockchain.
    c. **Deployment**: After successful compilation, the smart contract is deployed onto the Ethereum blockchain. This process involves specifying the contract's initial parameters, such as constructor arguments, and sending a deployment transaction to the network. Upon successful deployment, the smart contract is assigned a unique address on the blockchain, making it publicly accessible.
2. **Initialization stage**: Once deployed, the smart contract enters the initialization stage. Here, specific functions may be called to initialize the contract's state and

set initial values for variables. Initialization allows the contract to be customized according to its intended use and ensures that it is ready for execution.

3. **Execution stage**: The execution stage involves the active interaction and operation of the smart contract. Let us explore the key aspects:
   a. **External interaction**: Smart contracts can interact with external entities, such as users, other contracts, or even external data sources. Users can invoke specific functions defined within the contract, triggering the execution of pre-defined actions. Contracts can also interact with other contracts, exchanging data and invoking their functions.
   b. **State modification**: During execution, smart contracts can modify their internal state. This includes updating variables, changing data structures, or even interacting with other contracts to update their state. These state modifications are typically permanent and stored on the Ethereum blockchain, ensuring immutability and transparency.
   c. **Event emission**: Smart contracts can emit events during their execution. Events are an essential mechanism for communicating and notifying external entities about specific occurrences within the contract. These events can be subscribed to, allowing interested parties to react and take actions based on the emitted events.
4. **Termination stage**: The termination stage marks the end of a smart contract's lifecycle. Termination can occur under various conditions:
   a. **Self-destruction**: A smart contract can be programmed with a self-destruct function, allowing the contract to be terminated voluntarily. Self-destruction is typically used to free up storage space on the blockchain or in situations where the contract has fulfilled its intended purpose.
   b. **Expiry or condition fulfilment**: Contracts can be designed with predefined expiry dates or conditions. Once the expiry date is reached or the conditions are met, the contract can terminate automatically. This mechanism is particularly useful for time-bound agreements or specific contractual obligations.
   c. **External intervention**: In certain cases, external entities or external factors may trigger the termination of a smart contract. This can include legal or regulatory actions, consensus failures, or consensus upgrades that render the contract obsolete.

Smart contract programming using Solidity

Solidity, a high-level programming language specifically designed for smart contracts on the Ethereum platform, plays a vital role in developing these self-executing contracts.

Solidity is a statically-typed programming language that enables developers to write smart contracts for the EVM. Following are the key aspects to consider:

- **Syntax**: Solidity's syntax draws inspiration from popular programming languages such as JavaScript and C++, making it familiar and accessible to developers with prior programming experience.
- **Data types**: Solidity supports various data types, including integers, strings, arrays, structures, and mappings. These data types enable developers to define and manipulate variables within smart contracts.
- **Functions and modifiers**: Solidity allows the creation of functions, which encapsulate specific logic and actions within the contract. Modifiers, on the other hand, are used to modify the behavior of functions, ensuring proper access control and conditions.
- **Events**: Solidity facilitates event-driven programming by providing an event mechanism. Events allow smart contracts to emit notifications about specific occurrences, enabling external entities to react and respond accordingly.

Consider the following sample code:

```
// SPDX-License-Identifier: MIT

pragma solidity ^0.8.0;

// Contract declaration

contract MathContract {

    // State variable to store the result

    uint256 public result;

    // Function to add two numbers and store the result

    function addNumbers (uint256 _a, uint256 _b) public {

        // Adding the two input numbers and storing the result in the state
variable

        result = _a + _b;

    }

    // Function to get the stored result

    function getResult() public view returns (uint256) {

        // Retrieving and returning the stored result
```

```
        return result;
    }
}
```

Explanation:

- **`pragma solidity ^0.8.0;`**: This line specifies the version of Solidity being used. In this case, it is version 0.8.0.
- **`contract SimpleCounter { ... }`**: This defines a contract named **`SimpleCounter`** which contains the logic for the counter.
- **`uint256 private counter;`**: This declares a state variable named **`counter`** of type **`uint256`** (unsigned integer) and makes it **`private`**. State variables hold values that persist across function calls.
- **`constructor() { ... }`**: This is a special function that is executed only once when the contract is deployed. Here, it sets the initial value of the **`counter`** to zero.
- **`function incrementCounter() public { ... }`**: This function increments the **`counter`** value by one. The **`public`** keyword makes it accessible by anyone.
- **`function getCounter() public view returns (uint256) { ... }`**: This function retrieves the current value of the **`counter`**. The **`public`** keyword allows external entities to access it.
- The **`view`** keyword ensures that the function does not modify any state variables.

In this simple program, we have created a smart contract named **`SimpleCounter`** that allows users to increment the counter and retrieve its value. The **`incrementCounter`** function increases the counter value by one, while the **`getCounter`** function returns the current value of the counter.

Now, let us take it a higher level and consider a real case smart contract:

```
// Constructor function

constructor(string[] memory_candidates) {

    // Initialize the candidates array with the provided List

    candidates=_candidates;


    // Initialize the vote count for each candidate to zero

    for (uint256 i = 0; i < candidates.length; i++) {
        candidateVotes [candidates[i]] = 0;
```

```
    }
}

// Function to vote for a candidate
function vote(string memory candidate) public {
    // Check if  the candidate is valid
    require (candidateExists(candidate). "Invalid candidate");

    // Increment the vote count for the selected candidate
    candidateVotes [candidate]++;
}

// Function to retrieve the total votes for a candidate
function getVotesForCandidate (string memory candidate) public view returns
(uint256) {
    // Check if the candidate is valid
    require (candidateExists(candidate). "Invalid candidate");

    // Return the vote count for the selected candidate
    return candidateVotes (candidate);
}
// Function to check if a candidate exists
```

Explanation:

- **`pragma solidity ^0.8.0;`**: This line specifies the version of Solidity being used. In this case, it is version 0.8.0.
- **`contract VotingSystem { ... }`**: This defines a contract named **`VotingSystem`** which contains the logic for the voting system.
- **`mapping(string => uint256) private candidateVotes;`**: This declares a mapping named **`candidateVotes`** that maps a candidate's name (string) to the number of votes they have received (**`uint256`**). The **`private`** keyword makes it accessible only within the contract.

- `string[] private candidates;`: This declares an array named **`candidates`** to store the list of candidates. The **`private`** keyword makes it accessible only within the contract.
- `constructor(string[] memory _candidates) { ... }`: This is a special function that is executed only once when the contract is deployed. It takes an array of candidate names as a parameter and initializes the candidates array with the provided list. It also initializes the vote count for each candidate to zero.
- `function vote(string memory candidate) public { ... }`: This function allows users to vote for a candidate. It takes the name of the candidate as a parameter. It first checks if the candidate is valid by calling the **`candidateExists`** function. If valid, it increments the vote count for the selected candidate.
- `function getVotesForCandidate`(string memory candidate) **`public view returns`**
- `(uint256) { ... }`: This function allows users to retrieve the total votes for a candidate. It takes the name of the candidate as a parameter. It first checks if the candidate is valid by calling the **`candidateExists`** function. If valid, it returns the vote count for the selected candidate.
- `function candidateExists(string memory candidate) private view returns (bool) { ... }`: This function checks if a candidate exists in the candidates array. It takes the name of the candidate as a parameter. It iterates through the candidates array and compares each candidate's name with the provided candidate. If a match is found, it returns true; otherwise, it returns false.

Some major consideration while writing smart contracts are as follows:

- **Access control**: Implement proper access control mechanisms to restrict certain functions or data to authorized users. This helps prevent unauthorized users from executing critical functions.
- **Error handling**: Implement effective error handling mechanisms to gracefully manage unexpected situations and provide meaningful feedback to users.

Reentrancy in Solidity

Reentrancy refers to a scenario in which a contract can repeatedly call itself or another contract before the initial execution is complete. This can lead to unexpected and potentially malicious behavior. If a contract interacts with external contracts or sends Ether during its execution without proper safeguards, an external contract can exploit this by calling back into the original contract before its state is updated, potentially causing undesired effects. Developers can use mutex patterns, check-effects-interactions pattern, and reentrancy guards to prevent reentrancy vulnerabilities.

Let us look at some of the following points:

- **Overflow**: Arithmetic overflow occurs when a mathematical operation results in a value larger than the maximum representable value for a data type. For example, adding 1 to the maximum value of a `uint256` will result in overflow.
- **Underflow**: Arithmetic underflow is the opposite, occurring when a subtraction operation results in a value smaller than the minimum representable value for a data type.
- **Vulnerability**: If overflow or underflow is not handled properly, it can lead to unexpected behavior, vulnerabilities, or even loss of funds.
- **Prevention**: Developers should use `SafeMath` library functions or manually check for overflow/underflow conditions to ensure that arithmetic operations stay within the acceptable range.

Upgradeability of smart contracts

As smart contracts are immutable, we have a mechanism for upgradeability of smart contracts called **proxy contract**.

Proxy contracts are a technique used to achieve upgradability in smart contracts, allowing developers to update the logic of a contract without altering its address or state. This is particularly useful when dealing with immutable contracts on blockchain platforms like Ethereum. There are different types of proxy patterns, but the basic idea involves separating the storage and the logic of a contract into two separate contracts: a proxy contract and an implementation contract.

Here is a simplified explanation of how proxy contracts work:

- **Proxy contract**
  - o The proxy contract is the one that users interact with. It contains the address of the current implementation contract.
  - o When a function is called on the proxy contract, it forwards the request to the implementation contract.
- **Implementation contract**
  - o The implementation contract holds the actual logic of the smart contract.
  - o Upgrades involve deploying a new version of the implementation contract.
- **Upgrading process:**
  - o To upgrade the logic of the contract, a new version of the implementation contract is deployed.

- The proxy contract is then updated to point to the address of the new implementation contract.
- Users continue interacting with the proxy contract, unaware that the underlying logic has been updated.

- **Storage separation:**
  - The proxy contract retains storage data, ensuring that the state of the contract remains intact during upgrades.
  - This separation of storage and logic allows for the seamless transition between different versions.
- **Proxy patterns:**
  - There are various proxy patterns, such as transparent proxy, upgradeable proxy, and minimal proxy, each with its own characteristics and trade-offs.
  - The transparent proxy is a popular choice because it preserves the contract's interface, making the upgrade process smoother.
- **Security considerations:**
  - Proxy contracts introduce complexities, and security is a crucial concern.
  - Care must be taken to avoid vulnerabilities, and thorough testing and auditing are essential before deploying proxy-based contracts.
- **Governance mechanism:**
  - Upgradability often involves a governance mechanism where certain conditions or stakeholders decide when and how upgrades occur.
  - This helps prevent unauthorized or malicious upgrades.

Implementing proxy contracts requires careful consideration of the specific requirements and trade-offs of the application. It offers a flexible approach to upgradability, enabling developers to adapt and improve their smart contracts over time without sacrificing the benefits of immutability.

Introduction to MetaMask

MetaMask is a powerful and widely-used Ethereum wallet that provides users with a seamless and secure interface to interact with the Ethereum blockchain. In this comprehensive guide, we will explore the features, benefits, and working principles of MetaMask, shedding light on its significance in the world of DeFi and blockchain technology. MetaMask is a browser extension wallet designed specifically for Ethereum. It allows users to manage their Ethereum accounts, store ETH and other ERC-20 tokens, and interact with dApps directly from their web browsers. MetaMask acts as a bridge between users and the Ethereum network, simplifying the user experience and enhancing security.

Some key features of MetaMask are as follows:

- **Account management**: MetaMask enables users to create and manage multiple Ethereum accounts. Each account has a unique address and cryptographic key pair, ensuring secure ownership and access to funds.
- **Wallet integration**: MetaMask seamlessly integrates with popular web browsers like **Chrome** and **Firefox**, providing users with a user-friendly interface to manage their Ethereum assets. It offers easy access to account balances, transaction histories, and network status.
- **Ethereum dApp compatibility**: MetaMask serves as a gateway to the Ethereum ecosystem, allowing users to interact with a wide range of decentralized applications. Users can access and use various dApps, including decentralized exchanges, lending platforms, and gaming applications, all within the MetaMask interface.
- **Transaction management**: MetaMask simplifies the process of sending and receiving Ether and ERC-20 tokens. Users can set gas fees, customize transaction parameters, and sign transactions securely using their private keys.
- **Network connectivity**: MetaMask supports multiple Ethereum networks, including the mainnet, testnets (such as **Ropsten** and **Rinkeby**), and private networks. Users can switch between networks effortlessly to test and deploy smart contracts or explore different blockchain environments. Some benefits of MetaMask are as follows:
- **Enhanced security**: MetaMask employs robust security measures, such as encrypted storage of private keys, to protect user funds. It also utilizes phishing protection and warning systems to mitigate risks associated with malicious websites or scams.
- **User-friendly interface**: MetaMask offers a sleek and intuitive interface, making it accessible to users of all levels of technical expertise. Its simple design and clear navigation allow users to interact with the Ethereum blockchain seamlessly.
- **Interoperability with dApps**: MetaMask acts as a bridge between users and dApps, enabling effortless integration and interaction. Users can access a vast ecosystem of decentralized applications directly from their wallets, opening up opportunities for DeFi, gaming, and much more.
- **Customizable gas fees**: MetaMask allows users to customize gas fees according to their needs, balancing transaction speed and cost. This flexibility ensures efficient and cost-effective interactions with the Ethereum network.

- **Community and support**: MetaMask benefits from a vibrant and active community, with extensive documentation, forums, and support channels. Users can find resources, troubleshoot issues, and stay up-to-date with the latest developments in the MetaMask ecosystem.

Working principles of MetaMask

MetaMask is a highly popular wallet for its user-friendly interface, secure key management, and seamless dApp integration. However, there are some working principles of MetaMask that users and developers must be aware of. They are as follows.

- **Account creation**: Upon installation, MetaMask generates a new Ethereum account for the user, complete with a unique address and associated private key. Users must securely store their private keys, as they grant access to their funds and assets.
- **Browser integration**: MetaMask integrates seamlessly with popular web browsers, appearing as a small icon in the browser toolbar. Users can access their accounts, view balances, and initiate transactions directly from the browser interface.
- **Transaction signing**: When initiating a transaction, MetaMask prompts the user to review the details and confirm the action. The user must then sign the transaction using their private key, ensuring cryptographic verification and securing the transaction's integrity.
- **Smart contract interactions**: MetaMask facilitates interactions with smart contracts by automatically detecting contract addresses and providing a user-friendly interface for invoking functions, sending tokens, or interacting with contract-specific features.

Use cases of smart contracts

Now that you have understood how smart contracts work, let us look at some smart contract examples from the real world:

- **Clinical trials**: Efficient data sharing among institutions is crucial for successful clinical trials. Smart contracts facilitate seamless data sharing across the healthcare industry, revolutionizing the process. Additionally, blockchain technology can authenticate data, ensuring its accuracy and integrity. This breakthrough capability has far-reaching implications for launching expansive clinical trials, streamlining operations, and promoting collaboration among professionals.
- **Music industry**: Emerging music artists heavily rely on streaming income as they embark on their musical journey. Smart contracts offer a solution by simplifying royalty payments. These contracts can stipulate the distribution of royalty

income between the artist and the record label, ensuring a fair and transparent arrangement.

- Instant payments are enabled through smart contracts, benefiting all parties involved. For instance, Tune.fm leverages tokenized music economy using JAM tokens, allowing artists to receive direct payment for every second of their music streamed. Artists can even create and sell exclusive content as **non-fungible tokens** (**NFTs**) to fans in exchange for JAM tokens.
- **Supply chain management**: Smart contracts are a game-changer in supply chain management, operating autonomously without intermediaries or third parties. By designing a smart contract for end-to-end supply chain processes, daily management and auditing become obsolete. Deviations from the scheduled deliveries trigger pre-agreed escalation measures, ensuring a seamless and efficient operation. A notable example is **Datahash** (formerly Entrust), Australia's pioneering full-service agricultural supply chain platform, which combats the multi-billion-dollar fraudulent wine market using **Hedera Consensus Service** for trusted data tracing.
- **Property ownership**: Smart contract technology opens up the concept of fractional ownership in real estate. Instead of one person solely owning a property, ownership can be divided into tokens, allowing multiple individuals to invest in fractional shares. Each token represents a specific percentage of ownership, facilitating micro investments and democratizing access to the property market.
- **Mortgages**: The mortgage industry is ripe for disruption, burdened by costly intermediaries and time-consuming processes. Smart contracts address these challenges by ensuring lenders and loan seekers agree to clear terms and conditions, including proof-of-funds and payment planning. This emerging technology validates mortgage transactions without the need for lawyers or other intermediaries, streamlining the process and reducing costs.
- **Retail**: Smart contracts streamline administrative processes that often burden brick and mortar retailers. These contracts facilitate fast payments to contractors, digitize payroll administration in real-time, and provide visibility across supply chains by assigning unique blockchain identifiers to inventory units. Dropp, for example, enables micropayments in both cryptocurrency and traditional currencies, benefiting merchants and consumers alike.
- **Digital identity**: Smart contracts offer a secure means of managing digital identity, storing reputational data and digital assets. By connecting smart contracts to various online services, counterparties can gain insights about individuals without revealing their identities. Smart contracts can also incorporate credit scores, enabling lenders to assess potential risks. MyEarth ID, a decentralized

identity management system, empowers users to control their digital identity data securely and verify it with third parties.

- **Recording financial data**: Smart contracts play a crucial role in facilitating accurate and transparent financial data collection. These contracts significantly reduce auditing costs and ensure compliance by executing predefined financial rules without human intervention. This streamlined approach saves time for accountants and optimizes administrative workflows. **AllianceBlock**, a protocol bridging DeFi and **traditional financial services (TradFi)**, is building **AllianceBridge**—a validator network leveraging the Hedera Consensus Service.
- **Voting in elections**: Smart contracts can revolutionize the voting process by providing a secure environment that minimizes the risk of voter manipulation. Each vote recorded through a smart contract is protected on a tamper-proof ledger, making it extremely difficult to decode. With online systems powered by smart contracts, physical presence at a polling station becomes unnecessary, potentially increasing voter turnout.
- **Insurance sector**: Smart contracts have a pivotal role in automating policies and services within the insurance industry, mitigating disputes, reducing costs for insurers, and resulting in lower premiums. By leveraging smart contract technology, claims payment processes can be automated, ensuring policyholders receive payments faster compared to manual processes.

Opportunity and risks of smart contract

In the realm of blockchain technology, smart contracts have emerged as a disruptive innovation with the potential to revolutionize various industries. While smart contracts present numerous opportunities for efficiency and cost savings, they also come with inherent risks that must be carefully considered. This essay will delve into the risks and opportunities associated with smart contracts, shedding light on their transformative potential while acknowledging the challenges that lie ahead.

Here are some opportunities of smart contract:

- **Efficiency and automation**: One of the key advantages of smart contracts is their ability to automate processes, reducing human error and streamlining operations. By removing the need for intermediaries, smart contracts enable direct peer-to-peer interactions, significantly reducing transaction costs and processing times. This increased efficiency can lead to enhanced productivity and improved customer experiences.
- **Cost savings**: Smart contracts have the potential to dramatically reduce costs in various sectors by eliminating the need for traditional intermediaries, such as lawyers, auditors, and brokers. With automated execution and verification, smart

contracts minimize administrative overheads and operational expenses, making business processes more cost-effective.

- **Transparency and trust**: Blockchain technology, on which smart contracts are built, offers a transparent and immutable ledger that can be audited by all participants. This transparency instills trust and confidence in transactions, as all parties have access to the same information, reducing the likelihood of fraud or manipulation. Smart contracts enable verifiable and auditable transactions, fostering a more transparent and accountable business environment.
- **Disintermediation and decentralization**: Smart contracts empower individuals and businesses by removing the reliance on centralized authorities. With decentralized networks, smart contracts promote peer-to-peer interactions, facilitating direct transactions between parties. This disintermediation has the potential to democratize access to various industries, enabling greater participation and economic inclusivity.

Some risks associated with smart contracts are as follows:

- **Code vulnerabilities**: Smart contracts are written in code, and any flaws or vulnerabilities in the code can be exploited by malicious actors. These vulnerabilities can lead to security breaches, resulting in financial losses or unauthorized access to sensitive information. It is crucial for developers to ensure thorough code reviews, security audits, and testing to mitigate the risks associated with code vulnerabilities.
- **Legal and regulatory challenges**: As smart contracts operate in a decentralized and borderless environment; they can pose legal and regulatory challenges. The legal enforceability of smart contracts, especially across different jurisdictions, is still evolving. Additionally, the lack of a centralized authority to oversee smart contract transactions raises questions regarding liability, dispute resolution, and compliance with existing regulations.
- **Scalability and interoperability**: As blockchain networks, including those supporting smart contracts, grow in size and complexity, scalability and interoperability become significant challenges. The current limitations of blockchain technology, such as network congestion and slower transaction processing times, hinder the widespread adoption of smart contracts. Achieving seamless integration and compatibility between different blockchain platforms is also a technical hurdle that needs to be addressed.
- **Human error and irreversibility**: While smart contracts aim to eliminate human error, mistakes can still occur during the development or implementation phase. Once a smart contract is deployed on the blockchain, it becomes immutable and cannot be easily reversed. Any errors or bugs in the code can have long-lasting

consequences, making it imperative for thorough testing and auditing before deployment.

Smart contract deployment

In the realm of blockchain technology, smart contracts have gained significant attention for their ability to automate and enforce digital agreements. However, understanding the process of deploying smart contracts can be complex for newcomers to this concept. This comprehensive guide aims to explain the intricacies of smart contract deployment in a clear and accessible manner, providing insights into the steps involved and the considerations to be mindful of throughout the process.

Smart contract deployment refers to the process of making a smart contract functional and accessible on a blockchain network. It involves taking the code, which represents the terms and conditions of an agreement, and deploying it onto the blockchain so that it can be executed and interacted with by various parties.

Steps in smart contract deployment are as follows:

1. **Smart contract development**: Before a smart contract can be deployed, it must be developed. This entails writing the code that specifies the logic, conditions, and actions of the contract. Smart contracts are typically written in programming languages such as Solidity, which is widely used on the Ethereum blockchain. During the development phase, it is essential to thoroughly test the code to identify and address any bugs or vulnerabilities.
2. **Selecting the blockchain platform**: Choosing the appropriate blockchain platform for deployment is a crucial decision. Different platforms have their own unique features, capabilities, and ecosystems. Ethereum is one of the most popular choices due to its robustness and support for smart contracts, but other platforms like **Binance Smart Chain** and **Polkadot** also offer smart contract functionality. Factors such as scalability, security, and community support should be considered when selecting the blockchain platform.
3. **Deployment environment setup**: To deploy a smart contract, a suitable development environment must be set up. This typically involves using tools and frameworks provided by the chosen blockchain platform. For Ethereum, the development environment often involves using the **EVM** and development frameworks like Truffle or Hardhat. These tools facilitate the compilation, testing, and deployment of smart contracts.
4. **Compilation and testing**: Once the development environment is set up, the smart contract code needs to be compiled into a format that can be understood by the blockchain network. The compilation process verifies the syntax and structure of

the code, ensuring its validity. After compilation, rigorous testing is necessary to identify any potential vulnerabilities or logic flaws that could compromise the contract's functionality or security.

5. **Deploying to the Blockchain**: Deploying a smart contract involves uploading the compiled code to the blockchain network. This process requires paying a fee known as a gas fee, which covers the computational resources required to execute the contract on the network. The deployment transaction is recorded on the blockchain, and a unique address is assigned to the deployed contract. This address serves as a reference for interacting with the contract.
6. **Interacting with the deployed smart contract**: Once the smart contract is deployed, it becomes accessible to users and other smart contracts on the blockchain. Users can interact with the contract by invoking its functions, sending transactions, and accessing its data. Interactions are typically carried out using a web-based interface or through custom-built applications known as **dApps**. These interactions trigger the execution of the contract's predefined logic.

Nonetheless, there are some points which users must know when dealing with smart contracts. They are:

- **Security audits**: Smart contracts are immutable once deployed, making security audits a critical step. Conducting thorough audits by experienced professionals helps identify vulnerabilities and ensures that the contract's logic aligns with the intended functionality. Audits help mitigate the risk of potential exploits, which could lead to financial losses or compromised data.
- **Gas optimization**: Gas optimization involves writing efficient code to minimize the computational resources required for executing smart contracts. This optimization helps reduce transaction costs and ensures smoother contract execution. Techniques such as minimizing storage usage, avoiding unnecessary computations, and optimizing data structures contribute to gas efficiency.
- **Upgradeability and maintenance**: It is essential to consider the future upgradeability and maintenance of smart contracts. As blockchain technology evolves, it may become necessary to introduce updates or bug fixes to deployed contracts. Implementing upgradeability mechanisms from the beginning allows for seamless updates without disrupting the contract's functionality or requiring redeployment.
- **Compliance and legal considerations**: Smart contracts must comply with applicable laws and regulations. Depending on the jurisdiction, certain agreements may require legal enforceability. It is essential to seek legal advice and ensure that the smart contract's terms and conditions align with legal requirements to avoid any potential legal complications.

Truffle: Smart contract development

Truffle is a powerful development framework and suite of tools that simplifies and streamlines the process of building, testing, and deploying smart contracts on blockchain platforms. It is widely used by developers in the Ethereum ecosystem and has become an essential tool for creating dApps. This comprehensive guide provides an in-depth exploration of Truffle, its key features, and its significance in the world of smart contract development.

Some key features of Truffle are as follows:

- **Project structure and management**: Truffle provides a well-defined project structure that helps organize smart contract code, tests, and configurations. It utilizes a standardized directory layout, making it easy to navigate and maintain large-scale projects. Truffle also offers built-in project management features, such as package management using **Node Package Manager (npm)**, to efficiently handle dependencies and libraries.
- **Smart contract compilation and deployment**: Truffle simplifies the process of compiling and deploying smart contracts. It supports multiple blockchain platforms, including Ethereum, and integrates seamlessly with development networks like Ganache. Truffle's built-in compiler compiles Solidity contracts into bytecode, which can be easily deployed to the blockchain network. It also provides migration scripts to automate the deployment process across different environments.
- **Testing framework**: Testing smart contracts is crucial to ensure their functionality and security. Truffle incorporates a comprehensive testing framework that allows developers to write and execute unit tests, integration tests, and end-to-end tests for their contracts. Truffle's testing tools provide utilities for interacting with contracts, simulating different scenarios, and asserting contract behavior, enabling developers to validate contract functionality effectively.
- **Debugging and interactive console**: Truffle includes a powerful interactive console that facilitates contract interaction and debugging. Developers can use the console to interact with deployed contracts, execute contract functions, and inspect contract state. Additionally, Truffle integrates with popular debugging tools like **Geth** and **Ganache**, allowing developers to debug contracts and troubleshoot issues efficiently.
- **Contract management and upgrades**: Truffle provides features for contract management and upgrades. With Truffle, developers can easily manage multiple contract versions, track contract addresses, and handle contract upgrades. This feature is particularly valuable as it allows for seamless updates and bug fixes

while ensuring data continuity and minimizing disruption to dApps built on top of existing contracts.

- **Integration with development tools**: Truffle integrates well with various development tools and frameworks, enhancing the overall development experience. It integrates with popular code editors like **Visual Studio Code**, offering syntax highlighting, autocompletion, and code navigation features specific to Solidity. Truffle also integrates with testing frameworks like Mocha and assertion libraries like Chai, providing developers with a familiar and flexible testing environment.

Significance of Truffle in smart contract development

Truffle plays a vital role in empowering developers to build robust and efficient smart contracts. Its comprehensive set of features, coupled with its user-friendly interface, streamline the entire development lifecycle. By simplifying tasks like compilation, deployment, testing, and debugging, Truffle significantly reduces development time and enhances code quality.

Truffle's standardized project structure and management capabilities promote code organization and maintainability. Its integration with popular development tools and frameworks allows developers to leverage their preferred tools and workflows. Truffle's support for contract upgrades ensures that contracts can evolve over time without disrupting existing applications and data. Furthermore, Truffle's extensive community support, documentation, and active developer community make it a reliable and trusted choice for smart contract development. The Truffle ecosystem provides access to numerous plugins, libraries, and frameworks, enriching the development experience and expanding the possibilities for dApp creation. Let us look at the given steps for better understanding:

1. **Install Truffle Globally Bash**

   Terminal: `npm install -g truffle`

2. **Create a Truffle Project Bash**

   Terminal: `mkdir myTruffleProject cd myTruffleProject truffle init`

3. **Write a Smart Contract**: Create or edit a Solidity smart contract in the contracts/ directory. For example, create a file named **`MyContract.sol`**:

   Solidity:

```
// MyContract.sol  pragma solidity ^0.8.0;  contract MyContract {
uint public myNumber;
 function setNumber(uint _number) public {  myNumber = _number;
 }
```

```
}
```

4. **Compile the Smart** Contract bash

   Terminal: `truffle compile`

5. **Configure Deployment**

   Edit the **`migrations/2_deploy_contracts.js`** file to specify which smart contracts to deploy and any constructor arguments:

   Javascript:

```
// 2_deploy_contracts.js

/const MyContract = artifacts.require("MyContract");  module.exports
= function(deployer) {  deployer.deploy(MyContract);

};
```

6. **Deploy to a Development Blockchain (Ganache)**

   Make sure you have Ganache running or any other Ethereum development blockchain.

   Bash Terminal: **`truffle migrate`**

7. **Interact with Smart Contract**

   Start the Truffle console to interact with your deployed contract.

   Bash Terminal: **`truffle migrate`**

   Within the console, you can interact with your contract, by using the following code:

   Javascript:

```
let instance = await MyContract.deployed();  let result = await
instance.setNumber(42);  console.log(result);;
```

8. **Test smart contract**

   Write tests for your smart contract in the test/ directory.

   For example, create a file named **`myContract.js`**:

   Javascript:

```
// myContract.js

const      MyContract      =      artifacts.require("MyContract");
contract("MyContract", accounts => {  it("should set the number",
async () => { const instance = await MyContract.deployed();  await
instance.setNumber(42);  const result = await instance.myNumber();
assert.equal(result, 42);

    });
```

```
});
```

Let us run the tests.

Bash Terminal: `truffle test`

Some additional tips are as follows:

- Customize Truffle configurations in `truffle-config.js`.
- Use a development blockchain like Ganache for testing and debugging.
- Explore Truffle's documentation for more advanced features: **Truffle Documentation**

This flow provides a basic guide, and you can customize it based on your project requirements. Ensure to refer to Truffle's documentation for detailed information and updates.

Remix and test networks

When it comes to deploying smart contracts, two essential tools come into play: Remix, a widely used web-based IDE, and test networks specifically designed for testing and experimentation. In this comprehensive guide, we will delve into the use of Remix and test networks for deploying smart contracts, providing you with a clear understanding of these indispensable resources.

Remix: An accessible IDE

Remix serves as a user-friendly IDE that simplifies the process of developing smart contracts. Being a web-based tool, it eliminates the need for complex local setup and configuration, allowing developers to start coding immediately. Remix fully supports the Solidity programming language, which is extensively used for writing smart contracts on platforms like Ethereum.

Some key features of remix are as follows:

- **Code editing and compilation**: Remix offers a code editor equipped with features like syntax highlighting and autocompletion, enhancing the ease of writing and editing smart contract code. It also includes a built-in compiler that translates Solidity code into bytecode, which can subsequently be deployed to the blockchain.
- **Contract deployment**: With remix, developers can effortlessly deploy their smart contracts to various blockchain networks, including both local and test networks. By connecting Remix to a test network, you can deploy and interact with your contracts without incurring any costs or affecting the main blockchain network.

- **Debugging and testing**: Remix provides essential debugging capabilities, allowing developers to step through their smart contracts, examine variables, and identify potential issues. Additionally, Remix offers a testing framework that enables developers to write and execute unit tests, ensuring the accurate functionality of their contracts.

Importing from GitHub

Remix IDE allows you to import existing smart contracts from GitHub repositories directly. To do this follow the given steps:

1. Open Remix IDE in your browser.
2. On the left sidebar, find the *File Explorers* section.
3. Click on the GitHub icon.
4. Enter the GitHub repository URL or the path to the specific Solidity file.
5. Click *Import* to load the file into Remix.

Plugin management

Remix IDE supports plugins that enhance its functionality. To manage plugins:

1. Click on the plugin icon in the left sidebar.
2. Browse and install plugins from the available list.
3. Configure and customize the installed plugins based on your needs.

Deployment on testnets

Remix IDE provides an easy way to deploy your smart contracts on Ethereum testnets. Here is a general guide:

1. Write and compile your smart contract in Remix.
2. Go to the *Deploy and Run Transactions* tab in Remix.
3. Select the environment (JavaScript VM, Injected Web3, and so on.) and choose the appropriate network (Ropsten, Rinkeby, and so on.) from the dropdown.
4. Click *Deploy* to deploy your contract to the selected testnet.
5. Confirm the transaction in your connected wallet (if using MetaMask or another Ethereum wallet).

Note: Make sure you have testnet Ether in your testnet wallet to cover the deployment costs.

Additional features

Remix IDE offers various additional features for smart contract development:

- **Editor with syntax highlighting**: Write and edit your Solidity code with syntax highlighting for better readability.
- **Integrated debugger**: Debug your smart contracts step by step to identify and fix issues.
- **Gas estimation**: Estimate the gas cost of your transactions before deploying them.
- **Static analysis**: Remix provides static analysis reports to identify potential security vulnerabilities.

Remember that Remix IDE is a powerful tool, and its features may evolve over time. Always refer to the official Remix documentation and community resources for the most up-to-date and detailed information on using Remix IDE features.

Test networks: Simulating blockchains

Test networks serve as alternative blockchain networks that mimic the behavior of the main blockchain but operate in a simulated environment. These networks are purpose-built for testing and experimentation, allowing developers to deploy and test their smart contracts without involving real cryptocurrencies or affecting the live network.

Some benefits of test networks are as follows:

- **Cost-efficiency**: Test networks provide a cost-effective solution for deploying and testing smart contracts. Since these networks utilize test tokens with no real-world value, developers can experiment and iterate without the risk of losing actual funds.
- **Realistic simulation**: Test networks closely resemble the main blockchain network in terms of functionality and behavior. This enables developers to simulate real-world scenarios, interactions, and contract executions, ensuring that their smart contracts perform as expected.
- **Faster development**: By utilizing test networks, developers can significantly expedite the development process. They can deploy contracts, test functionalities, identify and resolve bugs, and refine their contracts without waiting for block confirmations or encountering congestion issues that may exist on the main network.
- **Community support and tooling**: Test networks boast vibrant developer communities that offer support, documentation, and specialized tools for their respective networks. This allows developers to leverage community resources and collaborate with fellow developers who are also utilizing the same test networks.

Some prominent test networks include **Ropsten**, **Rinkeby**, and **Kovan** networks for Ethereum. These networks closely resemble the Ethereum main network and are widely utilized by developers for testing and experimentation purposes.

In conclusion, Remix and test networks are vital components in the deployment of smart contracts. Remix serves as an accessible IDE, simplifying the development process, while test networks offer simulated environments for safe testing and experimentation. By utilizing Remix and test networks, developers can enhance their development workflow, ensure the functionality of their contracts, and gain confidence in their deployment process.

Conclusion

As the blockchain world continues to evolve, Ethereum is going to reach new heights in the coming years. By tackling challenges like scalability through upgrades like Ethereum 2.0, this blockchain network has continued its domination in the field. Experts are confident that it will continue to do so if it constantly updates itself to meet the ever-evolving market demands. This chapter has tried to explore all the dimensions of Ethereum through sections like EVM, MetaMask, Ethereum 2.0, and many more. Now that you know about permissionless blockchains, the next chapter will unveil permissioned blockchain, their architecture, use cases, applications, and more.

Questions and answers

1. **What is Ethereum, and how does it differ from Bitcoin?**

   Ans.: Ethereum is a decentralized blockchain platform that enables the development of smart contracts and dApps. Its main objective is to facilitate programmable contracts, going beyond just being a digital currency. On the other hand, Bitcoin is primarily a digital currency that focusses on peer-to-peer transactions.

2. **What are smart contracts?**

   Ans.: Smart contracts are self-executing contracts with predefined conditions. They automatically get executed when the predefined conditions encoded on the blockchain are met. This enables trustless interactions.

3. **What is gas on the Ethereum blockchain?**

   Ans.: Gas on the Ethereum blockchain refers to the transaction fees that users must pay to execute contracts. It reflects the number of resources needed for the execution of contracts.

4. **What is the life cycle of a smart contract?**

   Ans.: The life cycle of a smart contract involves several stages like creation, initialization, execution, and termination. Its understanding helps users create a strong and reliable smart contract.

5. **What are Ethereum test networks?**

   Ans.: Ethereum test networks can be called alternative blockchains that functions similar to the main Ethereum network. They are used for development and experimentation purposes without interacting with any real economic value.

Multiple choice questions

1. **What is the primary purpose of Ethereum?**
   a. Facilitating peer-to-peer transactions
   b. Enabling smart contracts and decentralized applications
   c. Providing a centralized banking system
   d. Mining Bitcoin

2. **What represents the computational cost of operations on the Ethereum network?**
   a. Bitcoin
   b. Token
   c. Gas
   d. Ledger

3. **What is the use of the Ethereum test network?**
   a. Real transactions and economic value
   b. Development, testing, and experimentation
   c. Mining real ETH
   d. Trading cryptocurrencies

4. **What does gas optimization primarily do?**
   a. Enhancing smart contract complexity
   b. Minimizing transaction speed
   c. Reducing computational resources consumed
   d. Increasing gas prices

5. **Which consensus mechanism does Ethereum 2.0 use?**
   a. Proof of authority (PoA)
   b. PoW
   c. Delegated proof of stake (DPoS)
   d. PoS

Answer

1. b
2. c
3. b
4. c
5. d

Join our book's Discord space

Join the book's Discord Workspace for Latest updates, Offers, Tech happenings around the world, New Release and Sessions with the Authors:

https://discord.bpbonline.com

CHAPTER 5

Permissioned Blockchain: Hyperledger Fabric

Introduction

In the realm of blockchain technology, two dominant paradigms have emerged: **permissionless** and **permissioned blockchains**. While both are built upon the fundamental principles of distributed ledger technology, they serve distinct purposes and exhibit contrasting characteristics. In this chapter, we embark on a journey into the realm of permissioned blockchain frameworks, exploring their core concepts, architecture, and applications.

Hyperledger Fabric is an open-source permissioned blockchain framework. It has been developed under the Hyperledger initiative of Linux. The primary use of Hyperledger Fabric is to facilitate the development of enterprise-grade blockchain-based applications. This chapter aims to dive deeper into the intricacies, features, and functionalities of Hyperledger Fabric. It will shed lights on this permissioned blockchain technology's advantages, challenges, and evolving landscape.

Structure

The chapter includes the following topics:

- Defining permissioned blockchains
- Architecture of Hyperledger Fabric
- Chaincode
- The ordering services
- Membership services
- Hyperledger project: Framework
- Structure of Hyperledger
- Introduction to Hyperledger Sawtooth
- Introduction to Hyperledger Iroha
- Introduction to Hyperledger Burrow
- Hyperledger Indy: Disrupting digital identity
- Hyperledger ecosystem
- Hyperledger tooling and utility libraries
- Blueprint of Hyperledger Fabric
- MSPs: The guardians of identity
- Chaincodes
- Nodes: The building blocks
- Chaincode: The logic of transactions
- Channels: Enabling privacy and segmentation
- Consensus mechanisms in Hyperledger Fabric
- Interoperability and scalability

Objectives

In this chapter, readers will get to learn its foundational concepts, practical implementations, architecture, smart contract capabilities, and more. The chapter will analyze the use cases of Hyperledger Fabric across various industries. Besides, its efficiency in facilitating decentralized solutions for a range of businesses will also be evaluated. This chapter will serve as a valuable guide for developers, enterprises, or blockchain enthusiasts seeking to comprehend Hyperledger Fabric.

Defining permissioned blockchains

Blockchain technology, as most of you are already aware, gained notoriety through its association with cryptocurrencies, particularly Bitcoin. However, blockchain's utility transcends the realm of digital currencies, and it has emerged as a versatile solution for various industries, ranging from finance and supply chain to healthcare and beyond. In our journey, we shall delve into the intricacies of blockchain technology, starting with an understanding of permissioned blockchains. Permissioned blockchains, often referred to as **consortium** or **private blockchains**, stand in stark contrast to their permissionless counterparts. The defining feature of a permissioned blockchain is its restricted access. Unlike permissionless networks such as **Bitcoin**, where anyone can participate without prior approval, permissioned blockchains operate within a controlled environment where access is limited to a select group of participants. These participants are typically known and trusted entities, which distinguishes permissioned blockchains as ideal choices for enterprises and institutions.

Some key characteristics of permissioned blockchain are as follows:

- **Access control**: Permissioned blockchains maintain strict access controls, ensuring that only authorized participants can validate transactions, propose new blocks, or access the blockchain's data. This control over network access aligns with the requirements of businesses seeking to maintain confidentiality and security.
- **Efficiency**: With a limited number of participants, permissioned blockchains can achieve higher transaction throughput and lower latency compared to their permissionless counterparts. This efficiency is vital for use cases where rapid transaction processing is essential.
- **Privacy**: Privacy is a paramount concern for many businesses. Permissioned blockchains offer configurable privacy features, enabling selective disclosure of transaction details. This empowers enterprises to protect sensitive information while still benefiting from the transparency of blockchain technology.

Architecture of permissioned blockchains

The primary difference between permissioned and permissionless blockchains lie in their architecture. The architecture of permissioned blockchains focuses on controlled access, privacy, and tailored governance structures. Understanding the architecture of permissioned blockchain frameworks is pivotal for grasping their operational mechanisms. Some of its critical elements are:

- **Nodes**: In a permissioned blockchain network, nodes are operated by authorized entities. These nodes can take on various roles, including validating transactions, maintaining the ledger, and executing smart contracts.

- **Consensus mechanisms**: Consensus algorithms in permissioned blockchains differ from those in permissionless networks. While **proof of work (PoW)** and **proof of stake (PoS)** are commonly used in permissionless blockchains, permissioned networks often opt for more efficient consensus mechanisms such as **Practical Byzantine Fault Tolerance** (**PBFT**) or Raft.
- **Identity management**: Identity management is a core component of permissioned blockchains. Participants are required to provide valid credentials, and their identities are often tied to cryptographic keys. This robust identity verification helps maintain the integrity of the network.

Use cases and applications

The adoption of permissioned blockchains has rapidly expanded across industries. They find application in a multitude of sectors, including finance, supply chain, healthcare, and government. It enables streamlined operations, secure data sharing, and improved traceability. Their characteristics make them well-suited for scenarios where confidentiality, regulatory compliance, and controlled access are imperative. Major sectors using permissioned blockchains are:

- **Supply chain management**: Tracking the provenance of goods and ensuring transparency in the supply chain is facilitated by permissioned blockchains. With permissioned blockchains, participants can record and verify the movement of products with confidence.
- **Financial services**: In the financial sector, permissioned blockchains are employed for the settlement and clearing of financial instruments, reducing processing time and enhancing security.
- **Education**: In the education sector, Hyperledger Fabric can be applied for secure and transparent management of academic credentials and certificates, reducing fraud in the certification process.
- **Real estate**: In real estate, permissioned blockchains are used for streamlining property transactions, managing land registries, and improving transparency in real estate dealings.
- **Energy and utilities**: Permissioned blockchains find application in energy trading, grid management, and supply chain traceability in the energy sector, enhancing efficiency and reducing operational complexities.
- **Insurance**: The insurance industry utilizes Hyperledger Fabric for enhancing the efficiency of claims processing, reducing fraud, and improving transparency in policy management.

- **Healthcare**: Managing patient records securely and ensuring that only authorized individuals can access sensitive medical data are challenges addressed by permissioned blockchain solutions.

As we can observe that the application of permissioned blockchains encompasses various industries, its integration is bound to increase in the years to come.

This section sets the grand stage for a comprehensive grasp of permissioned blockchain frameworks, paving the way for a more profound exploration of their complexities and potential in the chapters that lie ahead.

Architecture of Hyperledger Fabric

Before we delve into the intricacies of Hyperledger Fabric, it is crucial to understand its place within the broader Hyperledger ecosystem. Hyperledger, hosted by the Linux foundation, is a collaborative effort that seeks to advance cross-industry blockchain technologies. Within this ecosystem, Hyperledger Fabric emerges as a prominent player, offering a robust and highly customizable platform for building distributed ledger applications. *Figure 5.1* is the visual representation of the architecture of Hyperledger Fabric please refer to the following figure:

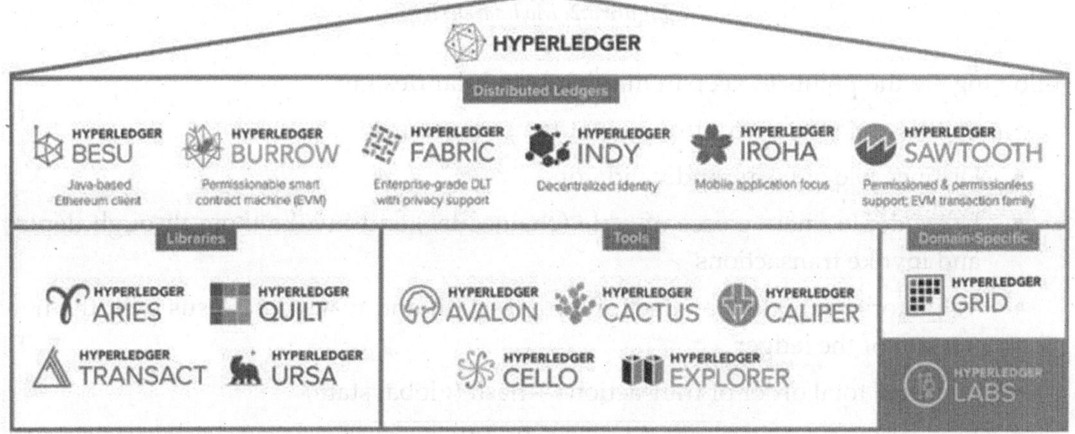

***Figure 5.1**: Hyperledger Fabric architecture*

The modular design

At the heart of Hyperledger Fabric lies its modular and pluggable architecture. This architectural elegance empowers developers and enterprises to tailor the blockchain network to their specific needs. Imagine it as a toolkit, where you can pick and choose the components that suit your project requirements.

Let me illustrate this with a real-life connection. Consider a multinational supply chain consortium aiming to increase transparency and traceability. Hyperledger Fabric's modular design allows them to integrate a range of components, such as a consensus algorithm suitable for their use case, identity management solutions for secure access, and smart contracts written in a language of their choice, be it Go, Java, or Node.js. This versatility is the key to unleashing the true potential of blockchain technology. Refer to *Figure 5.2* for the modular design:

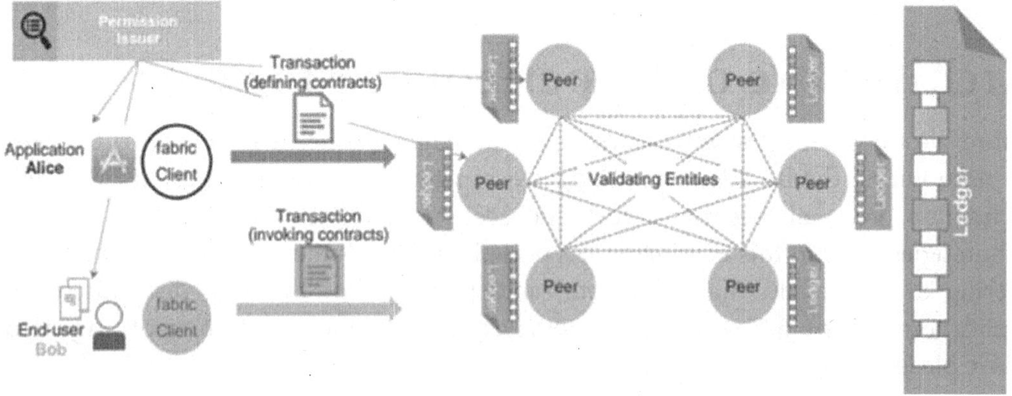

***Figure 5.2**: Modular design*

Following are the points to keep in mind for modular design:

- Permissioned system; strong identity management
- Distinct role of users, and validators
- Users deploy new pieces of code (chaincodes) and invoke them through deploy and invoke transactions
- Validators evaluate the effect of a transaction and reach consensus over the new version of the ledger
- Ledger = total order of transactions + hash (global state)
- Pluggable consensus protocol, currently PBFT and sieve

Why Hyperledger Fabric

Hyperledger Fabric's modular design sets it apart from other blockchain platforms. Unlike monolithic architectures, Fabric employs a modular approach that enhances flexibility and scalability. This modular design allows for the customization of components, enabling tailored solutions for diverse business needs.

Comparatively, platforms like Ethereum may follow a more integrated model. While Ethereum is renowned for its smart contract capabilities, Hyperledger Fabric excels in permissioned settings, providing finer control over access and privacy. Fabric's modular structure, with components like ordering service, **Membership Service Providers (MSPs)**, and channels, offers a comprehensive solution for enterprise blockchain applications.

In terms of chaincode, Hyperledger Fabric stands out with its support for smart contracts written in various programming languages. This flexibility facilitates easier integration and adoption for developers, allowing them to leverage existing skills. Other platforms might be limited to specific languages, potentially posing a learning curve for developers.

Hyperledger Fabric excels in some scenarios. These scenarios and advantages are as follows:

- **Privacy and confidentiality**
  - o **Scenario**: Financial institutions require privacy for transactions.
  - o **Advantage**: Hyperledger Fabric's channels allow the creation of private sub-networks, ensuring transaction confidentiality. This is crucial for financial transactions where privacy is paramount.
- **Selective endorsement**
  - o **Scenario**: Supply chain involving multiple parties with varying levels of trust.
  - o **Advantage**: Fabric's endorsement policies enable selective endorsement of transactions. In a supply chain, this ensures that only relevant participants validate transactions, enhancing efficiency and security.
- **Customizable consensus mechanisms**
  - o **Scenario**: Healthcare consortium requiring regulatory compliance.
  - o **Advantage**: Fabric supports pluggable consensus mechanisms. In scenarios with strict regulatory requirements, organizations can choose a consensus algorithm that aligns with compliance needs, ensuring trust and adherence to regulations.
- **Modular identity management**
  - o **Scenario**: Government agencies collaborating on a cross-agency blockchain.
  - o **Advantage**: Hyperledger Fabric's MSPs enable granular control over identities. In a government consortium, this ensures that each agency maintains control over its members' access, enhancing security and accountability.
- **Multi-language chaincode**
  - o **Scenario**: Global supply chain with diverse development teams.

- **Advantage**: Fabric's support for multiple programming languages allows development teams worldwide to contribute. This is advantageous in scenarios where diverse expertise and contributions are essential for a complex global system.

- **Scalability and performance**
  - **Scenario**: E-commerce platform managing a high volume of transactions.
  - **Advantage**: Fabric's architecture allows for scalable and efficient transaction processing. In scenarios where high transaction throughput is crucial, Hyperledger Fabric can handle the load effectively.

Chaincode

One of the cornerstones of Hyperledger Fabric is its support for smart contracts, referred to as chaincode. These chaincodes are the business logic that governs transactions within the network. Imagine a real estate agency employing Hyperledger Fabric to streamline property transactions. Chaincode enables them to automate the verification and transfer of property titles securely and efficiently.

The following *Table 5.1* shows the comparison between Ethereum smart contracts and Hyperledger Fabric:

Aspect	Hyperledger Fabric	Ethereum
Programming languages	Supports multiple languages (Go, JavaScript, and so on).	Primarily uses Solidity, requiring developers to learn a new language.
Execution model	Executes transactions in a deterministic, permissioned environment.	Runs on a global, decentralized network, allowing anyone to participate.
Privacy and confidentiality	Channels enable private transactions among specified participants.	All transactions are visible to all participants, potentially challenging privacy requirements.
Consensus mechanism	Supports pluggable consensus mechanisms (for example, Raft, Kafka).	Relies on **PoW**, transitioning to **PoS**.
Transaction cost	Transaction costs can be more predictable as they may be defined by the consortium.	Gas fees can vary based on network demand, leading to less predictable costs.
Finality	Achieves faster finality due to its permissioned nature.	Finality can take longer, especially in the **PoW** model.

Aspect	Hyperledger Fabric	Ethereum
Advantages of Hyperledger Fabric	Enhanced privacy features through channels.	Ideal for enterprise consortia where participants are known and trusted.
	Ideal for enterprise consortia where participants are known and trusted.	Allows flexibility in choosing consensus mechanisms.
Advantages of Ethereum	Operates on a global, decentralized network.	Smart contracts can be executed by anyone on the Ethereum network.

***Table 5.1**: Comparison between Ethereum smart contracts and Hyperledger Fabric*

Some advantages of Hyperledger Fabric are as follows:

- **Privacy**: Enhanced privacy features through channels.
- **Permissioned network**: Ideal for enterprise consortia where participants are known and trusted.
- **Pluggable consensus**: Allows flexibility in choosing consensus mechanisms.
- Some advantages of Ethereum are as follows:
- **Decentralization**: Operates on a global, decentralized network.
- **Global execution**: Smart contracts can be executed by anyone on the Ethereum network.
- **Ecosystem**: A large and established ecosystem with diverse **decentralized applications (DApps)**.

Understanding these differences can help organizations choose the right platform based on their specific use cases and requirements.

Lifecycle of a chaincode

Understanding the lifecycle of a chaincode is crucial for effective blockchain application management, ensuring continuous functionality, security, and adaptability to changing business needs. The lifecycle of a chaincode encompasses various distinct stages, each with its own process and outcome. These stages can be categorized as follows:

- **Deployment**
  - o It can also be termed as the stage of initialization.
  - o The chaincode is initialized and instantiated on the blockchain network.
  - o Initial parameters and configurations are set during this phase.

- **Endorsement and approval**
    - o The chaincode is endorsed by a subset of network participants.
    - o Approval from the majority of endorsing peers is required for deployment.
    - o The chaincode is endorsed according to the defined endorsement policy.
- **Instantiation**
    - o The approved chaincode is instantiated, and a new version becomes active on the network.
    - o Smart contracts are ready to process transactions.

Transaction processing

This stage involves two phases. They are as follows:

- **Invoke transactions**
    - o Applications invoke transactions by interacting with the deployed chaincode.
    - o Transactions are proposed, endorsed, and then committed to the ledger.
- **State updates**
    - o Chaincode execution may lead to updates in the world state (ledger).
    - o Updated state is replicated across all nodes in the network.

Upgrading

Under this stage, modifications and enhancements to the existing chaincode are invoked. It can involve the following elements:

- **Code changes**
    - o When an updated version of the chaincode is developed, incorporating bug fixes or new features.
- **Endorsement and approval for upgrade**
    - o Similar to deployment, the upgraded chaincode version is endorsed and approved by network peers.
- **Upgrade execution**
    - o The upgraded chaincode is installed on the peers.
    - o Existing instances are replaced by the new version.
- **Migration of state**
    - o If required, mechanism for migrating data from the old chaincode version to the new one is executed.

Maintenance

This stage is vital to ensure the stability and efficiency of the deployed blockchain. It includes:

- **Monitoring and diagnostics**
    - o Continuous monitoring of the chaincode's performance, health, and resource usage.
    - o Diagnostics to identify and address any issues promptly.
- **Patch deployment**
    - o Deploying patches or updates for security, stability, or performance improvements.

Scaling

This stage is crucial in scaling the network or adjusting resources to accommodate changing demands. This might involve adding new peers or adjusting existing configurations. It includes:

- **Periodic upgrades**
    - o Planning and executing periodic upgrades to ensure the chaincode remains aligned with evolving requirements and best practices.
- **Governance and policy**
    - o Adhering to network governance and policies for chaincode management.
    - o Updating access controls, policies, and configurations as needed

The ordering services

To maintain a consistent ledger across the network, Hyperledger Fabric employs an ordering service that sequences transactions into blocks. This ensures that all participants in the network have a uniform view of the ledger's history. Think of this as the conductor in a grand orchestra, orchestrating the harmonious execution of transactions.

Membership services

In any enterprise blockchain, identity management is paramount. Hyperledger Fabric offers membership services to authenticate participants and regulate access permissions. Consider a healthcare consortium, where only authorized personnel should access patient records.

Membership services ensure that sensitive medical data remains confidential.

Real-world deployments

Let us bring this all together with a real-life success story. IBM's Food Trust, powered by Hyperledger Fabric, revolutionized the food supply chain. It allows consumers to trace the journey of their food from farm to fork, enhancing food safety and transparency. Hyperledger Fabric's modular architecture played a pivotal role in creating this transformative solution.

The world of Hyperledger Fabric is a captivating realm of modularity, versatility, and real-world impact. As we progress through this module, we shall explore the tools and architecture that underpin this remarkable platform, uncovering its potential to reshape industries and create innovative solutions. Join me on this charismatic journey through the halls of Hyperledger Fabric, where blockchain technology meets the dynamic demands of the modern world.

Hyperledger project: Framework

Certainly, let us continue our exploration into the fascinating world of Hyperledger with a focus on the Hyperledger project framework. In this section, we will uncover the core aspects of this framework, which serves as the backbone of Hyperledger's collaborative efforts.

Collaborative innovation

At its essence, the Hyperledger project is a testament to the power of collaborative innovation. It is like a community garden tended by passionate individuals from diverse backgrounds, each contributing their unique expertise to cultivate the blockchain landscape. This framework, much like a well-maintained garden, thrives on cooperation and shared vision.

Open-source philosophy

What sets the Hyperledger project apart is its unwavering commitment to the principles of open source. Just as good neighbors share recipes over the garden fence, Hyperledger invites participation from all corners of the globe. The framework operates under the Linux foundation, ensuring transparency, trust, and accessibility to all who seek to engage in the blockchain revolution.

Hyperledger greenhouse

Imagine the Hyperledger project as a lush greenhouse filled with a rich variety of plants, each representing a different blockchain technology. This greenhouse is where various projects, such as Hyperledger Fabric, Sawtooth, and Indy, flourish. Each project has its unique characteristics and applications, providing a comprehensive toolkit for blockchain developers and enthusiasts.

Practical applications

In our down-to-earth exploration, we cannot overlook the practical applications of the Hyperledger project framework. Picture a local business consortium aiming to streamline their financial transactions. Hyperledger's modular approach allows them to select the most suitable project from the greenhouse, tailoring it to their specific needs. The result? Efficient and secure financial operations that benefit the community.

Down to earth approach

What makes the Hyperledger project truly remarkable is its down to earth approach, is not about grandiose promises or elusive blockchain fantasies. Instead, it is about rolling up one's sleeves and ge ing to work, tending to the needs of real-world businesses and organizations. The framework provides the tools and support for practical, tangible blockchain solutions.

The Hyperledger project framework is a fertile ground where collaborative innovation and open-source principles thrive. Just as a well-tended garden yields a bountiful harvest, the Hyperledger framework offers a diverse ecosystem of blockchain projects ready to meet the demands of industries worldwide.

Let us explore the structure of Hyperledger in simple and descriptive terms, making it easily understandable for all.

Structure of Hyperledger

Hyperledger, like a well-organized library, is structured to facilitate easy access to a wealth of blockchain tools and technologies. Its structure consists of open-source frameworks, tools, and libraries. All these components are tailored to address different aspects of blockchain technology. Since it consists of a range of frameworks and tools, enterprises get to alter its structure as per their requirements. Major components of Hyperledger structure are:

Hyperledger umbrella

At the heart of Hyperledger is the umbrella structure. Think of this as the library itself, with its various sections dedicated to different topics. Under this umbrella, you will find a collection of projects, each serving a distinct purpose and tailored for specific use cases.

Hyperledger projects

Now, let us venture into the library's sections, which correspond to individual Hyperledger projects. Imagine these projects as different series of books, each exploring a unique facet of blockchain technology.

Here are a few notable series you might encounter:

- **Hyperledger Fabric**: This series focuses on building enterprise-grade, modular blockchain applications. It is like the how to Build section in the library.
- **Hyperledger Sawtooth**: Think of this series as the experimental section. It is for those who want to experiment with different consensus algorithms and smart contract languages.
- **Hyperledger Indy**: In our library, this is the identity section. It is dedicated to projects that enhance identity management on the blockchain.
- **Hyperledger Besu**: This series is like the Ethereum integration section, offering compatibility with Ethereum clients.
- **Hyperledger Aries**: Consider this series as the Blockchain connectivity section. It deals with creating secure, interoperable blockchain-based solutions.

Diverse contributions

The beauty of the Hyperledger structure is that it is not just a library; it is also a community of authors. Developers, organizations, and enthusiasts worldwide contribute to these projects, adding new chapters and insights to the blockchain knowledge pool.

The structure of Hyperledger resembles a well-organized library, where each project is a series of books dedicated to specific aspects of blockchain technology. This structure ensures that you can find the resources you need to explore, experiment, and build your own blockchain solutions.

Hyperledger Fabric V1 architecture

Hyperledger Fabric V1, like the foundation of a sturdy house, has a fundamental architecture that supports its robustness. Imagine it as the blueprint for building a strong and reliable blockchain network.

Network components

In the world of Hyperledger Fabric V1, there are three core network components that work in harmony.

- **Peers**: Think of these as the workers in your blockchain network. They maintain the ledger and smart contracts, endorsing and validating transactions.
- **Ordering service**: This is like the post office. It ensures that transactions are processed in the correct order and added to the ledger consistently.
- **Membership services**: These are the gatekeepers of your network. They authenticate participants and manage permissions. It is like the bouncer at an exclusive club, only letting in the right guests.

Figure 5.3 shows network components of Hyperledger Fabric V1:

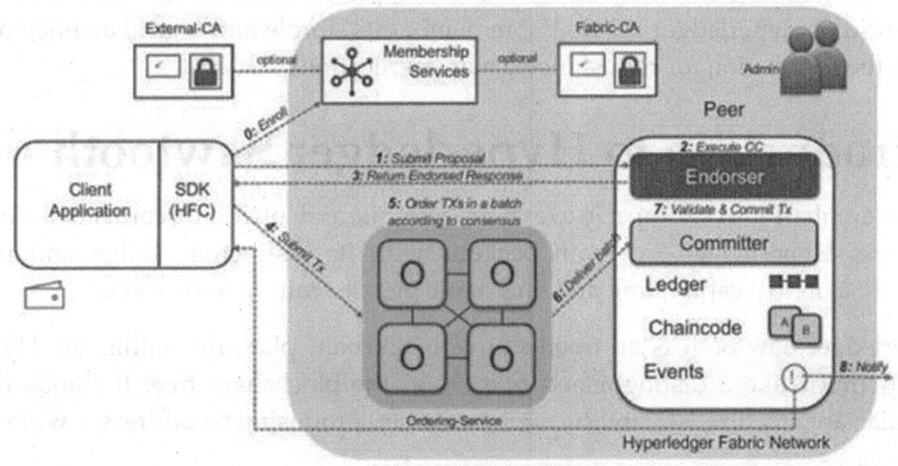

Figure 5.3: Hyperledger Fabric V1 architecture

Smart contracts and ledgers

Hyperledger Fabric V1 introduces a separation of powers, much like having separate books for accounting and inventory in a business. Here, we have:

- **Smart contracts (chaincode)**: These are the rules of your blockchain, like the rulebook of a board game. They define how transactions should behave.
- **Ledger**: Think of this as the accounting book. It records all transactions, providing an immutable history of the network's activity.

Channels for privacy

To maintain privacy, Hyperledger Fabric V1 introduces the concept of channels. Imagine a conference call where only specific people can hear the conversation. Channels allow for private communication within a network, ensuring that not everyone can see every transaction.

Consensus mechanisms

Just as a group of friends must agree on the movie they want to watch, a blockchain network needs a consensus mechanism to agree on the order of transactions. Hyperledger Fabric V1 offers pluggable consensus, allowing you to choose the mechanism that suits your needs, be it PBFT or Raft.

Hyperledger Fabric V1's architecture is like a well-structured house, with clear roles for each component. It offers a practical and reliable way to build enterprise-grade blockchain networks, ensuring that transactions are secure, private, and orderly. So, as you delve into the world of Hyperledger Fabric V1, remember its simple and logical architecture, which forms the foundation for robust blockchain applications.

Introduction to Hyperledger Sawtooth

Imagine embarking on a journey to explore a unique and intriguing corner of the blockchain universe. Hyperledger Sawtooth beckons with its distinctive design and innovative features, akin to a captivating and enigmatic puzzle waiting to be solved.

Hyperledger Sawtooth is an open-source blockchain platform within the Hyperledger family, much like a distinguished branch on the blockchain tree. It stands out for its modular architecture, scalability, and versatility, promising to address a wide spectrum of use cases.

The following *Table 5.2* shows a small comparison between Hyperledger Sawtooth and Hyperledger Fabric:

Feature	Hyperledger Fabric	Hyperledger Sawtooth
Consensus mechanism	Modular, supports PBFT, Kafka, and so on	**Proof of elapsed time (PoET)** for fairness and energy efficiency
Transaction families	N/A	Supports parallel processing with the concept of transaction families
Parallel transaction processing	Sequential processing within a block	Supports parallel processing of transactions within the same block

Feature	Hyperledger Fabric	Hyperledger Sawtooth
Smart contract language compatibility	Go, JavaScript, Java for chaincode development	Compatibility with Ethereum's solidity through a layer
Identity management	MSPs for identity management	Integrates with external identity management systems
Permissioned versus permissionless	Primarily designed for permissioned networks	Suited for both permissioned and permissionless networks
Global state merkle tree	Uses a versioned key-value store for ledger state	Maintains a global state Merkle tree structure

Table 5.2: Comparison between Hyperledger Sawtooth and Hyperledger Fabric

Modularity and components

At the core of Hyperledger Sawtooth lies its modular design, reminiscent of a finely crafted Swiss watch, with each component playing a precise role. These roles are:

- **Transaction families**: These are like the gears of the watch, responsible for processing specific types of transactions. Imagine one gear handling financial transactions while another manages supply chain operations.
- **Consensus engine**: Picture this as the heartbeat of Sawtooth, determining how transactions are validated and added to the ledger. It offers flexibility, allowing you to choose consensus mechanisms that suit your needs.
- **Validator nodes**: These are the guardians of the ledger, ensuring that transactions adhere to the rules defined by the transaction families. Validator nodes form a distributed network, enhancing security and decentralization.
- **Transaction processors**: Think of these as the skilled artisans who craft the gears for our watch. They execute transactions according to the rules defined by the transaction families, ensuring the ledger's integrity.

Hyperledger Sawtooth architecture

Hyperledger Sawtooth stands as an innovative and unique platform. Its architecture offers an adaptable platform for building enterprise-grade blockchain applications. This section will delve into the complex structure of Hyperledger Sawtooth, its distinctive features, and its real-world applications.

Features and benefits

Hyperledger Sawtooth boasts a set of features that make it a compelling choice for a diverse range of applications:

- **Permissioned and permissionless modes**: It caters to both private and public blockchain needs, offering flexibility for various use cases.
- **Parallel transaction execution**: Transactions can be processed concurrently, like different assembly lines in a manufacturing plant, increasing efficiency.
- **Smart contracts with WebAssembly (Wasm)**: Sawtooth supports smart contracts written in Wasm, making it accessible to a wide range of developers.
- **Scalability**: As your network grows, Sawtooth scales gracefully, ensuring that performance remains optimal even in demanding environments.
- **Simple yet powerful**: The platform's simplicity in design makes it accessible to developers while maintaining robustness for enterprise-grade applications.

Real-world applications

Consider a supply chain consortium seeking to improve transparency and traceability. Hyperledger Sawtooth, with its modular architecture and smart contract capabilities, can be tailored to create a custom solution that seamlessly tracks goods from production to distribution, ensuring authenticity and efficiency.

Hyperledger Sawtooth is a captivating chapter in the blockchain narrative, offering a modular, versatile, and scalable platform. Its unique design, akin to an intricately crafted timepiece, empowers developers and organizations to build tailored blockchain solutions.

Introduction to Hyperledger Iroha

Imagine strolling through a tranquil Japanese garden, where simplicity and efficiency harmonize. Hyperledger Iroha, like such a garden, offers a unique approach to blockchain technology, combining simplicity with practicality. Hyperledger Iroha is an open-source, permissioned blockchain platform within the Hyperledger family, designed with a specific focus on ease of use and minimalism. It draws inspiration from the traditional Japanese philosophy of Iroha, emphasizing simplicity, order, and clarity.

The following *Table 5.3* shows a contrast between Fabric, Sawtooth and Iroha:

Feature	Hyperledger Fabric	Hyperledger Sawtooth	Hyperledger Iroha
Consensus mechanism	**Pluggable (PBFT, Raft)**	**proof of elapsed time (PoET)**	**Yet Another Consensus (YAC)** (PBFT)
Smart contract execution	Modular chaincode (Go, JavaScript, Java)	Multiple languages, Ethereum solidity compatibility	Domain-driven C++ design

Feature	Hyperledger Fabric	Hyperledger Sawtooth	Hyperledger Iroha
Transaction model	Channels for transaction privacy	Transaction families for parallel processing	Simplified transaction model for mobile applications
Identity management	**Membership service providers (MSPs)**	External identity management systems (flexible)	Secure control and permissions over user roles and activities
Permissioned versus Permissionless	Primarily designed for permissioned networks	Suited for both permissioned and permissionless networks	Supports both permissioned and permissionless setups
Ease of use	Moderate learning curve due to modular architecture	Known for modular design and ease of use	Emphasizes simplicity, particularly for mobile applications
Use cases	Various industries (finance, supply chain, healthcare)	Supply chain, IoT applications, parallel processing	Asset management, identity control, simplicity in mobile apps

***Table 5.3:** Contrast between Fabric, Sawtooth and Iroha*

Core components of Hyperledger Iroha

At the heart of Hyperledger Iroha lies its core components, carefully orchestrated to deliver a streamlined blockchain experience. Some core components are:

- **Peer nodes**: Think of these as the participants in a traditional Japanese tea ceremony, each playing a specific role. Peer nodes execute transactions, maintain the ledger, and reach consensus efficiently.
- **Transactions**: These are like the carefully crafted tea utensils used in the ceremony. Transactions in Iroha are simple and compact, making them easy to understand and execute.
- **Consensus algorithm**: Much like the harmony and agreement sought in a tea ceremony, Iroha employs the **Yet Another Consensus** (YAC) algorithm to achieve consensus among peer nodes.
- **Command query language (CQL)**: This is the language of communication in Iroha, akin to the language used in a traditional ceremony. It allows users to interact with the blockchain in a straightforward and intuitive manner.

Hyperledger Iroha features

Hyperledger Iroha offers several key features that distinguish it in the blockchain landscape:

- **Simple yet powerful**: Iroha's minimalist design ensures that it is accessible to both developers and non-developers, making it an ideal choice for a wide range of applications.
- **Fast transaction processing**: Transactions in Iroha are quick to execute, ensuring efficiency in applications where speed is crucial.
- **Rich permission model**: It provides flexible permission management, allowing organizations to define access levels and roles easily.
- **Security and scalability**: Iroha offers robust security features and can be scaled to meet the demands of various use cases.

Real-world applications of Hyperledger Iroha

Consider a scenario where a local government wishes to create a blockchain-based system for managing citizen identities securely. Hyperledger Iroha's simplicity and user-friendly design make it an excellent choice for such a project. It can efficiently handle identity management, ensuring data integrity and security.

Hyperledger Iroha brings the elegance of simplicity to the blockchain world, much like a serene Japanese garden. Its minimalist design, user-friendly approach, and focus on efficiency make it a valuable addition to the Hyperledger family. As we continue our journey through the diverse landscape of blockchain technology, Hyperledger Iroha stands as a testament to the power of simplicity and clarity in the blockchain realm.

Introduction to Hyperledger Burrow

Picture a bespoke suit tailored to perfection, where every stitch and detail serves a specific purpose. Hyperledger Burrow can be likened to such a tailored creation in the world of blockchain technology. It is an open-source, permissioned blockchain platform that stands out for its unique characteristics. Hyperledger Burrow is akin to a specialized toolkit- a set of finely crafted tools designed for a particular purpose within the expansive Hyperledger ecosystem. It offers a distinctive approach to blockchain.

Hyperledger Burrow and Ethereum differ in their approach to executing smart contracts. Hyperledger Burrow, with its Tendermint consensus and permissioned design, offers fast and predictable transaction confirmation, making it efficient for known participants in enterprise settings. Ethereum, known for its public blockchain, faces variable confirmation times and gas fees, making it suitable for a broader range of decentralized applications. The choice depends on the desired level of permissioning, consensus mechanism, and the specific use case's efficiency requirements.

In addition to efficiency considerations, Hyperledger Burrow stands out with its deterministic execution, ensuring consistent outcomes for smart contracts. Its integration with the broader Hyperledger ecosystem provides interoperability benefits for comprehensive blockchain solutions. On the other hand, Ethereum's extensive ecosystem and developer community make it a preferred choice for decentralized finance and diverse public blockchain applications. Ultimately, organizations should weigh the advantages of permissioning, consensus models, and ecosystem support when deciding between Hyperledger Burrow and Ethereum for their smart contract execution needs.

EVM connection

What sets Hyperledger Burrow apart is its compatibility with the EVM. Think of it as a bridge that connects the world of Ethereum with the broader Hyperledger ecosystem. This bridge allows Ethereum smart contracts to run seamlessly within the Burrow blockchain.

Hyperledger Burrow boasts a set of distinctive features that make it a valuable addition to the blockchain toolkit. Some of these features are:

- **Ethereum compatibility**: Burrow's compatibility with Ethereum smart contracts opens up a world of possibilities, allowing developers to leverage existing Ethereum code and tools.
- **Permissioned blockchain**: It offers the control and security of a permissioned blockchain, making it an attractive choice for businesses and organizations with specific privacy and compliance requirements.
- **Modular architecture**: Burrow's architecture is modular, allowing for flexibility in configuring the network to suit various use cases.
- **Smart contract execution**: Much like a skilled artisan, Burrow excels in executing smart contracts efficiently, ensuring that transactions are processed smoothly.

Real-world applications

One of the major sectors where Hyperledger Burrow's permissioned blockchain is highly useful is finance. It can be used to facilitate secure and auditable financial transactions.

Hyperledger Burrow brings a unique perspective to the world of blockchain. It offers the elegance of Ethereum compatibility within the framework of a permissioned blockchain.

Hyperledger Indy, a prominent member of the Hyperledger family, offers a distinctive approach to blockchain technology, emphasizing digital identity and privacy.

Hyperledger Indy: Disrupting digital identity

Imagine sailing through uncharted waters, where trust and identity are the stars guiding your journey. Hyperledger Indy can be likened to a finely crafted compass, designed to navigate the intricate world of digital identity on the blockchain.

Hyperledger Indy is an open-source, decentralized platform tailored for managing digital identities securely and privately. It addresses the critical need for robust identity management in an increasingly digital world.

Hyperledger Indy components

At the heart of Hyperledger Indy are its core components, meticulously designed to address the challenges of digital identity. Some of its vital components are:

- **Decentralized Identifiers (DIDs)**: Think of DIDs as unique digital passports. They allow individuals and entities to create and manage their identities on the blockchain securely.
- **Verifiable credentials**: These are akin to digital certificates, enabling users to present proof of their identity or qualifications without revealing sensitive information.
- **Self-sovereign identity**: Hyperledger Indy champions the concept of self-sovereign identity, empowering individuals to have full control over their digital identities, much like possessing their own set of keys.

Besides, Hyperledger Indy offers a set of key features that elevate it as a trusted platform for digital identity management. They are as follows:

- **Privacy-preserving**: It ensures privacy by design, allowing users to disclose only the information necessary for a specific transaction or verification, safeguarding sensitive data.
- **Interoperability**: Hyperledger Indy is designed to work seamlessly with other blockchain platforms, enhancing its utility in a broader context.
- **Decentralization**: The platform's decentralized nature ensures that no central authority controls or owns users' identity information, fostering trust and security.
- **Open standards**: Hyperledger Indy adheres to open standards, promoting collaboration and interoperability in the digital identity space.

Real-world applications

Consider a scenario where individuals need to access healthcare services remotely. Hyperledger Indy's digital identity management can enable patients to securely share only relevant medical information with healthcare providers, ensuring both convenience and privacy. Hyperledger Indy is like a trusted companion on the journey of digital identity, offering privacy, control, and security. Its focus on self-sovereign identity aligns with the evolving needs of our digital age, where individuals seek to assert control over their digital personas. The Hyperledger project is a collaborative effort under the Linux foundation that aims to advance the development of open-source blockchain technologies and tools. It brings together a community of developers, organizations, and innovators to collectively work on building robust, enterprise-grade blockchain solutions.

Hyperledger ecosystem

Imagine a thriving ecosystem with diverse species of plants and animals, each contributing to the overall balance and growth. Similarly, the Hyperledger project, too, is an ecosystem where various tools and technologies coexist, each serving a unique purpose. These tools and technologies play a crucial role in its functioning. These tools and technologies are:

Hyperledger Fabric

Hyperledger Fabric, like the foundation of a sturdy house, is one of the flagship projects within the Hyperledger ecosystem. It offers a versatile and modular platform for building enterprise-grade blockchain applications. With features like smart contract support, permissioned networks, and pluggable consensus mechanisms, Fabric empowers organizations to design and deploy tailored blockchain solutions.

Hyperledger Sawtooth

Hyperledger Sawtooth, akin to a well-structured Swiss watch, is another blockchain framework designed for simplicity and scalability. It employs a unique consensus algorithm called **proof of elapsed time** (**PoET**) and allows for the development of smart contracts using various programming languages. Sawtooth's modular architecture and parallel transaction processing make it suitable for a wide range of use cases.

Hyperledger Indy

Hyperledger Indy, as we explored earlier, is a specialized tool for managing digital identities on the blockchain. It introduces the concept of self-sovereign identity, empowering individuals to have control over their digital personas while ensuring privacy and security.

Indy's components, such as **DIDs** and verifiable credentials, form the building blocks of a robust identity management system.

Hyperledger Besu

Hyperledger Besu, like a bridge connecting two worlds, is designed for Ethereum compatibility. It allows organizations to leverage Ethereum tools and smart contracts within the Hyperledger ecosystem. Besu's support for Ethereum mainnet and testnet networks makes it a valuable tool for enterprises seeking to integrate with the Ethereum blockchain.

Hyperledger Burrow

Hyperledger Burrow, with its EVM compatibility, serves as a versatile tool for running Ethereum smart contracts in a permissioned blockchain environment. It combines the benefits of Ethereum's smart contract capabilities with the control and security of a permissioned blockchain.

Hyperledger Aries

Hyperledger Aries focuses on enhancing blockchain interoperability and secure, peer-to-peer communication. It provides a set of protocols, tools, and libraries to enable the creation of decentralized identity and blockchain-interoperable applications.

The Hyperledger project is a vibrant ecosystem of tools and technologies that cater to a wide array of blockchain needs. Each tool and project within the Hyperledger ecosystem offers unique capabilities, allowing organizations to choose the right solution for their specific use cases.

Hyperledger tooling and utility libraries

Imagine entering a well-organized workshop, where various tools and utilities are neatly arranged on shelves, each serving a specific purpose. The Hyperledger ecosystem offers a rich assortment of tools and utility libraries that complement its blockchain frameworks. In this section, we shall explore some of these indispensable components.

Composer: A tool for rapid development

Hyperledger composer, like a skilled craftsman's toolbox, streamlines the development of blockchain applications. It provides a set of high-level abstractions and pre-built templates, allowing developers to define business networks and smart contracts in a simplified, intuitive manner. Composer accelerates the process of creating, testing, and deploying blockchain applications, making it a valuable asset for developers.

Caliper: Benchmarking and performance testing

Caliper, much like precision instruments in a laboratory, serves as a performance benchmarking tool for Hyperledger blockchain networks. It enables organizations to evaluate the speed, scalability, and reliability of their blockchain solutions. By simulating various workloads and transaction scenarios, Caliper helps in optimizing the performance of blockchain networks, ensuring they meet the demands of real-world applications.

Explorer: Visualizing the blockchain

Hyperledger Explorer is akin to a telescope that allows you to observe the inner workings of a blockchain network. It provides a web-based dashboard that displays real-time information about transactions, blocks, and network participants. Explorer simplifies monitoring and auditing, making it easier to track the activities and health of a blockchain network.

Quilt: Enabling interledger payments

Quilt, in the Hyperledger toolbox, serves as a bridge between different blockchain networks. It focuses on enabling interoperable payments using the **Interledger Protocol** (**ILP**). Quilt facilitates cross-chain transactions, making it possible to transfer value seamlessly between diverse blockchain ecosystems.

Ursa: A crypto-library repository

In the realm of cryptography, Ursa functions as a repository of cryptographic libraries for the Hyperledger community. It ensures that all Hyperledger projects use consistent and secure cryptographic implementations. Ursa enhances the security and reliability of Hyperledger blockchain networks by providing a standardized set of cryptographic tools.

Other utility libraries

The Hyperledger ecosystem encompasses several utility libraries that cater to specific needs, such as identity management, integration with external systems, and secure communication. These libraries act as the nuts and bolts of blockchain development, providing essential functionality and support to blockchain applications.

The Hyperledger ecosystem is not just about blockchain frameworks but also a well-equipped workshop filled with tools and utility libraries. These components play a crucial role in simplifying development, ensuring performance, enabling interoperability, and enhancing security.

Blueprint of Hyperledger Fabric

Imagine standing in the grand hall of a magnificent building, where every detail has been meticulously planned and executed. Hyperledger Fabric's architecture can be likened to such a masterpiece, designed with precision and versatility. It is a sophisticated architecture that offers enterprise-grade blockchain solutions. It is based on several key components that collectively contribute to its functionality. Refer to *Figure 5.4*:

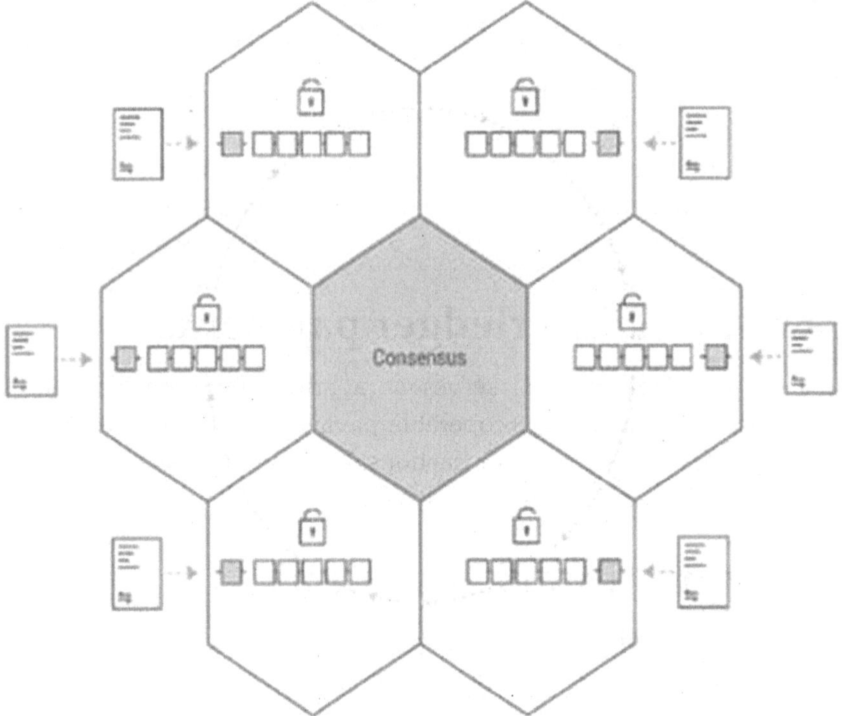

***Figure 5.4**: Hyperledger Fabric architecture*

Endorsement and validation

Imagine a document requiring multiple signatures for approval. In Fabric, transactions are endorsed by peer nodes, indicating their validity. These endorsements are collected and validated by peers, ensuring that only valid transactions are added to the ledger. This endorsement policy adds an extra layer of trust to the network, as shown in *Figure 5.5*:

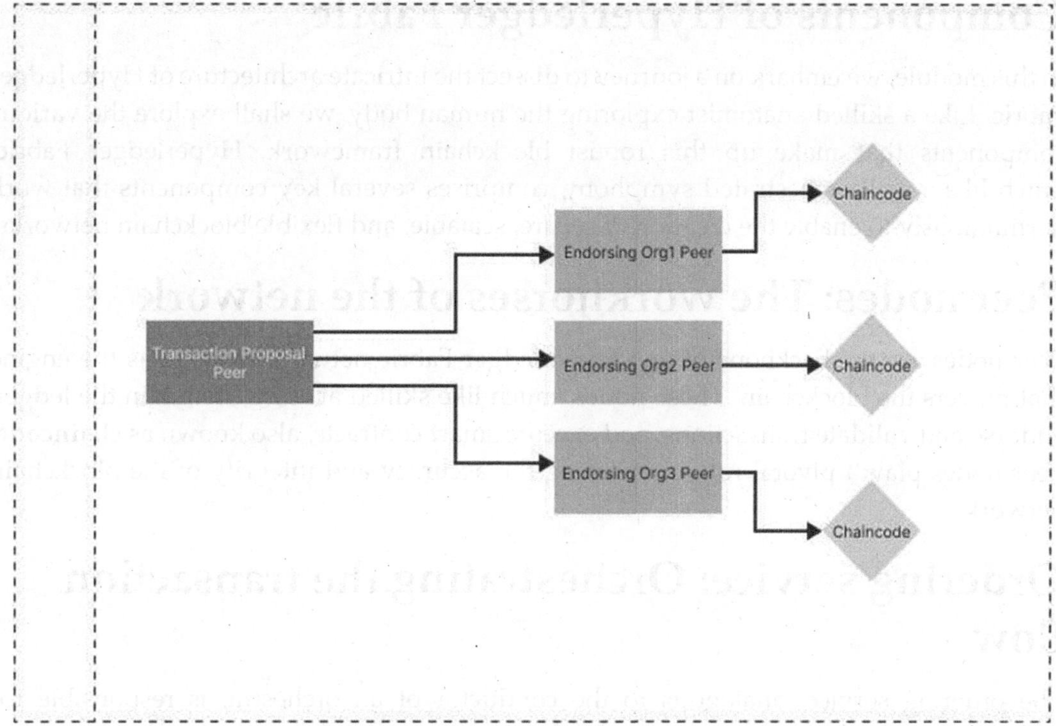

Figure 5.5: Transaction validation

Modular and pluggable design

Hyperledger Fabric's architecture is modular and pluggable, much like building blocks. This design allows organizations to tailor the network to their specific needs, integrating custom features and components. It promotes flexibility and extensibility.

Real-world applications

Consider a global supply chain consortium aiming to enhance transparency and traceability. Hyperledger Fabric's architecture allows the consortium to create a custom network with multiple channels, ensuring that each participant can access only the relevant data. Smart contracts automate supply chain processes, and the ledger maintains an immutable record of all transactions, bolstering trust among participants.

Hyperledger Fabric's architecture is like a well-orchestrated symphony, where each component plays a crucial role in creating a reliable and flexible blockchain network. Its modular design, channels for privacy, and support for various consensus mechanisms make it a versatile choice for a wide range of enterprise applications.

Components of Hyperledger Fabric

In this module, we embark on a journey to dissect the intricate architecture of Hyperledger Fabric. Like a skilled anatomist exploring the human body, we shall explore the various components that make up this robust blockchain framework. Hyperledger Fabric, much like a well-orchestrated symphony, comprises several key components that work harmoniously to enable the creation of secure, scalable, and flexible blockchain networks.

Peer nodes: The workhorses of the network

Peer nodes are the backbone of any Hyperledger Fabric network, serving as the engine that powers the blockchain. These nodes, much like skilled artisans, maintain the ledger, endorse and validate transactions, and execute smart contracts, also known as **chaincode**. Peer nodes play a pivotal role in ensuring the accuracy and integrity of the blockchain network.

Ordering service: Orchestrating the transaction flow

The ordering service, analogous to the conductor of an orchestra, is responsible for orchestrating the flow of transactions within the network. The ordering service ensures that transactions are arranged in the correct order and added to the ledger consistently.

Membership services: The gatekeepers

Membership services act as the gatekeepers of the Hyperledger Fabric network, managing the identities, authentication, and permissions of participants. Picture this as the gatekeeper.

Membership services ensure that only authorized participants can join the network.

Ledger: Recording the immutable history

The ledger, much like a historical archive, stores an immutable record of all transactions that have occurred on the Hyperledger Fabric network. The ledger stores a comprehensive history of all transactions on the network, providing transparency and immutability. It maintains transparency and data integrity.

Smart contracts

Smart contracts, also known as chaincode in Hyperledger Fabric, are the logic that governs transactions on the blockchain. Smart contracts enable automation and customization of transactions. They define the rules and logic for transactions.

Channels for privacy

To ensure privacy in a network, Hyperledger Fabric introduces the concept of channels. Imagine a private conference room within a bustling office. Channels allow for private communication among a subset of network participants. Transactions within a channel are visible only to those who are part of it, ensuring confidentiality.

Consensus mechanisms

Hyperledger Fabric offers flexibility in choosing a consensus mechanism. Much like different decision-making methods in a boardroom, Fabric supports various consensus algorithms, including **PBFT** and Raft. Consensus ensures that all network participants agree on the order and validity of transactions.

MSPs: The guardians of identity

In the intricate Fabric of a Hyperledger network, **Membership Service Providers (MSPs)** emerge as the guardians of identity and the keepers of trust. In this section, we shall embark on a journey to unravel the significance of MSPs in Hyperledger Fabric and understand their pivotal role in shaping the network's security and authenticity.

Role of MSPs

Much like vigilant sentinels, MSPs are responsible for managing the identities of participants within the Hyperledger Fabric network. Their primary roles include:

- **Identity verification**: MSPs verify the identity of participants by issuing digital certificates. These certificates act as digital passports, allowing individuals and entities to access the network securely.
- **Authentication**: MSPs ensure that only authorized participants can join the network. They verify the authenticity of certificates during the connection process, safeguarding against unauthorized access.
- **Permission management**: MSPs control access to the network by defining and enforcing permissions. They determine which participants can perform specific actions, maintaining granular control over network operations.
- **Revocation**: In the unfortunate event of a security breach or a participant's departure, MSPs have the power to revoke certificates, immediately denying access to the network.

MSP configuration in Fabric

Configuring an MSP within Hyperledger Fabric involves defining its structure, roles, and policies. Configuration includes specifying:

- **Root CA and intermediate CAs**: Identifying the authorities responsible for issuing certificates.
- **Admins and endorsers**: Designating network participants with administrative privileges and endorsement capabilities.
- **Revocation policies**: Defining the conditions under which certificates may be revoked.
- **Signing policies**: Specifying the conditions for approving transactions or changes to the network.

Chaincode

A following code is a chaincode sample which shows a crud operation for storing car information:

```
package main

Import (

    "encoding/json"

    *github.com/hyperledger/fabric/core/chaincode/shim"

    *github.com/hyperledger/fabric/protos/peer"

    "time"

)

type Car struct { ID, Title, Owner string; UpdatedAt time. Time }

type SimpleChaincode struct{}


func (t *SimpleChaincode) Invoke(stub shim. ChaincodeStubInterface) peer.
Response {

f, a :-stub.GetFunctionAndParameters()

    switch f {

    case "RegisterCar":
```

```
        return t. RegisterCar(stub, a)
    case "GetCar":
        return t.GetCar(stub, a)
    case "ListCars":
        return t.ListCars(stub)
    default:
        return shim.Error("Invalid function name.")
    }
}
func (t *SimpleChaincode) RegisterCar(stub shim.ChaincodeStubInterface, a []
string) peer.Response {
    if len(a) != 3 {
        return shim.Error("Incorrect number of arguments. Expecting 3.")
    }
    car:= Car{ID: a[0], Title: a[1], Owner: a[2], UpdatedAt: time. Now()}
    carJSON. _ :-Json.Marshal(car)
    stub. PutState(car.ID, carJSON)
    return shim.Success(nil)
}
func (t *SimpleChaincode) GetCar(stub shim ChaincodeStubInterface, a []
string) peer. Response {
    carJSON. _ :- stub.GetState(a[0])
    return shim.Success(carJSON)
}
func (t SimpleChaincode) ListCars(stub shim. ChaincodeStubInterface) peer.
Response {
    resultsIterator. _ :- stub.GetStateByPartialCompositeKey("CAR", []
    string())
```

```
    defer resultsIterator.Close()

    var cars []Car

    for resultsiterator.HasNext() {

        var car Car

        Json.Unmarshal(resultsIterator.Next().Value. &car)

        Cars = append(cars, car)

    }

    carsJSON. _ :- Json.Marshal(cars)

    return shim.Success(carsJSON)

}

func main() {

shim.Start(new (SimpleChaincode))

}
```

Explanation of the simplified code is as follows:

- **Car Struct**: Represents the structure of a car with **`ID`**, **`Title`**, **`Owner`**, and **`UpdatedAt`** fields.
- **SimpleChaincode Struct**: Implements the **`shim.Chaincode`** interface for the chaincode.
- **Invoke method**: Handles different functions based on the provided arguments. Supports **`RegisterCar`**, **`GetCar`** and **`ListCars`** functions.
- **RegisterCar method**: Registers a new car by accepting **`ID`**, **`Title`**, and **`Owner`** as arguments. Creates a **`Car`** instance, converts it to JSON, and stores it in the state.
- **GetCar method**: Retrieves information about a specific car by its ID.
- **ListCars method:** Lists all cars stored in the state.
- **Main Function:** Starts the chaincode.

The following figure elaborates the involvement of MSP in **Hyperledger Fabric** environment:

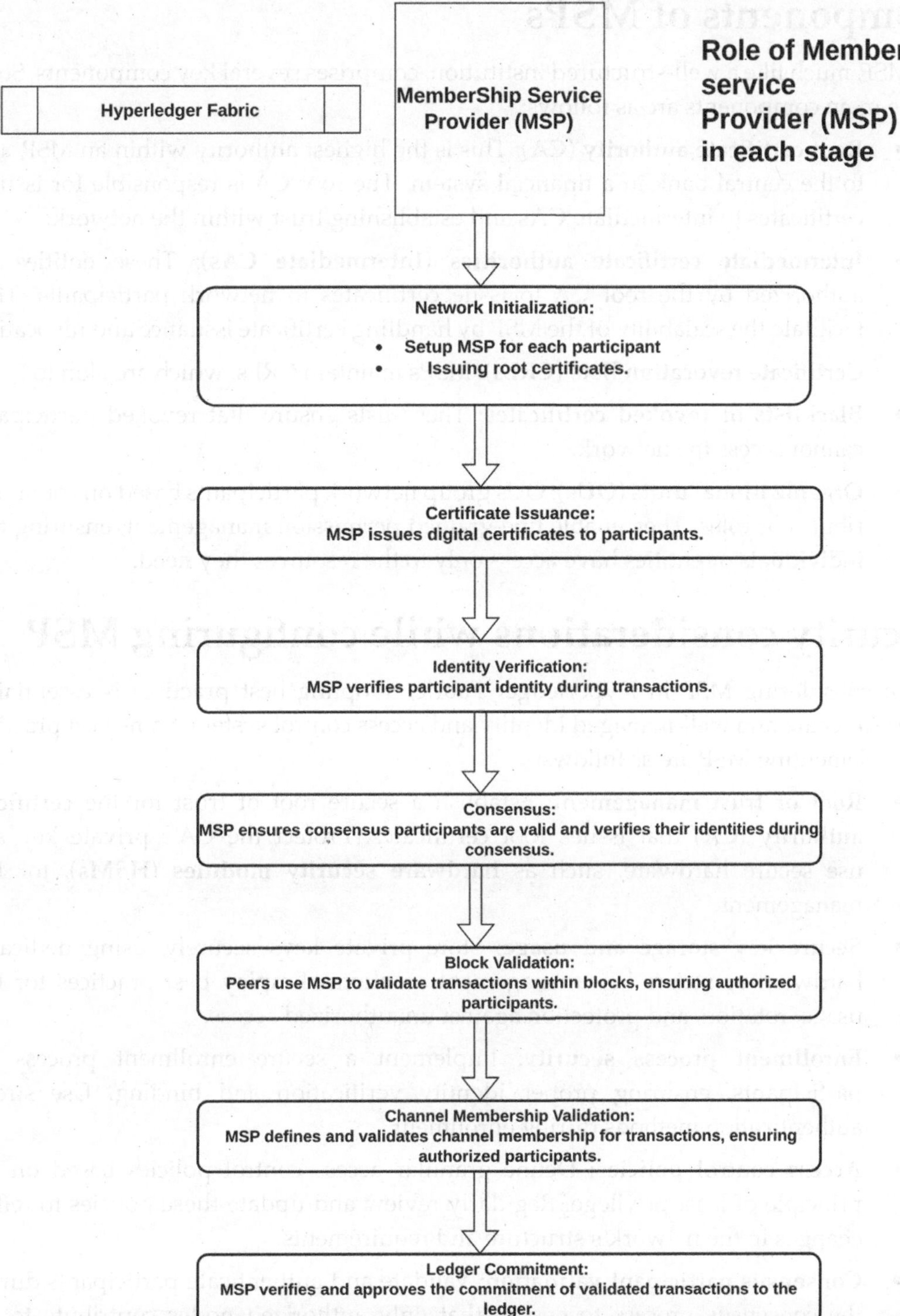

Figure 5.6: Involvement of MSP in Hyperledger Fabric environment

Components of MSPs

An MSP, much like a well-structured institution, comprises several key components. Some of the main components are as follows:

- **Root certificate authority (CA)**: This is the highest authority within an MSP, akin to the central bank in a financial system. The root CA is responsible for issuing certificates to intermediate CAs and establishing trust within the network.
- **Intermediate certificate authorities (Intermediate CAs)**: These entities are authorized by the root CA to issue certificates to network participants. They facilitate the scalability of the MSP by handling certificate issuance and revocation.
- **Certificate revocation lists (CRLs)**: MSPs maintain CRLs, which are akin to
- **Blacklists of revoked certificates:** These lists ensure that revoked participants cannot access the network.
- **Organizational units (OUs)**: OUs group network participants based on common a ributes or roles. They enable fine-grained permission management, ensuring that individuals or entities have access only to the resources they need.

Security considerations while configuring MSP

When considering MSP in Hyperledger Fabric, adopting best practices is essential to ensure a secure and well-managed identity and access control system. Some best practices for implementing MSP are as follows:

- **Root of trust management**: Establish a secure root of trust for the **certificate authority** (**CA**) that issues root certificates. Protect the CA's private key and use secure hardware, such as **hardware security modules** (**HSMs**), for key management.
- **Secure key storage and usage**: Store private keys securely, using dedicated hardware or secure key management solutions. Employ best practices for key usage, rotation, and protection against unauthorized access.
- **Enrollment process security**: Implement a secure enrollment process for participants, ensuring proper identity verification and binding. Use strong authentication methods during enrollment.
- **Access control policies**: Define granular access control policies based on the principle of least privilege. Regularly review and update these policies to reflect changes in the network's structure and requirements.
- **Consensus participant validation**: Validate and authenticate participants during the consensus process to ensure that only authorized nodes contribute to the agreement.

- **Channel membership validation**: Leverage Hyperledger Fabric's channel feature for private communication. Ensure that MSP validation of channel membership is robust to prevent unauthorized access.
- **Revocation and expiry policies**: Establish clear policies for certificate revocation and expiration. Regularly review and update these policies to maintain the security of the network.
- **Secure communication channels**: Use encrypted communication channels between nodes and participants to protect data in transit. Employ secure protocols and algorithms for communication.
- **Multi-signature and multi-party approval**: Implement multi-signature requirements and multi-party approval processes for critical operations. This adds an extra layer of security and prevents single points of failure.
- **Monitoring and auditing**: Implement comprehensive monitoring of MSP activities and regularly audit logs. Use tools for anomaly detection to identify potential security incidents.
- **Regular updates and patching**: Keep Hyperledger Fabric and MSP components up to date with the latest releases and security patches. Apply patches promptly to address any identified vulnerabilities.
- **Education and training**: Provide education and training to administrators and participants about security best practices. Foster a culture of security awareness within the organization.
- **Penetration testing**: Conduct regular penetration testing to identify and address potential vulnerabilities in the MSP setup. Perform security assessments to ensure robustness.
- **Documentation and procedures**: Maintain thorough documentation of MSP configurations, policies, and procedures. This documentation should be accessible to relevant stakeholders and updated regularly.
- **Continuous improvement**: Continuously assess the effectiveness of the MSP implementation and identify areas for improvement. Stay informed about emerging threats and adjust security measures accordingly.

By adhering to these best practices, organizations can enhance the security, reliability, and effectiveness of MSP in Hyperledger Fabric, contributing to the overall success of their blockchain network.

MSPs in action

Imagine a consortium of financial institutions collaborating on a blockchain network. MSPs play a crucial role in ensuring that only authorized banks can join the network, that transactions are signed and endorsed by trusted entities, and that certificates can be revoked if a bank's membership is terminated. MSPs form the foundation of trust in such a consortium. MSPs are the custodians of identity and trust within the Hyperledger Fabric network. Their role in managing identities, enforcing permissions, and maintaining security cannot be overstated.

Certificate authority

A **certificate authority** (**CA**) is a trusted entity that plays a vital role in ensuring the security of digital communications and authentication within a network or system. In the realm of cybersecurity and cryptography, a CA acts as a central authority responsible for issuing, verifying, and managing digital certificates.

Think of a situation where messages travel as sealed envelopes, and each envelope carries a seal of authenticity, ensuring that the message's sender is who they claim to be. In the digital sphere, a CA serves as the custodian of these digital seals, known as digital certificates. Let us explore the role and significance of a CA in the world of cybersecurity and cryptography.

A CA is a trusted entity that performs the following crucial functions. The role of a CA is as follows:

- **Issuance of digital certificates**: CAs issue digital certificates to individuals, devices, or entities. These certificates are akin to digital passports, containing key information such as the certificate holder's identity and a public key.
- **Authentication**: CAs verify the authenticity of certificate applicants before issuing certificates. This verification process ensures that the entity requesting a certificate is indeed who they claim to be.
- **Public key distribution**: Certificates include public keys, which are used for encryption and digital signatures. CAs distribute public keys securely, allowing secure communication between parties.
- **Revocation**: In cases of compromised certificates or when an entity's privileges change, CAs can revoke certificates. Revocation ensures that a compromised certificate cannot be used maliciously.

Certificate hierarchy

Much like a tree with roots and branches, CAs often operate within a hierarchical structure:

- **Root certificate authority (Root CA)**: At the top of the hierarchy sits the Root CA, the ultimate source of trust. It issues certificates to intermediate CAs and self-signs its own certificate. The root certificate is embedded in browsers and operating systems, establishing trust in the entire hierarchy.

- **Intermediate certificate authorities (Intermediate CAs):** These CAs are authorized by the Root CA to issue certificates to end entities, such as users or devices. They form an intermediate layer of trust within the hierarchy.
- **End entities:** End entities are the recipients of certificates issued by Intermediate CAs. They can be users, devices, or entities participating in a network.

Use cases

CA find extensive use in various scenarios. They are as follows:

- **Secure web communication**: In web browsers, CAs ensure the authenticity of websites by issuing SSL/TLS certificates, denoted by the padlock icon. This enables secure and encrypted communication between a user's browser and a website.
- **Email encryption**: CAs facilitate secure email communication by issuing S/MIME certificates. These certificates enable digital signing and encryption of email messages.
- **User authentication**: In corporate networks, CAs are used for user authentication.
- Users' digital certificates act as their credentials for accessing network resources.
- **IoT security**: CAs play a crucial role in securing the **Internet of Things (IoT)** by ensuring the authenticity and security of devices in IoT networks.

CA is the pillar of trust in the digital realm. It issues and manages digital certificates, securing digital communications and enabling secure authentication. Much like a trusted guardian, a CA ensures that the digital world remains a secure and reliable place for communication and transactions.

Nodes: The building blocks

In the intricate tapestry of a blockchain network, nodes emerge as the fundamental building blocks, akin to the bricks and mortar of a grand edifice. In this section, we shall embark on a journey to understand the significance of nodes within a blockchain ecosystem, with a focus on Hyperledger Fabric.

Nodes are the individual participants within a blockchain network, each with a specific role and responsibility. They serve as the workhorses of the network, collectively contributing to the network's security, transparency, and functionality. Nodes refer to the individual computing devices or servers that maintain the distributed ledger and support the network.

They play a vital role in validation and verification of transactions.

Hyperledger Fabric defines several types of nodes, each with its unique role. The various types of nodes in Hyperledger Fabric are as follows:

- **Peer nodes:** These nodes maintain the ledger, endorse and validate transactions, and execute smart contracts, also known as **chaincode**. Peer nodes serve as the core infrastructure of the network, ensuring its integrity and performance.
- **Ordering nodes:** Ordering nodes are responsible for arranging transactions into a consistent order and creating blocks for the ledger. They function as the network's timekeepers, ensuring that transactions are added to the ledger in the correct sequence.
- **Certificate authorities (CAs):** CAs, although not traditional nodes, play a pivotal role in issuing and managing digital certificates. They verify the identity of network participants and ensure the authenticity of certificates used for secure communication.
- **Endorser nodes:** In Fabric's unique transaction model, endorser nodes simulate the execution of smart contracts and provide endorsements for transactions. Their role is critical in achieving consensus and ensuring that transactions meet the required criteria.

Node hierarchy

Nodes within a blockchain network often operate within a hierarchical structure, much like an organization. Node hierarchy refers to the categorization of nodes based on their responsibilities, roles, and privileges. It helps understand the relationships between different types of nodes and their workings. The hierarchy of nodes is as follows:

- **Peer-to-peer network:** At the lowest level, individual peer nodes communicate directly with one another, forming a peer-to-peer network. They validate and endorse transactions, maintaining the network's integrity.
- **Ordering service:** Ordering nodes work together to form the ordering service, orchestrating the flow of transactions. They receive transaction proposals from peer nodes and create blocks for the ledger.
- **Consensus mechanisms:** Nodes within the network participate in consensus mechanisms, such as **PBFT** or **Raft**, to agree on the order and validity of transactions.

Nodes in Hyperledger Fabric have distinct roles and responsibilities. They are as follows:

- **Endorsing transactions**: Endorser nodes simulate transaction execution and provide endorsements, ensuring that proposed transactions meet the necessary criteria.

- **Validating transactions**: Peer nodes validate transactions by checking their correctness and consistency with the ledger's state. They maintain a copy of the ledger and endorse valid transactions.
- **Ordering transactions**: Ordering nodes arrange transactions into blocks and ensure that all nodes in the network agree on the order of transactions.
- **Maintaining security**: Nodes play a critical role in ensuring the security of the network, verifying digital signatures, and participating in consensus to prevent malicious actors.

Real-world applications

Consider a supply chain consortium utilizing Hyperledger Fabric. In this scenario, peer nodes could represent various participants, such as suppliers, manufacturers, and retailers. They endorse and validate transactions related to the movement of goods, ensuring transparency and trust among consortium members. Ordering nodes arrange these transactions into blocks, maintaining the chronological order of events.

Nodes are the elemental entities that form the backbone of a blockchain network. Their roles and interactions are crucial in achieving consensus, ensuring security, and maintaining the integrity of the ledger.

Chaincode: The logic of transactions

In the intricate design of a Hyperledger Fabric blockchain network, chaincode emerges as the vital logic that governs transactions, much like the laws that govern a society. In this section, we shall embark on a journey to understand the significance of chaincode, its role within Hyperledger Fabric, and how it empowers smart contracts.

Chaincode, also known as **smart contracts** in many blockchain platforms, is the logic responsible for defining and executing transactions within a blockchain network. It represents the rules, conditions, and business logic that govern the interactions and agreements between network participants.

In Hyperledger Fabric, chaincode is the encapsulation of business logic that enables participants to interact with the blockchain. Key attributes and functionalities of chaincode are as follows:

- **Transaction execution**: Chaincode defines how transactions are processed and executed within the network. It specifies the actions to be taken when a transaction is invoked.
- **Data manipulation**: Chaincode can read, write, and modify data on the blockchain ledger. It defines the rules for data storage and retrieval.

- **Endorsement and validation**: Chaincode is responsible for endorsing and validating transactions. It determines which nodes are required to provide endorsements and ensures that transactions meet the specified criteria.
- **Privacy and security**: Chaincode can implement privacy features, allowing selective disclosure of information to authorized participants. It also plays a role in enforcing access control and security policies.

Programming languages for chaincode

Hyperledger Fabric supports a variety of programming languages for writing chaincode, offering flexibility and accessibility to developers. Some of the supported languages include:

- **Go**: Chaincode can be written in Go, a popular systems programming language known for its efficiency and simplicity.
- **JavaScript (Node.js)**: JavaScript developers can write chaincode using Node.js, making it accessible to a wide developer community.
- **Java**: Chaincode can also be developed in Java, a language widely used in enterprise applications.
- **Other languages**: Hyperledger Fabric's pluggable architecture allows for the integration of other languages to write chaincode, catering to specific development preferences.

Real-world applications

Imagine a supply chain consortium using Hyperledger Fabric. Chaincode could be employed to automate and enforce business rules related to the movement of goods. For example, when a shipment reaches a specific checkpoint, the chaincode could trigger a smart contract to update the status and notify relevant participants. This automation enhances transparency, reduces errors, and streamlines operations.

Chaincode serves as the logic that breathes life into blockchain transactions. In Hyperledger Fabric, it defines how transactions are executed, data is manipulated, and agreements are enforced. Understanding the role and capabilities of chaincode empowers developers and organizations to design and implement efficient and secure blockchain solutions for various applications.

Channels: Enabling privacy and segmentation

In the intricate architecture of a Hyperledger Fabric blockchain network, channels emerge as the tool for enabling privacy and segmentation, akin to private conference rooms within a bustling office. In this section, we shall embark on a journey to understand the significance of channels, their role within Hyperledger Fabric, and how they empower secure and confidential communication.

Channels in Hyperledger Fabric are a mechanism for creating private and segregated communication pathways within a blockchain network. They serve as virtual sub-networks, allowing a subset of network participants to interact privately and securely, shielding their transactions and data from the broader network. Channels enable different groups of networks to create secure and separate environments for conducting transactions without disclosing sensitive information.

Channels provide several key benefits and functionalities within Hyperledger Fabric. Some of these key benefits are as follows:

- **Privacy**: Channels enable private and confidential communication. Transactions that occur within a channel are only visible to the participants of that channel, ensuring that sensitive information remains confidential.
- **Segregation**: Different groups or consortia within a network can create their own channels. This segregation allows each group to manage their transactions independently, with their own set of endorsing peers and ordering service.
- **Selective endorsement**: Channels support selective endorsement policies, meaning that only a predefined set of endorsing peers participates in the endorsement of transactions within the channel. This ensures that transactions meet specific criteria.
- **Network scalability**: Channels enhance network scalability by reducing the volume of transactions that all network nodes must process. This is particularly valuable in large-scale networks with numerous participants.
- **Efficiency**: Transactions within a channel can be processed more quickly and efficiently, as they involve a smaller subset of network nodes.

Creating and managing channels

Creating and managing channels in Hyperledger Fabric involves the following steps:

- **Channel creation**: An initial channel configuration is defined by the network administrators. This includes specifying the participating organizations, their endorsing peers, and the ordering service for the channel.
- **Joining a channel**: Organizations can join existing channels by configuring their peers to participate in the channel. This process establishes a connection to the channel and grants access to its transactions.
- **Updating channel policies**: Channel policies, including endorsement policies and access control, can be updated to reflect the changing needs of the participants.

Real-world applications

Imagine a consortium of healthcare institutions using Hyperledger Fabric. They create a private channel to handle patient data and healthcare records securely. This channel ensures that only authorized medical professionals and institutions have access to the sensitive patient information, while the broader network can remain unaware of these transactions, thus safeguarding patient privacy.

Channels in Hyperledger Fabric are the gateways to privacy and segmentation within a blockchain network. They enable private communication, selective endorsement, and efficient transaction processing, making them a powerful tool for organizations with diverse needs and privacy requirements.

Consensus mechanisms in Hyperledger Fabric

Consensus mechanisms are the decision-making processes that ensure that all participants in a blockchain network agree on the order and validity of transactions. In this section, we shall delve into three key consensus mechanisms used in Hyperledger Fabric: **Solo**, **Kafka**, and **Raft**, and explore their roles within the network.

Solo consensus: The lone decision maker

Solo consensus is a straightforward mechanism often used for development and testing environments. In this mechanism, a single node, usually the ordering node, makes all decisions regarding transaction ordering and validation. Solo consensus is suitable for small, non-production networks but lacks the robustness and fault tolerance required for enterprise use.

Kafka consensus: Distributed decision making

Kafka consensus, also known as the Kafka-based ordering service, introduces distributed decision making into the network. It employs Apache Kafka, a distributed streaming platform, to achieve consensus among multiple ordering nodes. Kafka consensus enhances network resilience, fault tolerance, and scalability by distributing the decision-making process across multiple nodes.

Raft consensus: A leader-follower model

Raft consensus is another distributed consensus mechanism used in Hyperledger Fabric. It operates based on a leader-follower model, where one ordering node serves as the leader, making decisions, while the others follow and replicate these decisions. Raft provides fault tolerance and ensures that the network continues to function even if some nodes fail.

Consensus mechanisms involve various roles and responsibilities:

- **Leader**: In the Raft consensus mechanism, the leader is responsible for proposing and deciding the order of transactions. In Kafka, Kafka brokers perform similar roles.
- **Followers**: Followers replicate the decisions made by the leader. They ensure consensus by confirming the leader's decisions.
- **Ordering service**: The ordering service in Hyperledger Fabric uses the chosen consensus mechanism to arrange transactions into blocks. It then broadcasts these blocks to the peer nodes for validation and endorsement.

Real-world applications

Consider a global supply chain consortium using Hyperledger Fabric with Kafka consensus. The consortium requires robust fault tolerance and scalability to handle the high volume of transactions involved in tracking goods across borders. Kafka consensus ensures that even if some ordering nodes experience issues, the network can continue to operate smoothly, maintaining transparency and trust among consortium members.

Consensus mechanisms are the backbone of a blockchain network, ensuring that all participants agree on the order and validity of transactions. In Hyperledger Fabric, Solo, Kafka, and Raft consensus mechanisms offer different levels of resilience and scalability to cater to various network requirements. Understanding these mechanisms equips network administrators with the knowledge to select the most suitable consensus mechanism for their specific use case, ensuring the reliability and efficiency of their blockchain network.

Interoperability and scalability

In the ever-evolving landscape of blockchain technology, two paramount challenges stand as formidable hurdles on the path to widespread adoption: interoperability and scalability. In this section, we shall embark on a profound exploration of these challenges, unveiling their complexities, consequences, and the strategies employed to overcome them.

Interoperability: Bridging the blockchain divide

Interoperability, the first cornerstone of our discussion, is the art of bridging the chasm between diverse blockchain networks, allowing them to communicate, share data, and collaborate seamlessly. Imagine this as the task of translating languages between different cultures to enable meaningful conversation.

Interoperability holds immense significance in the blockchain ecosystem. The significance of interoperability is as follows:

- **Network expansion**: Interoperability enables networks to extend their reach by connecting with other networks. This creates a broader ecosystem with increased utility.
- **Data sharing**: It facilitates data sharing across disparate networks, enhancing transparency, and streamlining processes.
- **Cross-chain transactions**: Interoperability allows for cross-chain transactions, where assets and data can move between different blockchains.
- **Marketplace integration**: Blockchain-based marketplaces can integrate with each other, creating a unified marketplace experience.

Challenges of interoperability

Interoperability is a complex challenge with various hurdles. Some of the challenges are as follows:

- **Diverse protocols**: Different blockchains often use different protocols, making it challenging to establish a common language for communication.
- **Consensus variability**: Variations in consensus mechanisms across blockchains can complicate interoperability.
- **Privacy concerns**: Ensuring privacy when sharing data across blockchains is a concern that must be addressed.

Scalability: Handling the growing load

Scalability, our second focal point, addresses the capacity of blockchain networks to handle increased loads as they grow. Picture this as a highway system that must expand to accommodate more traffic.

Scalability is pivotal for blockchain networks. The importance of scalability are as follows:

- **Mass adoption**: As blockchain technology gains popularity, networks must scale to cater to a broader user base.
- **Transaction speed**: Scalability enhances transaction processing speed, crucial for real-world applications.
- **Resource efficiency**: Efficient scaling ensures optimal use of network resources, reducing costs.

Scalability presents its own set of challenges. Some of the challenges of scalability are as follows:

- **Blockchain bloat**: As the blockchain grows, the data storage requirements increase substantially.
- **Consensus mechanisms**: Scaling while maintaining the integrity of consensus mechanisms can be complex.
- **Network congestion**: Scalability issues can lead to network congestion, affecting performance.

Improving channels' efficiency

Improving the efficiency of channels in Hyperledger fabric involves multiple strategies. These strategies are employed to optimize network operations and enhance their operations. They significantly streamline the transaction validation process and reduce latency. Some strategies are as follows:

- **Selective endorsement policies**: Tailor endorsement policies for each channel based on specific use cases and requirements. Channels in Hyperledger Fabric allow participants to define policies for endorsing transactions. By carefully selecting the set of endorsing peers for each channel, you can optimize the endorsement process and reduce the overall load on the network.
- **Dynamic membership**: Leverage the dynamic membership feature of Hyperledger Fabric channels to adapt to changes in the network. This allows organizations to dynamically join or leave channels, facilitating scalability as the network evolves. Dynamic membership helps in adding or removing participants without disrupting the entire network.

- **Data partitioning**: Consider partitioning data across channels based on logical groupings. This can enhance scalability by distributing the load and reducing contention for resources. By organizing channels around specific business processes or entities, you can achieve better parallelization and improved performance.
- **Private data collections**: Utilize private data collections within channels to share confidential information selectively. Private data collections allow specific participants to access certain data without revealing it to the entire network. This enhances privacy and reduces the volume of data that needs to be replicated across all nodes, contributing to improved scalability.
- **Channel configurations**: Optimize channel configurations, such as block size and timeout settings, to accommodate the expected transaction volume and network conditions. Adjusting these parameters can have a significant impact on the overall efficiency and responsiveness of the channel.
- **Off-chain processing**: For certain types of transactions that do not require immediate consensus, consider off-chain processing within channels. Off-chain processing involves executing transactions without immediate endorsement, deferring the endorsement process until later. This can be suitable for scenarios where real-time consensus is not critical.
- **Efficient chaincode design**: Design and implement chaincode with scalability in mind. Optimize the code for efficiency, minimize resource-intensive operations, and consider the data model to ensure efficient querying and updating of state.
- **Network topology**: Design an optimal network topology for communication within channels. Consider factors such as latency, bandwidth, and geographic distribution of peers. A well-architected network can contribute to faster transaction propagation and reduced communication delays.
- **Batching and aggregation**: Explore the use of transaction batching and aggregation techniques within channels. Grouping multiple transactions into a single batch can reduce the overhead associated with transaction validation and ordering, leading to improved throughput.
- **Caching mechanisms**: Implement caching mechanisms strategically to store frequently accessed data within channels. This can help reduce redundant data retrieval operations and improve response times for certain types of queries.
- **Regular performance testing**: Conduct regular performance testing to assess the scalability of channels under different conditions. Simulate various transaction loads and analyze the network's ability to handle increased demand.

Considerations for consensus mechanisms

Consensus mechanisms significantly influence the performance, security, and scalability of a blockchain network. Several factors are crucial to be considered before selecting the most suitable consensus mechanism, which can ensure optimal network performance and meet specific requirements. Some of these factors are as follows:

- **Algorithm selection**: Choose a consensus algorithm that aligns with the specific requirements of the blockchain network. Hyperledger Fabric supports pluggable consensus mechanisms, including PBFT, **Crash fault tolerance** (**CFT**), and others. Evaluate the trade-offs in terms of throughput, fault tolerance, and latency to select the most suitable algorithm.
- **Performance optimization**: Optimize the implementation of the chosen consensus algorithm for better performance. This may involve refining the codebase, reducing unnecessary computations, and optimizing network communication protocols.
- **Parallel processing**: Explore the possibility of parallelizing the consensus process. This can be achieved by dividing the transaction validation and agreement tasks among multiple nodes or subgroups, allowing for concurrent processing and improving overall throughput.
- **Asynchronous processing**: Consider adopting asynchronous consensus algorithms that allow nodes to process transactions independently and asynchronously. This can lead to reduced latency and improved responsiveness.
- **Adaptive consensus**: Implement adaptive consensus mechanisms that can dynamically adjust their behavior based on network conditions, load, or other factors. This adaptability can help the system maintain optimal performance under varying circumstances.
- **Permissioned network configuration**: In a permissioned blockchain network like Hyperledger Fabric, carefully configure the set of nodes participating in the consensus process. Limiting the number of nodes involved in consensus or selecting nodes with specific capabilities can impact the efficiency of the agreement mechanism.
- **Integration with hardware acceleration**: Leverage hardware acceleration technologies, such as HSMs or specialized hardware for cryptographic operations, to offload computationally intensive tasks related to consensus. This can enhance the security and performance of the network.
- **Continuous monitoring and analysis**: Implement robust monitoring tools to continuously assess the performance of the consensus mechanism. Analyze metrics related to latency, throughput, and fault tolerance to identify areas for improvement.

- **Research and development**: Stay informed about the latest advancements in consensus algorithms and participate in research efforts within the blockchain community. Continuous improvement often involves adopting new algorithms or adapting existing ones based on research findings.

Strategies and solutions

Addressing interoperability and scalability requires a blend of innovative strategies and robust solutions. The challenges of interoperability and scalability loom large on the blockchain horizon. Our exploration will shed light on the intricacies of these challenges and equip you with a profound understanding of the strategies and technologies that drive the blockchain ecosystem towards a more interconnected and scalable future.

Conclusion

In a nutshell, Hyperledger Fabric is a robust framework that is designed to meet the complex demands of enterprise-grade applications. This chapter has explored the architecture of Hyperledger Fabric and its real-world applications. Besides, the chapter has dissected some core components like nodes, smart contracts, consensus mechanisms, and identity management. As the fundamentals are covered, the next chapter will explore the hot arena of crypto assets and cryptocurrencies. Topics like fungible and non-fungible tokens will also be covered.

References

- Hyperledger Ecosystem: ps: **//www.hyperledger.org/wp-content/uploads/2021/03/hl_home_img.png**
- Hyperledger Fabric modular design: ps: **//hyperledger-fabric.readthedocs.io/en/release-2.2/_images/fabric-arch.png**
- IBM Food Trust: **ps://www.ibm.com/blogs/blockchain/wp-content/uploads/2021/03/Food-Trust-I nfographic-IBM-Blockchain-768x550.jpg)**

Questions and answers

1. **How is Hyperledger Fabric different from other blockchain frameworks?**

   Ans.: Hyperledger is an open-source, permissioned blockchain framework that is specifically designed for enterprise applications. It is different from other public blockchains as it operates in a permissioned setting. This allows for privacy and controlled access.

2. **What are the key components of Hyperledger Fabric's architecture?**

   Ans.: The key components of Hyperledger Fabric's architecture include smart contracts, MSPs, peers, and ordering services. They play a vital role in the proper functioning of Hyperledger Fabric.

3. **What role do nodes play in a Hyperledger Fabric architecture?**

   Ans.: Nodes in Hyperledger Fabric validate transactions, participate in consensus, and maintain ledger. There are different kinds of nodes in this blockchain framework. They primarily ensure the transparency and data integrity in transactions.

4. **In what industries is Hyperledger Fabric generally employed?**

   Ans.: Hyperledger Fabric finds applications in several major sectors, including finance, supply chain, healthcare, and governmental services. It addresses specific challenges in these sectors all while maintaining compliance and security.

5. **How does Hyperledger Fabric address scalability challenges?**

   Ans.: Hyperledger Fabric addresses scalability concerns through its modular architecture. It allows for parallel transaction execution across multiple channels. It utilizes multiple ordering nodes to enhance its scalability.

Multiple choice questions

1. **What is the primary difference between Hyperledger Fabric and other public blockchains?**
   a. Decentralization
   b. Permissioned network
   c. Proof-of-work consensus
   d. Transparent transactions

2. **Channels in Hyperledger Fabric are primarily used for:**
   a. Segregating private and confidential transactions
   b. Enforcing smart contract execution
   c. Achieving consensus among network nodes
   d. Synchronizing network nodes

3. **Which consensus mechanism is commonly associated with Hyperledger Fabric?**
   a. PoW
   b. Delegated proof of stake (DPoS)
   c. PBFT
   d. Proof of authority (PoA)
4. **In Hyperledger Fabric, what term is used for smart contracts?**
   a. Blockchain Scripts
   b. Script contracts
   c. Contract logic units
   d. Chaincode
5. **What does MSP stand for in Hyperledger Fabric?**
   a. Membership service provider
   b. Member security protocol
   c. Multi-party signatures
   d. Module security protocol

Answers

1. **b**
2. **a**
3. **c**
4. **d**
5. **a**

Join our book's Discord space

Join the book's Discord Workspace for Latest updates, Offers, Tech happenings around the world, New Release and Sessions with the Authors:

https://discord.bpbonline.com

CHAPTER 6

Crypto Assets and Cryptocurrencies

Introduction

The introduction of **crypto assets** and **cryptocurrencies** has made a revolutionary impact on the global financial landscape. These digital assets, based on blockchain technology, have triggered unparalleled interest across the globe. Cryptocurrencies and crypto assets have reshaped traditional notions of currency, investment, and technology. Since the inception of Bitcoin in 2009, the world of these digital assets has exploded and has captured the attention of investors, financial institutions, technologists, and even governments.

This chapter aims to deep dive into the ever-evolving world of crypto assets and cryptocurrencies. It will explore their fundamental principles, market dynamics, underlying technologies, and regulatory challenges. The chapter will also look into different types of cryptocurrencies and how they affect the market. Besides this, their role in investment portfolios and financial inclusion will also be explored. As the sphere of crypto assets and cryptocurrencies continue to evolve, a sound understanding of them is critical to navigate the complex financial landscape.

Structure

This chapter includes the following topics:

- ERC-20, ERC-721, and ERC-1155 tokens
- Defining a token
- ERC: A set of standards
- Fungible vs. non-fungible tokens
- Exploring NFTs
- NFT marketplaces
- Introducing initial coin offerings
- Security token offerings
- Diverse cryptocurrency landscape
- Cryptocurrencies in everyday life

Objectives

This chapter endeavors to provide a strong understanding of cryptocurrencies and crypto assets. It will comprehensively explore the fundamental concepts surrounding these digital assets, such as ERC-20 and ERC-721 token standards and fungible and **non-fungible tokens** (**NFTs**). The chapter will focus on the technical aspects, functionalities, and distinctions between different types of crypto assets. It will also analyze the present real-world use cases of crypto assets and empower readers with the latest knowledge.

ERC-20, ERC-721, and ERC-1155 tokens

In the realm of Ethereum and blockchain technology, tokens play a pivotal role in enabling a wide array of decentralized applications and ecosystems. In this section, we will look into the intricacies of three significant token standards: ERC-20, ERC-721, and ERC-1155.

ERC-20 tokens: The fungible tokens

ERC-20 tokens are category of digital assets within the cryptocurrency ecosystem. They represent the characteristics of fungibility, divisibility, and interchangeability. The ERC-20 standard outlines a set of rules and regulations for creating smart contracts on the Ethereum blockchain. ERC-20 tokens adhere to these standards. Notably, they are a cornerstone of the broader cryptocurrency landscape.

The anatomy of ERC-20 tokens

ERC-20 tokens possess distinct attributes and functionalities outlined by a set of rules. It contributes to their interoperability and widespread adoption across a range of decentralized applications. In this subtopic, we will explore the foundational aspects of ERC-20 tokens. Some of these aspects are as follows:

- **Token structure**: The structure of ERC-20 tokens, comprises of balance, allowance, and transfer functions.
- **Standard functions**: The standard functions such as transfer, approve, and transferFrom enable token transfers and interactions.
- **Total supply and decimals**: The total supply and decimal places provide flexibility in token representation.
- **Events**: The role of events is in broadcasting token transactions and status changes.

Use cases and real-world applications of ERC-20 tokens

ERC-20 tokens are used in a range of industries and functionalities. They are primarily used for **initial coin offerings (ICOs)**. They also form the backbone of **Decentralized Finance (DeFi)** protocols. In this subtopic, we explore the diverse applications and use cases of ERC-20 tokens. Some of the use cases are as follows:

- **ICO fundraising**: ERC-20 tokens are often used for ICOs to raise funds for blockchain projects.
- **Tokenized assets**: Real-world assets, such as real estate and art, are represented as ERC-20 tokens for fractional ownership.
- **DeFi ecosystem**: The role of ERC-20 tokens in the thriving DeFi ecosystem, includes lending, borrowing, and liquidity provision.
- **Gaming and collectibles**: ERC-20 tokens are employed in the gaming industry for in-game assets and collectibles.

ERC-721 tokens: The non-fungible tokens

The ERC-721 standard was introduced as a proposal in 2017. It revolutionized the concept of tokenization and ownership by enabling the creation of NFTs. ERC-721 tokens are notable because of their fungibility. Each ERC-721 token stays unique and irreplaceable. This standard has significantly contributed to the boom in the NFT market.

Understanding ERC-721 tokens

ERC-721 tokens have unlocked unprecedented opportunities for digital ownership, unique asset representation, and provable scarcity. They have disrupted how assets, collectibles, and digital properties are created and exchanged within the blockchain space. In this subtopic, we will delve into the unique characteristics and structure of ERC-721 tokens. Some of these unique characteristics are as follows:

- **Ownership and uniqueness**: ERC-721 tokens represent ownership of unique, indivisible assets.
- **Token metadata**: Token metadata plays a huge part in providing rich information about the NFT.
- **Transferring NFTs**: The process of transferring ERC-721 tokens differs from fungible tokens.
- **Interoperability**: ERC-721 tokens can be used to represent assets in virtual worlds and metaverse projects.

Applications and creative possibilities of ERC-721 tokens

ERC-721 tokens have redefined the concept of ownership in the digital world and transformed various industries. The applications of ERC-721 tokens continue to expand as developers are exploring its new use cases every now and then. In this subtopic, we will look at the myriad applications and creative possibilities unlocked by ERC-721 tokens, such as:

- **Digital art and collectibles**: Dive into the world of digital art marketplaces and the creation of unique digital collectibles using ERC-721 tokens.
- **Gaming and virtual realities**: NFTs are revolutionizing the gaming industry, from rare in-game items to virtual land ownership.
- **Tokenizing real-world assets**: The tokenization of real-world assets, such as real estate, using ERC-721 tokens are used for increasing liquidity and accessibility.
- **Provenance and ownership**: ERC-721 tokens are used to prove the ownership and authenticity of physical assets, including luxury goods and certificates.

ERC-20 and ERC-721 tokens are not just cryptographic assets but catalysts for innovation and transformation in the blockchain space. Understanding these token standards and their diverse applications empowers us to navigate the exciting world of DeFi, digital collectibles, and the metaverse, opening doors to creative possibilities and new economic paradigms.

ERC-1155 tokens: A multi-token standard

ERC-1155 is a **multi-token** standard supporting both fungible and non-fungible tokens within a single smart contract. The development of ERC-1155 has boosted the use cases of Ethereum token standards. Earlier, when a use case needed both ERC-21 and ERC-20 tokens, developers needed to create two separate smart contracts. But ERC-1155 has addressed this issue.

Highlights of ERC-1155 tokens

ERC-1155 is an efficient and versatile token standard on the Ethereum blockchain. It allows developers to create and manage a range of digital assets in a more efficient manner. Some of the highlights of ERC-1155 tokens are as follows:

- **Multi-token standard**: The ERC-1155 standard enables the creation of various types of tokens within the same contract.
- **Reduced gas costs**: Since ERC-1155 standard allows the development of both fungible and non-fungible tokens within the same contract, it significantly reduces the operation cost.
- **Versatility**: The ERC-1155 standard offers a more versatile approach to manage the tokens.

Use cases of ERC-1155 tokens

Due to its versatility and efficiency, the ERC-1155 token standard finds usability in various fields. It has unlocked a range of applications, benefitting various industries like finance, health, and many more. Some notable applications of ERC-1155 tokens are as follows:

- **Gaming**: ERC-1155 tokens are used primarily in the gaming sector. They are used to represent in-game characters, weapons, and other digital assets.
- **Tokenization**: The ERC-1155 token standard facilitates the tokenization of real-world assets. These assets can range from real estate to luxury collectibles.
- **Rewards**: ERC-1155 tokens can be used to create reward systems and loyalty points.
- **Governance**: Due to their multiple usability, ERC-1155 tokens are also used for governance purposes in decentralized organizations.

Defining a token

A **token**, in the context of blockchain technology, represents a unit of value or digital asset. It is a cryptographic representation of ownership or access rights to a specific resource.

Tokens can be used for various purposes, including transactions, digital identity, and access control.

Tokens are a fundamental component of blockchain ecosystems, enabling participants to interact, exchange value, and establish trust within decentralized networks. They serve as digital representations of real-world assets, virtual goods, or unique digital entities.

Tokens come in various forms, each designed to fulfil specific functions and use cases. Two prominent token standards in the Ethereum ecosystem are ERC-20 and ERC-721, which we will explore further in this module.

ERC: A set of standards

The term **Ethereum Request for Comment (ERC)** refers to a set of **technical standards** and **guidelines** that developers propose for Ethereum-based tokens and smart contracts. These standards define the rules, behaviors, and interfaces that tokens and contracts should adhere to, ensuring compatibility and interoperability within the Ethereum ecosystem.

ERCs serve as blueprints for creating tokens and smart contracts, providing a common language and structure for developers. They streamline the development process and enable the broader Ethereum community to understand and interact with these assets consistently.

ERCs are numbered sequentially, and each standard addresses specific functionalities or use cases. ERC-20 and ERC-721, for instance, are two of the most well-known standards within the Ethereum community.

Fungible vs. Non-fungible tokens

The landscape of blockchain-based assets is evolving around the distinction between fungible and NFTs. While fungible tokens represent uniformity and interchangeability, NFTs denote uniqueness and indivisibility. This section will delve into the fundamental differences between these two types of tokens. Understanding the difference between these two types of tokens is crucial for analyzing their applications.

Fungible tokens

Fungible tokens are digital assets that are entirely interchangeable with one another. Each unit of a fungible token is identical and holds the same value as any other unit of the same type. This ensures that no distinction exists between individual tokens. A classic example of fungible tokens is cryptocurrencies like Bitcoin or Ethereum. If you have one Bitcoin and exchange it for another, you still have one Bitcoin. Not only for cryptocurrencies, but fungible tokens have applications in other sectors as well.

Fungible tokens represent standardized units of value. This facilitates straightforward transactions and liquidity across various industries. Finance, supply chain management, and DeFi are among the biggest industries that benefit from fungible tokens.

NFTs

Non-fungible tokens, on the other hand, represent **unique and distinct assets**. Each NFT has a specific value, and no two NFTs are the same. They are indivisible and cannot be exchanged on a one-to-one basis. NFTs are commonly used to represent ownership of digital or physical assets, such as digital art, collectibles, virtual real estate, or even real-world property deeds. Given their uniqueness, NFTs cannot be substituted and traded with identical units.

The uniqueness of NFTs lies in their blockchain-based metadata. This metadata certifies the authenticity and ownership of these NFTs. This metadata includes information about the NFTs' creator, creation date, ownership history, and more authentic data.

NFTs are used in various industries, such as real estate, digital art, collectibles, gaming assets, and even music.

Some key differences between fungible and non-fungible tokens are as follows:

- **Interchangeability:** Fungible tokens are fully interchangeable, while non-fungible tokens are unique and non-interchangeable.
- **Ownership and uniqueness:** Fungible tokens do not carry ownership attributes or uniqueness, whereas NFTs represent unique ownership of specific assets.
- **Use cases:** Fungible tokens are suitable for currencies, tokens of value, and assets with uniform characteristics. NFTs are used for representing ownership, authenticity, and provenance of unique assets in various industries, including art, gaming, and collectibles.

Examples: Bitcoin and **ERC-20** tokens are examples of fungible tokens, while **CryptoKitties**, **Decentraland** parcels, and digital art represented as ERC-721 tokens are examples of non-fungible tokens.

Tokens are the digital keys that unlock the potential of blockchain technology. ERCs, as standards, provide the blueprint for creating these tokens, fostering compatibility and interoperability within the Ethereum ecosystem. Understanding the distinctions between fungible and non-fungible tokens empowers us to appreciate the diversity of digital assets and their transformative impact on industries ranging from finance to art and beyond.

Difference between ERC-721, ERC-20, and ERC-1155 tokens

Ethereum, with its versatile smart contract capabilities, has given rise to various token standards, three of the most prominent being ERC-721, ERC-20, and ERC-1155. These standards serve different purposes and exhibit distinct characteristics that cater to diverse use cases within the blockchain ecosystem.

Some key differences between ERC-721, ERC-20, ERC-1155 tokens are as follows:

- **Fungibility vs. non-fungibility:**
  - o **ERC-20**: ERC-20 tokens are fungible, meaning each token is identical and interchangeable with any other token of the same type. For example, if you have one ERC-20 token representing a cryptocurrency, it is equal in value and properties to any other token of the same kind.
  - o **ERC-721**: ERC-721 tokens are non-fungible, representing unique assets. Each ERC-721 token has distinct properties and value, and they are not interchangeable on a one-to-one basis. Each token stands alone, like a unique piece of art or a collectible.
  - o **ERC-1155**: ERC-1155 tokens offer a perfect blend of non-fungible and fungible traits. They facilitate the creation and management of both fungible and non-fungible tokens within a single contract.
- **Standard functions:**
  - o **ERC-20**: ERC-20 tokens adhere to a set of standard functions, including transfer, approve, and `transferFrom`. These functions facilitate token transfers, approvals, and interactions within the Ethereum network.
  - o **ERC-721**: ERC-721 tokens have a different set of functions designed for managing ownership of unique assets. They include functions like `transferFrom` for transferring ownership, `ownerOf` to check ownership, and approve for authorizing another address to manage an NFT.
  - o **ERC-1155**: ERC-1155 tokens offer a versatile set of functionalities. They help in managing and interacting with multiple token types within a single contract.
- **Use cases:**
  - o **ERC-20**: ERC-20 tokens are widely used as digital currencies and tokens of value. They serve as the foundation for numerous cryptocurrencies, utility tokens, and stablecoins. Examples include **Ethereum** (**ETH**), **Tether** (**USDT**), and **Basic Attention Token** (**BAT**).
  - o **ERC-721**: ERC-721 tokens are primarily used for representing ownership and authenticity of unique assets, making them ideal for digital collectibles,

virtual real estate, in-game items, art, and tokenized real-world assets. Popular examples include CryptoKitties, Decentraland parcels, and digital art NFTs.

  o **ERC-1155**: As it enables the management of both fungible and non-fungible tokens, the ERC-1155 token standard is used in various industries. Notable among them are tokenized and digital collectibles, gaming assets, and more.

- **Divisibility:**
  o **ERC-20**: ERC-20 tokens can be divisible into smaller units, with the level of divisibility determined by the number of decimal places specified in the token's smart contract. For example, one ETH can be divided into smaller fractions, like 0.1 ETH or 0.001 ETH.

  o **ERC-721:** ERC-721 tokens are indivisible, meaning they cannot be divided into smaller units. Each token represents a whole and unique asset, making them ideal for representing ownership of entire items or collectibles.

  o **ERC-1155:** The ERC-1155 token contract comes with both divisible and indivisible properties. They offer the maximum flexibility, depending upon the token type needs to be managed.

- **Representational use**:
  o **ERC-20:** ERC-20 tokens are well-suited for representing and transferring value, making them suitable for financial applications, decentralized exchanges, and payment systems.

  o **ERC-721:** ERC-721 tokens are designed for representing ownership, provenance, and authenticity, making them ideal for applications where uniqueness and scarcity are essential, such as digital art, gaming, and collectibles.

  o **ERC-1155:** This token contract offers a balanced representation of both non-fungible and fungible tokens. They are a good choice for the management of multiple token types within a single contract.

ERC-20 and ERC-721 tokens are distinct standards within the Ethereum ecosystem, each serving unique roles and catering to different use cases. ERC-20 tokens are fungible and primarily used for value transfer and financial applications, while ERC-721 tokens are non-fungible, representing ownership of unique assets in a wide range of creative and collectible contexts. Understanding these differences is crucial for harnessing the full potential of blockchain technology in various industries.

Exploring NFTs

NFTs have emerged as a revolutionary concept. This section will look into the unique characteristics, workings, applications, and significance of NFTs in the blockchain sphere.

NFTs possess distinct attributes that set them apart. Some key features of NFTs are as follows:

- **Uniqueness**: Each NFT is one-of-a-kind, representing a unique asset or item. This uniqueness is stored immutably on the blockchain.
- **Indivisibility**: NFTs cannot be divided into smaller units. They are whole and cannot be fragmented, making them ideal for representing complete assets.
- **Ownership proof**: NFTs provide indisputable proof of ownership. The blockchain ledger records the owner's address, ensuring transparency and security.
- **Interoperability**: NFTs can be used across different applications and platforms, enabling diverse use cases.

Working of NFTs

NFTs operate on blockchain technology, but their workings differ from cryptocurrencies like **Bitcoin** or **Ethereum**. They utilize smart contracts and decentralized ledgers to create, authenticate, and transfer unique digital assets. The working of NFTs involves a number of key components that contribute to their smooth operations. They are as follows:

- **Smart contracts**: NFTs are often created using smart contracts, self-executing agreements that define the rules and properties of the token.
- **Metadata**: NFTs include metadata that describes the asset they represent. This metadata can contain information about the asset's origin, ownership, and characteristics.
- **Token standards**: Standards like ERC-721 and ERC-1155 on the Ethereum blockchain define how NFTs should behave and be managed.
- **Ownership transfer**: NFT ownership is transferred by changing the ownership address in the token's smart contract. This transfer is recorded on the blockchain.

Examples of NFTs

NFTs have found applications in various fields, including:

- **Digital art**: Artists create and sell digital art as NFTs, providing provenance and ownership proof. Notable examples include the sale of Beeple's artwork for millions.
- **Gaming**: NFTs enable ownership of in-game assets and characters. Games like **Axie Infinity** and **Decentraland** rely on NFTs.
- **Collectibles**: Digital collectibles, such as CryptoKitties and NBA Top Shot, are sold and traded as NFTs.

- **Virtual real estate**: NFTs represent ownership of virtual land in metaverse projects like Decentraland and the Sandbox.

Usage of NFTs

NFTs serve diverse purposes. The multiple applications and use cases of NFTs have brought them to the fore in the blockchain world. From artworks and collectibles to gaming and real estate, NFTs have usability across industries. To understand their true impact, comprehending their creative potentials and the extensive range of utilities is vital. Their main applications are as follows:

- **Ownership proofs**: They prove ownership of physical or digital assets, ensuring authenticity.
- **Digital collectibles**: NFTs revolutionize the collection of digital items, from trading cards to virtual sneakers.
- **Tokenized real assets**: Real-world assets like real estate, art, and even tweets have been tokenized as NFTs for easier trading and ownership.
- **Content monetization**: Creators use NFTs to monetize their digital content, offering limited editions and royalties on resale.

Difference between NFTs and other cryptocurrencies

NFTs are different from other cryptocurrencies like Bitcoin and Ethereum due to their unique functionalities and characteristics. A proper understanding of the difference between NFTs and other cryptocurrencies is critical to analyze their respective roles. Major differences between NFTs and cryptocurrencies are:

- **Fungibility**: Cryptocurrencies are fungible, with each unit being interchangeable. NFTs are non-fungible and unique.
- **Use case**: Cryptocurrencies are primarily used as digital currencies for transactions. NFTs represent ownership of assets.
- **Interchangeability**: You can exchange one Bitcoin for another without any difference. NFTs represent distinct assets and are not interchangeable.

NFT marketplaces

NFT marketplaces are dedicated online platforms developed to facilitate the transactions involving non-fungible tokens. They can be called digital market hubs designed for NFTs. Through these marketplaces, people can buy, sell, or trade NFTs, including digital collectibles, artwork, virtual assets, and other items. These NFT marketplaces cater to artists, investors, collectors, and other enthusiasts.

While there are many NFT marketplaces in the market, **OpenSea** and **Magic Eden**, are prominent players in this space. The two marketplaces are briefly explained as follows:

- **OpenSea**: It is one of the most popular and largest NFT marketplaces. It has been developed on the Ethereum blockchain. This decentralized marketplace allows users to trade a range of digital assets, such as domain names, artwork, real estate, and many more. Notably, OpenSea supports both ERC-721 and ERC-1155 tokens. Here, users can create, sell, buy, or even bid NFTs using Ethereum.
- **Magic Eden**: It is the most popular NFT marketplace on the Solana blockchain, a leading rival to Ethereum. However, it is no more limited to the Solana blockchain. It has also expanded its offerings on the Ethereum and Polygon networks. Magic Eden also enables users to mint, list, buy, sell, and trade NFTs.

Note: Ethereum is a prominent platform for NFTs, with standards like ERC-721 and ERC-1155 dedicated to them. The Ethereum blockchain provides a secure and widely adopted infrastructure for creating, trading, and storing NFTs.

NFTs are a transformative force in the blockchain space, redefining ownership, creativity, and digital experiences. Understanding their key features, workings, real-world examples, applications, distinctions from cryptocurrencies, and relationship with platforms like Ethereum equips us with the knowledge to navigate this exciting frontier of blockchain technology.

Introducing initial coin offerings

In the dynamic realm of blockchain and cryptocurrency, **ICOs** have emerged as a significant fundraising mechanism. Under this mechanism, blockchain projects issue tokens to investors to raise capital. ICOs have helped projects and startups raise funds without opting conventional routes like venture capital and IPOs. In this section, we shall embark on an enlightening journey to understand the mechanics, advantages, disadvantages, and real-world examples of ICOs.

Functioning of the ICO mechanism

ICOs are a means by which blockchain projects and startups raise capital by issuing and selling their own digital tokens. The process typically follows these steps:

1. **Project concept**: A blockchain project conceives an idea or product that requires funding.

2. **Whitepaper**: The project team creates a detailed whitepaper outlining the project's goals, technical specifications, and the token's utility.
3. **Token creation**: The project team creates a new cryptocurrency token, often using blockchain platforms like Ethereum (ERC-20 tokens).
4. **Token sale**: The project team offers these tokens for sale to investors in exchange for established cryptocurrencies like Bitcoin or Ethereum.
5. **Crowdfunding**: Interested investors purchase these tokens during the ICO, providing the project with funding.
6. **Listing**: Once the ICO concludes, the project's token is often listed on cryptocurrency exchanges, enabling trading.

Some advantages and disadvantages of ICOs are as follows:

Advantages:

- **Access to capital**: ICOs provide a new way for startups and projects to raise capital without relying on traditional financial institutions.
- **Global reach**: ICOs have a global reach, allowing projects to attract investors from around the world.
- **Liquidity**: Tokens issued during ICOs can be traded on cryptocurrency exchanges, providing liquidity and potential for value appreciation.

Disadvantages:

- **Regulatory uncertainty**: The regulatory environment for ICOs is uncertain in many jurisdictions, leading to legal challenges and potential risks.
- **Scams**: The lack of regulation has given rise to fraudulent ICOs and scams, where investors may lose their funds.
- **Volatility**: The value of ICO tokens can be highly volatile, leading to significant price fluctuations.

Numerous blockchain projects have conducted successful ICOs. Some notable examples of ICO are as follows:

- **Ethereum**: Ethereum itself raised funds through an ICO in 2014, which played a pivotal role in the development of the Ethereum ecosystem.
- **Filecoin**: Filecoin conducted one of the largest ICOs in 2017, raising over $257 million to build a decentralized storage network.
- **Chainlink**: Chainlink's ICO in 2017 raised $32 million to develop a decentralized oracle network.
- **Polkadot**: Polkadot raised $145 million in its ICO to create a multi-chain network that enables different blockchains to interoperate.

ICOs have shaped the blockchain landscape, providing innovative projects with access to capital while posing regulatory and security challenges. Understanding how ICOs work, their advantages and disadvantages, and real-world examples equips us to navigate this fundraising mechanism and its role in the ever-evolving blockchain ecosystem.

ICOs and liquidity pool

Although ICOs and liquidity pool are two separate concepts, they intersect during a process. Let us consider, a project launches an ICO to raise funds for its new token. Once the ICO ends, the project allocates a portion of the funds raised to create a liquidity pool. Later, this liquidity pool enables users to trading the newly launched tokens with other cryptocurrencies. In essence, a liquidity pool improves token accessibility and enables smoother and more efficient trading for users. However, it is important to note that not all ICOs create liquidity pools.

Decoding crypto exchanges

The crypto trading has boomed in recent years. Even many investors are equating this to the trading of traditional assets like stocks and commodities. The trading of these digital assets is facilitated through dedicated crypto exchanges. These exchanges are digital platforms and help people buy, sell, and trade cryptocurrencies.

These crypto exchanges, in essence, act as intermediaries that connect sellers and buyers. They enable individuals to exchange a range of cryptocurrencies for other digital currencies or fiat currencies.

There are hundreds of crypto exchanges in the world, and Binance and Uniswap are the leading ones among them. Both these crypto exchanges offer unique services and features to their users.

Binance

It is one of the largest cryptocurrency exchanges in the world. It supports a wide range of cryptocurrencies and supports several trading pairs. Binance offers many features like spot trading, staking, and futures trading.

One of its noteworthy components is Binance launchpad. The launchpad facilitates ICOs and token sales. This enables users to buy tokens of promising projects vetted by Binance.

Uniswap

Uniswap is the leading **decentralized exchange** (**DEX**) and is built on the Ethereum blockchain. It operates as an open-source protocol and offers users a permissionless way to swap ERC-20 tokens directly from their wallets. Uniswap also boasts a massive liquidity pool.

Here, users can also earn money by becoming liquidity providers by staking their tokens to the liquidity pools of Uniswap. To maintain its pace with the evolving market trends, this decentralized exchange has rolled out its Uniswap v3.

Security token offerings

In the ever-evolving landscape of blockchain and finance, **security token offerings (STOs)** have emerged as a compelling method for raising capital while adhering to regulatory compliance. In this module, we delve into the world of STOs, exploring the types of security tokens and the benefits they offer.

Security tokens represent ownership in an asset or investment contract, offering various forms of financial rights. Three common types of security tokens are as follows:

- **Equity tokens**: These tokens represent ownership in a company, similar to traditional shares of stock. Equity tokens grant token holders a share of the company's profits and voting rights in corporate decisions.
- **Debt tokens**: Debt tokens are akin to bonds or loans. Holders of debt tokens are entitled to receive periodic interest payments and the return of the principal investment amount at maturity.
- **Asset tokens**: Asset tokens represent ownership in tangible or intangible assets such as real estate, art, or commodities. Token holders have a share of the asset's value and may receive dividends or rental income.

STOs offer several advantages as compared to traditional fundraising methods. Some of the benefits of STOs are as follows:

- **Regulatory compliance**: STOs are designed to comply with securities regulations, providing transparency and legal protection for investors.
- **Global access**: STOs enable a global pool of investors to participate, expanding the potential investor base.
- **Liquidity**: Security tokens can be traded on regulated secondary markets, enhancing liquidity and allowing investors to exit their positions more easily.
- **Fractional ownership**: Asset tokens, in particular, allow for fractional ownership, enabling smaller investors to access traditionally illiquid assets like real estate.
- **Reduced intermediaries**: STOs can streamline the fundraising process by reducing the need for intermediaries like investment banks and brokers.
- **Programmable features**: Smart contracts can be used to automate compliance, dividend distribution, and other processes, reducing administrative overhead.

STOs represent a bridge between traditional finance and the blockchain world, offering the benefits of regulatory compliance, global access, and enhanced liquidity. Understanding the types of security tokens and the advantages they bring empowers us to explore innovative ways of raising capital while maintaining investor protection and compliance with evolving financial regulations.

Diverse cryptocurrency landscape

Cryptocurrencies are digital or virtual currencies that rely on cryptographic techniques to secure transactions and control the creation of new units. They are decentralized and typically operate on a distributed ledger technology called **blockchain**. Key features of cryptocurrencies are as follows:

- **Decentralization:** Cryptocurrencies are not controlled by any central authority, such as a government or central bank.
- **Security:** Cryptography ensures the security of transactions and the creation of new units.
- **Transparency:** Transactions on the blockchain are transparent and recorded on a public ledger, accessible to anyone.
- **Pseudonymity:** While transactions are transparent, the identities of users are often pseudonymous, represented by cryptographic addresses.

Cryptocurrencies come in various forms, each with its unique features and use cases. Here are some notable examples of the diverse range of cryptocurrencies:

- **Bitcoin (BTC):** The pioneering cryptocurrency, created by an anonymous entity known as *Satoshi Nakamoto*. Bitcoin serves as digital gold and a store of value.
- **Ethereum:** Beyond being a cryptocurrency, Ethereum is a platform for smart contracts and DApps.
- **Ripple (XRP):** Designed for fast and low-cost cross-border payments, Ripple has gained popularity among financial institutions.
- **Litecoin (LTC):** Often referred to as **silver** to Bitcoin's **gold**. Litecoin is known for its fast transaction confirmation times.
- **Bitcoin Cash (BCH):** A fork of Bitcoin, Bitcoin cash focuses on scalability and lower transaction fees.
- **Cardano (ADA):** Cardano is known for its research-driven approach to blockchain, emphasizing security and sustainability.
- **Polkadot (DOT):** Polkadot aims to enable interoperability between different blockchains, allowing them to communicate and share data.

- **Chainlink (LINK):** Chainlink provides decentralized oracle services, connecting smart contracts with real-world data.
- **Stellar (XLM):** Stellar focuses on facilitating cross-border payments and has partnerships with various financial institutions.

Cryptocurrencies in everyday life

Cryptocurrencies are not just digital assets; they are also becoming integral to various aspects of everyday life:

- **Digital payments:** Cryptocurrencies can be used for online purchases, peer-to-peer payments, and remittances.
- **Investment:** Many people buy cryptocurrencies as a form of investment, hoping that their value will increase over time.
- **DeFi:** DeFi platforms use cryptocurrencies to offer financial services such as lending, borrowing, and trading.
- **NFTs:** They represent unique digital assets and are often bought and sold using cryptocurrencies.
- **Blockchain applications:** Cryptocurrencies are used to pay transaction fees and interact with blockchain-based applications.

Cryptocurrencies have transformed the way we think about money and digital assets. Understanding the fundamentals of cryptocurrencies and their diverse range empowers us to navigate this revolutionary technology and its applications in various aspects of our lives.

Conclusion

The sphere of cryptocurrencies and crypto assets is extremely dynamic and is defined by innovation and transforming potential. This chapter has elucidated the intricate concepts like ERC-20 and ERC-721 tokens, NFTs, initial coin offerings, and security token offerings. As we conclude this chapter, we can observe that the crypto world continues to evolve and presents both opportunities and challenges. In the next chapter, we will focus on blockchain applications and case studies. It will offer practical knowledge to readers.

Questions and answers

1. **What is the difference between ERC-20 and ERC-721 tokens?**

   Ans.: ERC-20 tokens are fungible tokens on the Ethereum blockchain. They usually represent digital currencies or utility tokens. On the contrary, ERC-721 tokens are non-fungible tokens. They represent unique assets like collectibles, in-game items, and artworks. Unlike ERC-20 tokens, each ERC-721 token is distinct and non-interchangeable.

2. **What are the primary applications of NFTs?**

   Ans.: NFTs have a range of applications, which include art ownership, digital collectibles, gaming assets, and more. They have revolutionized digital ownership by providing verifiable scarcity and provenance.

3. **How do initial coin offerings work?**

   Ans.: Through **ICOs**, startups and projects raise funds by issuing tokens. Investors purchase these tokens in exchange for established cryptocurrencies. However, several factors affect ICOs of a project. They include team expertise, regulatory compliance, and project's market viability.

4. **In what industries are ERC-721 tokens finding applications?**

   Ans.: The application of ERC-721 tokens encompasses various industries. These tokens are primarily used in the gaming, supply chain, real estate, and entertainment industries. However, ERC-721 tokens find application in many more industries.

5. **How do fungible tokens ensure uniformity and interchangeability?**

   Ans.: Fungible tokens ensure uniformity and interchangeability by being identical and interchangeable with tokens that are of the same type. This feature facilitates easy transactions and fosters liquidity on cryptocurrency exchanges.

Multiple choice questions

1. **Which term describes the unique characteristics of NFTs?**
   a. Indivisibility
   b. Fungibility
   c. Interchangeability
   d. Uniformity

2. **Which fundraising method allows startups to raise capital by issuing tokens directly to investors?**
   a. Venture capital
   b. Initial public offering (IPO)
   c. ICO
   d. Security token offering (STO)

3. **What is the difference between security token offerings (STOs) and ICOs?**
   a. STOs involve offering utility tokens, while ICOs involve security tokens.
   b. STOs are regulated offerings compliant with securities laws, while ICOs often lack regulatory compliance.
   c. STOs are exclusively for accredited investors, while ICOs are open to all.
   d. STOs are not subject to investor protection laws, unlike ICOs.

4. **Which blockchain feature ensures the privacy of users during transactions?**
   a. Anonymity
   b. Identity verification
   c. Pseudonymity
   d. Centralized control

5. **Which one of the following cryptocurrencies focuses on facilitating fast and low-cost cross-border payments?**
   a. Ethereum (ETH)
   b. Bitcoin Cash (BCH)
   c. Litecoin (LTC)
   d. Ripple (XRP)

Answers

1. a
2. c
3. b
4. c
5. d

Join our book's Discord space

Join the book's Discord Workspace for Latest updates, Offers, Tech happenings around the world, New Release and Sessions with the Authors:

https://discord.bpbonline.com

CHAPTER 7

Blockchain Applications and Case Studies

Introduction

Through previous chapters, we have gained a deep understanding of blockchain technology, cryptocurrencies, and their intricate concepts. From the Diffie-Hellman key exchange method to cryptography to fungible and non-fungible tokens, we have covered several crucial concepts that are poised to shape the landscape of technology in future.

In this chapter, we will comprehensively explore the symbiotic relationships between these technologies. The chapter will look into how blockchain technology can be used in the real-world setting. It will analyze the convergence of emerging technologies like blockchain, **Internet of Things (IoT)**, and **artificial intelligence (AI)**.

Structure

This chapter contains the following topics:

- Blockchain and IoT
- Blockchain with AI
- Blockchain improving cybersecurity

Objectives

The chapter will shed light on blockchain, IoT, and AI and their dynamic intersections. The chapter will provide readers with the knowledge about collaborative potential of these technologies. It will illustrate how these technologies can enhance security, transparency, and operational efficiency. Through case studies and real-world examples, the chapter will highlight how these technologies can benefit a range of industries, including healthcare, finance, supply chain, and more.

Blockchain in IoT

Blockchain technology and the **IoT** are two of the most transformative innovations of our era. When combined, they create a potent synergy that holds immense potential for reshaping industries, enhancing security, and fostering new levels of connectivity. In this section, we will delve into the convergence of blockchain and IoT, exploring its applications, real-world implementations, and the promising future it holds.

Understanding IoT and its challenges

First, let us demystify IoT. At its core, IoT is the interconnection of everyday devices and objects to the internet. These smart devices can range from your thermostat to your refrigerator, and even to industrial machines and autonomous vehicles. They collect data, communicate with each other, and often make autonomous decisions based on this data. These devices are equipped with sensors, software, and other connectivity features.

In short, the IoT is a network of interconnected devices that exchange data and communicate with each other through internet. These data can then be analyzed and processed for making automated decisions. This improves efficiency and enables new functionalities.

However, this connectivity comes with its own set of challenges. Some of the challenges of IoT are as follows:

- **Security**: As billions of devices communicate through the internet, the risk of cyberattacks and data breaches skyrockets.
- **Privacy**: IoT devices often collect sensitive personal data, raising concerns about privacy and data ownership.
- **Interoperability**: Different devices from various manufacturers may not seamlessly communicate with each other due to interoperability issues.
- **Scalability**: As the number of IoT devices grows exponentially, traditional centralized systems struggle to scale efficiently.

Blockchain and IoT together

Blockchain technology provides a distributed, secure, and transparent ledger system, which offers potential solutions to these IoT challenges:

- **Enhanced security:**
  - o **Immutable record**: Blockchain records transactions in a tamper-proof manner. Once data is added to a block, it becomes nearly impossible to alter, ensuring data integrity.
  - o **Decentralization**: The decentralized nature of blockchain reduces the risk of a single point of failure. Even if one node is compromised, the network remains secure.
- **Privacy and data ownership:**
  - o **Smart contracts**: Blockchain allows for the creation of smart contracts, which can automate interactions between devices while preserving privacy and enforcing data ownership rights.
- **Interoperability and trust:**
  - o **Interoperability**: By establishing a common protocol for data exchange, blockchain can facilitate interoperability among diverse IoT devices.
  - o **Immutable identity**: Each IoT device can have a unique, immutable identity on the blockchain, fostering trust in device interactions.
- **Scalability:**
  - o **Off-chain solutions**: To address scalability issues, some blockchain platforms use off-chain solutions, such as state channels and sidechains, to reduce the burden on the main blockchain.

Real-world implementations

Blockchain's marriage with IoT is no longer a theoretical concept; it is a reality in various sectors. It has revolutionized the sphere of connectivity, security, and data integrity. The intertwining of these two technologies has made a transformative impact on various industries and sectors. Some of them are as follows.

- **Supply chain management**: Companies are using blockchain and IoT to track the movement of goods in real-time, enhancing transparency and reducing fraud in supply chains.
- **Energy sector**: IoT devices, like smart meters, communicate energy consumption data to blockchain networks, enabling efficient energy trading and distribution.

- **Healthcare**: IoT-enabled medical devices securely transmit patient data to blockchain networks, ensuring patient privacy and data accuracy.
- **Smart cities**: Municipalities use IoT and blockchain for waste management, traffic control, and public service delivery, improving city efficiency.

Given its potential, a promising future for the convergence of blockchain and IoT lies ahead. This technological revolution will reshape industries, enhance security, and foster new levels of connectivity. However, challenges remain, particularly in terms of standardization, scalability, and regulatory frameworks. But these challenges are not insurmountable.

Blockchain with artificial intelligence

AI and blockchain are two technological marvels that have captured the imagination of innovators and industry leaders alike. In this section, we embark on an exciting journey to explore the convergence of blockchain and AI, uncovering the real-world challenges it addresses and the transformative solutions it offers.

At first glance, AI and blockchain may seem like distant cousins in the world of technology. While AI deals with data processing, machine learning, and predictive analytics, blockchain focuses on decentralized ledger technology, transparency, and security. However, the fusion of these two domains creates a powerful synergy that addresses critical issues in AI.

AI in blockchain governance models

AI has played a vital role in enhancing blockchain governance models by introducing automation and efficiency. AI algorithms can monitor transactions, track compliance with rules, and execute decisions based on predefined criteria. This streamlines governance mechanisms and reduces potential human errors. Consequently, it can improve data security and integrity, privacy, and reliability of blockchain governance systems.

Benefits of AI's predictive analysis

Blockchain technology can greatly benefit from the predictive analysis of artificial intelligence, revolutionizing several industries. For instance, in the financial sector, AI's predictive analysis can develop smarter investment strategies, risk assessment, and fraud detection. It can also help individuals forecast market fluctuations and optimize portfolios by analyzing historical market trends. Additionally, in healthcare, AI can enhance patient care, disease prediction, and treatment plans.

Challenges in collaboration of blockchain and AI

AI, despite its remarkable capabilities, faces several challenges. Some of them are as follows:

- **Data privacy**: AI algorithms require vast amounts of data, often personal or sensitive. Ensuring data privacy and security is paramount.
- **Data quality**: Garbage in, garbage out. AI models heavily depend on the quality and accuracy of the data they are trained on.
- **Trust and accountability**: AI decision-making can be opaque, making it challenging to understand or hold AI accountable for its actions.
- **Decentralized learning**: Collaborative AI models involve multiple parties, each holding their data. Coordinating and maintaining trust in a decentralized learning environment is complex.

The blockchain solution

Blockchain technology brings several solutions to these challenges. It boasts a range of features, including immutability, traceability, transparency, decentralization, smart contracts, and consensus mechanism, among others. These features can significantly benefit AI, as discussed in the following points:

- **Data privacy and security**: Blockchain's encryption and decentralized nature ensure data privacy and security. Access to data can be controlled through smart contracts.
- **Data immutability**: Once data is recorded on the blockchain, it cannot be altered, ensuring the integrity of training data.
- **Transparency and accountability**: Blockchain records all transactions transparently. AI decision-making can be traced, enhancing accountability.
- **Decentralized learning**: Blockchain enables secure, decentralized AI models where participants maintain control over their data.

Real-world applications

Now that we know how blockchain can help AI improve processes, let us see how their integration can perform in real-world scenarios. These technologies together have the potential to benefit and revolutionize several, if not all, industries. Some real-world applications of these technologies are as follows:

- **Healthcare**: Blockchain secures patient data, while AI-driven diagnostics and personalized medicine enhance healthcare outcomes.

- **Finance**: Fraud detection and risk assessment are bolstered by AI models, while blockchain ensures the security and transparency of financial transactions.
- **Supply chain**: AI optimizes supply chain operations, and blockchain verifies the provenance and authenticity of products.
- **Energy**: AI-driven energy management meets blockchain's secure energy trading, enabling efficient and green energy ecosystems.
- **Intellectual property**: Blockchain records intellectual property rights, while AI identifies and protects against IP infringement.

The future of blockchain in AI

As we look ahead, the synergy of blockchain and AI holds the promise of transforming industries, enhancing trust, and advancing the capabilities of AI systems. However, it is essential to address challenges such as scalability, standardization, and regulatory frameworks.

The fusion of blockchain and AI is a testament to human innovation. It is a journey into a future where trust, security, and transparency converge with intelligence, opening doors to unprecedented possibilities. As this partnership continues to evolve, it will undoubtedly shape the way we interact with technology, revolutionizing industries and improving the quality of our lives.

Blockchain improving cybersecurity

Cybersecurity is an ever-escalating battleground where defenders and attackers engage in an unceasing war of wits. However, blockchain technology has emerged as a panacea as far as digital security and data privacy is concerned. Its decentralized and immutable nature makes its highly resistant to cyberattacks or unauthorized alterations. It employees cryptographic techniques and each data within a blockchain is linked and hashed. Any attempt to alter information in one block would require changes in all subsequent blocks across the chain, which is an impossible task without detection.

In this section, we will look at the remarkable fusion of blockchain technology and cybersecurity, exploring how it addresses real-world security challenges and fortifies our digital world against an array of threats.

Understanding the threat landscape

Cybersecurity threats have evolved in complexity, from phishing attacks and malware to sophisticated nation-state cyber espionage. As per the data from Statista, about 73%

of businesses have reported falling victim to cyberattacks. Moreover, different types of cyberattacks have sprung up in recent years. Some of the major challenges are:

- **Data breaches**: Massive data breaches expose sensitive information, causing financial and reputational damage.
- **Identity theft**: Criminals exploit identity data to commit fraud and cybercrimes, jeopardizing individuals and organizations.
- **Insecure supply chains**: Vulnerabilities in the supply chain can lead to compromised hardware or software.
- **Lack of trust**: Trust is elusive in a digital realm fraught with misinformation, deepfakes, and cyber threats.

Blockchain's defensive arsenal

Blockchain technology offers a robust arsenal of defensive measures to combat these threats. It is **distributed ledger technology** (**DLT**) has already redefined data security. Besides, when combined with artificial intelligence, blockchain can prevent cyberattacks effectively. Features that help blockchain tackle the issue of data threats are as follows:

- **Immutability**: Once data is recorded on the blockchain, it becomes virtually immutable, preventing unauthorized alterations or deletions.
- **Decentralization**: Blockchain's decentralized nature eliminates single points of failure, reducing the risk of breaches due to centralized targets.
- **Cryptographic security**: Blockchain employs advanced cryptographic techniques to secure data and transactions.
- **Smart contracts**: Self-executing smart contracts can automate security measures and trigger actions in response to predefined conditions.

Real-world applications

Blockchain technology can easily address the challenges in the sphere of data security and privacy. It can help businesses and individuals operate securely in an interconnected digital world. A few of the many real-world applications of blockchain are as follows:

- **Secure identity management**: Blockchain ensures secure and tamper-proof identity verification, mitigating identity theft risks.
- **Supply chain security**: Blockchain traces the provenance of products, enhancing transparency and security in supply chains.
- **Encrypted communication**: Blockchain-based secure messaging platforms protect communication channels from eavesdropping.

- **Decentralized DNS**: Blockchain-based **domain name systems** (**DNS**) are resistant to domain hijacking and censorship.
- **Secure file sharing**: Blockchain-backed file sharing platforms enable encrypted and decentralized sharing, reducing data exposure risks.
- **Strengthening IoT devices**: Blockchain technology offers robust data security for IoT devices. Its immutable ledger provides secure device authentication and tamper-proof data storage. This reduces vulnerabilities to cyber threats in an IoT ecosystem.
- **Anti-fraud system in finance**: Blockchain creates transparent and immutable transactions records. It facilitates secure peer-to-peer transactions without the need for intermediaries. Besides, blockchain technology enables real-time monitoring of transactions, reducing the risk of fraudulent activities.

The future of blockchain in cybersecurity

As we gaze into the future, blockchain's role in cybersecurity is set to expand. However, challenges such as scalability, integration with legacy systems, and regulatory frameworks must be addressed.

In the series of technological advancements, quantum blockchain security has garnered a massive attention. As quantum computers can quickly solve complex mathematical problems that power blockchains, they pose a threat to traditional cryptographic algorithms. To tackle this looming threat, quantum blockchain are being developed.

Quantum blockchain will be an encrypted, decentralized, and distributed database that will be based on quantum computation. It will become highly improbable to maliciously tamper the data after it is recoded in the quantum blockchain. This system aims to develop quantum-resistant cryptography, which will create encryption methods that can withstand attacks even from quantum computers.

The integration of blockchain and cybersecurity is a testament to human ingenuity in the face of evolving digital threats. It is a journey into a future where trust and security form the bedrock of our digital interactions. As this partnership continues to evolve, it will undoubtedly shape the landscape of digital security, fortifying our defenses and allowing us to navigate the digital frontier with greater confidence.

Conclusion

It is now quite evident that the integration of blockchain, IoT, and AI can reshape global industries. Their amalgamation has shown remarkable growth potential across a variety of sectors. As the technological world is evolving, these technologies are likely to play a major role in the coming years. This chapter has tried to explore the true and vast potential of blockchain, IoT, and AI through case studies and real-world examples. Hopefully, the readers would have gained the fundamental knowledge about these technologies and concepts discussed in previous chapters.

Questions and answers

1. **What are some common IoT devices?**

   Ans.: IoT has a significant impact on people's daily lives. Some of the common IoT devices include wearable fitness trackers, thermostats, connected home security systems, voice-controlled assistants, and many more.

2. **How does blockchain enhance the security of IoT networks?**

   Ans.:. The immutability feature of blockchain ensures that data transmitted between IoT devices stay tamper-proof and immune to alterations. This, in turn, increases the trust and transparency in the IoT ecosystem.

3. **Provide a real-world example where the integration of blockchain and IoT works.**

   Ans.: The integration of blockchain and IoT devices can significantly benefit the supply chain management. For instance, IoT devices can facilitate data collection while blockchain can secure the data from tampering and altering. It ensures authenticity and reduces counterfeit goods.

4. **How can smart contracts benefit AI applications?**

   Ans.: Blockchain's smart contracts automate and enforce predefined rules in AI-powered transactions or agreements. It facilitates secure and transparent interactions between users and AI developers.

5. **How do blockchain and AI technologies address challenges in data security?**

   Ans.: AI's data processing and blockchain's encryption capabilities can establish permissioned and secure access to sensitive data. This way data can be shared with only authorized parties.

Multiple choice questions

1. **Which feature of blockchain ensures that recorded data stays tamper-proof?**

   a. Decentralization

   b. Transparency

c. Immutability

d. Smart contracts

2. **What is a common real-world application of blockchain and IoT integration?**

a. Cryptocurrency mining

b. Supply chain management

c. Weather forecasting

d. Social media networking

3. **Which technology records AI decisions in a transparent and auditable manner?**

a. Blockchain

b. Machine learning

c. IoT

d. Smart contracts

4. **What is one challenge associated with IoT implementation?**

a. Limited device connectivity

b. High data security

c. Low scalability

d. Interoperability issues

5. **What is a common example of an IoT device used in households?**

a. Smart thermostat

b. Desktop computer

c. Microwave oven

d. Landline telephone

Answers

1. c
2. b
3. a
4. d
5. a

Index

Symbols

A

B

C

D

E

F

G

H

I

K

L

M

Q

R

S